CW00336116

P.O. Box 1375

Barrhead

Glasgow

G78 1JJ

Tel: 0141 880 6839

Fax: 0870 124 9189

e-mail: teejaypublishers@btinternet.com

web page: www.teejaypublishers.co.ok

TeeJay Publishers

Level 4⁺ Textbook

Produced by members of the TeeJay Writing Group

T Strang, J Geddes and J Cairns.

Level 4⁺ Textbook

The book can be used to cover the entire contents of the CfE Level 4 Course, and, with our Book N5, will also cover, in depth, the National 5 Course.

- Those pupils going onto a National 5 Course should complete the contents of CfE Book 4⁺ possibly by the end of Secondary 3, some earlier and some later.

- There are no A and B exercises. The book covers the entire Level 4 CfE course without the teacher having to pick and choose which questions to leave out and which exercises are important. They all are !

- The book contains a 5 page "Chapter Zero", which primarily revises all those strands from CfE Level 3 that have been covered in TeeJay's Books 3a and Book 3b.

- Each chapter will have a "Remember, Remember" exercise as a summary.

- Teachers are encouraged, at the end of various chapters, to consider assessing the pupils using the corresponding TeeJay Outcome Assessment*.

- Pupils could sit Unit Assessments along the way, or take part in an end of course exam to confirm they are progressing satisfactorily at Level 4, in preparation for attempting the National 5 course the following year.

- Note :- Various outcomes, those involving practical aspects of the course or discussion topics, such as MNU 4-03a, MNU 4-09a, MNU 4-10a, MNU 4-11a, MTH 4-12a and MNU 4-20a,0 are not mentioned in our Index but are an integral part of the course.

  We make no apologies for the multiplicity of colours used throughout the book, both for text and in diagrams - we feel it helps brighten up the pages !!

T Strang, J Geddes, J Cairns

(June 2013)

---

* TeeJay's CfE Level 4 Assessment Pack is available and is of the same format as our highly successful CfE Early to Level 3 Packs, which have sold now to over 90% of Scottish Primary and Secondary Schools.

Contents

CfE Level 4⁺

* E2·1 etc - Indicates an Outcome that is also part of the National 5 Course

You **should** be able to do this exercise without a calculator.

1. Round to 2 decimal places :-
   - (a) 5·5416
   - (b) 0·15602
   - (c) 11·065
   - (d) 9·99611.

2. Round to 2 significant figures :-
   - (a) 7·657
   - (b) 1 236 545
   - (c) 11·4999
   - (d) 59 512 332.

3. Write down how many significant figures each of these numbers has :-
   - (a) 0·010
   - (b) 5·004.

4. By rounding, find an approximate answer to :-
   - (a) 83 654 ÷ 189
   - (b) 62 974 × 293.

5. A farmer's crop of 60 kg of carrots is sealed into 1·5 kg plastic bags. He sells the bags at £0·60 each.

   How much money will he make ?

6. A second hand scooter was on sale for £880. I bought it using a hire purchase agreement :-

   - I paid an initial deposit of 25% of the cash price.

   - I then made ten payments of £75·50 each.

   - (a) How much did it cost me paying it up this way ?
   - (b) How much would I have saved if I had paid cash ?

7. Find :-
   - (a) 12 × 30
   - (b) 3450 × 400
   - (c) 80 000 ÷ 200
   - (d) 345 000 ÷ 500.

8. What is the answer to :-
   - (a) 5 + 2 × 3
   - (b) 15 − 10 ÷ 5 + 3 ?

9. Find :-
   - (a) (−10) − 4
   - (b) 15 − (−12)
   - (c) 69 + (−70)
   - (d) (8) × (−4)
   - (e) (−45) ÷ (−5)
   - (f) 172 ÷ (−3)
   - (g) $(-2)^6$
   - (h) $(-1)^{71}$.

10. Find the lowest common multiple of :-
    - (a) 3 and 4
    - (b) 8 and 6
    - (c) 2, 3 and 6
    - (d) 5, 6 and 8.

11. Find the highest common factor of :-
    - (a) 10 and 15
    - (b) 24 and 42
    - (c) 480 and 720
    - (d) 21, 42 and 63.

12. List all the prime numbers between :-
    - (a) 40 and 50
    - (b) 90 and 110.

13. As a product of its prime factors, 60 can be written as :- 2 × 2 × 3 × 5. Write each as a product of its prime factors :-
    - (a) 42
    - (b) 100
    - (c) 36
    - (d) 128.

14. Find :-
    - (a) 6^2
    - (b) 30^2
    - (c) 3^3
    - (d) 4^4
    - (e) $\sqrt{49}$
    - (f) $\sqrt{40000}$.

15. Change to a decimal :-
    - (a) $\frac{1}{2}$
    - (b) $\frac{3}{5}$
    - (c) 13%
    - (d) 9%.

16. Change to a percentage :-
    - (a) 0·5
    - (b) 0·4
    - (c) $\frac{3}{4}$
    - (d) $\frac{2}{3}$.

17. A greenhouse is priced at £800. In a sale, a discount of 15% is given.

    How much would I pay for the greenhouse in the sale ?
    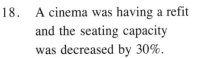

18. A cinema was having a refit and the seating capacity was decreased by 30%.

    The old cinema had an original maximum audience of 750.

    How many can the revamped cinema hold ?

19. Change each to a top heavy fraction :-

    (a) $3\frac{1}{2}$ (b) $3\frac{2}{3}$

    (c) $7\frac{5}{6}$ (d) $12\frac{5}{6}$.

20. Change each to a mixed number :-

    (a) $\frac{27}{4}$ (b) $\frac{33}{2}$

    (c) $\frac{173}{5}$ (d) $\frac{4863}{8}$.

21. Find :-

    (a) $\frac{1}{2} + \frac{1}{3}$ (b) $3\frac{3}{4} + 1\frac{5}{8}$

    (c) $7\frac{1}{3} - 2\frac{1}{5}$ (d) $8\frac{1}{7} - 7\frac{2}{3}$.

22. (a) If a lift takes 33 seconds to climb 6 floors, how long will it take to climb 1 floor ?

    (b) The lift can carry a maximum of 12 people.

How many trips will it have to make to take 140 people to the top floor ?

23. 1 chocolate chip cookie costs 45p. I got a pack of 8 for £3.

    Did I get a bargain ?
    (*Justify your answer*).

24. 5 trips to the dump with my car when clearing out my loft took 2 hours 5 minutes.

    How much longer would an **extra** 3 trips take ?

25. Olive oil is sold in 700 ml bottles and in 2 litre cans ?

£6·30   £16·00

    Which is the better buy here ? (*Explain*).

26. Georgio is a waiter in a hotel and earns £12 per hour.
He was called in at the weekend to help at a wedding.
Overtime is paid at time and a half.
Over the weekend, he put in 12 hours overtime.

    How much was he paid for his overtime work ?

27. Avril is a primary teacher. Her gross monthly pay is £2350.

Her monthly deductions are :-
    Income Tax - £370,
    National Insurance - £115 and
    Graduated Pension - £108.

    What is Avril's net monthly pay ?

28. (a) A truck covers 260 miles in 4 hours. What is the truck's average speed ?

    (b) The Hubble telescope travels round the earth at 7·5 km/second.

How far will it fly in 8 seconds at this speed ?

    (c) A car is towed at a steady speed of 40 km/hr.

How long will it take it to cover a distance of 90 km ?

29. This graph shows the distance a plane travels as it flies from Glasgow to Athens in Greece.

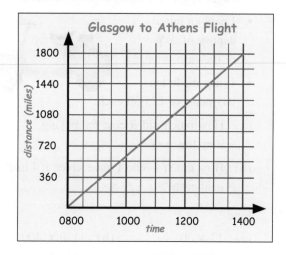

    Calculate the average speed of the plane.

30. Calculate the area of each of these shapes :-

    (a)
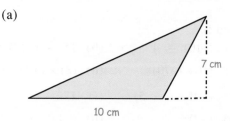
7 cm

10 cm

30. (b)

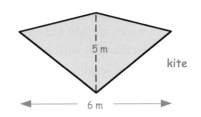

kite

31. Calculate the **circumference** of this no entry sign.

It has a radius of 70 centimetres.

32.

The diameter of this circular wooden lid is 40 cm.

Calculate the **area** of the lid.

33. Calculate the **capacity** of this water tank, in litres.

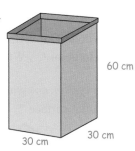

60 cm

30 cm   30 cm

34. Calculate the area of this shape.

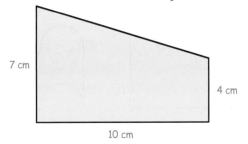

7 cm

4 cm

10 cm

35. Write the next two numbers in the following sequences :-
    (a) 187, 178, 169, 160, ..., ...
    (b) 2, 6, 12, 20, ..., ...
    (c) 1, 1, 2, 3, 5, 8, 13, ..., ...

36. This table shows the height of a tomato plant over a 5 day period.

No. of day's (d)	1	2	3	4	5
Height in cm (H)	15	21	27	33	39

Use the table to devise a formula connecting H and d.

37. Simplify :-
    (a) $12x - 4y - 5x + y$ (b) $p + 3q - p - 2q$
    (c) $5a \times 4b$ (d) $16abc \div 4ab$.

38. Multiply out the brackets :-
    (a) $3(2x - 4)$ (b) $2m(3m - 2n)$
    (c) $-4(3x - 5y)$ (d) $\frac{1}{2}g(4 - 2g)$.

39. Simplify fully :-
    (a) $9t + 6s - 3(t - 4s)$ (b) $4(k - 3) + 13$
    (c) $10 - 3(h - 7)$ (d) $12j - 6(2j + 1) - 6$.

40. If $p = 13$, $q = 4$ and $r = -3$, find :-
    (a) $p + q + r$ (b) $pq - r$
    (c) $3q - 4r$ (d) $\frac{p - 4q}{r}$.

41. Solve :-
    (a) $2x - 1 = 17$ (b) $4x = 18$
    (c) $5x - 2 = 18$ (d) $12x - 3 = 30$
    (e) $2x + 3 = x - 5$ (f) $6x + 5 = 3x + 29$
    (g) $4(2x - 3) = x + 2$ (h) $\frac{1}{2}x - 9 = 13$.

42. Solve these inequalities :-
    (a) $4x > 24$ (b) $5x - 2 > 28$
    (c) $2x + 3 \leq 3x - 1$ (d) $\frac{1}{3}x + 7 \leq 22$.

43. (a) Write down a formula for the area (A) of this shape in terms of a, b, c and d.

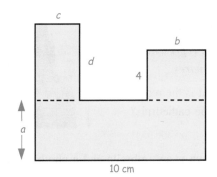

c

b

d

4

a

10 cm

(b) Evaluate the formula, given :-
    $a = 3.5$, $b = 4.5$, $c = 3$ and $d = 6$.

44. Copy each diagram and fill in **all** the missing angles :-
    (a)   (b)

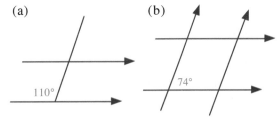

110°

74°

44. (c)
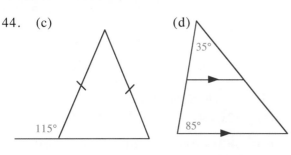

(d)

(e)
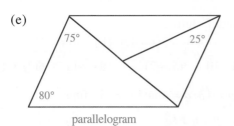
parallelogram

45. What is the 3 figure bearing representing :-

    (a)   South   (b)   West

    (c)   East   (d)   North East ?

46. What is the compass direction corresponding to the 3 figure bearing :-

    (a)   225°   (b)   315° ?

47. As the captain of a ship sails on a bearing of 050°, he notices another ship going in the exact opposite direction.

Write down the bearing of the 2nd ship.

48. This drawing of a Cathedral was done to a scale :-

1 cm represents 40 metres.

What is the real height of the cathedral ?

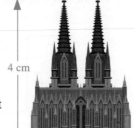

4 cm

49. Shown is an umbrella and a photograph of it.

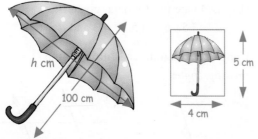

h cm

100 cm

5 cm

4 cm

Calculate the scale factor and use it to determine the span (*h* cm) of the blue nylon part of the umbrella.

50. A map is to show the distance between two train stations which are 140 km apart. The distance on the map must be between 5 cm and 10 cm in length.

Write down a suitable scale for the map.

51.
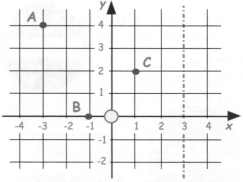

(a) Write down the coordinates of point A.

(b) Write down the coordinates of a 4th point D such that ABDC is a rhombus.

(c) Point C is reflected over the dotted line to point C'. Write the coordinates of C'.

52. State (*yes or no*) which of these shapes would tile a flat surface ?

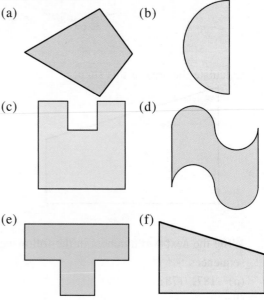

53. The ages of a group of people are as shown :-

          1, 2, 2, 5, 7, 31.

Find the :–

    (a) range   (b) mode

    (c) median   (d) mean.

54. Which of the averages in question 53 would **best** indicate the "average" age.

    (*Explain why you think so*).

55. Here are the bank balances of 10 students :-

£55,   £20,   –£15,   £50,   –£25,
£115,   £90,   £50,   –£55,   £40.

(a) What is the range of the bank balances ?

(b) What is the modal balance ? *(the mode)*.

(c) What is the median balance ?

(d) What is the mean balance ?

56. James' mean mark for his three tests was 62.

He scored 52 in English and 46 in French.

What must his mark have been in his Maths test ?

57. Four finals in the Olympics were being shown on TV at the same time. The pie chart shows which sport a group of women chose to watch.

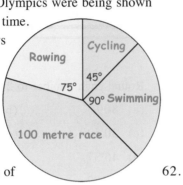

(a) What fraction of the women chose to watch the 100 m race ?

(b) If 180 women took part in the survey, how many of them watched the 100 m race ?

58. The ages of people waiting in a bank queue were recorded as follows :-

35	24	47	18	57	45	12
40	53	62	68	42	29	27
14	24	65	52	11	45	23
34	51	16	50	28	48	23
52	47	52	63	25	58	59

Construct an ordered stem and leaf graph to show this information.

59. This pack contains 1 yellow, 3 blue, 5 red and 6 green pencils.

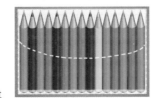

What, in its simplest form, is the probability the first pencil chosen from the pack is green ?

60. From a group of people, the number wearing glasses is noted. The probability of choosing one from the group who is actually wearing glasses is 0·25.

In fact, 5 from the group were wearing glasses.

How many were not wearing glasses ?

61. State the order of symmetry and the turn symmetry, if any, for each of the following shapes :-

(a)
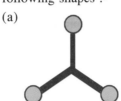

(b)

(c)
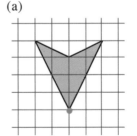

(d)
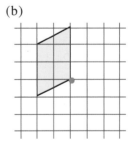

62. Make a copy of each of the following shapes, neatly and carefully.

Create a shape which has half turn symmetry by rotating each shape by 180° around the red dot :-

(a)
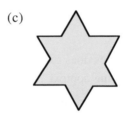

(b)
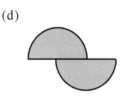

(c)
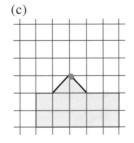

(d)
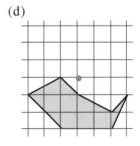

> ## Rounding - Significant Figures
>
> A figure or digit in a number is "significant" if it gives some sense of QUANTITY & ACCURACY.
>
> > "ZEROS" can be complicated - when do we count them ? – when do we leave them out ?
> >
> > **If zeros are used** only to show where the position of the decimal point is,
> > **then they are** NOT **significant.**
>
> **Example 1 :-**
>
> 607 has .... 3 significant figures.   60·7 has .... 3 significant figures.
>
> 6·07 has .... 3 sig. figs.   0·607 has .... 3 sig. figs.
>
> **0·06070** has .... **4** sig. figs. (Front zero positions the decimal point, but trailing zero shows accuracy).
>
> **Example 2 :-**
>
> 4386 rounded to 1 sig. fig. is **4000**   39 264 rounded to 3 sig. figs. is **39 300**
>
> 5·746 rounded to 3 sig. figs. is **5·75**   0·008 317 rounded to 2 sig. figs. is **0·0083**

Exercise 1·1

1. How many significant figures does each number have in the following context ?

   (a) There are **400** ten pences in forty pounds.

   (b) Approximately **70** boys attended the dance.

   (c) To the nearest million pounds, the football transfer fee was **£12 000 000**.

   (d) The altitude of Ben Nevis is **1344** metres.

2. Write down how many significant figures there are in each of these numbers :-

   (a) 41·0   (b) 9·00

   (c) 7·006   (d) 479

   (e) 70·1   (f) 25·80

   (g) 0·099   (h) 2·000 005

   (i) 0·000 80   (j) 6·000 003

   (k) 154·000   (l) 0·000 000 010.

3. Round each number to 1 sig. fig. :-

   (a) 53   (b) 478

   (c) 6478   (d) 22 364

   (e) 4499   (f) 4599

   (g) 1·96   (h) 0·426

   (i) 0·789   (j) 0·0021

   (k) 0·019   (l) 3 750 000

   (m) 0·000 785   (n) 79·99.

4. Round each number to 2 sig. figs :-

   (a) 809   (b) 7139

   (c) 30 700   (d) 181 129

   (e) 46·37   (f) 19·52

   (g) 7·192   (h) 0·339

   (i) 0·003 684   (j) 89·816.

5. Round each number to 3 sig. figs :-

   (a) 5841   (b) 25 081

   (c) 73 853   (d) 482 199

   (e) 15·826   (f) 12·817

   (g) 0·287 45   (h) 0·293 54

   (i) 0·001 677   (j) 0·049 999.

6. Find the weight of a set of 300 DVD's, if each DVD weighs 49 grams.

   (*Give your answer in grams to 2 sig. figs.*).

7. I deposited £25 531 in the Building Society, receiving an interest rate of 1·8% per annum.

   Calculate my interest for the year, correct to 2 sig. figs.

8. Miss Mace purchased a vacuum cleaner for £361·14 + V.A.T. at 20%.

   Calculate the V.A.T. correct to 4 sig. figs.

Estimating using Significant Figures

Significant Figures can be used to estimate an answer to any calculation.

Examples :- Round each number to **1 significant figure** and estimate :-

1. 5892 + 2176	2. 574 x 286	3. 5184 ÷ 49
=> 6000 + 2000	=> 600 x 300	=> 5000 ÷ 50
= **8000**	= **180 000**	= **100**

Exercise 1·2

1. Round each number to **1** significant figure to estimate each calculation :-

   (a) 4621 + 1883   (b) 57 638 – 12 629   (c) 128 331 + 721 110

   (d) 41 182 – 10 714   (e) 123 x 51   (f) 351 x 189

   (g) 1272 x 485   (h) 347 x 666   (i) 492 ÷ 11

   (j) 1935 ÷ 246   (k) 222 554 ÷ 97   (l) 21 761 ÷ 484

   (m) 495 123 x 316   (n) 5 219 787 ÷ 4998   (o) 12 663 ÷ 19 .

2. Round each number to **2** significant figures to estimate each calculation :-

   (a) 891 + 113   (b) 682 – 487   (c) 299 x 147

   (d) 7965 + 1452   (e) 62 284 – 11 618   (f) 1897 x 196

   (g) 10 137 x 124   (h) 95 501 ÷ 478   (i) 543 321 ÷ 998

   (j) 264 339 + 32 246   (k) 387 ÷ 1344   (l) 1 484 002 ÷ 29 946 .

3. Round each number to **1** significant figure to estimate each calculation (remember BOMDAS ?) :-

   (a) 285 + 132 x 18   (b) 416 x 593 – 23 718   (c) 3920 ÷ 38 + 273

   (d) 2·41 + 2·8 x 4·9   (e) 19·7 – 3·75 x 5·277   (f) 53·2 ÷ 9·96 + 24·75

   (g) 1·2 + 4·8 x 38   (h) 19·7 – 26·3 ÷ 2·8   (i) 3·27 x 4·76 – 2·564 ÷ 3·36 .

4. Round each number to 1 significant figure to estimate each calculation :-

   (a) A jar of jelly beans contains an average number of one hundred and eighty five beans.
   How many jelly beans are there in 32 jars ?

   (b) There are 9137 pages in 312 identical magazines.
   How many pages are in each magazine ?

   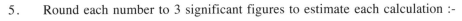

5. Round each number to 3 significant figures to estimate each calculation :-

   (a) A company's three top executives each earned £718 925 last year.
   How much was that in total ?

   (b) A football club's 2 star players are valued at £7 249 500 and £34 515 900.
   What is their mean value, correct to 3 sig figs. ?

   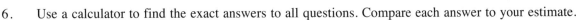

6. Use a calculator to find the exact answers to all questions. Compare each answer to your estimate.

The Order of Operations - a Reminder of **BOMDAS**

You hopefully remembered in Question 3 of the previous exercise that many calculations have to be completed in a specific order. Here is a further reminder of **BOMDAS**.

Example :-   For $120 - 20 \times 6$ .... the answer is **NOT** .... $100 \times 6 = 600$.

The answer **IS** ...... $120 - 120 = 0$.

The easy way to remember which part of a calculation comes first is using the mnemonic **BOMDAS**.

B (rackets)
O (f)
M (ultiply)
D (ivide)
A (dd)
S (ubtract)

Example 1 :-	**Example 2 :-**	**Example 3 :-**
$15 + 9 \times 5$	one fifth of $80 - 15$	$(52 + 18) \div (7 \times 5)$
Multiply first	*Of first*	*Brackets first*
$= 15 + 45$	$= 16 - 15$	$= 70 \div 35$
$= 60$	$= 1$	$= 2$

• *Multiply & Divide rank equally*
• *Add & Subtract rank equally*

1	2	3	4
B	O	M or D	A or S

• *After you have applied **B** and **O**, go from left to right using any **M** or **D** as you find them.*

• *Then go from left to right doing any **A** or **S** as you find them.*

Exercise 1·3

1.   Use **BOMDAS** to help you calculate :-

(a) $14 + 8 \times 7$ (b) $80 - 9 \times 6$ (c) $30 \times 3 + 10$

(d) $79 - 72 \div 8$ (e) $200 - 80 \div 20$ (f) $32 - 54 \div 2$.

2.   Calculate :-

(a) $40 - 16 + 6 - 20$ (b)   one third of $75 \div 5$ (c)   one quarter of $102 - 6$

(d) $\frac{1}{2}$ of $108 \div 9$ (e) $12 + \frac{1}{4}$ of 72 (f) $23 - \frac{1}{3}$ of $18 + 15$

(g) $7 \times 9 - 200 \div 4 + 10$ (h) $6 \times 8 - 3 \times 9 + 56 \div 7$ (i) $12 - \frac{1}{5}$ of $(74 - 19)$.

3.   Find, showing two more steps each time :-

(a) $51 + (54 \div 6)$ (b) $125 \div (27 - 22)$ (c) $9 \times (18 + 32)$

(d) $500 \div (190 + 60)$ (e) $8 \times (7 + 4) - 77$ (f) $(8 + 2) \times (13 - 9) - 66$.

4.   **Copy** each of the following and **insert brackets** to make each calculation correct :-

(a) $4 + 8 \times 2 = 20$ (b) $37 - 7 \times 5 = 2$ (c) $20 + 28 \div 2 = 24$

(d) $30 + 50 \div 8 \times 5 = 2$ (e) $25 + 50 \div 28 - 3 = 3$ (f) $4 + 9 \times 4 - 8 + 5 = 27$.

5.   Find :-

(a) $500 \div 5 + 4 \times 10$ (b)   one sixth of $(67 + 5)$ (c) $3 \times (47 + 13)$

(d) $8 \times 8 - 4$ (e) $18 + 6 \times 7$ (f) $17 + (7 \times 9)$

(g) $300 - \frac{1}{3}$ of 90×5 (h) $\frac{1}{10}$ of $(\frac{1}{5}$ of $450)$ (i) $((48 \div 6) + 2) \times 9 - (67 + 13)$.

You have already found how to add, subtract, multiply and divide integers in CfE Level 3.
As you will frequently use these operations in CfE Level 4 and National 5, the exercise below will help you recall how to carry them out.

Examples :-

$-18 + 27$	$(-25) - 15$	$-7 \times 6p$	$-6a \times -9a$	$-2000 \div -40$
$= \boxed{9}$	$= \boxed{-40}$	$= \boxed{-42p}$	$= \boxed{54a^2}$	$= \boxed{50}$

Exercise 1·4

1. Simplify :-

   (a) $6 + (-7)$

   (b) $(-8) + (-10)$

   (c) $(-17) + (21)$

   (d) $30 - 75$

   (e) $(-8) - 9$

   (f) $(-12) - 1$

   (g) $(-12) - 15 - 6$

   (h) $(-3) + 9 + 6$

   (i) $7 - 12 - 5$

   (j) $(-3) + (-2) + 10$

   (k) $103 + 109 - 2$

   (l) $(-200) - 400 - 10.$

2. Simplify these algebraic expressions :-

   (a) $4x + 9x$

   (b) $x + (-6x)$

   (c) $8a - a$

   (d) $(-y) + 7y$

   (e) $(-3b) - 5b$

   (f) $(-8e) + 17e$

   (g) $(-5m) - 5m$

   (h) $(-2x) - 5x + 9x$

   (i) $2x + 9x - 10x$

   (j) $5c + (-8c) + 2c$

   (k) $(-7w) - 7w - 7w$

   (l) $5a + 7b - a - 2b.$

3. If $x = 6$ and $y = -4$, write down the value of :-

   (a) $3 - x$

   (b) $7 + y$

   (c) $x - 14$

   (d) $y + 20$

   (e) $(-x) + 15$

   (f) $(-x) + y$

   (g) $x + y$

   (h) $y - x.$

4. Simplify :-

   (a) $7 - (-1)$

   (b) $17 - (-3)$

   (c) $(-4) - (-6)$

   (d) $(-7) - (-1)$

   (e) $(-9) - (-10)$

   (f) $(-15) - (-15)$

   (g) $5x - (-3x)$

   (h) $0 - (-11x)$

   (i) $(-4x) - (-5x)$

   (j) $(-9x) - (-x)$

   (k) $-(-4x) - (-x)$

   (l) $(-8x^2) - (-8x^2).$

5. If $p = -2$, $q = -1$ and $r = -3$, find the value of :-

   (a) $p + q$

   (b) $p - q$

   (c) $q - r$

   (d) $q + r$

   (e) $p - r$

   (f) $r + p.$

   (g) $(-p) - r$

   (h) $-(-r) + q.$

6. Work out the answers to the following :-

   (a) $3 \times (-3)$

   (b) $(-7) \times 5$

   (c) $9 \times (-1)$

   (d) $(-20) \times 0$

   (e) $5 \times (-2a)$

   (f) $(-7y) \times 3$

   (g) $2x \times (-3x)$

   (h) $(-40) \div 4$

   (i) $(-50x) \div 5$

   (j) $(-18p) \div 9$

   (k) $(-15m) \div 3m$

   (l) $7 \times (-1) \times 4$

   (m) $((-5) - 1) \times 8$

   (n) $((-17) - 13) \div 3$

   (o) $(-7) \times (-10)$

   (p) $(-40) \times (-5)$

   (q) $(-35) \div (-7)$

   (r) $(-90) \div (-9)$

   (s) $5 \times (-2) \times (-4)$

   (t) $((-19) + (-9)) \div -7$

   (u) $(-2a) \times (-6a)$

   (v) $(-7)^2$

   (w) $(-2)^6$

   (x) $(-4)^2 - (-2)^3.$

7. If $a = 5$, $b = 0$ and $c = -2$, find the value of :-

   (a) abc

   (b) $a + b + c$

   (c) $a^2 + b^2 + c^2$

   (d) $ab + bc + ca$

   (e) $a^2 + b - c$

   (f) $4a^2 + 2c^2$

   (g) $a^3 + c^3$

   (h) $a^2 - 5c^2$

   (i) $(a + c)(c - a)$

   (j) $b(a^3 + c^2 - 5ac).$

Remember Remember..... ?

1. Round each number to 1 sig. fig. :-

(a) 62   (b) 369

(c) 5279   (d) 47 261

(e) 3·76   (f) 0·418

(g) 0·046   (h) 7 350 000

(i) 0·000 395   (j) 49·99.

2. Round each number to 2 sig. figs. :-

(a) 708   (b) 7147

(c) 50 800   (d) 272 666

(e) 58·29   (f) 69·73

(g) 8·174   (h) 0·449

(i) 0·001 6793   (j) 39·828.

3. Round each number to 3 sig. figs. :-

(a) 6942   (b) 34 074

(c) 62 951   (d) 731 188

(e) 13·838   (f) 13·296

(g) 0·396 52   (h) 0·293 54

(i) 0·001 778   (j) 0·037 777.

4. Round each number to 1 significant figure to estimate each calculation :-

(a) 5723 + 1122   (b) 62 438 − 11 748

(c) 329 221 + 694 330

(d) 471 × 185   (e) 789 ÷ 21

(f) 345 687 ÷ 98   (g) 412 555 × 196

(h) 8 719 232 ÷ 3198

(i) Avone Hotels are being built with 478 rooms. To date, 23 hotels have been built. How many rooms in total ?

5. Round each number to 2 significant figures to estimate each calculation :-

(a) 792 + 223   (b) 584 − 369

(c) 52 294 − 21 116   (d) 41 182 − 10 714

(e) 1985 × 179   (f) 301 × 189

(g) 10 165 × 5980   (h) 362 ÷ 178

(i) Trevor earned £386 250 last year. Jane earned £274 650. How much less did Jane earn ?

6. Calculate :-

(a) one fifth of 100 ÷ 20

(b) $14 + \frac{1}{4}$ of 56

(c) $33 - \frac{1}{3}$ of 39 + 13

(d) 7 × 8 − 4 × 9 + 63 ÷ 7

(e) $23 + \frac{3}{4}$ of 20 − 38

(f) $250 - \frac{1}{8}$ of 400 × 5.

7. Simplify :-

(a) $x + (-9x)$ (b) $(-4p) - 8p$

(c) $(-7n) - 7n$ (d) $3g + (-6g) + 2g$

(e) $(-y) - y - (-y)$ (f) $4a + 8b - a - 7b$

(g) $(-4w) - (-6w)$ (h) $0 - (-40x)$

(i) $-(-5m) - (-m)$ (j) $(-10x^2) - (-4x^2)$.

8. Work out :-

(a) $7 \times (-6)$ (b) $15 \times (-2a)$

(c) $(-9y) \times 3$ (d) $4x \times (-5x)$

(e) $(-80x) \div 8$ (f) $(-20m) \div 2m$

(g) $(-6k) \times (-9k)$ (h) $(-5)^2$

(i) $(-2)^5$ (j) $(-8)^2 - (-4)^3$.

9. If $a = 4$, $b = 0$, $c = -2$ and $d = -1$,

Find :-

(a) $a + c$ (b) $b - d$

(c) $d - 2a$ (d) $2c - 3d$

(e) $(-c) - (-a)$ (f) $(-a) + cd$

(g) $b + cd$ (h) $a + c - d$

(i) $(-a) - c - 2d$ (j) $(-5c) - 3a - d$

(k) acd (l) $ac - d$

(m) $a^2 + b^2 + c^2$ (n) $ab + bc + ca$

(o) $a^2 + b - c$ (p) $4a^2 + 2d^2$

(q) $a^3 + c^3$ (r) $(-d^2) - 5c^2$.

10. Find :-

(a) $17 + 11 \times 2$ (b) $\frac{1}{4}$ of (8 + 12) × 5.

Basic Revision Work - a Reminder !

The angles round a point always add to give **360°**.	Two angles making a straight line always add to give **180°**.	Angles opposite each other at a cross **are equal**.

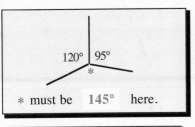

120° 95°

* must be **145°** here.

140° *

* must be **40°** here.

32° *

* must be **32°** here.

The 3 angles of every triangle always add to give **180°**.	Two of the angles in an **isosceles** triangle are equal.	All three of the angles in an equilateral triangle **are equal**.

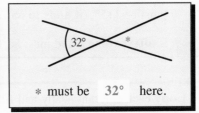

40° * 35°

* must be **105°** here.

50° *

* must be **80°** here.

* * *

* must be **60°** here.

Exercise 2·1

1. Calculate the sizes of the angles marked a, b, ...

2. Calculate the sizes of the angles marked m, n, ...

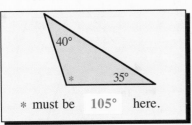

$a°$ 122°

69°
$c°$

$b°$ 46°

$d°$ 82°
$d°$

40° 90° $e°$

34° $f°$ 34°

$g°$
41°

77°
$h°$

52°
$i°$

$j°$ 105°

$k°$
19·5°

$l°$

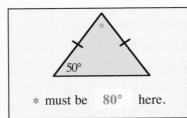

$m°$ 32°
29°

$n°$ 61°
42°

53°
$o°$

$p°$
101° 151°

$q°$
53°

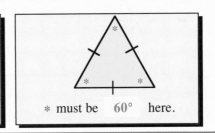

65°
$r°$

38° $s°$

42°
$t°$

94°
$u°$

$v°$

48°
$w°$

38°
$x°$

 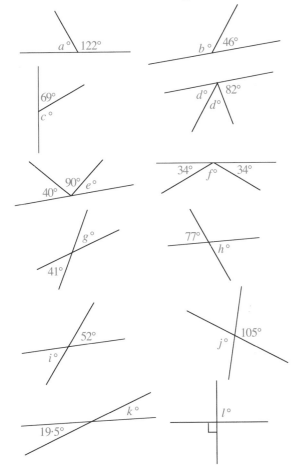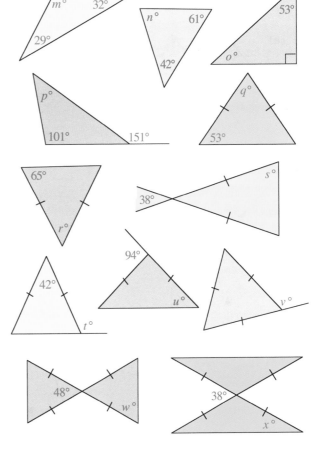

The following should also be known :-

- *e* is **corresponding** to *a* and must be 65°.

- *c* is **(vertically) opposite** *a* and must be 65°.

- *b* must be 115°, **(it adds to 65 to give 180)**.

- *h* is **alternate** to *b* and must be 115° also.

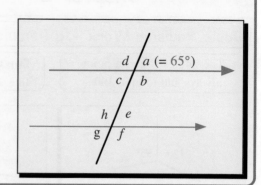

3. **Copy** each diagram neatly and fill in the sizes of **every** angle.

(a)

(b)

61°

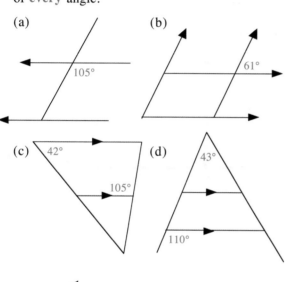

(c) 42°

105°

(d) 43°

110°

(e)

40°

(f) 136°

(g)

29°

(h)

(i)

125°

35°

(j) 63°

75°

(k)

290°

(l)

146°

112°

(m)

113°

(n) 32°

(o) 115°

93°

(p) 70°

(q) 32°

112°

(r) 278°

29°

(s)

Two congruent
equilateral triangles

(t) 86°

32°

Parallelogram

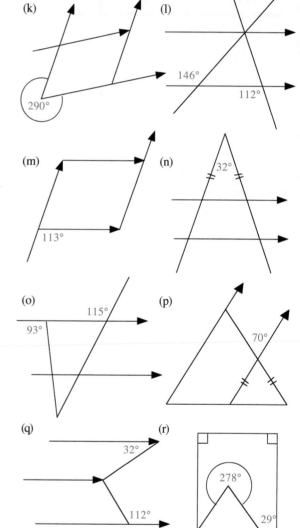
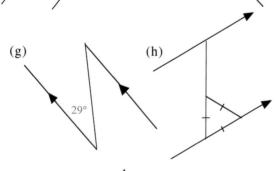
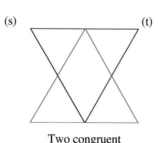
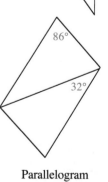

Quadrilaterals - A Reminder

You should know by this stage that the :-

"4 angles of a **quadrilateral** always add to give **360°**."

$$a + b + c + d = 360$$

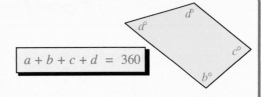

You should also be able to calculate missing angles in any of the 5 main quadrilaterals.

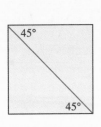 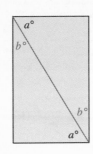 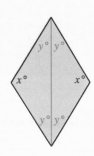 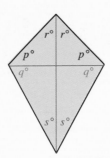 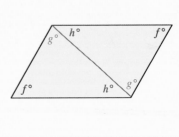

Exercise 2·2

1. **Sketch** the following quadrilaterals, name them and mark in the sizes of all the angles :-

(a)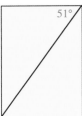
51°

(b)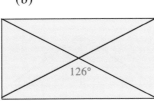
126°

(c)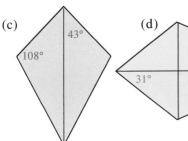
43°
108°

(d)
31°   50°

(e)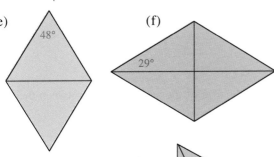
48°

(f)
29°

(g)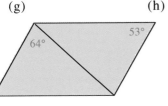
64°   53°

(h)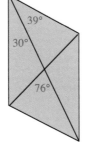
39°
30°
76°

2. This shape consists of a rectangle with a trapezium on top and it has 1 **vertical** line of symmetry.

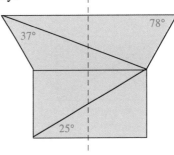
37°   78°
25°

Sketch it and fill in **ALL** the missing angles.

3. This shape is made from a rhombus and a kite.

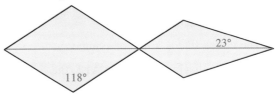
23°
118°

Sketch it and fill in **ALL** the missing angles.

4. ABCD and DEFG are a pair of **congruent** rhombuses and BF is a line of symmetry.

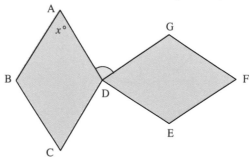
A
$x°$
G
B
D
F
E
C

Let ∠BAD = $x°$. Prove that ∠ADG = 90°.

1. **Copy** each figure and fill in the sizes of **all** the missing angles.

(a)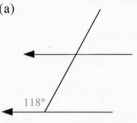

(b)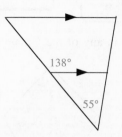

(c)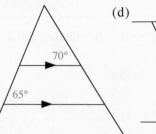

(d)

(e)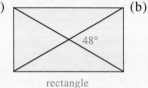

(f)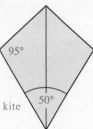

(g)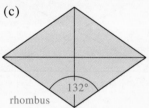

(h)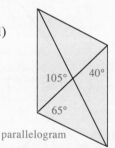

2. **Copy** each figure and fill in the sizes of **all** the missing angles.

(a)
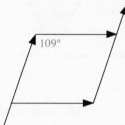
rectangle

(b)
95°
50°
kite

(c)
132°
rhombus

(d)
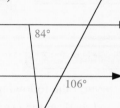
105°   40°
65°
parallelogram

3. This shape consists of two congruent rectangles (ABCD and PQRS) and trapezium BPSC.

The dotted line is a line of symmetry.

Copy the diagram and fill in **ALL** the missing angles.

B   65°   P

A

C S

Q

D   70°   R

4.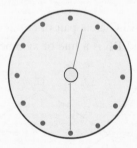

Calculate the size of the smaller angle between the two hands at half past 12.

5. Repeat question 4 for the time :- (a) quarter to 5 (b) quarter past 3.

Finding a Percentage without a Calculator

Many **percentages** can be reduced to simple fractions.

e.g.   To find **25%** of a quantity, **divide by 4.**   **20%** of a quantity, **divide by 5.**

        75% of a quantity, **divide by 4**, then multiply by 3.   etc ....

To find $75\% \text{ of } £120 = \frac{3}{4} \text{ of } £120 = (£120 \div 4) \times 3 = £90$

percentage	50%	25%	75%	$33\frac{1}{3}\%$	$66\frac{2}{3}\%$	20%	40%	60%	80%	10%	30%	70%	90%
fraction	$\frac{1}{2}$	$\frac{1}{4}$	$\frac{3}{4}$	$\frac{1}{3}$	$\frac{2}{3}$	$\frac{1}{5}$	$\frac{2}{5}$	$\frac{3}{5}$	$\frac{4}{5}$	$\frac{1}{10}$	$\frac{3}{10}$	$\frac{7}{10}$	$\frac{9}{10}$

Examples :-

To find 9% .....

• first, find 1%, ($\div$ 100)

• then times by 9. ($\times$ 9)

To find 70% .....

• first find 10%, ($\div$ 10)

• then times by 7. ($\times$ 7)

To find 19% .....

• first find 10%, ($\div$ 10)

• then find 9% (see Ex.1)

• then add them both.

Exercise 3·1

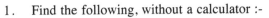

1. Find the following, without a calculator :-

(a) 10% of £18   (b) 70% of £30

(c) 20% of £10·10   (d) 80% of 560 kg

(e) 25% of 1152 cm (f) $33\frac{1}{3}\%$ of £54

(g) 75% of £5·16   (h) 1% of 240 g

(i) 60% of 3700 m (j) 50% of £3·2 million

(k) $66\frac{2}{3}\%$ of £27·90 (l) 10% of £9

(m) 3% of £1200   (n) 5% of £3

(o) 8% of £15 000 (p) $7\frac{1}{2}\%$ of £400.

2. Calculate, set down with working :-

(a) 11% of £40   (b) 15% of £80

(c) 3% of £28   (d) 8% of 5000 km

(e) 5% of 2480 cm (f) 2% of 64 000 miles

(g) 12% of £150   (h) 15% of £3200

(i) 90% of 62 000 g (j) $12\frac{1}{2}\%$ of £2400

(k) 4% of £2280   (l) 120% of £3000

(m) 0·5% of 4800 kg (n) 1·5% of £900

(o) 2·5% of £20 000 (p) $37\frac{1}{2}\%$ of £12.

3. Abby got 20% discount when buying a coat in a sale.

If the coat was originally priced at £250, what did Abby pay for it ?

4. Joseph has £38 000 to invest.

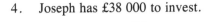

Scotco Bank
1·5% interest p.a.

Scots Bank
2% interest p.a.

How much more money will he gain over a year if he puts his money in Scots Bank ?

5. Ross County announced that season ticket sales were up by $12\frac{1}{2}\%$ on the previous season.

Last season, 1200 season tickets were sold.

How many this season ?

6. Out of 500 people surveyed at a supermarket, 30% liked duck, 15% liked pheasant, 45% liked chicken, while the rest preferred rabbit.

How many of those surveyed liked :-

(a) duck   (b) pheasant

(c) chicken   (d) rabbit ?

When using a calculator, remember to show ALL of your working.

Example :-   Find 65% of £8250

$$\frac{65}{100} \times £8250$$
$$= (65 \div 100) \times £8250$$
$$= 5362 \cdot 5$$
$$= £5362 \cdot 50$$

note the "0"

Exercise 3·2

1. Find the following, using a calculator :-

   (a) 14% of £1200   (b) 76% of 240 miles

   (c) 24% of £25·50   (d) 85% of 780 kg

   (e) 22·5% of 60 cm   (f) 33% of 960 g

   (g) 48% of £90   (h) 8·5% of 3500 km

   (i) 64% of 4400 m   (j) 16% of 8 mm

   (k) $66\frac{2}{3}$% of £85·50 (l) 29% of £4·5 million.

2. On St. Andrew's Day, 95% of the pupils at Crieff High School wore a tartan ribbon.

   If there were 820 pupils in attendance on that day, how many wore a ribbon ?

3. Diana weighed 85 kg a week ago, but on her return from holiday found that her weight had increased by 4%.

   What is her weight now ?

4. In a survey outside a butcher's, 72% of those asked, said they preferred mince pie to steak pie.

   If 650 people took part, how many voted for mince pie ?

5. Manic Menswear have jackets on offer with an 18% discount.

   What's the discounted price of a jacket, originally priced £94·50 ?

6. (a) 4500 people visited a golf driving range.

   27% of them had never played golf before.

   How many was that ?

   (b) As they were new to the sport, they were offered $12\frac{1}{2}$% off the normal fee of £8·40 for a hundred balls.

   How much did each of them have to pay ?

7. For the St Mirren v Hearts League Cup Final in 2013, the Saints were allocated 17 500 tickets.

   Hearts were given 33% more than that.

   How many tickets did Hearts get ?

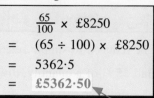

8. Slimline cameras were on sale in a shop, priced £340.

   The shopkeeper decided to increase their price by $7\frac{1}{2}$%.

   (a) How much was the increase ?

   (b) What's the new price ?

   The shopkeeper reduced the price of a £40 camera case by $2\frac{1}{2}$%.

   (c) How much would it be now to buy a Slimline camera with a case ?

9. Holiday travel company Jet4 had a holiday to the Algarve on offer at £825 per person.

   Rival company Easyfly, presented the same holiday, priced £650.

   Jet4 reduced their prices by 18%, while Easyfly increased theirs by 4·5%.

   Which holiday company is now the cheaper ?

10. Two bungalows are each valued at £280 000.

    By the end of next year, Bungalow 1 is expected to be worth 3·25% more whereas Bungalow 2's value is expected to drop by 1·08%.

    (a) Calculate the new expected value of each bungalow.

    (b) How much of a difference is there between the new values of the 2 bungalows.

Linking Fractions, Decimals & Percentages

You have already learned that finding a percentage of a quantity can be worked out in at least 4 ways :-

e.g   40% of £8 can be done :- $\frac{2}{5}$ × £8 or Find 10% of £8, then × 4 or $\frac{40}{100}$ × £8 or 0·40 × £8.

Each time the answer will be £3·20.

The following exercise gives you the opportunity to link fractions with decimals, and with percentages.

Examples :-   Change each of these fractions into a decimal, then into a percentage :-

$$\frac{12}{50} = 12 \div 50 = 0·24 = 24\%$$

$$\frac{3}{8} = 3 \div 8 = 0·375 = 37·5\%$$

Exercise 3·3

1. **Copy** and complete :-

   (a) $\frac{14}{25} = 14 \div 25 = 0·.... = ...\%$

   (b) $\frac{7}{10} = ... \div ... = 0·.... = ...\%$

   (c) $\frac{30}{40} = ... \div ... = 0·.... = ...\%$

   (d) $\frac{5}{8} = ... \div ... = 0·.... = ...\%.$

2. Change each of the given fractions into a **decimal**, then into a **percentage** :-

   (a) $\frac{32}{40}$ (b) $\frac{3}{40}$

   (c) $\frac{21}{28}$ (d) $\frac{92}{200}$

   (e) $\frac{6}{150}$ (f) $\frac{37}{370}$.

3. Change these **fractions** to **percentages** :-

   (a) $\frac{1}{10}$ (b) $\frac{21}{105}$

   (c) $\frac{18}{20}$ (d) $\frac{44}{220}$

   (e) $\frac{18}{60}$ (f) $\frac{333}{5550}$.

4. Maria sat 3 tests. She scored :-

   $\frac{24}{40}$ for Art

   $\frac{38}{70}$ for Music

   $\frac{56}{90}$ for Graphics.

   (a) Change her marks to percentages.

   (b) In which subject did she perform best ?

5. Change these marks into percentages :-

   (a) Andy   30 out of 80

   (b) Beth   33 out of 44

   (c) Carole   21 out of 35

   (d) Donnie   45 out of 72

   (e) Elsie   48 out of 60.

6. Put each of the lists in order, largest first :-

   (a) 0·45, $\frac{11}{20}$,   47%

   (b) 89%, $\frac{70}{80}$,   0·825%

   (c) $\frac{4}{80}$,   0·02, $\frac{1}{9}$,   3%.

7. Put each of the lists in order, smallest first :-

   (a) $33\frac{1}{3}\%$ of £279, $\frac{4}{7}$ of £147,   0·62 × £145

   (b) 0·125 × £40, $\frac{4}{9}$ × £12·60,   72% of £8

   (c) 65% of 160,   0·85 × £120, $\frac{1}{2}\%$ of £21 000.

8. Henry was quoted £12 000 at Melvins Garage for a new Mezdo car.

   Vardon Motors asked for 92% of Melvin's price.

   Williamson Cars would give Henry 0·2 off Vardon's offer.

   Henry finally bought his new Mezdo from Taylor Autos for seven eighths of Williamson's price.

   What did he pay for his new car ?

No Calculator to be used in Qu's 1-7.

 Calculator can be used from Qu 8 onwards.

1. Change the percentages to a decimal and then to a fraction in its simplest form :-

    (a) 35%   (b) 18%

    (c) 52%   (d) 12·5%

    (e) $66\frac{2}{3}$ %   (f) $62\frac{1}{2}$ %.

2. Change each of these into a percentage :-

    (a) 0·66   (b) 0·1

    (c) 0·04   (d) 0·875

    (e) $\frac{4}{5}$ (f) $\frac{17}{20}$

    (g) $\frac{21}{25}$ (h) 1·25.

3. Work out :-

    (a) $\frac{5}{9}$ of 1188 km   (b) $\frac{11}{20}$ of £60·60

    (c) $\frac{3}{40}$ of 80p   (d) 70% of 90p

    (e) $12\frac{1}{2}$ % of £2440   (f) $33\frac{1}{3}$ % of 72 kg

    (g) 0·4 of £240   (h) 0·025 of £2000.

4. Robert bought a guitar for £630.

    He sold it later for $\frac{7}{9}$ of that price.

    How much did he get for it ?

5. 92% of the packs of burgers were removed from a supermarket's shelves.

    Of the 300 packs on the shelves how many remained ?

6. In 2011 my car insurance cost me £500.

     In 2012 it was increased by 4% and there was a further 5% increase in 2013.

    How much did it cost me to insure it in 2013?

7. Jeff puts £1200 into his current account with Scotia bank, earning him a poor 0·5% interest per annum.

    How much should he expect to have in his account after one year ?

8. Calculate :-

    (a) 18% of £510   (b) $\frac{2}{9}$ of £72

    (c) 0·45 of £7·20   (d) $87\frac{1}{2}$ % of £40 000

    (e) $\frac{19}{25}$ of 4250 kg   (f) 0·07 of £28

    (g) $\frac{1}{2}$ % of 225 g   (h) 0·4 of $12\frac{1}{2}$ % of £40.

9.  Gas prices have increased by 6% over the last few months.

    Before the increase, my bills were working out at £90·50 per month.

    How much will they be now ?

10. The managing director's salary last year was £420 000.

    This year he got a 7·5% pay rise.

    (a) What is his new salary ?

    (b) How much is that per month ?

11.  A new jar of coffee claims to have 17·5% more coffee.

    The old jar stated that there was enough coffee to have 80 decent sized cups.

    How many cups of coffee should you get from the new jar ?

12. List these people in order, beginning with the person with the largest new salary.

    Trevor, £510 per week, gets rise of £38 per week.

    Paula, £28 000 per year, gets 2·5% wage rise.

    Senga, £2280 per month, gets $\frac{1}{20}$ pay rise.

13. Mrs Parkin bought a freezer which was priced £368 by putting down a 37·5% deposit and paying the remainder over 10 months.

    As she had paid such a large deposit she didn't have to pay any extra money over the period.

    What was her monthly payment ?

1.   Round each of the following to the number of significant figures indicated in **red** :-

(a) 3·784 **(2)**   (b) 1452   **(2)**

(c) 9·091 **(1)**   (d) 812617 **(3)**.

2.   At a local football match the number of spectators **to 2 significant figures** was reported as 3500.

What was the **minimum** number of spectators ?

3.   Find :-   (a) $3 + 5 \times 2$

(b) $2 - 6 \div 3$ (c) $24 - 4 + 3 \times 6 \div 2$.

4.   Insert brackets to make each of the following correct :-

(a) $3 + 4 \times 3 = 21$ (b) $24 \div 3 + 5 = 3$

(c) $12 + 6 \times 2 \div 3 + 1 - 10 = 2$.

5.   **Copy** the following and simplify :-

(a) $9 - (-3)$ (b) $(-2) - (-11)$

(c) $(-9x) - (-x)$ (d) $(-6x^2) - (-6x^2)$

(e) $(-8y) \times 4$ (f) $3x \times (-5x)$

(g) $(-40x) \div 8$ (h) $(18p) \div (-9)$

(i) $5 \times (-2) \times 6$ (j) $(-42) \div (-7)$

(k) $(-3) \times (-2) \times (-4)$ (l) $(-6a) \times (-7a)$.

6.   Given $a = 3$, $b = 2$, $c = -1$ and $d = -2$, find :-

(a) $a + c$ (b) $b - d$

(c) $d - 2a$ (d) $2c - 3d$

(e) $(-c) - (-a)$ (f) $(-a) + cd$

(g) $a^2 + b - c$ (h) $(-d^2) - 5c^2$.

7.   Find :-

(a) $\frac{5}{9}$ of 8109 km   (b) $\frac{11}{20}$ of £50·20

(c) $\frac{3}{40}$ of 1200 kg   (d) 70% of 80 cm

(e) $12\frac{1}{2}$% of £168   (f) $33\frac{1}{3}$% of 81 km

(g) 0·4 of £120   (h) 0·025 of $3000

(i) 15% of £8   (j) 17·5% of 80 mm.

8.   Sketch each of these and fill in the sizes of **all** the missing angles :-

(a)   (b)

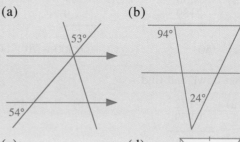

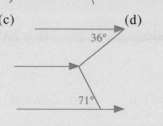

(c)   (d)

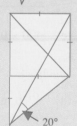

9.   Find the reflex angle between the hands of a clock at ten past twelve (*to the nearest degree*).

You may use a calculator for questions 10 - 12.

10. A sales manager earned £42 000 last year.

This year he got a 3·5% pay rise.

(a) What is his new salary ?

(b) How much is that per month ?

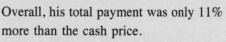

11. Larry earned £414 a week, but now gets a 5% pay increase.

Louise had an annual salary of £21 600, but receives a $\frac{1}{25}$ pay rise.

If they are both paid monthly (*12 monthly payments per year*), who now gets a **higher** *monthly* pay **and** by how much ?

12. Mr Jonah bought a motorbike which was priced £4680 by putting down a 43% deposit and paying the remainder over 10 months.

Overall, his total payment was only 11% more than the cash price.

What was his monthly payment ?

Turn off that Calculator...

1. Set down and find :-

   (a) $\begin{array}{r} 6000 \\ -\ 2189 \\ \hline \end{array}$ (b) $\begin{array}{r} 397 \\ \times\ 9 \\ \hline \end{array}$ (c) $\begin{array}{r} 1376 \\ \times\ 600 \\ \hline \end{array}$ (d) $\begin{array}{r} 59 \\ \times\ 27 \\ \hline \end{array}$ (e) $9\overline{)8073}$

   (f) 50^2 (g) $66\,500 \div 70$ (h) $30 - 9 \times 3$ (i) $8 \times (9 + 5) - 7$ (j) $34 - 18 \div 2.$

2. Set down and find :-

   (a) $\begin{array}{r} 5 \cdot 172 \\ -\ 1 \cdot 879 \\ \hline \end{array}$ (b) $8 - 2 \cdot 457$ (c) $9\overline{)43 \cdot 74}$ (d) $\begin{array}{r} 3 \cdot 178 \\ \times\ 7 \\ \hline \end{array}$

   (e) $400 \times 0 \cdot 416$ (f) $748 \div 200$ (g) $\dfrac{7 \times 25 \cdot 4}{1000}$ (h) $19 \cdot 6 \div 10\,000.$

3. Change :-

   (a) 3720 m to km   (b) 0·06 km to m   (c) 54 cm to m   (d) 3096 g to kg.

4. Find :-   (a) $\frac{3}{8}$ of 64   (b) $\frac{4}{5}$ of 2000   (c) $\frac{5}{9}$ of 1530 .

5. Simplify :-   (a) $\dfrac{32}{48}$ (b) $\dfrac{35}{49}$ (c) $\dfrac{21}{91}$.

6. Find :-   (a) $\frac{3}{4} - \frac{1}{2}$ (b) $3\frac{1}{2} + 2\frac{1}{4}$ (c) $4 - 1\frac{1}{8}$ (d) $3 \times 5\frac{1}{3}$.

7. Express as a fraction :-   (a) 80%   (b) $12\frac{1}{2}\%$ (c) $133\frac{1}{3}\%$.

8. Find :-   (a) 75% of £1600   (b) 5% of £2400   (c) $33\frac{1}{3}\%$ of £4·44

   (d) 40% of £150   (e) $12\frac{1}{2}\%$ of £560   (f) 3% of £4.

9. Find :-   (a) $28 + (-13)$ (b) $141 + (-19)$ (c) $(-29) + 15$

   (d) $(-18) + (-22)$ (e) $14 - 20$ (f) $(-9) - 32$ (g) $14 - (-6)$

   (h) $(-11) - (-15)$ (i) $0 - (-29)$ (j) $(-6) - (-7)$ (k) $(-2) - 3 - 4.$

10. Find :-

    (a) $(-4) \times 13$ (b) $8 \times (-21)$ (c) $(-6) \times (-7)$ (d) $(-15) \div 3$

    (e) $(-11)^2$ (f) $210 \div (-7)$ (g) $(-40) \div (-8)$ (h) $\dfrac{(-4) \times (-12)}{(-6)}$.

11. Convert to 24 hour format :-   (a) 8·25 am   (b) 7·45 pm   (c) $\frac{1}{4}$ to midnight.

12. How long is it from :-   (a) 7·50 am to 2·25 pm   (b) 2·43 pm to 7·16 pm ?

13. A show starts at 4·45 pm and lasts for two and three quarter hours. At what time does it end ?

14. (a) How far will a plane travel in 2 hours 20 minutes at an average speed of 360 m.p.h. ?

    (b) A train covered the 640 km from Glasgow to London in 5 hours.   Calculate its average speed.

Wages and Salaries

Payment for work done by you is called your **pay**, **wage** or **salary**.

An **income** is generally regarded as a weekly, monthly or yearly (**annual**) salary.

Overtime is extra work above your normal number of hours.

It is usually paid at a **higher rate** of pay :-

Time and a Half	1·5 × the normal rate
Double Time	2 × the normal rate
Treble Time	3 × the normal rate

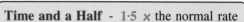

Exercise 4·1

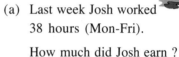

1. Calculate the **weekly** salaries for :-

    (a) Andrew - £9 per hour   - works 40 hrs.

    (b) Sarah - £8·25 per hour   - works 38 hrs.

    (c) Chloe - £10·66 per hour - works 52 hrs.

    (d) David - £12·68 per hour - works 44·5 hrs.

2. Calculate these **annual** salaries :-

    (a) Gregor earns £380 per **week**.

    (b) Natalie earns £824 per **week**.

    (c) Calum earns £1325 per **month**.

    (d) Russell earns £2376 per **month**.

3. Calculate each person's **monthly** salary :-

    (a) Scott earns £19 800 **annually**.

    (b) Zoe earns £36 000 **per year**.

    (c) Lyle earns £42 586·56 **per annum** (yearly).

4. Calculate each person's **weekly** salary :-

    (a) Stephen earns £29 265·60 annually.

    (b) Ryan earns £38 012·52 yearly.

    (c) Ross earns £50 445·20 per annum.

5. Calculate these **weekly** salaries :-
    (a)

    > **Joiner's Assistant**
    > **9 am - 6 pm (Mon to Fri)**
    > £7·20 per hour.

    (b)

    > **Secretary**
    > **8·30 am - 5 pm (Mon to Fri)**
    > £8·42 per hour.

6. Calculate the **annual** salaries for the joiner and the secretary in question 5.

7. Josh earns £7 an hour as a plumber's mate.

    He also gets paid **double time** on a Saturday.

    (a) Last week Josh worked 38 hours (Mon-Fri).

    How much did Josh earn ?

    (b) Last Saturday Josh worked for 6 hours. How much did he earn last Saturday ?

    (c) How much did he earn last week **in total** ?

8. Mark earns £9·50 an hour as a labourer.

    He gets paid **time and a half** on a Saturday and **treble time** on a Sunday.

    Last week Mark worked :-

    > 9 am to 4 pm (Mon - Fri),
    > 5 hours on Saturday and
    > 4 hours on Sunday.

    Calculate his **total weekly wage**.

9. Amy works 36 hours a week at £7·44 per hour.

    She worked 4 hours on Friday night at **time and a half,** and 3 hours on Saturday at **double time**.

    (a) How much did Amy earn that week ?

    (b) What would be her **annual** wage if these were her usual working times every week ?

10. Sam earns £6·80 per hour at the Supermarket.

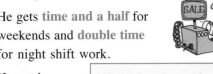

He gets **time and a half** for weekends and **double time** for night shift work.

He works :–

Mon-Fri from 9 am to 3 pm
Thursday nights 8 pm to 4 am
Saturdays from 11 am to 6 pm.

Calculate Sam's **annual** wage.

11. Andrew earns the same hourly rate as Sam.

He starts work (Mon-Fri) at 9 am and also works the same hours as Sam does on a Thursday and a Saturday.

Andrew earns £350·20 a week.

What time must he finish work on a weekday ?

12. Claudia earned £244·80 for 12 hours overtime.

She *thought* she was being paid **double time** but *actually* only got paid at **time and a half**.

How much **less** did she get than she expected ?

Commission is usually paid as a **percentage** of the amount of sales.

Example :– Sean is paid 5% **commission** on £18 000 worth of cars he sold.

Commission = 5% of £18 000
= 0·05 × 18 000
= £900

---

13. (a) Last month Sean sold £24 600 worth of cars. How much commission (5%) did he earn ?

(b) Leah earns 6% commission on all her sales. How much commission would she earn on £32 000 worth of sales ?

(c) Kimmi earns 12·5% commission. How much would she earn on £4500 sales ?

14. Laura has a basic wage of £12 000 **p.a.** (*p.a. is short for per annum*).

She also earns 8% **commission**, but this time it is only awarded on any sales **over** £10 000.

Last year Laura sold £35 000 worth of clothes.

(a) What commission did she earn last year ?

(b) What were her total earnings last year ?

15. Lyndsay has a basic wage of £16 000 per year.

She sold £120 000 worth of windows for which she earned 4·5% **commission**.

How much did Lyndsay earn **in total** ?

16. Two adverts for salespeople are as shown.

CARS - R - US	CELLCARS
£600 per month	**£800 per month**
PLUS	PLUS
8% commission	**7% commission**

A good sales person would be expected to sell £30 000 worth of cars each month.

With which company would a salesperson earn more (*based on £30 000 sales*) ?

17. Craig is paid £7·90 an hour basic rate as a computer salesman, working 9 am to 3 pm (Mon to Fri).

He also works 10 am - 6 pm on a Saturday (paid at **time and a half**).

Craig also earns 3% **commission** on all sales.

Last week Craig sold £9300 worth of goods.

What was his **total** wage last week ?

18. A sales company pays commission as follows :–

Total Sales	Commission
£5000 - £15 000	3·25%
£15 001 - £25 000	5·5%
over £25 000	7·5%

(a) Calculate the commission on sales of :-

(i) £12 800   (ii) £33 480

(iii) £41 942   (iv) £25 000.

(b) Paula earned £3000 in commission. What were her **total sales** worth ?

19. Alison earned £1514 in total last month.

Her basic wage of £1250 is supplemented by a percentage commission on all sales.

Last month her total sales were £17 600.

What percentage commission did Alison get ?

Gross pay is the amount that an employer pays you.

Deductions are taken from your gross pay and include things like :-

Superannuation - a type of extra pension for when you retire.

National Insurance - (N.I.) to pay for loss of earnings if you are sick / unemployed.

Income Tax - tax paid to the government to pay for education, health, transport, etc.

Net pay is the amount that you *take home* after deductions are made.

Net Pay = Gross Pay – Deductions

Exercise 4·2

1. Calculate each **annual net** (take home) **pay** :-

	Name	Gross Pay	Deductions
(a)	Stephanie	£18 000 p.a.	£3270
(b)	Bianca	£24 500 p.a.	£4010
(c)	Daniel	£2125 *(per month)*	£477 *(per month)*

2. Harry has a gross pay of £28 000 per annum. He pays £5240 in deductions.

   (a) Calculate his annual **net** pay.

   (b) What is Harry's **weekly** take home pay ?

3. Jack has an **annual** salary of £15 200. He has to pay the following deductions :-

Superannuation	: £920
National Insurance (N.I.)	: £1200
Income Tax	: £1152

   (a) Calculate Jack's total deductions.

   (b) Calculate his annual **net pay**.

4. Ethan is paid £635 a week. His weekly deductions are as follows :-

Income Tax	: £91
National Insurance (N.I.)	: £76
Superannuation	: 5% of gross wage

   Calculate Ethan's weekly **net pay.**

5. Will has a monthly **net** wage of £2460.

   His monthly deductions are £786.

   Calculate his monthly **gross** wage.

6. Frank has an annual **net** pay of £34 000. His deductions are £8275 per annum.

   Calculate Frank's **gross** pay.

7. Ivan works a 40 hour week, earning a gross pay of £346.

   As well as this, he worked 10 hours overtime, paid at **time and a half.**

   Last week, he paid £36 Income Tax, £42 N.I. and 8% superannuation (*based on his total wage*).

   Calculate his **take home pay** for last week.

   (*You will need to calculate his basic rate of pay first*).

8. Last year, Alicia had a gross pay of £76 000, and a took home a net pay of £59 765.

   16235

   She paid £6840 towards her superannuation and paid £5320 in N.I. contributions.

   What did she pay in Income Tax last year ?

9. (*Hard*) Olivia has a take home pay of £39 880 per annum as a managing director of an IT company.

   She pays 6% of her gross pay towards superannuation, which comes to £3480.

   Her NI payments are £4640.

   Calculate her **Income Tax** payment.

Income Tax

Income Tax calculation is a difficult and sometimes very confusing process.

The Inland Revenue - (the tax people !) - do not calculate your tax bill purely on your gross income. Instead, they give you **allowances** and **relief** on part of your income - other factors are taken into consideration. (Are you employed or self-employed ? What assets or liabilities do you have ? Expense accounts, Capital Gains, the list goes on...)

The Inland Revenue determines your **Taxable Income** (earnings that will be taxed) from the above.

In 2013 the Income Tax calculations were as shown in the table below.

Rates of Tax :–

- first £32010 of taxable income **20%**

- £32011- £150000 of taxable income **40%**

- all remaining taxable income **45%** (over £150000)

Example 1 :-

Mr Greig has a **taxable income** of £18400.		
20% of £18400	=	£3680
Total Income Tax due is		**£3680**

Example 2 :-

Mrs Bishop has a **taxable income** of £68400.		
20% of £32010	=	£6402
40% of £36390	=	£14556
Total Income Tax due is		**£20958**

Exercise 4·3

1. Mr Fleming has a **taxable income** of £23650. Copy and complete :-

20% of £23650	=	£ ....
Total Income Tax due is		£............

2. Mr Bond has a **taxable income** of £58400. Copy and complete :-

20% of £32010	=	£ ....
40% of £............	=	£ ....
Total Income Tax due is		£............

3. Dr No has a **taxable income** of £155000. Copy and complete :-

20% of £32010	=	£ ....
40% of £117990	=	£ ....
45% of £............	=	£ ....
Total Income Tax due is		£............

4. Calculate the income tax due on each **taxable income** below :-

   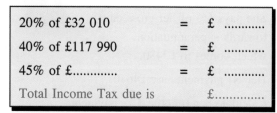

   (a) Mr Kenobi - £29780

   (b) Ms Leia - £30000

   (c) Mr Yoda - £51360

   (d) Mr Solo - quarter of a million pounds.

5. Mr Ford, a joiner, is self employed and earned a **gross income** of £42200.

   He estimates his taxable income will be £31080.

   (a) Calculate his *estimated* income tax due.

   His *actual* taxable income was £32760.

   (b) Calculate how much **more** Mr. Ford has to pay above his original estimate.

6. Ms Fisher has a taxable income of between £40000 and £45000.

   Her income tax bill is £10 402.

   Calculate her exact **taxable income**. (*Tricky*)

Value Added Tax (VAT)

The government also raises money by charging **V.A.T.**.

Most items that you purchase are charged VAT (*usually at 20%*).

However, some items like heating, are charged at only 5%.

Items like medicines and school books are zero-rated (0% VAT).

Example :- A 3D - DVD costs £18·80 plus VAT.

How much does the DVD cost in total ?

Method 1	Method 2
VAT is **20%** of £18·80	**120%** of £18·80
= 0·2 × 18·80	= 1·2 × 18·80
= £3·76	= £22·56
Total Cost is (£18·80 + £3·76) = £22·56	

Exercise 4·4

 ✓

1. Find the total cost for each item.
   (*Using VAT at 20%*).

   (a) A DVD costing £16 + VAT.

   (b) A car costing £3500 + VAT.

   (c) A fridge/freezer costing £275 + VAT.

   (d) A laptop computer at £1876 + VAT.

2. Find the final cost of each item after **adding** VAT, (*at 20%*).

(a)
£16·80

(b)
£200

(c)
£860

(d)
£425

(e) £8000

(f)
£17 500

3. **Copy** and complete each bill :-

(a)

DINO'S CAFE

Drinks	£ 8·60
Food	£23·40
Subtotal	....
VAT (20%)	....
Total cost	....

(b)

JO-JO'S GARAGE

Labour	£176·60
Parts	£ 73·40
Subtotal	....
VAT (20%)	....
Total cost	....

4. James bought a car priced £4500 + VAT.

   How much would he have saved if VAT was charged at 17·5% instead of 20% ?

5. Phil uses 350 units of gas at 3·4 pence per unit.

   The gas company also added a £36·10 service charge.

   Find the total bill **including VAT at 5%**.

6. A tractor is valued at £14 800 + 20% VAT. A 15% discount is to be given to a customer.

The customer wants the discount taken off **before** the VAT is added.

The tractor company want to give the discount **after** VAT has been added.

Is there any difference to the final price ? (Explain).

7. **Copy** and complete each bill :-

(a)

Den's Repairs

Parts	....	£ 80·00
Paint	....	£ 46·00
Labour (4 hrs at £8·50/hr)	£	_____
Subtotal	....	
VAT (20%)	....	
Total cost	....	_____

(b)

Gas Bill

Gas used	....	£153·20
Standing Charge	....	£ 38·80
Subtotal	....	_____
VAT (5%)	....	
Total cost	....	_____

(c)

Paul's Paintshop

New bumper	....	£ 80·00
Paint	....	£ 45·50
Labour (3 hrs at £12/hr)	£	_____
Subtotal	....	
VAT (20%)	....	
Total cost	....	_____

8. A plumber's bill is as follows :-

> 4 m of plastic pipe at £1·50 / m
> 5 knuckle joints at £1·20 each
> Labour (3 hours at £15 / hr)

Find the total cost including VAT (20%).

9. An electrician's bill is as follows :-

> 3 m of wire at £2·95 / m
> 5 m of gold wire at £5·10 / m
> Labour (4·5 hours at £12·80/ hr)

Find the total cost including VAT (20%).

10. A toy is sold for £7·50 **including** VAT.

How much was the selling price before VAT was added ? (*i.e. 120% = £7·50*)

11. **Tricky.** Each price below is **inclusive** of VAT. Calculate the original price **before** VAT.

(a)
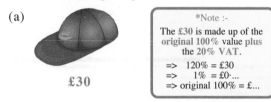
£30

> *Note :-
> The £30 is made up of the original 100% value plus the 20% VAT.
> => 120% = £30
> => 1% = £0·...
> => original 100% = £...

(b) £84   (c) 96p

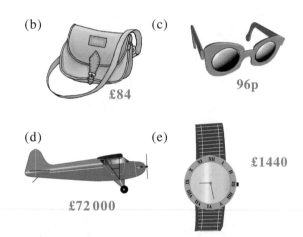

(d) £72 000   (e) £1440

12. A 3 kg box of Kittilitter costs £2·82 **inclusive** of VAT.

A 10 kg box costs £8·20 **excluding** VAT.

Which box gives the better value ? (Explain).

13. Look at the cafe bill below :- (*Tricky*)

Dario's Diner

Drinks	....	£
Food	....	£23·40
Subtotal	....	
VAT (20%)	....	_____
Total cost	....	£54·00

Calculate the amount spent on **drinks**.

Hire Purchase (H.P.)

Receiving goods by making an initial part payment, (**deposit**), and paying the remaining cost over a required number of weeks or months is called **Hire Purchase (H.P.)**.

The disadvantage to paying by H.P. is that the goods tend to be a little more expensive.

Example :-   Ann buys a dishwasher by making a £30 deposit, and agreeing to pay 12 monthly instalments of £45.

How much did she pay for the dishwasher **in total** ?

Deposit	£30
Payments (12 x £45)	£540
Total price	**£570**

Exercise 4·5

1. Frank buys a new bed. He pays a **£50 deposit** and makes 22 payments of £12·60.

   How much did he pay in total ?

2. Find the total price paid for each item :-

   (a) Fridge - £60 deposit, 12 payments of £35.

   (b) Car - £800 deposit, 24 payments of £126.

   (c) TV - £50 deposit, 26 payments of £22·73.

   (d) Hi-Fi - £45 deposit, 36 payments of £1·28.

3. Aisha bought a new suite, paying £1124 in total.

   She paid a deposit of £80 followed by 12 equal monthly instalments.

   How much was each monthly instalment ?

4. Binnie paid a total of £770 for a new oven. She paid a deposit and made 18 equal monthly payments of £35·50.

   How much of a deposit did Binnie pay ?

5. Kurt paid £680 for a cinema surround system.

   He paid a **10% deposit** and made 12 equal payments.

   How much was each payment ?

6. Celia paid £1460 for a bathroom suite. She paid a **20% deposit** and 40 equal payments.

   How much was each payment ?

7. A motorised go-cart has a cash price of £250. It could also be bought on Hire Purchase by making a **15% deposit** and 12 equal payments of £22·63.

   How much cheaper is it to pay by cash ?

8. Three companies offer different rates of payments for a £3000 conservatory.

	Deposit	Equal payments
CheapCons	£400	12 at £265 each
Cons-R-Us	10%	18 at £185 each
ConservCo	12·5%	16 at £175 each

   Calculate the total price for each company, and state which is the dearest.

9. Alan's new snooker table cost £540. He paid a deposit and made 24 equal payments of £18·90.

   Calculate the deposit he paid **and** express the deposit as a percentage of the cost price.

10. The **cash price** on a motorcycle was £4000. Ken paid a 20% deposit and 32 equal payments.

    He ended up paying 20% more than the cost price. How much was each payment ?

Insurance

Paying a sum of money, to cover you in case an unfortunate event might happen, is called insurance. For example, a fire, a theft or a breakage. Life insurance is sometimes called assurance.

Payments to insurance or assurance companies vary depending on many different factors. The tables shown below give examples of the type of payments.

House and Contents insurance
(Monthly premiums per £10 000)

Group	Buildings Ins.	Contents Ins.
1	£1·90	£5·90
2	£2·80	£6·20
3	£3·25	£8·00

These groupings depend on the area you live in, how likely you are to be burgled etc.

Life Assurance
25 year term policy - monthly premiums
Life Insurance (for every £100 000 insured)

Age		Non-smoker	Smoker
Male	*Female*		
16-24	16-31	£6·10	£11·40
25	32	£6·50	£11·60
26	33	£6·65	£11·80
27	34	£6·80	£12·50
28	35	£7·10	£12·70
29	36	£7·40	£12·90
30	37	£7·70	£13·80
31	38	£8·20	£14·50

Exercise 4·6

Use the tables above to answer each question.

1. Keri lives in a Group 2 house. She insures the **contents** for £30 000.

   Copy and complete to find her monthly premium.

   > For £10 000 → *premium* = £6·20
   >
   > For £30 000 → *premium* = £6·20 x 3 = ...

2. Calculate each monthly premium :-

   (a) Group 3, contents insurance of £40 000.

   (b) Group 1, buildings insurance of £70 000.

3. Harry lives in a Group 2 house worth £150 000. His contents are worth an estimated £40 000.

   Calculate his total house **and** contents insurance.

4. Find the house and contents insurance for :-

   (a) £160 000 Group 2 house, contents £45 000.

   (b) £215 000 Group 1 house, contents £57 000.

5. Jeremy pays a £17·10 monthly premium for his Group 1 house.

   How much is his house worth ?

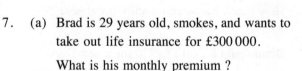

6. Each person below takes out a 25 year life insurance policy for £100 000.

   Find their monthly premiums (payments).

   (a) Bob, 22 year old, non-smoker.

   (b) Alice, 30 year old, smoker.

   (c) Sally, 37 year old non-smoker.

7. (a) Brad is 29 years old, smokes, and wants to take out life insurance for £300 000.

   What is his monthly premium ?

   (b) Paula is a 30 year old non-smoker who takes out a £200 000 policy.

   How much is her **annual** premium ?

   (c) Claudia is a 35 year old smoker who takes out a quarter of a million pound life insurance policy.

   Calculate her **annual** premium.

Great Britain uses the pound (GBP) as its currency.
Many European countries use the euro.
In April 2013 the exchange rate was :-

£1 ⟶ 1·15€

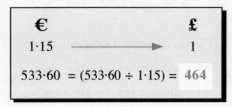

Example 1 :-   Change £123 into euros.

£	€
1	⟶ 1·15
123 = (123 × 1·15) =	**141·45**

Example 2 :-   Change 533·60 euros into pounds.

€	£
1·15	⟶ 1
533·60 = (533·60 ÷ 1·15) =	**464**

Exercise 4·7

1. Change each of the following into euros :-

    (a) £40   (b) £175   (c) £1200

    (d) £8500   (e) £45 000   (f) £200 000.

2. Change the price of each item into euros :-

    (a)   (b)

    £120

    £285

3. Change each of the following into GBP (£'s) :-

    (a) 1173€   (b) 232·53€   (c) 552·46€

    (d) 658·72€   (e) 517 500€   (f) 1·38€.

4. Decide in each case which is the better buy :-

    (a) DVD player   - £176 or 250·20€

    (b) Car   - 18 200€ or £16 500

    (c) House   - £80 000 or 91 000€

    (d) Carpet   - 414€ or £360.

5. Lorna changed £700 into euros for her holiday.

    On holiday she spent 667€ and exchanged the
    remaining amount into pounds on her return.

    How many £'s did she have on her return ?

6. Elle changed 1633€ into £'s and spent £940.

    How many euros did she return home with ?

This table shows other currencies and exchange rates.

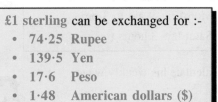

> **£1 sterling** can be exchanged for :-
> • 74·25 Rupee
> • 139·5 Yen
> • 17·6   Peso
> • 1·48   American dollars ($)

7. Change each of the following :-

    (a) £18 to yen   (b) £63 to peso's

    (c) £250 to rupees   (d) £450 to $

    (e) 11 160 yen to £   (f) $57·72 to £

    (g) 4306·5 rupees to £ (h) 7392 peso's to £

    (i) 1 527 525 yen to £ (j) $2501·20 to £.

8. Christian changed £600 into yen.
    On holiday he spent 80 910 yen.

    How many GBP could he change this for ?

9. Sahi took 62 370 rupees on holiday to the UK.
    He had to borrow another £85 on holiday.

    How much did he spend in total ?

10. Bart had $2100 to take on holiday. He spent
    £600 in the UK and 111 600 Yen in Japan.

    How many dollars did he have left ?

11. Which is greater :-   131 130 yen or $1406 ?

12. (a) Change 53 460 rupees into yen.

    (b) Change $127·28 into pesos.

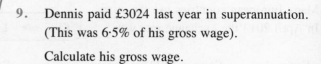

1. Calculate each **annual** income :-

    (a) Olive earns £416 weekly.

    (b) Jack earns £1045 a month.

    (c) Aziz earns £625·40 weekly.

2. Tia has an **annual** salary of £28 080.

    (a) Calculate her **monthly** wage.

    (b) Calculate her **weekly** wage.

3. Eddie is a handyman who earns £7·20 per hour.

    He works :-

    | Mon-Fri 9 am to 3 pm. |
    | Saturday 3 hours (*time and a half*). |

    Calculate his **weekly** wage.

4. Baz earns £14 560 annually.

    If he works 40 hours per week, what is his hourly rate ?

5. Ronnie earns a basic annual pay of £12 000 **plus 7·5% commission** on all his sales.

    Last year Ronnie sold £78 000 worth of toys.

    (a) Calculate his commission.

    (b) What was his total earnings for last year ?

6. Yorak earned £412·50 in commission last month from his sales worth £7500.

    What percentage commission did he receive ?

7. Lara has a gross income of £22 500 and her total deductions are £3650.

    Calculate her net income.

8. Patrick has a gross income of £27 800.

    He pays income tax of £448, N.I. £206 and 6% of his gross wage on Superannuation.

    (a) Calculate his annual **take home** pay.

    (b) Calculate his **weekly** take home pay.

9. Dennis paid £3024 last year in superannuation. (This was 6·5% of his gross wage).

    Calculate his gross wage.

10. The table shows the income tax rates.

    Calculate the amount of income tax if the taxable income was :-

Rate of Tax on
first £32 010 of taxable income   20%
£32 010 – £150 000 taxable income   40%
all remaining taxable income   45% (over £150 000)

    (a) £18 900.

    (b) £53 460.

    (c) £200 000.

11. Calculate the total amount including VAT (*at 20%*), on each of these items :-

    (a)

    £12·80 +VAT

    (b)

    £186 +VAT

12. James bought a TV, making a £75 deposit. He also made 24 monthly payments of £24·60.

    How much in total did he pay for the TV ?

13. The guitar shown can be paid for by making a 15% deposit of the cash price, followed by 18 equal monthly payments of £29·75.

    Cash price £560

    How much **dearer** is this than the cash price ?

14. INSURA-CO charges £3·25 per £10 000 in insurance. How much is Ali's monthly premium for a £175 000 policy ?

15. Using the exchange rate of :-

    (a) change £450 into euros.

    (b) change $959·78 into £'s.

    (c) change 4600 euros into dollars ($).

£1
= 1·15€
= $1·48.

Multiplication in Algebra

Examples :-

Collecting Like Terms (*a reminder*)

$x + x + x + x \quad = \quad 4x$

$7a - 4a \quad = \quad 3a$

$6p + q - p + 8q \quad = \quad 5p + 9q$ (**not** $14pq$)

$10 + 2m - 6 \quad = \quad 4 + 2m$ (**not** $6m$)

$b^2 + b^2 + b^2 \quad = \quad 3b^2$ (**not** b^6)

Multiplying and Dividing Terms

$9 \times c \quad = \quad 9c$

$a \times 3 \quad = \quad 3a$

$x \times x \quad = \quad x^2$ (**not** $2x$)

$5p \times 6p \quad = \quad 30p^2$ (**not** $30p$)

$2m \times 5n \quad = \quad 10mn$

$10c \div 5 \quad = \quad 2c$

$24ab \div 4a \quad = \quad 6b$

$6p^2q^3 \div 2pq \quad = \quad 3pq^2$

$5a^2b \times 4ab \quad = \quad 5 \times a \times a \times b \times 4 \times a \times b = 20a^3b^2$

Note :- "unlike" terms, such as $2x$ and $3y$, **cannot** be added - but they **can** be multiplied.

Exercise 5·1

1. Simplify by collecting like terms :-

   (a) $3m + 9m$

   (b) $p + p - p + p$

   (c) $5x + x + 7x + x$

   (d) $3b + c - b + 6c$

   (e) $v + w + v - w$

   (f) $5g - 2r + 5g - r$

   (g) $9a^2 + h^2 - 8a^2 - 2h^2$

   (h) $x^2 - 5y^2 + 3x^2 + 5y^2 - 4x^2$.

2. Simplify by multiplying :-

   (a) $15 \times c$

   (b) $u \times 18$

   (c) $t \times t$

   (d) $p \times p \times 6$

   (e) $s \times 9 \times s$

   (f) $3y \times 2k$

   (g) $7 \times 3c$

   (h) $4u \times 5$

   (i) $6a \times 9a$

   (j) $3v \times 2v \times 7$

   (k) $3 \times h \times h \times h$

   (l) $3n \times 2n \times 8n$

   (m) $3p \times 5p$

   (n) $(8w)^2 \quad (\neq 8w^2)$

   (o) $(2k)^3$

   (p) $(3f)^3$

   (q) $(2xy)^2$

   (r) $(3km)^3$

   (s) $(2mn)^4$

   (t) $(4vw)^2 \times vw$.

3. Simplify (harder) :-

   (a) $4x \times 2y$

   (b) $5x^2 \times 3y$

   (c) $6x \times 4y^2$

   (d) $7xy \times y$

   (e) $2xy \times x$

   (f) $8x^2y \times x$

   (g) $9xy^2 \times y$

   (h) $3x^2y \times x^2$

   (i) $12x^2y \times y^2$

   (j) $10x^2y^2 \times y$

   (k) $6x^2y^2 \times x$

   (l) $3x^2y^2 \times xy$

   (m) $4xy \times 4xy$

   (n) $3x^2y \times 2xy^2$

   (o) $8x^2y \times 3xy$

   (p) $5x^2y^2 \times 2x^2y^2$.

4. Try these divisions :-

   (a) $12b \div b$

   (b) $30c \div 10c$

   (c) $16pq \div 8p$

   (d) $3gh \div h$

   (e) $22vw \div 11vw$

   (f) $30lmn \div 3lm$

   (g) $4x^2 \div x$

   (h) $8a^2b \div b$

   (i) $8a^2b \div a$

   (j) $8a^2b \div 2a$

   (k) $8a^2b \div 2b$

   (l) $8a^2b \div 2ab$

   (m) $8a^2b \div 2a^2b$

   (n) $3x^2y^2 \div xy$.

Examples :-

1. $3(a + 4)$

$= 3a + 12$

2. $4(2x - 3y)$

$= 8x - 12y$

3. $c(c + 5)$

$= c^2 + 5c$

4. $5m(2m - 7n)$

$= 10m^2 - 35mn$

5. $-3(x + 6)$

$= -3x - 18$

6. $-7(y - 1)$

$= -7y - 7 \times -1$

$= -7y + 7$

(Note the double
negative = +ve)

7. $2(x + 3) - 5$

$= 2x + 6 - 5$

$= 2x + 1$

8. $4(3v + 2w) - 7w$

$= 12v + 8w - 7w$

$= 12v + w$

9. $3(x + 5) + 2(x - 3)$

$= 3x + 15 + 2x - 6$

$= 5x + 9$

10. $3(2a + 4) - 3(a - 1)$

$= 6a + 12 - 3a + 3$

$= 3a + 15$

11. $8 - 2(x + 1)$

$= 8 - 2x - 2$ [not $6(x + 1)$!]

$= 6 - 2x$

Exercise 5·2

1. Multiply out the brackets :-

(a) $2(b + 4)$ (b) $5(a + 1)$ (c) $8(d - 6)$ (d) $9(1 - g)$

(e) $3(m + n)$ (f) $7(c - t)$ (g) $11(3 + y)$ (h) $30(x - 5)$

(i) $3(6p + 1)$ (j) $5(3 - 4q)$ (k) $8(11x - 7y)$ (l) $a(b + 7)$

(m) $g(h - 10)$ (n) $x(6 + x)$ (o) $k(3e + 8g)$ (p) $4u(10u - v)$

(q) $3(4a + 7b + 2)$ (r) $9(p + q - 4r)$ (s) $6(3 - 5f - 2g)$ (t) $x(x - y - 9z)$

(u) $-5(a + 1)$ (v) $-x(3 + x)$ (w) $-g(6g - 1)$ (x) $-x(7y - 11x)$.

2. Multiply out the brackets and collect like terms :-

(a) $2(q + 4) + 3$ (b) $3(e + 1) + 6$ (c) $5(t + 4) + 2$

(d) $6(u + 2) - 7$ (e) $4(p + 2) - 7$ (f) $3(s + 6) - 20$

(g) $2(f + 4) + 8f$ (h) $9(h + 1) + h$ (i) $4(k + 5) - 3k$

(j) $6(z + 2) - 2z$ (k) $10(5 + c) - 3c$ (l) $7b + 7(b + 2)$

(m) $8m + 9(m - 1)$ (n) $5w + 2(4w + 3)$ (o) $7r + 4(3r - 2)$

(p) $5y + (y - 1)$ (q) $6a + 10(a + 3p)$ (r) $g + 10(5g + 2h)$

(s) $20x + 2(5x - 15y)$ (t) $80v + 10(7v + n)$ (u) $7 + 2(q + 1)$

(v) $8(5w - 3e) - 36w$ (w) $3 + 2(x - 1)$ (x) $12 - 2(x - 5)$.

3. Simplify :-

(a) $3(m + 2) + 4(m + 1)$ (b) $5(b + 2) + 2(b + 4)$ (c) $8(c + 1) + 3(c + 6)$

(d) $4(k - 1) + 2(k + 5)$ (e) $6(g - 2) + 3(g + 4)$ (f) $2(a - 6) + 7(a + 2)$

(g) $3(4 + p) + 7(1 - p)$ (h) $9(1 - u) + 3(1 + u)$ (i) $10(2y + 3) + 2(3y - 11)$

(j) $2(8t - 2) + 5(2t + 4)$ (k) $6(4 - 5e) + 7(2 + 4e)$ (l) $3(2x + 4y) + 5(3x - y)$.

4.   Simplify :-

(a) $5(x + 1) - 2(x + 2)$

(b) $8(x + 2) - 7(x + 2)$

(c) $4(x + 6) - 3(x + 7)$

(d) $4(2x + 1) - 3(x + 2)$

(e) $7(3x + 4) - 4(x + 6)$

(f) $8(x + 3) - 6(x - 1)$

(g) $9(x + 1) - 6(x - 2)$

(h) $10(1 + 2x) - 10(1 - x)$

(i) $2(2 - x) - 6(1 - x)$

(j) $x(x + 1) + 5(x - 1)$

(k) $x(x + 3) - 5(x + 1)$

(l) $x(8x - 2) - 2(3x - 8)$.

5.   Simplify :-

(a) $9 - 2(y + 4)$

(b) $6 - 6(p - 1)$

(c) $8 - (d - 1)$

(d) $7 + 6(h + 2)$

(e) $2 + 9(2 - c)$

(f) $12 - 2(1 - u)$

(g) $10(b - 2) - 1$

(h) $-2(n - 1) + 8$

(i) $m + 3(m - 20)$

(j) $x - (100 - x)$

(k) $7k - 2(k + 11)$

(l) $4w - 2(1 - 5w)$.

Factorising Algebraic Expressions - "The Common Factor"

Earlier, when we multiplied out the brackets, $4(2x + 3)$, we obtained :- $8x + 12$
   If we **start** with the expression $8x + 12$,   we can **reverse** the process
   and we can see, from above, that we obtain $4(2x + 3)$.

When you are given the algebraic expression, $8x + 12$ and you are asked :–

   "What is the HIGHEST factor of the two terms, $8x$ and 12 ?" => Answer is 4.

   Now take the 4 outside a set of brackets   =>   4(.........)
   and decide what goes in the bracket so that when multiplied, you obtain $8x + 12$.

   | Example :- $8x + 12$ |
   This is called "**FACTORISING**" the expression.
   | $= 4(2x + 3)$ |

* Note - In the above example, the "4" is the **highest common factor"** (*h.c.f.*)

   You must always use the h.c.f. if the expression is to be factorised FULLY !

Further Examples :-

Factorise fully :-	1. $5x + 10$	2. $12a - 16b$	3. $pq + pr$	4. $12x - 18x^2$
Check answers by removing the brackets	$= 5(x + 2)$	$= 4(3a - 4b)$	$= p(q + r)$	$= 6x(2 - 3x)$
	5 is *h.c.f.*	4 is *h.c.f.*	p is *h.c.f.*	6x is *h.c.f.*

Exercise 5·3

1.   **Copy** and complete :-

(a) $5a + 5b = 5(..........)$

(b) $2x + 8y = 2(..........)$

(c) $6g + 4h = 2(..........)$

(d) $pq + pr = p(..........)$

(e) $cd + c = c(..........)$

(f) $mn + n^2 = n(..........)$

(g) $vw^2 + v = v(..........)$

(h) $3ab + 3ac = 3a(..........)$

(i) $8x + 12y = 4(..........)$

(j) $40b - 16a = 8(..........)$

(k) $4cd - 8d = 4d(..........)$

(l) $6p + 21p^2 = 3p(..........)$.

2. Factorise the following, by considering the highest common factor in each case :-

   (a) $5a + 25$ (b) $3x + 12$ (c) $9p - 36$ (d) $11v + 11w$

   (e) $6p - 6q$ (f) $10c - 20h$ (g) $7m - 28$ (h) $12n + 60$

   (i) $4x + 6y$ (j) $14u - 21v$ (k) $20x - 25y$ (l) $4r - 32u$

   (m) $9s + 24$ (n) $22u - 11$ (o) $24x - 56y$ (p) $18a + 12c$.

3. Factorise fully :-

   (a) $5b + bc$ (b) $7x - vx$ (c) $pq + pr$ (d) $a^2 + 6a$

   (e) $8t - t^2$ (f) $c^2 - 4c$ (g) $4xm + 4xn$ (h) $5ad - 10ae$

   (i) $17rs - 17s$ (j) $3y^2 + 7y$ (k) $12x^2 - 20xy$ (l) $6q^2 + q$

   (m) $6d + 14d^2$ (n) $a - 13a^2$ (o) $3y^2 - 24cy$ (p) $24mn + 32n^2$.

4. Completely factorise :-

   (a) $a^2 + 4ab - 7a$ (b) $8xy - 8xz + x$ (c) $p^3 + p^2$ (d) $4d^3 - 16d$

   (e) $a^2c + ac^2$ (f) $18rs^2 - 30rs$ (g) $8x^2 - 12xa$ (h) $\frac{1}{5}gh + \frac{1}{5}hj$.

Remember Remember..... ?

1. Simplify :-

   (a) $9a + a$ (b) $9a \times a$ (c) $9a \div a$ (d) $9a^2 \div 3a$

   (e) $24 \times x$ (f) $g \times g$ (g) $8a \times 4b$ (h) $(5p)^2 \times 2$

   (i) $4mn \times m$ (j) $3x\,q^2 \times q$ (k) $20c \div c$ (l) $12x^2y \div 3y$.

2. Multiply out the brackets :-

   (a) $5(a + 2)$ (b) $-2(3x + 1)$ (c) $a(9 + a)$ (d) $m(n - m)$

   (e) $4(2 - 6r)$ (f) $-5k(k - 4)$ (g) $-2x(3x - 6y)$ (h) $-p^2(7p - pq)$.

3. Simplify :-

   (a) $3(x + 1) + 7$ (b) $9(y + 4) - 8y$ (c) $10 - 3(a - 2)$

   (d) $4(w + 1) + 5(w + 2)$ (e) $10(1 - d) + 2(4 + d)$ (f) $7(2 - 3q) - 3(4 - 8q)$

   (g) $20 - 5(u + 3)$ (h) $8 - 2(1 - k)$ (i) $8m^2 - 2(m - 4m^2)$.

4. Factorise fully :-

   (a) $9x + px$ (b) $ab - bg$ (c) $m^2 + 3m$ (d) $12h - h^2$

   (e) $5vw - 5xw$ (f) $7kr + 14kp$ (g) $2q^2 + 9q$ (h) $12x^2 - 18xy$

   (i) $24x^2 + 32ax$ (j) $36ab - 45a^2$ (k) $y^3 - y^2$ (l) $6q^3 - 42q$

   (m) $mn^2 - nm^2$ (n) $16ab^2 + 40ab$ (o) $8tax^2 - 12x^2t$ (p) $\frac{1}{2}cd + \frac{1}{4}ad^2$.

Line Symmetry – Revision

A **line of symmetry** occurs in a shape if, when the shape is folded over the line, the two pieces, either side of the line, fit **exactly** on top of each other.

Some shapes have more than 1 line of symmetry.

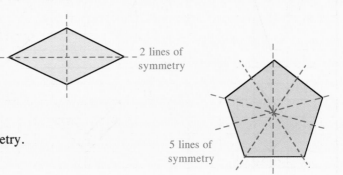

2 lines of symmetry

5 lines of symmetry

Exercise 6·1 – Revision Work

1. State how many lines of symmetry, if any, are in each of the following :-

    (a) square   (b) rectangle

    (c) parallelogram   (d) semi-circle

    (e) isosceles triangle (f) equilateral triangle

    (g) *regular* pentagon (*all sides & angles same*)

    (h) regular hexagon (i) regular decagon

    (j) regular heptagon (k) regular nonagon.

2. Make a neat tracing of each shape and show any **lines of symmetry** on your tracings :-

    (a) 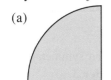   (b)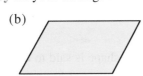

    (c) 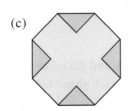   (d)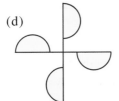

    (e) 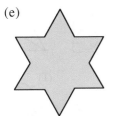   (f)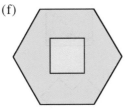

    (g)    (h)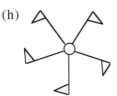

2. (i)   (j)

  (k)   (l)

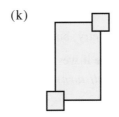

3. Copy and complete each shape so that the dotted line is a **line of symmetry** :-

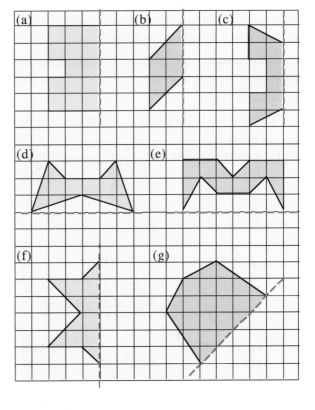

4. Copy and complete each shape so that the **red** lines are **lines of symmetry** :-

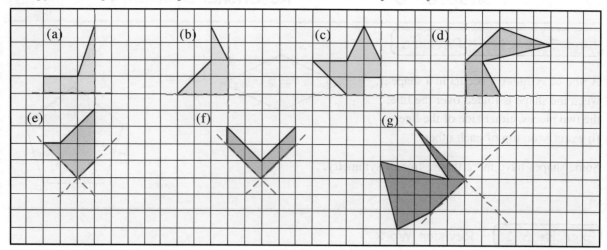

5. List all the capital letters of the alphabet (A B C D E....). State how many lines of symmetry each has.

Rotational Symmetry

Some shapes have no line symmetry, but have **rotational** or **turn symmetry**.

This shape will fit its own outline if we "spin" the shape by 180° (*a half turn*).

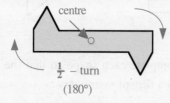

This shape is said to have $\frac{1}{2}$ turn symmetry or **Rotational** Symmetry of **order 2**.

This shape will fit its own outline if we "spin" the shape by 120° (*a third turn*).

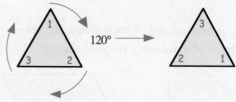

This shape is said to have $\frac{1}{3}$ turn symmetry or **Rotational** Symmetry of **order 3**.

Exercise 6·2

1. Which of the following have **half turn** symmetry ?

   (a)   (b)   (c)

   (d)   (e)   (f)

   (g)   (h) (i)

2. State the **turn symmetry** **and** the **order** of rotational symmetry for each shape below :-

   (a) (b) (c)

   (d)   (e)   (f)

   (g)   (h)   (i)

3. State the **turn symmetry** *and* the **order** of rotational symmetry for each shape below :-

(a)   (b)   (c)

(d)  (e)   (f)

(g)  (h) regular octogon (i) regular decagon

4. Make a copy of each shape below, and rotate each by $\frac{1}{2}$- **turn** around the red dot :-

(a) 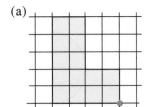 (b)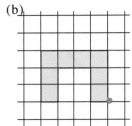

(c) 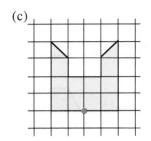 (d)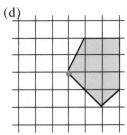

(e) 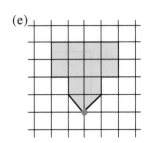 (f)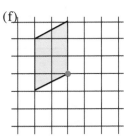

(g) 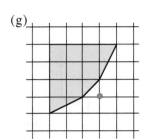 (h)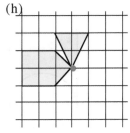

5. Copy each of the following shapes onto $\frac{1}{2}$ centimetre squared paper.

Complete each shape so that it has rotational symmetry about O in the given order :-

(a) 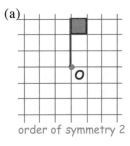 (b)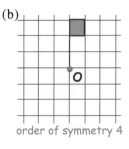

order of symmetry 2   order of symmetry 4

(c) 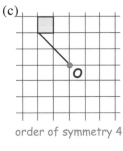 (d)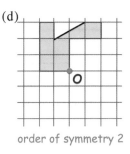

order of symmetry 4   order of symmetry 2

(e) 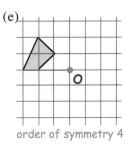 (f)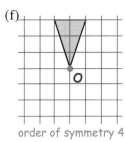

order of symmetry 4   order of symmetry 4

(g) 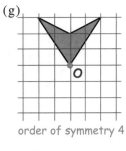 (h)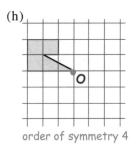

order of symmetry 4   order of symmetry 4

(i) 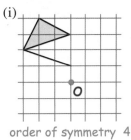 (j)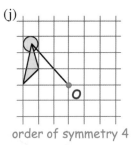

order of symmetry 4   order of symmetry 4

6. Create some rotational symmetry questions of your own and test your partner.

7. Investigate where symmetry is used in the real world. Report your findings to the class.

Translational (Slide) Symmetry

A **translation** is simply a movement (*sliding*) from one place to another.

A **translation** is part of the group of **transformations** (*you will learn more about transformations later*).

Shown is a 3 by 2 rectangular tile. It is easy to see that if you have lots of tiles **congruent***
to this one, you can cover an area using them, with **NO** gaps.

In Mathematics terms, we say :-
"The rectangle tiles the surface".
(or "tiles the **plane**").

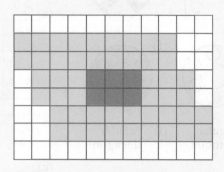

***congruent** -
two shapes are congruent
if they are exactly the
same size and shape.

Exercise 6·3

1. **Copy** each shape onto squared paper. Shade or colour it, then completely surround it with **congruent** tiles to show that the shape will "**tile the plane**".

(a)

(b)

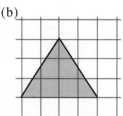

(c)

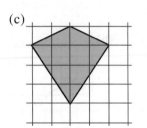

(d)

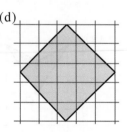

(e)

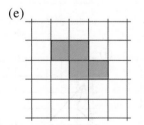

(f)

(g)

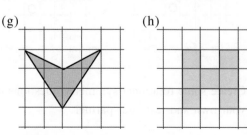

(h)

2. Shown below are various shapes.

Without actually drawing them, decide which shapes are most likely to "**tile the plane**".

(a)

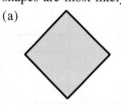

(b)

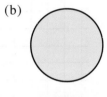

(c)

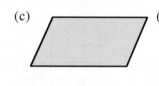

(d)

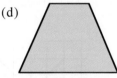

(e)

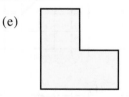

(f)

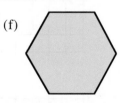

(g)

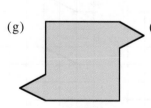

(h)

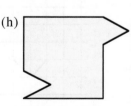

(i)

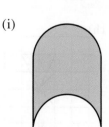

(j)

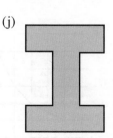

1. State how many lines of symmetry, if any, are in each of the following :-
    (a) square
    (b) regular hexagon

    (c)
    (d)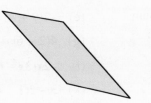

2. Copy and complete each shape so that each dotted line is a **line of symmetry** :-

    (a)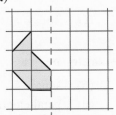
    (b)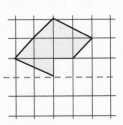

    (c)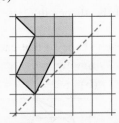
    (d)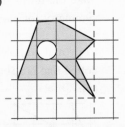

3. State the **turn symmetry** and the **order** of rotational symmetry for each shape below :-

    (a)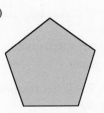
    (b)

    (c)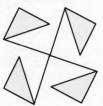
    (d)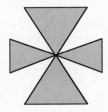

4. Copy each of the following shapes on to half centimetre squared paper.
    Complete each shape so that it has rotational symmetry about O in the given order :-

    (a)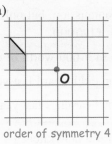
    (b)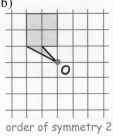

    order of symmetry 4   order of symmetry 2

    (c)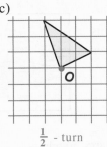
    (d)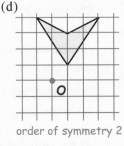

    $\frac{1}{2}$ - turn   order of symmetry 2

5. Shown below are various shapes.

    Without actually drawing them, decide which shapes are most likely to "**tile the plane**".

    (a)
    (b)

    (c)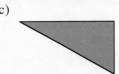
    (d)

6. **Copy** each shape onto squared paper.
    Shade or colour it, then completely surround it with **congruent** tiles to show that the shape will "**tile the plane**".

    (a)
    (b)

    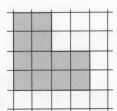

1. Clara has an annual income of £25 740.

   (a) Calculate her monthly wage.

   (b) Calculate her weekly wage.

2. Jamie has a basic salary of £25 000 per annum. He also earns 15% commission, but only on annual car sales over £120 000.

   Last year Jamie sold £136 000 worth of cars.

   (a) What commission did he earn last year ?

   (b) What were his total earnings last year ?

3. Tabatha paid £4800 for a new kitchen.

   She paid a 30% deposit and spread her payments equally each month over two years.

   How much was each payment ?

4. At the cash & carry Harry bought :-

   Soft drinks - £122 + 20% VAT
   Electricity vouchers - £75 + 8% VAT
   School jotters - £46 (no VAT).

   How much was his total bill ?

5. Penny has a gross income of £23 920. She pays income tax of £345, N.I. £227 and 8% of her gross wage on Superannuation.

   (a) Calculate her annual take home pay.

   (b) Calculate her weekly take home pay.

6. Using the exchange rate of :-

   (a) change £860 into euros.

   (b) change $814 into £'s.

   (c) change 828 euros into dollars ($).

   | £1 |
   | = 1·15€ |
   | = $1·48. |

7. Mr Andrews took £1400 with him when he set off for France and then America. He spent 920€ in France and when he arrived home from America, he had £140 left.

   How many dollars had he spent in America ?

8. Simplify :-

   (a) $8a + 3a$ (b) $7b \times b$

   (c) $43pq \times p$ (d) $12x^2y \div 4xy$

   (e) $-2(9 + a)$ (f) $m(n - m)$

   (g) $4(2 - 6r)$ (h) $-5k(k - 4)$

   (i) $-2x(3x - 6y)$ (j) $-p^2(7p - pq)$.

   (k) $3 - 2(1 - k)$ (l) $10 - 3(a - 2)$

   (m) $4(w + 1) + 5(w + 2) - 5(3w + 3) - 1$.

9. Factorise fully :-

   (a) $3p + 9$ (b) $15t - 12$

   (c) $18kg - 21k$ (d) $8pqr + 2qr$

   (e) $p^2k^2v - p^2kv^2$ (f) $16t^3 - 80t^2$.

10. How many lines of symmetry are in a :-

    (a) rectangle   (b) square

    (c) kite   (d) parallelogram ?

11. State the turn symmetry and the order of symmetry for each of the shapes in Q10.

12. Copy and complete each shape so that each dotted line is a line of symmetry :-

    (a)   (b)

    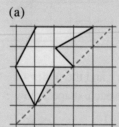 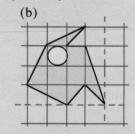

13. Copy each of the following shapes onto half centimetre squared paper.

    Complete each shape so that it has rotational symmetry about the red dot :-

    (a)   (b)

    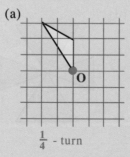 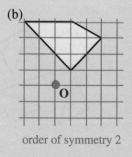

    $\frac{1}{4}$ - turn   order of symmetry 2

1. Set down and find :-

    (a) 413×62

    (b) $5016 \div 8$

    (c) 312×400

    (d) 30^2

    (e) 7^3

    (f) $6000 - 529$

    (g) $18 - 5 \times 3$

    (h) $7\overline{)5054}$.

2. Set down and find :-

    (a) $4 \cdot 156 \times 6$

    (b) $17 \cdot 2 + 8 \cdot 876$

    (c) $9\overline{)833 \cdot 58}$

    (d) $17 \cdot 43 \times 600$

    (e) $38 \div 200$

    (f) $9 - 8 \cdot 279$

    (g) $\frac{2}{1000}$

    (h) $30 \cdot 4 \div 4000$.

3. Find :-

    (a) $\frac{7}{8}$ of 120

    (b) $\frac{3}{7}$ of 560

    (c) $\frac{9}{11}$ of 880.

4. Simplify :-

    (a) $\frac{28}{49}$

    (b) $\frac{16}{72}$

    (c) $\frac{13}{52}$

    (d) $\frac{65}{85}$.

5. Find :-

    (a) $\frac{1}{3} + \frac{1}{3}$

    (b) $3\frac{1}{4} + 2\frac{1}{4}$

    (c) $4 - 1\frac{2}{3}$

    (d) $2 \times 5\frac{1}{5}$.

6. Express as a simple fraction :-

    (a) 60%

    (b) 48%

    (c) $2\frac{1}{2}$%.

7. Find :-

    (a) $66\frac{2}{3}$% of £180

    (b) 125% of £120

    (c) $2\frac{1}{2}$% of 360 g

    (d) 5% of 600 ml

    (e) 15% of £640

    (f) 11% of £9.

8. Express :-

    (a) 42 as a percentage of 60

    (b) 15 as a percentage of 45.

9. A shopkeeper bought a box of a dozen toilet rolls for £3·00. He sold them at 35p each.
    Find his total profit and express it as a percentage of the cost price.

10. Find :-

    (a) $(-6) + 21$

    (b) $(-7) - 13$

    (c) $(-30) + 19$

    (d) $6 - (-12)$

    (e) $-15 - (-8)$

    (f) $(-8) \times (-6)$

    (g) $(-200)^2$

    (h) $48 \div (-6)$

    (i) $(-63) \div (-7)$

    (j) $\frac{11 - (-14)}{(-5)}$

    (k) $-3(-10 - (-8))$.

11. Solve the following equations :-

    (a) $3x + 14 = 2$

    (b) $1 - 4x = -19$

    (c) $5x - 5 = 5$

    (d) $10 - x = x$.

12. How long is it from :-

    (a) 9·55 am to 12·37 pm

    (b) 1547 to 1702 ?

13. Change to hours and minutes :-

    (a) 0·3 hours

    (b) 2·45 hours

    (c) $1\frac{2}{3}$ hours.

What is Tolerance ?

When a car manufacturer orders steel bolts to help build his car engines, he would like them to be 35 millimetres long **exactly**.

This is not always possible, so the manufacturer allows a "little error" either side of this.

He might be willing to accept any bolt as long as it lies between 33 mm and 37 mm.
This means he will accept a bolt which is **within 2 mm** of the 35 mm he asked for.
This is referred to as the **tolerance** for the measurement.

35 mm

He will then specify the *acceptable limits* as =>   (35 ± 2) mm

and this means   **minimum** length is (35 – 2) mm = **33 mm**.
                              maximum length is (35 + 2) mm = **37 mm**.

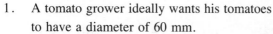
Exercise 7 · 1

1. A tomato grower ideally wants his tomatoes to have a diameter of 60 mm.

    He states the tolerance as (60 ± 3) mm.

    (a) What is the minimum acceptable diameter (60 – 3 = ... mm) ?

    (b) What is the maximum acceptable diameter ?

2. For each of the following tolerances, write down the minimum (min) and maximum (max) allowable sizes :-

    (a) (20 ± 1) mm   (b) (35 ± 5) kg

    (c) (16 ± 2) m   (d) (15 ± 3) kg

    (e) (150 ± 4) cm   (f) (75 ± 2) mm

    (g) (350 ± 10) km   (h) (120 ± 15) mg

    (i) (100 ± 20) ft   (j) (9·6 ± 0·1) cm

    (k) (7·5 ± 0·2) m   (l) (19·7 ± 0·3) kg

    (m) (23·2 ± 0·1) cm   (n) (10 ± 0·3) cm

    (o) (30 ± 0·5) ml   (p) (85 ± 0·5)°C

    (q) (4·2 ± 0·3) litres   (r) (50 ± 1·5) cm.

3. Write down the maximum and minimum values given by these tolerances :-

    (a) (9·23 ± 0·01) cm   (b) (6·45 ± 0·03) m

    (c) (18·25 ± 0·05) km (d) (0·84 ± 0·04) km

    (e) (10·23 ± 0·05) kg (f) (24·57 ± 0·03)°C

    (g) (4·98 ± 0·02) g   (h) (3·147 ± 0·002) g

    (i) (8·063 ± 0·004) millilitres.

4. In the manufacture of washing machines, the bolts required to secure the back plate are required to be (45 ± 3) mm long.

    (a) Write down the minimum and maximum acceptable lengths.

    (b) State which of the following bolts should be **rejected** :-

    (i)   47 mm   (ii)   42 mm

    (iii) 49 mm   (iv)   50 mm

    (v)   40 mm   (vi)   43 mm

    (vii) 44·2 mm   (viii) 47·9 mm.

5. A hole has to be drilled in a metal plate so that it lines up with a bolt projecting from a wall.

    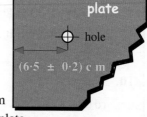
    plate
    hole
    (6·5 ± 0·2) c m

    The hole is to be at a distance of (6·5 ± 0·2) cm from the left side of the plate.

    (a) What is the minimum and maximum acceptable distance ?

    (b) It is discovered that the hole has been drilled 6·29 cm in from the left hand side of the plate. Is this O.K. ?

6. To bake a cake in a oven, a particular recipe recommends a temperature of (190 ± 5)°C.

    State which of the following temperatures are acceptable :-

    (a) 195·5°C   (b) 189°C

    (c) 185°C   (d) 184·8°C.

7.  Most stopwatches are only accurate to a certain degree.

When Andy Holtz ran the 100 metres final, his time was given as $(10 \cdot 23 \pm 0 \cdot 02)$ seconds.

    (a)   What was Andy's fastest possible time, (from the tolerance) ?

    (b)   What was his slowest time ?

8.   To make a batch of fruit scones, the amount of castor sugar used is important. The recommended weight is $(0 \cdot 035 \pm 0 \cdot 005)$ kg.

    (a)   What is the minimum weight of castor sugar required ?

    (b)   What is the maximum weight of castor sugar required ?

9.   When "Eau de Glesca" fill their bottles of perfume, they expect the bottles to hold (150 ± 5) ml.

    (a)   What is the minimum and maximum acceptable volume ?

    (b)   A bottle is found to contain 146 ml of perfume. Is this O.K. ?

Using Tolerance Notation

Example 1 :- When blowing up balloons for an office party, the manager decides that, for effect, the diameters should be between 25 and 35 centimetres.

This can be put into **"tolerance form"** as follows :-

    Step 1 –   Find the **"middle"** of 25 and 35 => $\dfrac{(25+35)}{2}$ = 30.

    Step 2 –   Write it as (30 ± 5) **cm.**

Example 2 :- The diameter of a drilled hole is to be between 6·4 and 6·8 centimetres.

    => Midpoint is $\dfrac{(6 \cdot 4 + 6 \cdot 8)}{2}$ = 6·6 => Tolerance is $(6 \cdot 6 \pm 0 \cdot 2)$ **cm.**

Exercise 7·2

1.   The length of a football pitch should be between 80 and 100 yards.

Put this into tolerance notation $(.... \pm ....)$ yards.

             length

2.  The working temperature in an office should be between 20°C and 26°C.

Write this in tolerance form.

3. Write each of the following in tolerance form :-

(a) min = 18 cm
    max = 20 cm

(b) min = 50 cm
    max = 60 cm

(c) min = 10 cm
    max = 11 cm

(d) min = 120 m
    max = 140 m

(e) min = 4 kg
    max = 5 kg

(f) min = 37 mm
    max = 43 mm

(g) min = 6·2 m
    max = 6·6 m

(h) min = 10·1 cm
    max = 10·5 cm

(i) min = 0·9 cm
    max = 1·1 cm

(j) min = 20·2 cm
    max = 20·8 cm

(k) min = 9·8 cm
    max = 10·2 cm

(l) min = 700 km
    max = 900 km.

4. **Harder**. Put the following into tolerance form :-

(a) min = 6·32 cm
    max = 6·34 cm

(b) min = 8·05 cm
    max = 8·09 cm

(c) min = 0·24 cm
    max = 0·28 cm

(d) min = 10·71 cm
    max = 10·77 cm

(e) min = 9·38 cm
    max = 9·42 cm

(f) min = 0·05 cm
    max = 0·09 cm

(g) min = 0·95 cm
    max = 1·05 cm

(h) min = 0·062 cm
    max = 0·068 cm.

5. In a recording studio, the sound engineer tries to keep the volume between 6·2 and 6·8 decibels.

(a) Write this in tolerance notation.

(b) Say whether the following are "too quiet", "too loud" or "just right" :-

(i) 6·1 db
(ii) 6·67 db
(iii) 6·31 db
(iv) 6·81 db.

6. A plane, flying across the Atlantic Ocean, tries to maintain a steady height of between 30 000 ft and 34 000 ft.

Write this in tolerance notation.

7. A typist claims she can type between 100 and 112 words per minute.

Write this in tolerance notation.

8. Whilst following a recipe for coffee cake, Mrs Jones uses between 35 grams and 45 grams of coffee.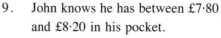

Express this in tolerance notation.

9. John knows he has between £7·80 and £8·20 in his pocket.

(a) Write this in tolerance form.

(b) Is it possible he has a £5 note, two £1 coins and three 50p coins in his pocket ?

10. All 8 runners in the 400 metre race took between 52 and 60 seconds to complete the race.

Write this in tolerance notation.

11. The weight of a metal washer, stamped out in a factory press, should weigh between 3·24 grams and 3·30 grams.

(a) Write this in tolerance form.

(b) State which of these are acceptable weights for washers :-

(i) 3·29 g
(ii) 3·23 g
(iii) 3·30 g
(iv) $3\frac{1}{2}$ g.

12. In a chemist shop, when medicine is poured into a bottle, each bottle should contain between 340 ml and 360 ml.

(a) Write this in tolerance form.

(b) Is 361 ml acceptable ?

13. Presco Stores have a rule that all watermelons which they sell must have a diameter between 14 cm and 23·5 cm.

Write this in tolerance form.

14. Regulations state that foods which need temperature control for safety must be held either :-

 HOT at or above a minimum of 63°C or CHILLED at or below a maximum of 8°C. In between is called the DANGER AREA.

Write the temperatures for this danger area in tolerance form.

Remember Remember..... ?

1. When a pianist played a melody, the time he took was given as (125 ± 10) seconds.

   (a) What was his quickest time ?

   (b) What was his slowest time ?

2. For each of the following, write down the minimum and maximum values :-

   (a) (30 ± 2) mm   (b) (75 ± 5) m   (c) (240 ± 20) kg

   (d) (1600 ± 150) m   (e) (8·6 ± 0·1) litres   (f) (19·2 ± 0·3) mg

   (g) (28·3 ± 0·5) tonnes   (h) (370 ± 30) m.p.h.   (i) (0·8 ± 0·2) m.

3. The weight of a particular ingredient in making chocolate macaroons should be quite accurate. It is given as :-

   (0·332 ± 0·005) g.

   (a) What is the maximum permitted weight ?

   (b) What is the minimum permitted weight ?

4. The diameter of any tomato grown on a plant should have a certain value in order for a supermarket to purchase it :-

   diameter = (4·8 ± 0·3) cm.

   Which of the following are acceptable diameters :-

   (a) 5·75 cm   (b) 5·01 cm   (c) 4·95 cm   (d) 5·11 cm ?

5.

   Brockie is a boxer. In any week, depending on how hard he trains, his weight varies between 52 kg and 56 kg.

   Write this in tolerance form as (.... ± ....) kg.

6. Put the following into tolerance form :-

   (a) min = 60 g   (b) min = 128 cm   (c) min = 1500 m
       max = 70 g   max = 132 cm   max = 1700 m

   (d) min = 8·4 cm   (e) min = 19·7 cm   (f) min = 0·6 kg
       max = 8·6 cm   max = 20·3 cm   max = 0·9 kg.

7. (a) A tolerance is given as (.... ± 0·3) m.
      The maximum value allowed is 7·1 m.

      What must the minimum value be ?

   (b) A tolerance is given as (.... ± 4·25) m.
      The minimum value allowed is 3·75 m.

      What must the maximum value be ?

Gradients

We can measure how steep a hill or road is, or how steeply a ladder is resting against a wall.

This is called the **slope** or the **GRADIENT** of the hill or ladder.

The **gradient** of a hill is usually written as a **fraction**.
(*It can be given as a decimal or as a percentage*).

Hill Street has a **gradient** of 1 in 10.

This is written as :- $\boxed{\text{gradient} = \frac{1}{10}}$

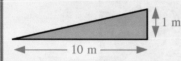

This means that for every 10 metres moved across (**horizontally**), the road rises by 1 metre (**vertically**).

How to Calculate the GRADIENT of a Hill

Example :- New Street rises by 4 metres.
It is 80 metres (horizontally)
from one end to the other.

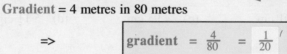

Gradient = 4 metres in 80 metres

=> $\boxed{\text{gradient} = \frac{4}{80} = \frac{1}{20}}$

Can you see that $\frac{1}{20}$ is **smaller** than $\frac{1}{10}$? —> this means New Street is **less** steep than Hill Street.

Definition :- $\boxed{\text{Gradient} = \frac{\text{vertical distance}}{\text{horizontal distance}}}$

Exercise 8·1

1. Look at this picture of Dunn Street.

    (a) Calculate its **gradient** like this :-

    Copy :-

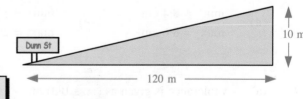

$$\text{Gradient} = \frac{\text{vertical distance}}{\text{horizontal distance}}$$

$$=> \text{gradient} = \frac{10}{120} \quad => \quad \text{gradient} = \frac{?}{?}$$

    (*Simplify the fraction* $\frac{10}{120}$).

    (b) Compare the **gradient** of Dunn Street with that of Hill Street and New Street.

    Which of the three is the :- (i) steepest (ii) least steep ?

2. Look at each hill shown.

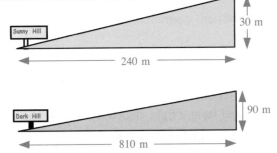

(a) Calculate the gradient of each hill.

(b) Compare the gradient of Sunny Hill with that of Dark Hill.

Which of the two is steeper ?

3. Four hills have gradients :-

$$\frac{8}{50}, \quad 0\cdot24, \quad 19\% \quad \text{and} \quad 0\cdot2.$$

Write the gradients in order, (steepest first).
(Hint : change them all to decimals).

4. Two car ramps are shown below.

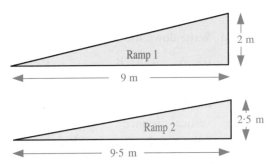

(a) Calculate the gradient of each ramp.

(b) Change each gradient to a decimal.

(c) Compare the gradients to find which ramp is the steeper.

5. A ladder is placed against a wall as shown.

Calculate the gradient of the ladder.

6. Two ladders are placed against a wall shown.

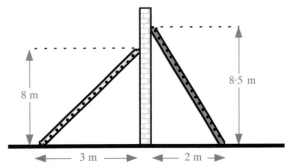

For safety reasons, a ladder must have a gradient with a value between 4 and 5.

Which of the ladders shown above is/are safe ?

7. A fire engine uses an extended ladder.

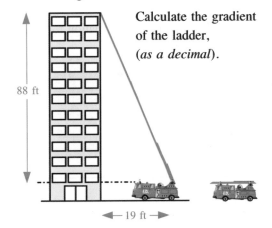

Calculate the gradient of the ladder, (as a decimal).

8. A ramp, with vertical height of 2 metres, has a gradient of 0·25.

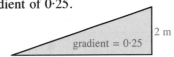

gradient = 0·25

Calculate the horizontal distance.

9. A cable car travels from a base point to the top of a mountain as shown.

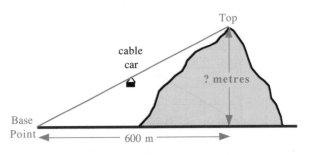

If the gradient of the cable is 0·4, calculate the height of the mountain.

Finding the Gradient of a Line from a Coordinate Diagram

The gradient of a line can be found from a coordinate (or Cartesian) diagram.

Any 2 given points on a straight line can be used to form a right angled triangle.
Vertical and horizontal **changes** can be found, using points on the line, and the formula used as before.

Example :-

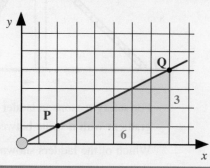

Pick any two coordinates - P(2, 1) and Q(8, 4) and form a right-angled triangle as shown.

Horizontal change is **6**.

Vertical change is **3**.

$$Gradient = \frac{\text{vertical distance}}{\text{horizontal distance}} = \frac{3}{6} = \frac{1}{2}$$

1. Copy and complete the calculation to find the **gradient** of the line shown.

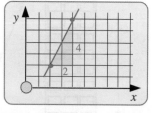

   Horizontal dist = 2.
   Vertical dist = 4.

$$Gradient = \frac{\text{vertical distance}}{\text{horizontal distance}} = ... = ...$$

2. Calculate the gradient of each line in the Cartesian diagrams below :-

   (a)   (b)

3. The diagram shows three coloured lines.

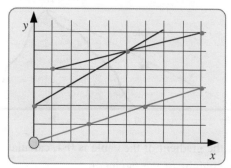

   Find the gradient of each line.

4. Plot each set of points and calculate the gradient of the line passing through each set :-

   (a) (1, 1), (2, 2), (3, 3)

   (b) (0, 2), (2, 3), (6, 5)

   (c) (0, 0), (1, 4), (2, 8).

5. The line AB is shown in a Cartesian diagram.

   (a) Write down the coordinates of :-

      (i) A   (ii) B.

   (b) By writing down the horizontal and vertical distance from A to B, calculate the gradient of the line AB.

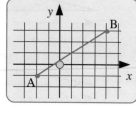

6. Calculate the gradient of each line below :-

   (a)   (b)

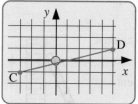   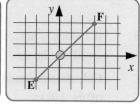

7. Each set of points represents a straight line. Calculate the gradient of each :-

   (a) (−2, 1), (1, 4)   (b) (−4, 2), (6, 4)

   (c) (−1, −2), (2, 4)   (d) (−4, −3), (5, 0)

   (e) (−12, −61), (4, 3)   (f) (−0·5, 1), (1·5, 3).

The gradient of a line AB can be written as m_{AB}.

Any line which slopes **upwards** from left to right has a **positive** gradient.
Any line which slopes **downwards** from left to right has a **negative** gradient.

Example :- Find the **gradient** (*m*) of the line CD.

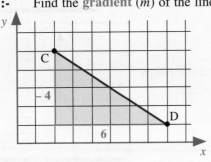

Vertical change is −4
Horizontal change is 6.

$$Gradient\ (m_{CD}) = \frac{vertical\ distance}{horizontal\ distance} = \frac{-4}{6} = \frac{-2}{3}$$

$$m_{CD} = -\frac{2}{3}$$

8. Copy and complete the calculation to find the gradient of the line shown.

Vertical change is ....

Horizontal change is ...

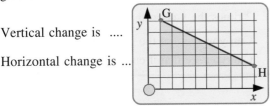

$$m_{GH} = \frac{vertical\ distance}{horizontal\ distance} = \frac{-?}{8} = -\frac{?}{?}$$

9. Calculate the gradient of each line in the Cartesian diagrams below :-

(a) 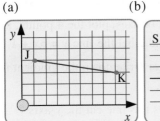   (b)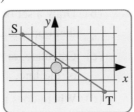

10. (a) Calculate the gradient of each line below.

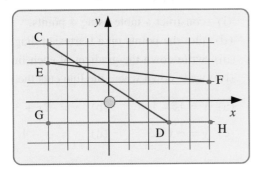

(b) Notice the gradient of line GH.

What can you say about the gradient of **ALL** horizontal lines ? Explain.

11. (a) Calculate the gradient of each **parallel** line.

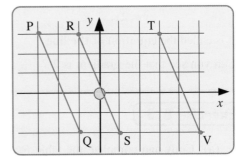

(b) What can you say about the gradient of lines which are **parallel** to each other ?

12. (a) Find :- (i) m_{AB} (ii) m_{BC}
        (iii) m_{CD} (iv) m_{AD}.

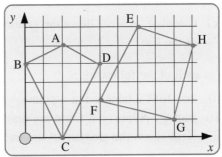

(b) Find the gradient of each side of EFGH.

(c) Use your answers to (b) to explain why EFGH is **not** a parallelogram.

13. A quadrilateral, STUV, has coordinates S(0, 5), T(2, 7), U(6, −1) and V(0, −7).

Find the gradients of both its **diagonals**.

14. Prove, **without** actually drawing a coordinate diagram, that the points A(−6, 1), B(−1, 0) and C(4, −1) all lie on the same straight line.

The Equation of a Line - a Formula

Consider the equation $y = 2x$.

A table of values can be constructed

x	−1	0	1	2
y	−2	0	2	4

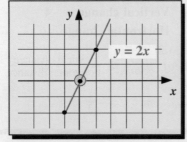

and the points plotted.

The formula connecting the points on this line can be written as

$$y = 2x.$$

It is called the **equation of the line**.

Can you see that the gradient is 2 ?

Consider the equation $y = 2x + 3$.

A table of values can be constructed

x	−1	0	1	2
y	1	3	5	7

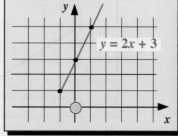

and the points plotted.

The formula connecting the points on this line can be written as $y = 2x + 3$.

(The y-coordinate of any point on the line is 2 times the x-coordinate **plus** 3).

Can you see that the gradient is also 2 ?
Can you see that it cuts the y-axis at $(0, 3)$?

Exercise 8·3

1. (a) Copy and complete the table for $y = 3x$.

x	−1	0	1	2
y	−3	...	...	...

   (b) Draw a set of axes, plot the 4 points, join them up and label the line $y = 3x$.

   (c) Calculate, or write down the gradient (m) of the line.

2. For each of the following :-

   (i) construct a table using 4 points.
   (ii) plot the points on a Cartesian diagram.
   (iii) write down the gradient of the line formed.

   (a) $y = 4x$ (b) $y = x$

   (c) $y = \frac{1}{2}x$ (d) $y = -x$.

   > Any straight line through the origin will have its equation $y = mx$ where m is the gradient.

3. Write down the **gradient** of each line below :-

   (a) $y = 6x$ (b) $y = \frac{1}{5}x$

   (c) $y = -12x$ (d) $y = 0·5x$.

4. (a) Copy and complete the table for the equation $y = 3x + 1$.

x	−1	0	1	2
y	−2	...	...	...

   (b) Draw a set of axes, plot the 4 points, join them up and label the line $y = 3x + 1$.

   (c) Calculate, or write down the gradient (m) of the line.

   (d) Where does this line cut the y-axis ?

5. For each of the lines below :-

   (i) construct a table using 4 points.
   (ii) plot the points on a Cartesian diagram.
   (iii) write down the gradient of each line.
   (iv) write down where the line cuts the y-axis.

   (a) $y = 4x - 1$ (b) $y = -2x + 3$

   (c) $y = \frac{1}{2}x + 3$ (d) $y = -x - 4$.

6. For the line $y = 5x + 2$,

   (a) write down its gradient.

   (b) write down where it meets the y-axis.

The Equation of a Straight Line

The equation of any line (**a linear equation**) takes the form :–

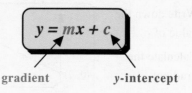

$$y = mx + c$$

Where m represents the **gradient** of the line   gradient   y-intercept
and c represents the **y-intercept**. (*i.e. - where it cuts the y-axis*).

Examples :-
1. $y = 3x + 4$ has gradient **3** and y-intercept **4**.

2.   A line with y-intercept **–2** and gradient $\frac{3}{4}$ has equation $y = \frac{3}{4}x - 2$.

3.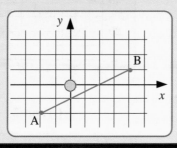

$m_{AB} = \frac{3}{6} = \frac{1}{2}$ y-intercept is **–1**

=>   Equation of line AB is $y = \frac{1}{2}x - 1$

Exercise 8·4

1.   Write down the **gradient** and **y-intercept** in
each of these equations :-

(a) $y = 3x + 2$ (b) $y = 5x - 3$

(c) $y = x + 1$ (d) $y = -2x + 5$

(e) $y = \frac{1}{2}x + 2$ (f) $y = -\frac{1}{3}x - 1$

(g) $y = 0\cdot5x + 9$ (h) $y = -0\cdot1x + 2$

(i) $y = 4 + 2x$ (j) $y = 15 - x$.

2.   Write down the **y-intercept** of the line given by
the equation :- $y = 4x$.

3.   Write down the **equation** of each of these lines :-

(a) $m = 2$, and the y-intercept is 3.

(b) $m = 4$, and the y-intercept is – 2.

(c) y-intercept is 6, and the gradient is 4.

(d) gradient is – 2, and it passes through $(0, 3)$.

(e) gradient is $\frac{1}{3}$, and it passes through $(0, -1)$.

(f) $m = 12$ and line passes through the origin.

4.   Line AB cuts the y-axis at the point $(0, 4)$ and
is **parallel** to a line with equation $y = 2x - 3$.

(a) Write down the **gradient** of the line AB.

(b) Write the equation of this line AB.

5.   For each of the six lines below,

(i)   calculate its gradient

(ii)   write down its y-intercept

(iii) write the equation of the line.

(a)   (b)

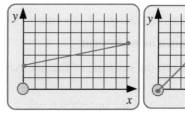

(c)   (d)

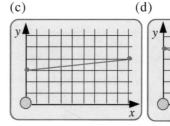

(e)   (f)

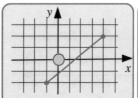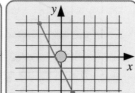

6. The line shown has equation $y = mx + c$.

   (a) Write down the value of c.

   (b) Calculate the gradient.

   (c) Write down the **equation** of the line.

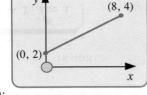

7. Write down the equation of each line below :-

   (a)   (b)

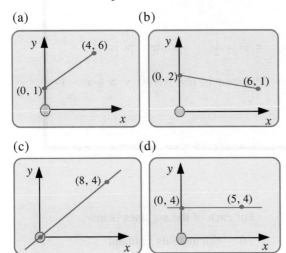

   (c)   (d)

8. The line AB passes through points A(0, 2) and B(4, 4).

   (a) Show the line AB on a Cartesian diagram.

   (b) Calculate the gradient of this line.

   (c) Write down its y-intercept.

   (d) Write down the equation of the line AB.

9. Find the **equation** of the line shown below.

   (*Hint : look at the scale on each axis carefully*).

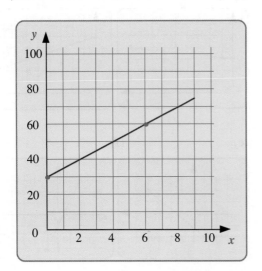

10. Which of the two lines below is steeper ?
    (*Careful!*)

Graph 1

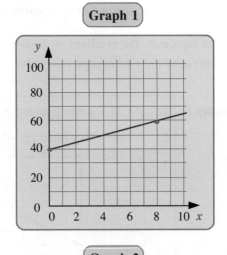

Graph 2

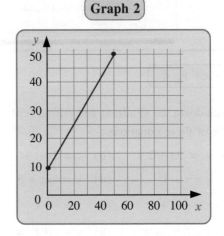

11. Write down the equation of each of the four lines below :-

    (a)   (b)

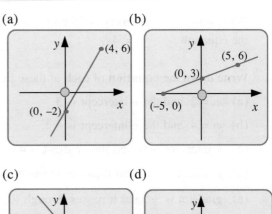

    (c)   (d)

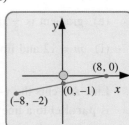

12. Match each of the following equations with their corresponding graphs shown below :-

(a) $y = 3x$ (b) $y = 2x - 1$

(c) $y = -5x$ (d) $y = -x - 1$

(e) $y = \frac{1}{2}x + 3$ (f) $y = -5$.

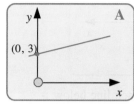
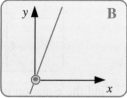
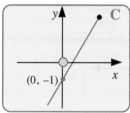
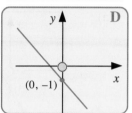
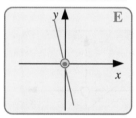
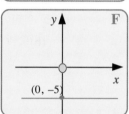

13. Find the equation of the line passing through each set of points below :-

(a) C(0, 1), D(4, 5) (b) E(0, 5), F(6, 6)

(c) G(–2, 6), H(0, –2) (d) J(0, –5), K(3, 4).

14. Show that the line through the pair of points (0, 1), (4, 7) and the line through (0, –3) and (4, 3) are **parallel** to each other.
(*Remember : parallel lines have equal gradients*).

15. Show that the line through the pair of points (1, –8) and (12, –3) and the line through (–5, –5), and (21, 6) are **NOT parallel** to each other.

16. Write down the equation of the line :-

(a) which goes through the point (0, 3) and is **parallel** to the line $y = 5x + 1$.

(b) **parallel** to the line $y = -x$ and lies on the point (0, –6).

Remember Remember..... ?

1. Calculate the **gradient** of this ramp.

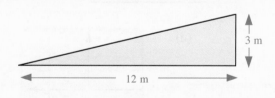

2. The gradients of four ramps are given below :-

    car ramp   20%,

    ski jump ramp   0·15,

    skateboard ramp $\frac{1}{2}$,

    bike ramp   0·3.

    List the ramps in order, **steepest** first.

3. Calculate the gradient of each line below :-

(a)   (b)

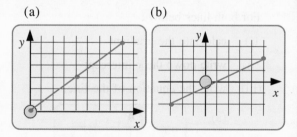

(c)   (d)

4. Calculate the gradient of :-

(a) the line AB which passes through the points A(–2, –1) and B(3, 4).

(b) the line CD which passes through the points C(–4, 5) and D(3, 5).

(c) the line EF which passes through the points E(–6, 5) and F(4, –5).

(d) the line GH which passes through the points G(5, 2) and H(5, –1).

5. Write down the **gradients** and the **y-intercepts** of these lines :-

(a) $y = 2x + 7$ (b) $y = 1 - x$

(c) $y = \frac{1}{2}x + 2$ (d) $y = 7 + \frac{1}{4}x$

(e) $y = x - 8$ (f) $y = -2x + 9$

(g) $y = -\frac{1}{5}x - 1$ (h) $y = -1 - \frac{1}{3}x$

(i) $y = 0 \cdot 2x + 4$ (j) $y = -0 \cdot 9x - 9$.

6. Write down the **equation** of each line :-

(a) $m = 3$, with its y-intercept is –2.

(b) gradient of –1, through the point (0, 7).

(c) $m = -5$ and passing through the origin.

(d) $m = 0$ and passing through (2, –1).

(e) infinite gradient and passing through (–1, 0).

7. For both lines below :-

(i) calculate the gradient

(ii) write down the y-intercept

(iii) write the equation of the line.

(a)

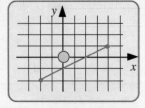

(b)

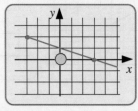

8. Write down the equation of this line.

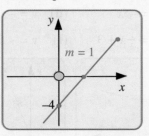

9. Find the equation of each line below :-

(a)

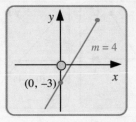

(b)

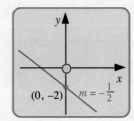

(c)

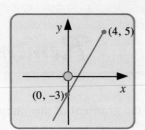

(d)

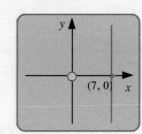

(e)

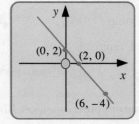

Solving Equations

There are various ways of solving equations.

We shall use the "CHANGE SIDE - CHANGE SIGN" method. *

* Your teacher may show you an alternative method.

Examples :-   Solve the following :-

Move the +7 to the other side ... change it to –7.

$$x + 7 = 11$$
$$\Rightarrow \quad x = 11 - 7$$
$$\Rightarrow \quad x = 4$$

Move the × 4 to the other side and change to ÷ 4.

$$4x = 22$$
$$\Rightarrow \quad x = 22 \div 4$$
$$\Rightarrow \quad x = 5\tfrac{1}{2}$$

Move the –7 to the other side and change to +7

Move the × 2 to the other side and change to ÷ 2.

$$2x - 7 = 11$$
$$\Rightarrow \quad 2x = 11 + 7$$
$$\Rightarrow \quad 2x = 18$$
$$\Rightarrow \quad x = 9$$

Move the 3x to the left side and change to –3x

Move the –2 to the right side and change to +2

Move the × 5 to the other side and change to ÷ 5.

$$8x - 2 = 3x + 28$$
$$\Rightarrow \quad 8x - 3x = 28 + 2$$
$$\Rightarrow \quad 5x = 28 + 2$$
$$\Rightarrow \quad 5x = 30$$
$$\Rightarrow \quad x = 6$$

Multiply out the brackets

Double Change side
Change sign
Tidy up

Divide by 7.

$$2(4x + 1) = x + 16$$
$$\Rightarrow \quad 8x + 2 = x + 16$$
$$\Rightarrow \quad 8x - x = 16 - 2$$
$$\Rightarrow \quad 7x = 14$$
$$\Rightarrow \quad x = 2$$

Multiply out brackets
(Watching –ve × –ve)

Tidy up

Double Change side
Change sign
Tidy up

Divide by 2.

$$3(2x + 4) - 2(x - 2) = 2x + 36$$
$$\Rightarrow \quad 6x + 12 - 2x + 4 = 2x + 36$$
$$\Rightarrow \quad 4x - 2x = 36 - 16$$
$$\Rightarrow \quad 2x = 20$$
$$\Rightarrow \quad x = 10$$

Exercise 9·1

1.   **Copy** each equation and solve to find the value of x :-

    (a) $x + 7 = 9$ (b) $x + 15 = 15$ (c) $x - 4 = 8$

    (d) $x - 17 = 0$ (e) $x - 80 = 70$ (f) $x + 7 = 5$

    (g) $x + 14 = 0$ (h) $7 + x = 12$ (i) $3 + x = 2$

    (j) $5 + x = 5$ (k) $20 + x = 13$ (l) $11 + x = -9$.

2.   **Copy** each equation and solve to find the value of the letter :-

    (a) $2x = 14$ (b) $5a = 40$ (c) $3b = 27$

    (d) $8p = 8$ (e) $4e = 6$ (f) $7c = 0$

    (g) $6d = 3$ (h) $3y = 150$ (i) $6r = 27$

    (j) $4q = 11$ (k) $5s = 28$ (l) $7t = 20$

    (m) $10k = 35$ (n) $5n = 4$ (o) $8h = 2$.

3. Find the value of x in the following equations :-   (*Show each step of working carefully*).

(a) $2x + 1 = 9$ (b) $3x + 4 = 19$ (c) $5x + 3 = 33$

(d) $4x + 8 = 16$ (e) $8x - 1 = 31$ (f) $6x - 4 = 14$

(g) $8x - 9 = 47$ (h) $7x - 7 = 0$ (i) $10x - 8 = 72$

(j) $5x - 10 = 45$ (k) $2x + 14 = 20$ (l) $7x - 1 = 69$

(m) $2x + 3 = 1$ (n) $12x + 12 = 0$ (o) $2x - 9 = 0$

(p) $4x + 20 = 4$ (q) $4x + 5 = 14$ (r) $6x - 8 = 19.$

4. Copy and complete :-

(a) $7x + 2 = 3x + 14$
$\Rightarrow 7x - 3x = 14 - ....$
$\Rightarrow 4x = ...$
$\Rightarrow x = ...$

(b) $4x - 5 = x + 16$
$\Rightarrow 4x - ... = ... + ...$
$\Rightarrow 3x = ...$
$\Rightarrow x = ...$

5. Solve these equations using the same method as shown in Question 4 :-

(a) $3x + 1 = x + 7$ (b) $4x + 5 = 2x + 15$ (c) $6x + 1 = 3x + 13$

(d) $7x - 6 = 3x + 22$ (e) $8x - 1 = 2x + 29$ (f) $10x - 2 = 6x + 24$

(g) $9x - 1 = 7x + 14$ (h) $10x - 2 = 5x + 29$ (i) $12x - 12 = 2x + 11.$

6. These equations look a little "**different**", but solve them in the same way as Question 5 :-

(a) $4x = 3x + 9$ (b) $6x = 2x + 28$ (c) $6x = 3x + 21$

(d) $7x = 5x + 3$ (e) $8x = 4x + 30$ (f) $7x - 44 = 5x$

(g) $4x - 27 = x$ (h) $9x + 8 = 7x$ (i) $3x - 55 = -7x.$

7. Solve these equations by multiplying out the brackets first :-

(a) $2(x + 3) = 12$ (b) $3(x + 5) = 27$ (c) $4(x - 5) = 32$

(d) $7(x + 1) = 56$ (e) $10(x - 2) = 50$ (f) $2(x - 1) = 11$

(g) $5(x - 9) = 0$ (h) $8(x - 6) = 8$ (i) $3(x + 4) = -6.$

8. Solve these equations :-

(a) $2(2x + 1) = 18$ (b) $3(4x - 8) = 36$ (c) $6(5x - 1) = 24$

(d) $2(3x + 4) = 20$ (e) $4(2x - 3) = 4x + 12$ (f) $2(1 + 5x) = 3x + 51$

(g) $6(3x - 5) = 13x$ (h) $11(2x - 3) = 15x + 2$ (i) $10(x + 13) = -3x.$

9. Solve :-

(a) $2(x + 4) - x - 6 = 11$ (b) $3(x + 2) + 3x - 3 = 21$

(c) $5(x - 1) + 4x = 13$ (d) $2x + 5 + 6(x - 1) = 31$

(e) $3(x - 2) + 2(x + 4) = 17$ (f) $5(2x + 1) + 6(1 - 2x) = 1$

(g) $2(3x + 1) + 3(x - 4) = 4x + 5$ (h) $4(3x - 6) + 5(x + 1) = 5x + 5$

(i) $4(x + 5) - 2(x + 1) = 30$ (j) $2(4x + 1) - 3(x - 3) = x + 35.$

10. Dave bought 5 bags of toffees. His friend Jan, bought 1 bag, but she already had 120 loose toffees.

They then discovered that they had **exactly** the same number of toffees.

(a) Make up an equation to show this information.
     (Let x represent the number of toffees in 1 bag).

(b) Solve the equation to determine how many toffees there were in each bag.

Equations with Fractions

Fractions are a complication in equations we could well do without.

But we can **remove the fractions** quite easily ....

> **Rule :-** Always **ELIMINATE** the fractions at the very beginning .....
>
> by **MULTIPLYING** every term by the l.c.m. of all the fractional denominators.

Remember - l.c.m. means "lowest common multiple".

Example 1 :-

Multiply BOTH sides by **2** to eliminate the fraction $\frac{1}{2}$.

$$\frac{1}{2}x + 5 = 9$$
$$2 \times \frac{1}{2}x + 2 \times 5 = 2 \times 9$$
$$=> \quad x + 10 = 18$$
$$=> \quad \boxed{x = 8}$$

* note - every term must be multiplied by 2

Example 2 :-

Multiply BOTH sides by **20** to eliminate the two fractions, since the l.c.m. of 4 and 5 is **20**.

$$\frac{3}{4}x + \frac{2}{5} = 1$$
$$20 \times \frac{3}{4}x + 20 \times \frac{2}{5} = 20 \times 1$$
$$=> \quad 15x + 8 = 20$$
$$=> \quad 15x = 12$$
$$=> \quad x = \frac{12}{15} = \boxed{\frac{4}{5}}$$

Exercise 9·2

1. Copy and complete the following two equations :-

(a)
$$\frac{1}{3}x + 2 = 6$$
$$3 \times \frac{1}{3}x + 3 \times 2 = 3 \times 6$$
$$=> \quad x + \ldots = \ldots$$
$$=> \quad x = \ldots$$

(b)
$$\frac{4}{5}x - 5 = \frac{1}{2}x + 1$$
$$10 \times \frac{4}{5}x - 10 \times 5 = 10 \times \frac{1}{2}x + 10 \times 1$$
$$=> \quad 8x - \ldots = \ldots x + \ldots$$
$$=> \quad \ldots x = \ldots$$
$$=> \quad x = \ldots$$

2. Solve each of these equations, by first multiplying every term by the l.c.m. of all the fractional denominators.

This will eliminate the fractions.

(a) $\frac{1}{2}x - 1 = 4$

(b) $\frac{1}{4}x + 5 = 6$

(c) $\frac{1}{8}x - 2 = 0$

(d) $\frac{2}{3}x - 4 = 6$

(e) $3 + \frac{3}{5}x = 9$

(f) $\frac{3}{8}x + 10 = 19$

(g) $\frac{3}{4}x - \frac{1}{2} = 1$

(h) $\frac{1}{2}x + \frac{1}{5} = 4$

(i) $\frac{2}{5}x - \frac{1}{3} = 3$

(j) $\frac{1}{2}x - 4 = \frac{1}{4}$

(k) $\frac{2}{3}x + 3 = \frac{1}{3}$

(l) $\frac{3}{4}x - 1 = \frac{1}{5}$

(m) $\frac{1}{2}x + 2 = \frac{1}{3}x + 5$

(n) $\frac{3}{4}x - 4 = \frac{3}{5}x + 2$

(o) $1 + \frac{3}{8}x = \frac{1}{3}x + 2$

(p) $\frac{1}{2}x + \frac{1}{3} = \frac{1}{4}$

(q) $\frac{1}{4}x + \frac{1}{2} = \frac{2}{5}$

(r) $\frac{1}{2}x - \frac{1}{3} = \frac{2}{5}x + \frac{1}{4}$.

More Equations with Fractions (harder)

Example 1 :-

$$\frac{x + 1}{3} + 2 = 8$$

Multiply both sides by **3** to eliminate the **3** in the denominator.

$$\cancel{3} \times \frac{x + 1}{\cancel{3}} + 3 \times 2 = 3 \times 8$$

$$\Rightarrow \quad x + 1 + 6 = 24$$

$$\Rightarrow \quad x = 24 - 7$$

$$\Rightarrow \quad \boxed{x = 17}$$

Example 2 :-

$$\tfrac{3}{4}(2x - 1) + \tfrac{1}{3}x = 1$$

Multiply both sides by **12** to eliminate the two denominators, **4** & **3**.

$$\cancel{12} \times \tfrac{3}{4}(2x - 1) + \cancel{12} \times \tfrac{1}{3}x = 12 \times 1$$

$$\Rightarrow \quad 9(2x - 1) + 4x = 12$$

$$\Rightarrow \quad 18x - 9 + 4x = 12$$

$$\Rightarrow \quad 22x = 21$$

$$\Rightarrow \quad x = \tfrac{21}{22}$$

Exercise 9·3

1. **Copy** and complete to solve the following two fractional equations :-

(a)

$$\frac{x - 2}{5} - 3 = 7$$

$$\cancel{5} \times \frac{x - 2}{\cancel{5}} - 5 \times 3 = 5 \times 7$$

$$\Rightarrow \quad x - \ldots - \ldots = 35$$

$$\Rightarrow \quad x = \ldots + \ldots + \ldots$$

$$\Rightarrow \quad x = \ldots$$

(b)

$$\tfrac{2}{5}(2x + 1) - \tfrac{1}{3}x = 2$$

$$\cancel{15} \times \tfrac{2}{5}(2x + 1) - \cancel{15} \times \tfrac{1}{3}x = 15 \times 2$$

$$\Rightarrow \quad 6(2x + \ldots) - \ldots x = 30$$

$$\Rightarrow \quad 12x + \ldots - \ldots x = 30$$

$$\Rightarrow \quad 7x = \ldots$$

$$\Rightarrow \quad x = \frac{\ldots}{7}$$

2. Multiply each term by the l.c.m. of the denominators to eliminate the fractions and solve :-

(a) $\dfrac{x + 2}{5} = 4$

(b) $\dfrac{x + 7}{4} = 5$

(c) $\dfrac{x - 9}{2} = 3$

(d) $\dfrac{x + 4}{3} - 1 = 2$

(e) $\dfrac{3x - 4}{5} + 2 = 9$

(f) $5 + \dfrac{x - 2}{4} = 0$

(g) $\tfrac{2}{3}(2x + 4) - 2 = 0$

(h) $\tfrac{3}{4}(3x - 1) - 1 = 2$

(i) $\tfrac{5}{8}(x + 3) - \tfrac{1}{2}x = 2$

(j) $\tfrac{2}{5}(2x + 3) - \tfrac{1}{3}x = 4$

(k) $\tfrac{5}{6}(2x + 1) = \tfrac{3}{4}x + 7$

(l) $8 + \tfrac{3}{10}(3x + 2) = \tfrac{1}{3}x + 1$

(m) $\tfrac{2}{3}(2x + 5) + \tfrac{1}{2}(x - 2) = 5$

(n) $\dfrac{x}{2} + \dfrac{x + 2}{4} = 5$

(o) $\dfrac{x + 2}{3} + \dfrac{x + 3}{4} = 1$

(p) $\dfrac{2x - 1}{5} + \dfrac{x + 2}{10} = 3$

(q) $\dfrac{x - 1}{2} - \dfrac{x - 2}{5} = 1$

(r) $\dfrac{3x - 5}{6} - \dfrac{x - 7}{3} = 4.$

Chapter 9   this is page 58   Eqns. & Ineqlts

$3x + 1 = 9$ and $7(x + 2) = 5x + 11$ are two examples of **equations**.

Inequalities are very similar, except the "=" sign is replaced with one of "<", ">", "≤" or "≥".

Solving an inequality is almost identical to solving the corresponding equation.

equation	inequality
$2x - 5 = 11$	$2x - 5 < 11$
$2x = 11 + 5$	$2x < 11 + 5$
$2x = 16$	$2x < 16$
$x = 8$	$x < 8$

The solution this time is
"x can be any number
'smaller' than 8"
(not just $x = 8$)

equation	inequality
$2(2x - 1) = x + 7$	$2(2x - 1) \geq x + 7$
$4x - 2 = x + 7$	$4x - 2 \geq x + 7$
$4x - x = 7 + 2$	$4x - x \geq 7 + 2$
$3x = 9$	$3x \geq 9$
$x = 3$	$x \geq 3$

The solution this time is
"x can be any number
'bigger' than or equal to 3"
(not just $x = 3$)

Remember :- "<" - means "less than".

"> " - means "greater than"

"≤" - means "less than **or** equal to"

"≥" - means "greater than **or** equal to"

Example 1 :-

$$3(x + 1) - 10 \geq x$$
$$\Rightarrow \quad 3x + 3 - 10 \geq x$$
$$\Rightarrow \quad 3x - x \geq 10 - 3$$
$$\Rightarrow \quad 2x \geq 7$$
$$\Rightarrow \quad x \geq 3 \cdot 5$$

Example 2 :-

$$8 - 2a < 12$$
$$\Rightarrow \quad -2a < 12 - 8$$

Change the > sign
to < in last line $\Rightarrow \quad -2a < 4$

$$\Rightarrow \quad a > -2$$

note

Note * | If you have to divide by a negative number, you must reverse the inequality symbol.

Exercise 9·4

Solve each of the inequalities in questions 1 – 3.

1. (a) $x + 2 > 4$ (b) $y + 6 < 5$ (c) $p + 5 > 9$ (d) $t - 2 < 0$

    (e) $v + 6 \geq 7$ (f) $g + 7 \leq -7$ (g) $d - 8 \geq 0$ (h) $e - 4 > -3$

    (i) $q - 5 \geq 2$ (j) $k + 12 \leq 12$ (k) $b + 7 \leq 5$ (l) $m + 21 < 18$.

2. (a) $2x > 8$ (b) $5y < 20$ (c) $7m > 14$ (d) $3p < -12$

    (e) $5b < -5$ (f) $7n \leq 49$ (g) $10k \geq -40$ (h) $2u \leq -11$.

3. (a) $2x + 1 > 5$ (b) $3a - 4 < 8$ (c) $5b - 2 < 23$ (d) $7c + 7 > 0$

    (e) $4d + 5 < 21$ (f) $8e + 2 > 10$ (g) $6g + 3 \leq 0$ (h) $9h + 9 \geq 9$

    (i) $4k - 2 \leq 0$ (j) $10y - 20 \geq -50$ (k) $6p + 7 \leq -23$ (l) $\frac{1}{2}r + 6 < -1$

    (m) $3r + 7 > 1$ (n) $2c - 9 > -12$ (o) $11y + 11 \leq -33$ (p) $\frac{1}{3}w - 1 \geq 9$.

4. By solving each inequality, find the **smallest whole number** which makes it true.

    (a) $2x + 6 > 8$ (b) $5x - 7 \geq 14$ (c) $3x + 9 \geq 20$ (d) $8x - 2 > 0$.

5. By solving each inequality, find the **largest whole number** which makes it true.

    (a) $4x + 5 < 17$ (b) $4x + 5 \leq 17$ (c) $7x - 2 < 40$ (d) $6x - 1 \leq 3$.

Solve the following inequalities.   (*Watch for the inequality sign requiring to be reversed !*)

6. (a) $-x > 4$ (b) $-a < 2$ (c) $-b < -6$ (d) $-2c > -11$

    (e) $-3d < 18$ (f) $1 - g > 2$ (g) $9 - h \geq 4$ (h) $12 - n \leq -1$.

7. (a) $3x + 3 > x + 9$ (b) $5x + 8 < 3x + 18$ (c) $7x - 3 > 3x + 29$ (d) $7x + 1 \geq 13 - x$

    (e) $13 - 2x \leq 3x - 7$ (f) $24 - 3x \geq x + 12$ (g) $x - 1 \leq 9x - 57$ (h) $15 - 7x \geq 12 - x$.

8. (a) $2(x + 3) + 3 > 17$ (b) $2(p + 5) - 1 > 3$ (c) $5(2y - 1) + 7 \leq 3$

    (d) $8 - 2(r - 2) \geq 20$ (e) $9 - (1 - k) < 4$ (f) $1 - 3(m - 5) \geq -2$

    (g) $3(1 - 2x) \leq 27$ (h) $2(5x - 1) > 0$ (i) $-\frac{1}{2}(4x - 5) \leq -2$

    (j) $-6(x + 2) \leq 3x + 24$ (k) $2(2x + 4) \geq 36 - 6x$ (l) $3(1 - 2x) < 13 - 5x$

    (m) $2(5x + 10) > 10(2x + 1)$ (n) $2(4x - 7) \leq 3x - 14$ (o) $9(2x + 2) < 22x$.

9. A gardener pours 1100 ml of water and 6 cups of weedkiller, each holding x ml of weedkiller, into a **two litre** watering can.

    (a) Show that $1100 + 6x \leq 2000$.

    (b) Solve the inequality to find the maximum volume of water each cup can hold.

10. Mrs Emery, the maths teacher, has £245 to spend on **Teejay** Maths Books which cost £10 each.

The delivery charge is £15. She orders y books.

Make up an inequality and solve it to find the **maximum** number of books she can buy.

11. A village fayre costs £320 to run. A raffle, held locally, raised £70 towards the cost of the fayre.

x entry tickets were sold, priced at £2·50 each.

Form an inequality and solve it to find the **minimum** number of tickets that had to be sold to avoid a loss.

TAYLOR'S TENTS
£12
PLUS
£5 per DAY

12. (a) Write down the hire cost for d days with each hire company.

    (b) Make an inequality if Taylor's cost is known to be **less** than Camper's for the d days, and solve it.

    (c) Suggest a reason why most people hire their tents from Taylor's.

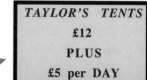

CAMPER TENT HIRE
£5
PLUS
£12 per DAY

Remember Remember..... ?

1. Copy each equation and solve to find the value of x :-

   (a) $17 + x = 12$ (b) $6x = 9$ (c) $2x + 8 = 19$

   (d) $6x - 2 = 40$ (e) $8x + 4 = 2x - 8$ (f) $10x - 3 = 5x + 17$

   (g) $10x = 3x + 56$ (h) $2(x - 5) = 20$ (i) $4(2x - 3) = 4x + 30$

   (j) $3(x - 3) + 2(x + 5) = 16$ (k) $2(6x + 1) - 3(x - 4) = x + 34$ (l) $2(5x - 3) - 3(4x - 6) = 0$.

2. Solve :-

   (a) $\frac{1}{2}x - 1 = 5$ (b) $\frac{2}{5}x - \frac{1}{4} = 1$ (c) $\frac{2}{3}x - 1 = \frac{3}{4}x + 2$

   (d) $\frac{1}{4}x - \frac{1}{2} = \frac{4}{5}$ (e) $\frac{x + 2}{5} = 3$ (f) $1 + \frac{x - 2}{4} = 0$

   (g) $\frac{2}{5}(2x + 3) - 4 = 0$ (h) $\frac{5}{6}(2x + 2) = \frac{1}{4}x + 3$ (i) $\frac{x + 1}{3} + \frac{x + 4}{4} = 2$

   (j) $\frac{2x - 1}{3} + \frac{x + 2}{6} = 1$ (k) $\frac{x - 1}{5} - \frac{x - 2}{2} = 9$ (l) $\frac{7x - 1}{8} - \frac{x - 2}{4} = 3$.

3. Solve these inequalities :-

   (a) $a + 7 < 8$ (b) $b - 11 \geq 0$ (c) $5c \leq -45$

   (d) $2d + 1 > 12$ (e) $2e - 9 > -17$ (f) $1 - f > -14$

   (g) $7g + 1 \geq 13 - g$ (h) $38 - 3h \geq h + 6$ (i) $2(i + 1) + 5 > 25$

   (j) $11 - (1 - j) \geq -2$ (k) $2(2k + 7) \geq 19 - 6k$ (l) $2(1 - l) \leq 3(2l - 2)$.

4. To rent a DVD movie from **Electroshow** costs :-

   - membership free   • then £4 per DVD.

   To rent from **Moviebuster**, the charge is :-

   - £3 for membership   • but their DVD's are cheaper to rent at £2·50 each.

   (a) Take x as the number of DVD's rented and make an inequality showing that Electroshow is **dearer** than Moviebuster for renting movies.

   (b) Solve the inequality and make a recommendation about which company you should go to rent :-

        (i) 1 DVD   (ii) 2 DVD's   (iii) 3 DVD's.

1.   Explain in a short sentence or two the meaning of the mathematical term **tolerance**.

2.   For each of the following, write down the minimum and maximum values :-

    (a) (11 ± 2) mm   (b) (84 ± 0.5) m

    (c) (2.42 ± 0.8) kg   (d) (1.9 ± 0.01) m.

3.   A bolt design gives a diameter tolerance of 0.045 cm. The minimum diameter is given as 8.4 mm.

    State the maximum diameter.

4.   Calculate the gradient of the line joining the 2 points A$(-1, 3)$ and B$(5, -1)$.

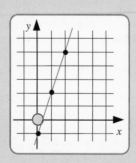

5.   Write down both the **gradient** and the **y-intercept** of each of these two lines :-

    (a) $y = \frac{1}{2}x - 2$ (b) $3y + 2x - 6 = 0$.

6.   Write down the **equation** of this line.

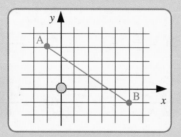

7.   Make a neat sketch of the following lines showing all the important points :-

    (a) $m = 2$ through the point $(0, 3)$

    (b) passing through $(0, -2)$ with $m = 0.5$

    (c) $y = \frac{2}{3}x + 2$

    (d) $y = -2x - 3$

    (e) $m = a$ (where $a < 0$) passing through $(0, b)$ where $b > 0$.

8.   Write down the equations of these lines :-

    (a)

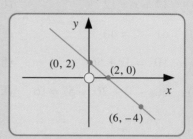

    (b)

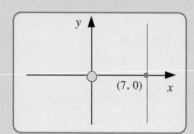

    (c)

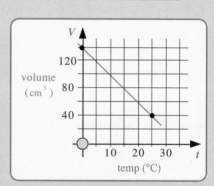

9.   Solve the following equations, showing each step of your working :-

    (a) $7x - 2 = 40$ (b) $8x + 3 = 2x - 9$

    (c) $10x = 3x + 56$ (d) $5(2x - 3) = 7x + 12$.

10. Solve, showing **ALL** working :-

    (a) $\frac{3}{5}x - \frac{2}{3} = 2$ (b) $\frac{2x - 3}{7} = 3$

    (c) $\frac{x + 1}{3} + \frac{x - 2}{4} = 1$.

11. Solve the following inequalities :-

    (a) $x + 3 \le 4$

    (b) $2x - 1 > -6$

    (c) $25 + 3x \ge x + 37$

    (d) $10 + (3 - 2x) \ge 1$

    (e) $3(2x - 4) + 6 < 3 - (x - 3)$.

1. Set down and find :-

   (a) 263
        × 25

   (b) 9 ⟌ 7533

   (c) 5 × 72

   (d) 3420
        × 8

   (e) 25 × 500

   (f) 700 × 9000

   (g) 70400 ÷ 80

   (h) 8000 − 964.

2. I deposit £185 in the bank each month. How much will I have deposited after 1 year ?

3. Set down and find :-

   (a) 38 ÷ 8

   (b) 9·1 − 2·384

   (c) 20 − 9·749

   (d) 54 ÷ 300

   (e) 0·035 × 2000

   (f) 19·274
        × 6

   (g) 19·2 − 11·93 + 16·174

   (h) 8 ⟌ 17·344.

4. Find :-

   (a) $\frac{4}{5}$ of 330

   (b) $\frac{3}{4}$ of 84

   (c) $\frac{2}{7}$ of 2100.

5. Simplify :-

   (a) $\frac{10}{15}$

   (b) $\frac{24}{27}$

   (c) $\frac{34}{51}$

   (d) $\frac{19}{76}$.

6. Find :-

   (a) $\frac{1}{2} + \frac{3}{4}$

   (b) $7 - 2\frac{1}{4}$

   (c) $4 \times 2\frac{1}{4}$

   (d) $\frac{1}{2}$ of $\frac{1}{2}$.

7. Of 180 pupils, $\frac{5}{6}$ do not wear glasses. $\frac{2}{3}$ of those without glasses have brown hair.

   How many have brown hair and don't wear glasses ?

8. VAT is charged (at 20%) on luxury goods.

   Calculate the final cost of the following items if these are the pre–VAT prices :-

   (a) Widescreen T.V. — £240

   (b) P.C. game — £20

   (c) Speakers — £36.

9. Find :-

   (a) 25% of £6·40

   (b) 70% of £6

   (c) 3% of £32·00

   (d) 15% of £60

   (e) $33\frac{1}{3}$% of £225

   (f) $2\frac{1}{2}$% of £1200.

10. I deposit £1600 in the bank. I receive 4% interest **per annum**.

    How much will I have in my bank account after 6 months ?

11. Find :-

    (a) (−6) + 13

    (b) (−17) − 12

    (c) 7 + (−24)

    (d) 15 − (−25)

    (e) (−79) − (−19)

    (f) (−3) × 15

    (g) $(-11)^2$

    (h) 35 ÷ (−7)

    (i) $(-5) \times (-3)^2$

    (j) $\frac{(-10) \times 4 \times (-6)}{5 \times (-8)}$

    (k) −6((−2) − (−5))

    (l) (−70) ÷ (−2).

12. The temperature fell from 19°C at noon to − 17°C at midnight. By how much had it fallen ?

13. Today is 13th June. My birthday was 3 weeks ago. On what date was my birthday ?

Squares, Roots and Powers

Reminders :-   To **square** a number means to **multiply it by itself.** $\boxed{7^2 = 7 \times 7 = 49}$

             To **cube** a number means to **multiply it by itself, then itself again.** $\boxed{5^3 = 5 \times 5 \times 5 = 125}$

The smaller number on the right shoulder is known as an **index** (plural "indices") or a **power.**

Higher Powers - the Use of a Scientific Calculator.

If you have a scientific calculator, it will have a button like this ....

        $\boxed{x^y}$ or $\boxed{y^x}$.   This is useful for finding powers of a number.

Example 1 :-   Find 4^8 by writing it as $4 \times 4 \times 4 \times 4 \times 4 \times 4 \times 4 \times 4$ and working it out.

Example 2 :-   To find 4^8, using the $\boxed{x^y}$ do the following :-   Press $\boxed{4}$ $\boxed{x^y}$ $\boxed{8}$ $\boxed{=}$

              You should get the same answer as in example 1, (65 536) but a lot quicker !

Exercise 10·1

1.   Do not use a calculator in this question.

     Copy and complete the following :-

     (a) $4^2 = 4 \times 4 = ...$ (b) $6^2 = 6 \times 6 = ...$

     (c) $8^2 = 8 \times ... = ...$ (d) $10^2 = ...$

     (e) 11^2 (f) 12^2

     (g) 1^2 (h) 30^2

     (i) $(-1)^2$ (j) $(-5)^2$

     (k) $(\frac{1}{2})^2$ (l) $(-\frac{1}{4})^2$

     (m) $4^3 = 4 \times 4 \times 4 = ...$

     (n) $9^3 = 9 \times 9 \times ... = ...$

     (o) $10^3 = ... \times ... \times ... = ...$

     (p) $(-4)^3 = ... \times ... = ...$ (q) $(-1)^3$

     (r) $(10)^4$ (s) $(-1)^{12}$

     (t) $(-2)^6$ (u) $(\frac{1}{3})^5$.

2.   You can use a calculator this time.

     Find the value of :-

     (a) 19^2 (b) 28^2

     (c) 105^2 (d) $(-64)^2$

     (e) 8^3 (f) 25^3

     (g) $(-9)^3$ (h) $(-40)^4$

     (i) 7^4 (j) 5^6

     (k) 10^7 (l) 9^5

     (m) 3^7 (n) 6^5

     (o) 1^{15} (p) 0^{12}

     (q) 2^{14} (r) 12^4

     (s) 3^8 (t) $(\frac{1}{2})^8$

     (u) $4^{10} + 3^4$ (v) $100^5 - 80^5$

     (w) $10^4 + 1^{15}$ (x) $2^{12} - 4^6$

     (y) $(-4)^8 + (-3)^5$ (z) $(-5)^7 - (-2)^7$.

Square Roots, Cube Roots & Harder Roots

$\sqrt[5]{7776}$

You already know how to find the **square root** and **cube root** of a number :-

e.g. $\sqrt{49}$ - by asking - "what number, times itself, gives 49 ?" $\sqrt{49} = 7$.

The cube root e.g. $\sqrt[3]{27}$ is found by asking - "what number $\times$ itself, $\times$ itself again gives 27 ?" $\sqrt[3]{27} = 3$.

Harder Roots - the Use of a Scientific Calculator.

On your scientific calculator, look **above** the y^x power button and you should see $\sqrt[x]{y}$.

Now follow 【3】【shift】【y^x】【27】【=】 and you will find the answer to $\sqrt[3]{27}$ again.

*note - depending on the make of your calculator, the root button may vary from the one in the example. Check with you teacher !

Example :- Find $\sqrt[3]{7962624}$. On your calculator ... 【5】【shift】【y^x】【7962624】【=】 **24**

Exercise 10·2

1. Without the use of a calculator, write down the answer to :-

    (a) $\sqrt{25}$ (b) $\sqrt{81}$ (c) $\sqrt{1}$ (d) $\sqrt{2500}$

    (e) $\sqrt{0·64}$ (f) $\sqrt{90000}$ (g) $\sqrt{1210000}$ (h) $\sqrt{64}$.

2. Use your calculator to find the following, to 2 decimal places :-

    (a) $\sqrt{7}$ (b) $\sqrt{28}$ (c) $\sqrt{69}$ (d) $\sqrt{105}$

    (e) $\sqrt{500}$ (f) $\sqrt{2000}$ (g) $\sqrt{102·2}$ (h) $\sqrt{100000}$.

3. On your calculator find the $\sqrt[3]{x}$ button and use it to work out :-

    (a) $\sqrt[3]{125}$ (b) $\sqrt[3]{512}$ (c) $\sqrt[3]{343}$ (d) $\sqrt[3]{1000}$

    (e) $\sqrt[3]{3375}$ (f) $\sqrt[3]{21952}$ (g) $\sqrt[3]{1331000}$ (h) $\sqrt[3]{64000000}$.

4. Calculate :-

    (a) $\sqrt[4]{81}$ (b) $\sqrt[5]{243}$ (c) $\sqrt[4]{625}$ (d) $\sqrt[5]{1024}$

    (e) $\sqrt[3]{729}$ (f) $\sqrt[6]{64}$ (g) $\sqrt[7]{2187}$ (h) $\sqrt[10]{1024}$

    (i) $\sqrt{17 + 8}$ (j) $\sqrt{75 - 11}$ (k) $\sqrt[3]{15 + 12}$ (l) $\sqrt[3]{1442 - 111}$

    (m) $\sqrt[3]{6^2 + 8^2}$ (n) $\sqrt[3]{13^2 - 12^2}$ (o) $\sqrt[4]{194481} - \sqrt[5]{161051} - \sqrt{100}$.

Very Large Numbers - Standard Form

A number like 4700 can be written in a different way.

$$4700 = 470 \times 10 = 47 \times 10 \times 10 = 4\cdot7 \times 10 \times 10 \times 10 = 4\cdot7 \times 10^3.$$

$4\cdot7 \times 10^3$ is called the "Standard Form" of 4700.

It is also said to be in Scientific Notation when the number at the start, (the 4·7), lies between 1 and 10.

How to change a "normal" number into a number in Scientific Notation.

95800   -> **Step 1**   move the decimal point until it comes between the 1st and the 2nd digits.   9·58

         Step 2   now count how many places the decimal point was moved (4 places here).   9·5800

         Step 3   finally, write this number, (the 4), as the power of 10. $9\cdot58 \times 10^4$

Example :- Write 14 000 000 in scientific notation, $a \times 10^n$. $14\,000\,000 = 1\cdot4 \times 10^7$

Exercise 10·3

1. Write 6400 in scientific notation.

     6400 =>   (6·400) => $6\cdot4 \times 10^{\cdots}$ (3)

2. Use the method shown above to write the following numbers in scientific notation :-

(a) 73 (= $7\cdot3 \times 10^{\cdots}$) (b) 516

(c) 8540   (d) 6421

(e) 7000   (f) 10 000

(g) 29 000   (h) 34 500

(i) 9   (j) 60

(k) 412 000   (l) 658 200

(m) 630   (n) 5 000 000

(o) 4 800 000   (p) 3 710 000

(q) 42 000 000   (r) 55 500 000

(s) 300 000 000   (t) 453 100 000.

Remember :-

25 million	=	25 000 000
1·86 million	=	1 860 000
$4\frac{1}{2}$ million	=	4 500 000

---

3. Write out each of the following in full, then change into scientific notation.

(a) 3 million = 3 000 000 = $3\cdot0 \times 10^{\cdots}$

(b) 2·5 million = 2 500 000 = ... $\times 10^{\cdots}$

(c) 6·29 million = ... = ...

(d) $9\frac{1}{2}$ million   (e) 3·6 million

(f) $15\frac{1}{2}$ million   (g) 7·632 million

(h) $44\frac{1}{4}$ million   (i) $50\frac{3}{4}$ million

(j) Rovers sold their star player for £12·4 million.

(k) The population of Iceland is two hundred and eighty five thousand.

4. Write the following decimal numbers in scientific notation.

(a) 35·6   (b) 2·15

(c) 250·1   (d) 462·55

(e) 6470·5   (f) 82 700·1

(g) 200 000·1   (h) 33·3333.

Reversing the Process

How to change from Scientific Notation back to "normal" form.

Example :- Write $3\cdot85 \times 10^4$ in normal form.

$3\cdot85 \times 10^4 \quad \rightarrow$ **Step 1** Write down the 385 **without** the decimal point.

Step 2 Move the point (4) places to the right from where it was.

4 places

$3\cdot85 \times 10^4 \quad = \quad 3\,8\,5\,0\,0 = \quad 38\,500$

(Can you see why we need the two extra zeroes ?)

Further Example :- $3\cdot852 \times 10^7 \quad = \quad 38\,520\,000$

5. Each of the following is written in scientific notation, $a \times 10^n$.

   Change each one back into **normal** form.

   (a) $2\cdot3 \times 10^2$ (b) $6\cdot41 \times 10^3$

   (c) 8×10^5 (d) $7\cdot73 \times 10^4$

   (e) $9\cdot102 \times 10^3$ (f) $6\cdot004 \times 10^4$

   (g) $4\cdot913 \times 10^6$ (h) $1\cdot1 \times 10^5$

   (i) $8\cdot71 \times 10^7$ (j) $2\cdot143 \times 10^5$

   (k) $1\cdot9 \times 10^8$ (l) $3\cdot555 \times 10^5$.

   When large numbers appear on a scientific calculator, they sometimes do so in scientific notation form.

   The calculator below shows the number .....

   $3\cdot95 \times 10^8$

   | 3·95 | 8 |

   On/Off
   Shift
   (7) (8) (9) (+)

   $= 395\,000\,000$

6. What numbers are shown on these calculators ?

   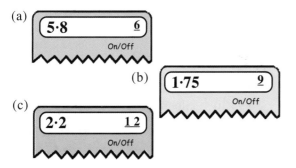

   (a)
   | 5·8 | 6 |
   On/Off

   (b)
   | 1·75 | 9 |
   On/Off

   (c)
   | 2·2 | 12 |
   On/Off

7. A cafe sells $7\cdot73 \times 10^5$ litres of cola each year. Write this amount as a normal number.

8. Lottery Extra stands at £$4\cdot25 \times 10^6$. Write this amount as we would know it.

9. There are $3\cdot156 \times 10^7$ seconds in a solar year. Write this number of seconds out fully.

10.

The distance from Neptune to the sun is $4\cdot497 \times 10^9$ km. Write this in normal form.

11. The hospital vending machines made a profit of £$8\cdot105 \times 10^3$ last year. Write the profit in normal form.

12.

The population of China is $1\cdot298 \times 10^9$. Write the population of China in normal form.

13. Chelsea paid Marseille £$2\cdot43 \times 10^7$ for a striker called Didier Drogba.

Write this transfer fee in normal form.

Very Small Numbers

It is also possible to write very small numbers (decimal numbers) in **Scientific Notation**.

It is a process of moving the decimal point to a position just after the first **non-zero** whole number.

Example 1 :- $0.00052 \Rightarrow 00005.2 \times 10^{-4} = 5.2 \times 10^{-4}$

4 places

note :- the NEGATIVE sign

Example 2 :- $0.0467 \Rightarrow 004.67 \times 10^{-2} = 4.67 \times 10^{-2}$

2 places

Example 3 :- $0.0000093 = 9.3 \times 10^{-6}$

Exercise 10·4

1. Write each of the following small numbers in scientific notation :-

   (a) 0·05   (b) 0·007

   (c) 0·9   (d) 0·0004

   (e) 0·00006   (f) 0·000001

   (g) 0·043   (h) 0·0097

   (i) 0·00035   (j) 0·000066

   (k) 0·00147   (l) 0·358

   (m) 0·000249   (n) 0·00000963

   (o) 0·000000003   (p) 0·000000000018.

2. Rewrite each sentence, expressing the number in scientific notation.

   (a) The radius of the lead in a pencil is 0·0012 m.

   (b) The weight of a single eyelash is 0·00000024 kg.

   (c) Jenny Peters beat Alice Duff by 0·099 seconds to win the race.

   (d) A thin film of grease is approximately 0·000000755 mm thick.

   (e) An hour is 0·000114 of a year.

   (f) Pluto's mass is 0·0025 times that of the mass of the Earth.

Changing from a number in Scientific Notation, back to "normal" form.

Simply move the point **LEFT** to express the number in full.

Example 1 :-

$2.6 \times 10^{-3} \Rightarrow .0026 = 0.0026$

3 places

Example 2 :-

$7.15 \times 10^{-5} \Rightarrow .0000715$

5 places

$= 0.0000715$

3. Write these numbers in **decimal** form :-

   (a) 4.7×10^{-3} (b) 3.4×10^{-3}

   (c) 5×10^{-2} (d) 9×10^{-6}

   (e) 8.01×10^{-4} (f) 3.002×10^{-3}

   (g) 4.775×10^{-6} (h) 6.283×10^{-5}

   (i) 1.111×10^{-2} (j) 5.442×10^{-3}

   (k) 9.9×10^{-7} (l) 3.8874×10^{-1}.

4. A bread ring weighs 5.9×10^{-2} kilograms.

   Is this more or less than 60 grams ?

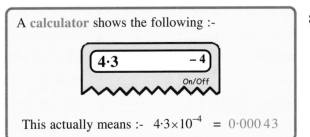

A **calculator** shows the following :-

4·3   – 4
On/Off

This actually means :- $4 \cdot 3 \times 10^{-4} = 0 \cdot 000 \, 43$

5.   What do these readings mean ?

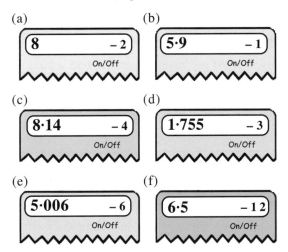

(a)
8   – 2
On/Off

(b)
5·9   – 1
On/Off

(c)
8·14   – 4
On/Off

(d)
1·755   – 3
On/Off

(e)
5·006   – 6
On/Off

(f)
6·5   – 12
On/Off

6.   Write out in full :-

(a) 3×10^{-3} (b) 7×10^{2}

(c) $2 \cdot 5 \times 10^{-2}$ (d) $8 \cdot 2 \times 10^{3}$

(e) $4 \cdot 87 \times 10^{4}$ (f) $6 \cdot 03 \times 10^{-4}$

(g) $7 \cdot 123 \times 10^{-6}$ (h) $3 \cdot 85 \times 10^{5}$

(i) 2×10^{-5} (j) $7 \cdot 009 \times 10^{8}$.

7.   Write in scientific notation :-

(a)   0·0006   (b)   49

(c)   9310   (d)   0·02

(e)   0·3   (f)   885 000

(g)   0·089   (h)   1 950 000

(i)   0·000 000 55   (j)   69 000 000 .

8.   Each of the following numbers can be written
as $a \times 10^{n}$, where a lies between 1 and 10.

Find the values of a and n in each case.

(a)   The attendance at the Rugby
World Cup final in Australia
in 2003 was 82 950.

8.   (b)   The distance from
the sun to Mars is
217 million kilometres.

(c)   The average diameter of a human hair
is 0·000 09 metres.

(d)   The population of Alaska is 627 000.

(e)   The average time taken
to blink is 0·4 seconds.

(f)   105 million people
voted in the last
election in the USA.

(g)   A NASA space probe was recorded
travelling at a speed of 13 650 mph.

(h)   The thickness of a sheet of thin paper
is 0·000 001 metres.

(i)   A beam of light
travels 5 kilometres in
0·000 016 5 seconds.

(j)   The stem of a rose is
0·009 metres thick.

(k)      A fast computer took
0·000 085 seconds
to complete a calculation.

(l)   A high speed train
in Japan can reach
a top speed of
443·5 km/hr.

(m)   A **billion** is another name for a
"thousand million".

Write, in scientific notation :-

(i)   2 billion   (ii)   3·1 billion

(iii)   96 billion   (iv) $17\frac{1}{2}$ billion.

Scientific Notation and the Calculator

Your calculator is equipped to handle numbers in standard form (**scientific notation**).

Look for the (Exp) button (or the (**EE**) button) on your calculator.

Example 1 :- Calculate $6 \times (3.25 \times 10^3)$ giving your answer in scientific notation.

In your calculator enter :-

The answer is **19 500**   In this case, the answer has not appeared in scientific notation.

You have to do this yourself as shown earlier. 1.95×10^4.

Example 2 :-   Calculate $(1.57 \times 10^{-5}) \div 7$, giving your answer in scientific notation, correct to 3 significant figures.

In your calculator enter :-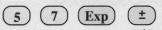

this might be different on your calculator

The answer may appear as 2.242×10^{-6}.

It is then rounded to 2.24×10^{-6} (to 3 sig. figs).

Note :-   the answer may appear as $0.000\,002\,242$.

(if it does, you have to change this into scientific notation and round).

Exercise 10·5

1. Use your scientific calculator to work out the following :-

    Answer in scientific notation.

    (a) $5 \times (4.26 \times 10^5)$ (b) $6 \times (2.97 \times 10^8)$

    (c) $9.23 \times (3 \times 10^5)$ (d) $1.4 \times (7.5 \times 10^4)$

    (e) $2.75 \times (6 \times 10^{-4})$ (f) $(8.55 \times 10^{-7}) \times 2$

    (g) $3.8 \times (4.5 \times 10^{-8})$ (h) $(3.7 \times 10^{-3}) \times 4.4$.

2. Work out the following, giving your answers in scientific notation, (*rounded to 3 significant figures when necessary*).

    (a) $(5.8 \times 10^3) \div 9$ (b) $(8.1 \times 10^7) \div 2$

    (c) $(3.1 \times 10^5) \div 1.9$ (d) $(4.5 \times 10^2) \div 8.8$

    (e) $3 \div (1.27 \times 10^4)$ (f) $8 \div (3 \times 10^8)$

    (g) $5.9 \div (8.2 \times 10^{-3})$ (h) $7.9 \div (2.6 \times 10^{-8})$.

3. Try these, answering in scientific notation :-

    (a) $(5.8 \times 10^3) + 7$ (b) $(1.5 \times 10^4) + 500$

    (c) $(9.8 \times 10^3) - 40$ (d) $(4.3 \times 10^{-2}) + 10$

    (e) $20 - (7.5 \times 10^{-1})$ (f) $7000 - (6.2 \times 10^3)$

    (g) $654 - (6 \times 10^2)$ (h) $0.15 - (3.8 \times 10^{-3})$.

4. Do the following calculations :-

    Give your answers in **"normal"** form, rounded to 3 significant figures.

    (a) $(8.2 \times 10^3) \times (3.1 \times 10^2)$

    (b) $(5.69 \times 10^4) \times (4.7 \times 10^{-7})$

    (c) $(2.8 \times 10^{10}) \div (5.3 \times 10^{-3})$

    (d) $(5 \times 10^6) \div (8 \times 10^{-4})$

    (e) $(9.1 \times 10^5)^3$

    (f) $(3.2 \times 10^{-7}) \times (9 \times 10^6)^3$.

In the following questions, express each of your answers in **scientific notation**.

5. There are 3.156×10^7 seconds in a solar year.

    How many seconds are there in 5 solar years ?

6.   The Lotto jackpot of $£8.4 \times 10^6$ was shared equally among 3 winners. How much did each receive ?

7. Last year, Robertsons Jam factory made a profit of $£7 \times 10^7$.

    This year they made $£1.2 \times 10^5$ more than that.

    How much profit was made this year ?

8. A carbon atom weighs 2.03×10^{-23} grams. What do 1000 carbon atoms weigh ?

9. The formula for the surface area of a sphere is

    $$\text{Area} = 4\pi r^2 \text{ , where } \pi = 3.14.$$

    A small electrically charged particle is spherical in shape, and has radius $r = 2.3 \times 10^{-8}$ cm.

    Calculate its surface area, giving your answer correct to 3 significant figures.

10.  Light travels at a speed of 3×10^5 km per second.

    How long would it take (in minutes and seconds) for a beam of light to travel from the sun to the Earth, a distance of 1.476×10^8 km ?

11. The planet Mars is at a distance of 2.3×10^8 km from the Sun.

    The speed of light is 3×10^5 km per second.

    How long does it take light from the Sun to reach Mars ?

    Give your answer to the nearest minute.

12. The new Hubble telescope, in orbit around the Earth, can now detect 3.8×10^{11} galaxies.

    If each galaxy has on average, 4.7×10^{13} visible stars, how many stars can the telescope detect ?

13. The total mass of argon in a flask is 5.23×10^{-2} grams.

    Given that the mass of a single atom of argon is 6.63×10^{-23} grams, find to 3 significant figures the approximate number of argon atoms in the flask.

14. A cyclotron produces high speed particles.

    A particle moving inside the cyclotron takes 9.4×10^{-23} seconds to travel 2.1×10^{-1} metres.

    Calculate the speed of the particle in metres per second.

15. The total number of visitors to The Modern House Exhibition was 1.425×10^5 .

    The exhibition was open each day from the 1st June to 14 September **inclusive**.

    Calculate the average number of visitors per day to the exhibition, to 3 significant figures.

16. The annual profit of a company was around $£3.2 \times 10^9$ during the year 2013.

    Approximately how much profit did the company make per second ?

17. The Aircraft Journal reported :-

    "The top airline's oldest jumbo jet has now flown 3.58×10^7 miles".

    (*This is equivalent to 150 trips from the earth to the moon*).

    Calculate the distance from the earth to the moon, giving your answer correct to 3 sig. figs.

1. Write down the value of :-

    (a) 2^9

    (b) $(-5)^3$

    (c) $\sqrt{4900}$

    (d) $\sqrt{0.0016}$.

2. Write each of these in **scientific notation** :-

    (a) 860 $(= 8.6 \times 10^{\cdots})$

    (b) 7210

    (c) 95 200

    (d) 126 800

    (e) 16.82

    (f) 5 240 000

    (g) 6 million

    (h) 243 million

    (i) $5\frac{1}{2}$ million

    (j) $1\frac{3}{4}$ million.

3. Copy and complete :-

    $$0.000\,623 \;=\; 6.23 \times 10^{\cdots}$$

4. Write each of these in **scientific notation** :-

    (a) 0.0036

    (b) 0.0521

    (c) 0.000 077

    (d) 0.0008

    (e) 0.989

    (f) 0.000 000 42.

5. Write out each of the following numbers in "**normal**" number form :-

    (a) 5.9×10^3

    (b) 8.08×10^5

    (c) 7.1×10^2

    (d) 2.81×10^4

    (e) 4×10^6

    (f) 3.2×10^9

    (g) 1.001×10^7

    (h) 3.5×10^{12}.

6. Write out each of the following numbers in "**decimal**" form :-

    (a) 5.8×10^{-3}

    (b) 9.9×10^{-2}

    (c) 6.2×10^{-5}

    (d) 2.3×10^{-1}

    (e) 3×10^{-7}

    (f) 4×10^{-4}.

7. Write in scientific notation :-

    (a) 42 000

    (b) 0.0801

    (c) 137 000

    (d) 0.000 34

    (e) 0.000 006 5

    (f) $9\frac{1}{2}$ million

    (g) 34 000 000

    (h) 0.000 02.

8. Rewrite the following numbers out fully :-

    (a) 7.3×10^6

    (b) 49×10^{-3}

    (c) 3.61×10^4

    (d) 8×10^{-5}

    (e) 8×10^8

    (f) 5.5×10^{-2}

    (g) 3.03×10^5

    (h) 4.2×10^{-1}.

9. Calculate :-

    (a) $\sqrt[3]{216}$

    (b) $\sqrt[4]{4096}$.

10. Use your EE or EXP buttons to find the following :-

    (*Give each answer in scientific notation*).

    (a) $150 \times (3.8 \times 10^8)$

    (b) $(2.31 \times 10^6) \times (1.35 \times 10^5)$

    (c) $(5.4 \times 10^{13}) \times (2.5 \times 10^{-4})$

    (d) $(6.8 \times 10^{15}) \div (4 \times 10^4)$

    (e) $(5.22 \times 10^8) \div (1.8 \times 10^{-5})$

    (f) $(3.2 \times 10^{10})^2$

    (g) $(1.3 \times 10^{-4})^3$

    (h) $\dfrac{(4.2 \times 10^8) \times (2.5 \times 10^7)}{(3 \times 10^{-4})}$.

11. Calculate the **area** of this rectangle, and answer in scientific notation.

(1.3×10^6) mm

(6.4×10^5) mm

12. Light travels at 2.998×10^8 metres per second.

    How far will a beam of light travel in :-

    (a) an hour   (b) a day   (c) a year ?

13. The formula for the **volume** of a sphere is $V = \frac{4}{3}\pi r^3$. where r is its radius. ($\pi = 3.14$)

    Calculate the volume of the Earth which has a radius of 6.4×10^3 km.

Circumference

Remember that the **perimeter**, or the **circumference**
of a circle can be measured by the formula :-

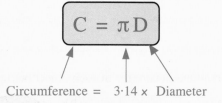

Circumference =   3·14 x Diameter

(Your teacher will go over this with you if you have not met this before).

Example :-   Calculate the **circumference** of this circle,
which has a diameter of 9 centimetres :-

=> | $C = \pi D$
=> | $C = 3·14 \times 9$
=> | $C = 28·26$ cm

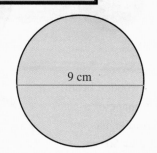

9 cm

Exercise 11·1

1.   Calculate the **circumference** of a circle
which has a diameter of 8 cm.

Copy and complete :-

=> | $C = \pi D$
=> | $C = 3·14 \times 8$
=> | $C = $ .... cm.

2.   Calculate the circumference of each
circle below :-
(*Show 3 lines of working for each*).

(a)   (b)

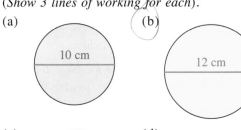

10 cm   12 cm

(c)   (d)

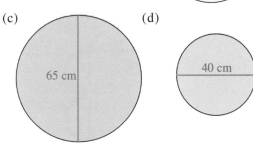

65 cm   40 cm

(e)   (f)   A circle with
diameter 1 cm.

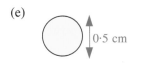

0·5 cm

3.   Find the circumference of each object below :-
(a)   (b)

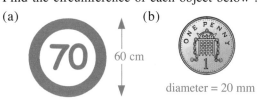

70   60 cm

diameter = 20 mm

(c)   (d)

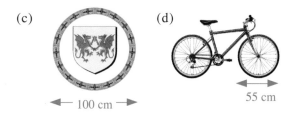

100 cm   55 cm

Remember if you are given the **radius**
you need to **double** it to find the diameter.

4.   Calculate the circumference of a circle
with radius 10 cm.

Copy and complete :-

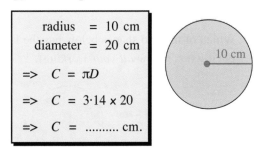

radius   = 10 cm
diameter = 20 cm

=> $C = \pi D$

=> $C = 3·14 \times 20$

=> $C = $ .... cm.

10 cm

5. Calculate the circumference of each circle :-

(a)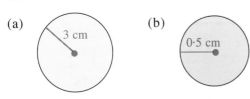
3 cm

(b)
0·5 cm

6. Find the **perimeter** of each object below :-

(a)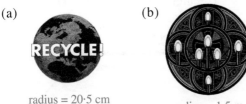
RECYCLE!
radius = 20·5 cm

(b)
radius = 1·5 m

7. A red wooden beam, in the shape of a semi-circle, has **diameter** 50 cm.

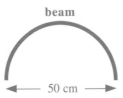
beam
50 cm

Calculate the length of the red wooden beam.

8. A semi-circular garden has a diameter of 8 metres.

Calculate the **perimeter** of the garden.

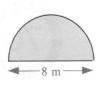
8 m

9. Calculate the perimeter of a semi-circular garden with a **radius** of 5 metres.

10. A garden path has a fence made from strips of metal rod bent into semi-circles.

Each semi-circle has a diameter of 20 centimetres.

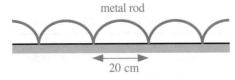
metal rod
20 cm

Find the length of metal rod needed to make the fence which has to be 5 metres long.

11. Which of the two shapes below has the larger **perimeter**. (*Show all your working*).

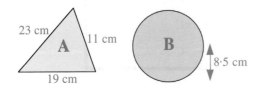
23 cm
A
11 cm
19 cm
B
8·5 cm

12. Calculate the **perimeter** of each shape below :-

(a)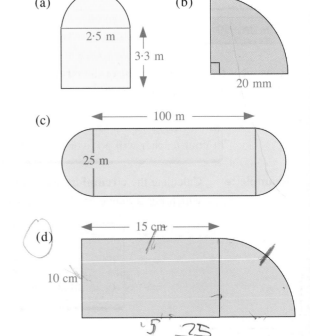
2·5 m
3·3 m

(b)
20 mm

(c)
100 m
25 m

(d)
15 cm
10 cm
5   25

13. Push'n'Go Pram company has a large logo made from steel bars. The design consists of 2 straight bars each 2 metres long, two circular bars each with 1 metre diameter and a three quarter circular bar as shown.

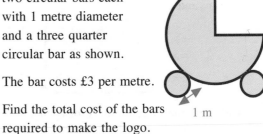
1 m

The bar costs £3 per metre.

Find the total cost of the bars required to make the logo.

14. A jeweller designs a brooch from gold wire using the design shown below.

Two straight 9 cm wires joined at right angles.
One arc, (a quarter circle), joining the wires.
Three identical semi-circles at the top.
Two other identical semi-circles at the side.

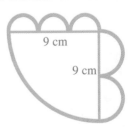
9 cm
9 cm

The gold wire costs £1·40 per centimetre.

Calculate the total cost to make the brooch.

Finding the Diameter

You can use the formula $C = \pi D$ to calculate the **diameter** of a circle if you know its circumference.

Example :-   Find the diameter of a circle with circumference 94·2 cm.

$$C = \pi D$$
$$94\cdot2 = 3\cdot14 \times D$$
$$D = \frac{94\cdot2}{3\cdot14} = 30 \text{ cm}$$

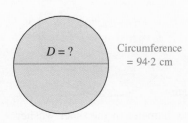

$D = ?$ Circumference $= 94\cdot2$ cm

The formula needed to
calculate the diameter is :–

Diameter $\longrightarrow$ $D = \dfrac{C}{\pi}$ $\longleftarrow$ Circumference

$\longleftarrow$ 3·14

Exercise 11·2

1. Find the diameter of a circle with a
   circumference of 21·98 cm.

   Copy and complete :-

   $$D = \frac{C}{\pi}$$
   $$\Rightarrow \quad D = \frac{21\cdot98}{3\cdot14}$$
   $$\Rightarrow \quad D = \text{........ cm}$$

   D

   Circumference
   $= 21\cdot98$ cm

2. Calculate the diameter of each circle below :-
   (*Show 3 lines of working for each*)

   (a)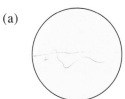

   $C = 492\cdot98$ cm

   (b)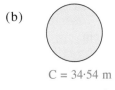

   $C = 34\cdot54$ m

   (c)

   $C = 3\cdot14$ mm

   (d)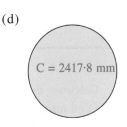

   $C = 2417\cdot8$ mm

3. Find the diameter of a circle with circumference :-

   (a) 157 cm   (b) 386·22 mm

   (c) 6280 m   (d) 0·314 km.

4. Write down the **radius** of each of the circles
   in question 3.

5. Find the **radius** of a circle with circumference
   471 millimetres.

6. Find the radius of a circle which has
   perimeter 3 kilometres.
   (*Give your answer to the nearest metre*).

7. (*Give all answers to one decimal place*).

   (a) Determine the
       diameter
       of the
       tyre,
       given
       that its
       circumference
       is 200 centimetres.

   (b) Find the **diameter** of a circular button
       if its circumference is 8 centimetres.

   (c) The circumference of a large birthday
       cake is 0·5 metres.
       Determine the
       radius of the cake,
       in centimetres.

   (d) Find the **radius** of a circle with
       circumference :-

       (i) 18 cm   (ii) 1056 m.

8. A small circular washer has an outer
   circumference of 30 millimetres.

   The hole has a radius of 1 millimetre.

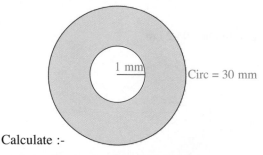

   Circ = 30 mm

   Calculate :-

   (a) the diameter of the outer washer.

   (b) the circumference of the hole.

9. A clock company uses a logo made from three
   quarters of large circular rod and six rods
   welded at right angles.

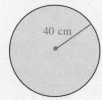

   The logo needs red trim
   as shown opposite.

   Find the total length of red trim needed if the
   circle has a circumference of 3 metres.

   (*Answer to the nearest centimetre*).

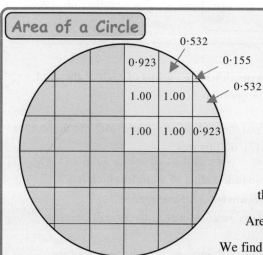

The **blue** area (quarter circle) has been put onto a
square centimetre grid and the area for each part has
been measured and is given in the diagram.

The total **blue** area (*quarter circle*) is **7·065 cm²**

This means the total area of the circle is :-

$$7·065 \times 4 = 28·26 \text{ cm}^2.$$

There is a formula (or rule) we can use to calculate
the area of a circle as long as you know its radius.

Area generally uses two measurements (... cm × ... cm).

We find that if we calculate $r \times r$ (or r^2), and multiply it by π,
we also get an answer of **28·26 cm²**,

which is the same value as we found by measuring !

To find the area of a circle we can use :- $\pi \times r \times r$ **or** $\boxed{A = \pi r^2}$ *Area* = $\pi \times r \times r$

Example :- Calculate the area of a circle with radius 40 cm.

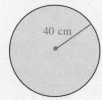

40 cm

$$A = \pi r^2$$
=> $$A = 3·14 \times 40 \times 40$$
=> $$A = 5024 \text{ cm}^2$$ (square centimetres)

1. Find the **area** of a circle with radius 4 cm.

   Copy and complete :-

   $$A = \pi r^2$$
   => $$A = 3·14 \times 4 \times 4$$
   => $$A = ... \text{ cm}^2$$

2. Calculate the **area** of each circle below :-
   (You **must** set down 3 lines of working).

   (a)

   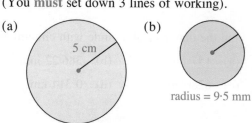

   5 cm

   (b)

   radius = 9·5 mm

3. Find the area of each object below :-

(a)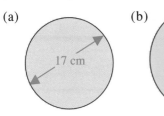

radius of light
= 27 cm

(b)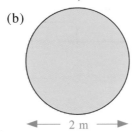

5·25 cm

4. Find the area of each circle below :-
(*Remember you must use the* radius)

(a)

17 cm

(b)

2 m

5. (a) Find the area of a circular poster with **diameter** 60 centimetres.

(b) Find the area of a circular place-mat, whose radius is 13 centimetres.

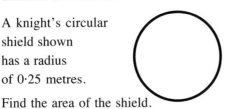

(c) Find the area of a circular rug with diameter 2·2 metres.

(d) A knight's circular shield shown has a radius of 0·25 metres.

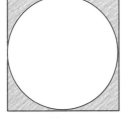

Find the area of the shield.

(e) A circular serving plate has a diameter of **half a metre**.

Calculate the area of the plate.

6. A square metal machine plate with side 35 centimetres has a circular hole cut from it.

Find :-

(a) the area of the plate.

(b) the area of the hole.

(c) the area of steel plate remaining. (*shown shaded*).

35 cm

7. Two semi-circular mirrors of radius 60 centimetres are placed side by side on a light blue frame as shown.

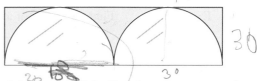

Find the area of light blue frame **not** covered by the mirrors.

8. (a) Find the area of a circular glass panel with **diameter** 100 centimetres.

(b) A circular field has a **diameter** of 1 km. Find the area of the field.

9. A garden pond is in the shape of a semi-circle.

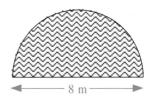

8 m

Find the area of the pond.

10. A garden is designed as shown using a square of side 6 metres and four semicircles.

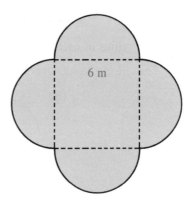

6 m

Find the total area of the garden.

11. A cylindrical snake tank has a base with diameter 75 centimetres.

The base has to be treated with a special paint which costs 2·5p per square centimetre.

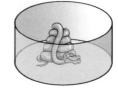

Find the cost of painting the base of the tank.

You can use the formula $A = \pi r^2$ to calculate the **radius** of a circle if you know its area.

Example :-   Find the radius of a circle with area 78·5 cm².

$$A = \pi r^2$$

$$78·5 = 3·14 \times r^2$$

$$r^2 = 78·5 \div 3·14 = 25$$

$$r = \sqrt{25} = \boxed{5 \text{ cm}}$$

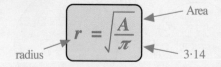

Area = 78·5 cm²

A special formula, which can be used
to calculate the radius, given the area, is :-

$$r = \sqrt{\frac{A}{\pi}}$$

Area

radius   3·14

1.   Find the radius of a circle with area 314 cm².

Copy and complete :-

$$r = \sqrt{\frac{A}{\pi}} \quad \Rightarrow \quad r = \sqrt{\frac{314}{3·14}}$$

$$\Rightarrow \quad r = \sqrt{.... } \text{ cm}$$

$$\Rightarrow \quad r = \text{ .... cm}$$

2.   Calculate the radius of each of these :-

(Show 3 lines of working for each)

(a)   (b)

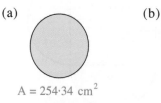

A = 254·34 cm²

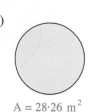

A = 28·26 m²

(c)   (d)

Speaker Area
= 530·66 cm²

Table-top area
= 22 686·5 cm²

3.   Calculate the **radius** of a circle with an area
of 628 square centimetres.

4.   Calculate the **diameter**
of the circle shown.

A = 1256 cm²

5.   Calculate the **diameter** of a circle with area :-

   (a)   4710 cm²   (b)   2041·785 cm² .

6.   Circular biscuits, each
with an **area** of 78·5 cm² ,
are baked on a rectangular
tray 100 centimetres by
80 centimetres as shown.

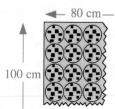

80 cm

100 cm

What is the **maximum** number of biscuits
that can be baked, like this, on one tray ?

7.   Bart has a square piece of card which has an
area of 400 cm² .

Explain why he cannot cut out a circular piece
from it with an area of 325 cm² .

8.   A cylinder with a base area of 113·04 cm²
fits **exactly** into a box with a square base.

Calculate the lengths
of the sides of the base.

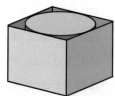

9.   A circle has area 1384·74 square centimetres.

Calculate the **perimeter** of the circle.

A Mixture of Problems

Remember :- when finding :-

> the area of a **semi-circle** .... find the area of the whole circle and **half** it.
>
> the area of a **quarter circle** ... find the area of the whole circle and **divide by four**.
>
> a **composite** area .... find the area of each part and **add** them together.

Exercise 11·5

1. Find the area of each shape :-

(a)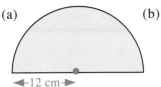
←12 cm→

(b)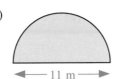
← 11 m →

(c)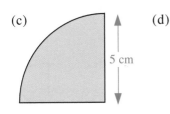
5 cm

(d)
Quarter circle with
a 1 metre diameter

2. For each of the three shapes below, find :-
   (i) its area
   (ii) its perimeter.

(a)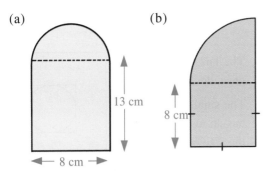
13 cm
← 8 cm →

(b) 8 cm

(c)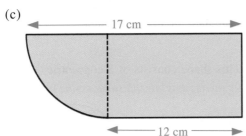
← 17 cm →
← 12 cm →

3. A circle has **circumference** 157 centimetres.

   Calculate the **area** of the circle.

4. A circle has an area of 11 683·94 cm² .
   Calculate the **perimeter** of the circle.

5. The semi-circular garden shown below has a diameter of 12 metres.

   A semi-circular brick pathway **one metre wide** partly surrounds the grass lawn.

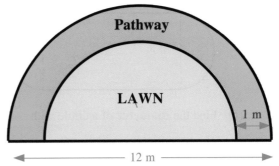
Pathway
LAWN
1 m
← 12 m →

   Find the perimeter of :-

   (a) the grass lawn   (b) the brick path.

6. A company logo uses five circles, each with a **circumference** of 100 cm, which overlap as shown.

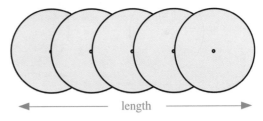
← length →

   Find the total length of the company logo.

7. A **semi-circle** has an area of 401·92 cm² .
   Calculate the perimeter of the semi-circle.

8. A quarter circle has an area of 854·865 cm² .

   Calculate the perimeter of the quarter circle.

Area = 854·865 cm²

1. Calculate the **circumference** of each circle ✓
   below. *(Show 3 lines of working)* :-

   (a)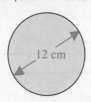
   12 cm

   (b)
   5·5 cm

2. Calculate the **perimeter** of each shape below :-

   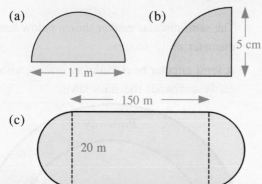

   (a) 11 m

   (b) 5 cm

   (c) 150 m   20 m

3. (a) Find the **diameter** of a circle with :-

   (i) circumference 20·41 cm

   (ii) perimeter 4·71 km.

   (b) Find the **radius** of a circle with
   circumference 329·7 mm.

4. Calculate the **area** of each of these :-
   (Show at least 3 lines of working)

   (a)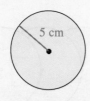
   5 cm

   (b)
   12 m

   (c)
   40 m

   (d)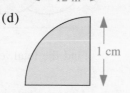
   1 cm

5. Find the **area** of a circle with :-

   (a) 15 cm radius   (b) 23 cm diameter.

6. Calculate the :-

   (a) **radius** of a circle with area 7·065 m².

   (b) **diameter** of a circle with area 0·785 mm².

7. A white square with
   sides 8 centimetres has
   four identical quarter
   circles cut out from
   each corner as shown.

   Find the white area.

   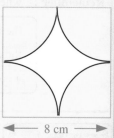
   8 cm

8. For each shape below, find the :-

   (a) **perimeter**   (b) **area**.

   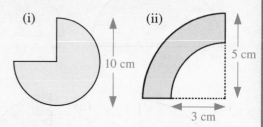

   (i) 10 cm

   (ii) 5 cm   3 cm

9. The shape shown
   is **one eighth** of
   a circle which
   has a radius of
   6 centimetres.

   Calculate the area
   of this shape.

   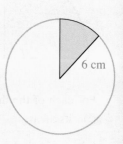
   6 cm

10. The large square
    has side 2 metres.

    The smaller square
    has an **area** a quarter
    the size of the larger
    area.

    Calculate the total pink area.

    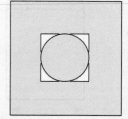

11. This shape consists of 3 concentric* circles
    (* *means having the same centre*).

    Determine the
    combined areas
    which are shaded
    pink.

    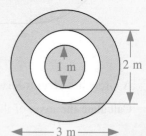
    1 m   2 m   3 m

Chapter 12

Coordinates and Transformations

Coordinates – Revision

Revision :-   You should know what a Coordinate diagram, (or a **Cartesian** diagram), looks like.

- x–axis (*or horizontal axis*).
- y–axis (*or vertical axis*).
- the **origin** (O).

A is 3 (*right*) and 4 (*up*) from the origin.

$=>$ A(3, 4), has x–coordinate 3 and y–coordinate 4.

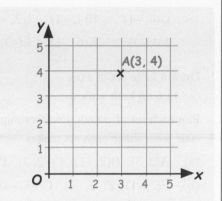

Remember :-

We also extended the set of x and y axes **backwards** and **downwards**.

The point B is 4 (*to the right*) and 2 (*down*) from the origin

$->$ B(4, –2).

The point C is 2 (*to the left*) and 3 (*up*) from the origin

$->$ C(–2, 3).

The point D is 4 (*to the left*) and 1 (*down*) from the origin

$->$ D(–4, –1).

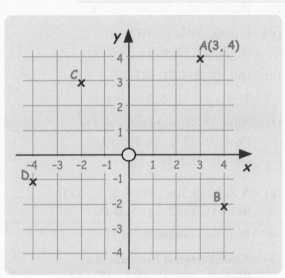

Exercise 12·1   Revision Work

1. Look at the coordinate diagram below.
    The coordinates of E are **E(–3, 3)**.
    Write down the coordinates of the other points.

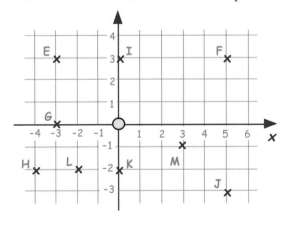

2. From the diagram in question 1, write down all the coordinates :-

    (a) that lie on the x-axis

    (b) that lie on the y-axis

    (c) that has an x-coordinate of 3

    (d) that has an x-coordinate of –4

    (e) that has a y-coordinate of –3

    (f) that have the same x-coordinate

    (g) that have the same y-coordinate

    (h) that have the same x and y-coordinate.

3. (a) Copy the Cartesian coordinate grid from question 1.

    (b) Plot each of the following coordinates on your diagram :-

    A(6, 3)   B(2, 0)   C(0, 4)

    D(–4, 2)   E(–2, 0)   F(–2, –3)

    G(0, –1)   H(4, –1)   I(2, –3)

    J(0, –3)   K(6, –1)   L(–3, –3).

4. Draw a large set of axes (–8 to 8 on both scales).

    Plot each set of points, join them up and state what shape each set makes.

    (a) A(2, 3), B(2, –1), C(–2, 3), D(–2, –1).

    (b) E(2, –1), F(–3, –1), G(–3, –3).

    (c) H(2, 0), I(0, –2), J(–3, 1), K(–1, 3),

    (d) L(3, 4), M(7, 1), N(3, –2),
         N(–2, –2), O(–6, 1), P(–2, 4),

    (e) Q(0, 4), R(4, 2), S(1, –3),
         T(–1, –3), U(–5, 2).

    (f) A(0, –1), B(–2, –1), C(–4, 1),
         D(–4, 3), E(–2, 5), F(0, 5),
         G(2, 3), H(2, 1).

5. (a) A rectangle has vertices at A(–1, 1), B(1, –1), C(–2, –4), and D.

        State the coordinates of D.

    (b) A parallelogram has vertices at E(–3, 2), F(0, 3), G(2, –1) and H.

        State two possible coordinates for H.

    (c) A kite has vertices at I(4, 3), J(0, –3), K(–3, –4) and L.

        State the coordinates of L.

    (d) An isosceles triangle has vertices at

        M(–3, –2), N(4, –2) and P.

        State the two possible coordinates of P.

    (e) An isosceles triangle has vertices at Q(3, 3), R(–1, –1) and S.

        State two possible coordinates for S.

    (f) A rhombus TUVX has vertices at T(2, –2), U(1, 3), V(–4, 4) and X.

        State the coordinates of X.

6. Determine the size of the Cartesian diagram you need and plot each set of points joining them up as you go to see who you have drawn.

    Arm :   (–24, –15) (–24, –6) (–26, –4) (–22, –4)
            (–22, –2) (–21, –1) (–20, –1) (–19, –3)
            (–19, –2) (–15, –4) (–15, –6) (–13, –6)
            (–13, –8) (–16, –10) (–16, –13)
            (–14, –14) (–13, –12) (–8, –10)
            (–6, –7) (–5, –6) (–5, –8) STOP
            (–19, –3) (–20, –5) (–19, –6) (–18, –6)
            (–16, –4) (–15, –4) STOP

    Arm :   (24, –15) (25, –13) (26, –9) (25, –4)
            (27, –3) (28, –2) (27, –1) (24, –1)
            (25, 2) (24, 3) (22, 1) (19, 1) (18, 0)
            (18, –3) (17, –4) (16, –3) (14, –4)
            (14, –5) (17, –6) (18, –7) (17, –11)
            (14, –11) (13, –9) (8, –9) (7, –7)
            (6, –6) (6, –8) (3, –9) (1, –13)
            (–1, –10) (–6, –7)   STOP
            (19, 0) (20, 0) (21, –2)
            (23, –2) (22, 1)   STOP
            (7, –7) (6, –8) (6, –4)   STOP

    Mouth : (–5, –6) (–5, –1) (–4, 1) (–1, 3) (–1, 2)
            (0, 1) (1, 1) (2, 1) (2, 3) (5, 1) (6, –2)
            (6, –4) (5, –6) (2, –8) (–1, –8) (–4, –6)
            (–5, –4) STOP
            (0, –5) (0, –4) (1, –4) (1, –5) (0, –5)

    Eye :   (7, 3) (5, 2) (4, 2) (2, 3) (1, 5) (1, 7)
            (2, 8) (4, 9) (5, 9) (8, 8) (9, 7) (8, 5)
            (8, 3) (8, 2) (8, 1) (7, 0) (6, 0) STOP
            (5, 3) (5, 4) (6, 4) (6, 3) (5, 3) STOP

    Eye :   (–6, 3) (–4, 2) (–3, 2) (–1, 3) (0, 5)
            (0, 7) (–1, 8) (–3, 9) (–4, 9) (–6, 8)
            (–7, 7) (–7, 5) (–6, 3) (–7, 3) (–7, 1)
            (–6, 0) (–5, 0)   STOP
            (–5, 3) (–5, 4) (–4, 4)
            (–4, 3) (–5, 3)   STOP

    Head : (–7, 7) (–6, 12) (–5, 15) (–4, 16)
            (–1, 17) (2, 17) (5, 16) (6, 15) (7, 12)
            (8, 7)   STOP

    Hint : (12, 5) (12, 10) (13, 10) (14, 9) (14, 7)
            (13, 5) (12, 5)   STOP
            (15, 6) (15, 9) (16, 10) (17, 10) (18, 9)
            (18, 6) (17, 5) (16, 5) (15, 6)   STOP
            (19, 5) (19, 10)   STOP
            (22, 5) (22, 10)   STOP
            (19, 8) (22, 8)   STOP.

In mathematics, a **transformation** simply means a movement or changing of a point or shape.

This movement or change is sometimes called a "*mapping*"(*you will learn more about mappings later*).

There are 4 types of transformation (you have used them in previous work but they were not defined) :-

Reflection – Rotation – Translation – Dilatation (*or dilation*)

Reflection – where a point or shape is reflected usually over a line of symmetry (*used in Chapter 6*).

Example :-   A Triangle with vertices ABC is as shown.

When reflected over the *x*-axis, the images of the vertices are A'(2, –4), B'(3, –1) and C'(1, –1).

When triangle A'B'C' is reflected over the *y*-axis, the images of these vertices are A"(–2, –4), B"(–3, –1) and C"(–1, –1).

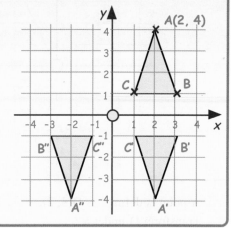

> **N.B.**   Under a reflection in the *x* axis
>
> $$P(x, y) \rightarrow P'(x, -y)$$
>
> Under a reflection in the *y* axis
>
> $$Q(x, y) \rightarrow Q'(-x, y).$$

Exercise 12·2

1. (a) Copy the diagram below using the coordinates to draw the F-shape :-

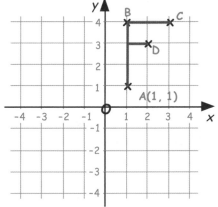

    (b) Reflect ABCD over the *x*-axis and label the images A'B'C'D'.

    (c) Write down the coordinates of A'B'C'D'.

    (d) Reflect A'B'C'D' over the *y*-axis and label them A"B"C"D".

2. A square has vertices E(2, 2), F(5, –1), G(2, –4) and H.

    (a) Write down the coordinates of H.

    (b) Reflect the square over the *x*-axis and state the vertex images (Write as E'(....) etc...).

    (c) Reflect E'F'G'H' over the *y*-axis and state the images of the vertices.

3. A point is defined as J(3, –2). The point is mapped under a reflection over the *x* axis **and** then over the *y*-axis.

    State the new coordinates of the image of J.

4. A triangle has vertices K(1, 4), L(2, 3) and M(2, 0).

    Triangle KLM is mapped under a reflection over the *y* axis **and** then over the *x*-axis.

    State the coordinates of the image of ΔKLM.

5. A triangle has vertices P(–2, 5), Q(1, –3) and R(–4, –3).

    (a) Sketch these points on a Cartesian grid.

    (b) Show the line *x* = 2 as a dotted line.

    (c) Show the images of P, Q and R after a reflection over the dotted line.

6. For each point and its image, describe the reflection that has occurred :-

    (a) S(4, 1)   ->   S'(4, –1)

    (b) T(7, –3)   ->   T'(–7, –3)

    (c) U(–3, –3)   ->   U'(3, –3)

    (d) V'(7, 11)   ->   V"(–7, 11)

    (e) A(–x, –y)   ->   A'(–x, y)

    (f) B(–a, b)   ->   B'(a, b).

- where a coordinate or shape is rotated about a point, usually the origin (*used in Chapter 6*).

Example 1 :- Under a 90° clockwise rotation about O
A(2, 4) –> A'(4, –2)
Under a 180° rotation about O
A(2, 4) –> A''(–2, –4).

Example 2 :- Triangle ABC has been given a 180° rotation about the origin.

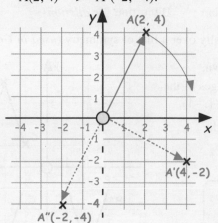

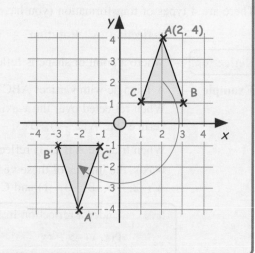

7. A point is defined as D(3, 2).
   Transform D under a :-

   (a) 180° rotation about the origin O.

   (b) 90° clockwise rotation about the origin.

8. For each point below, apply a :-

   (i) 180° rotation about the origin
   (ii) 90° clockwise rotation about the origin.

   (a) E(6, 1)   (b) F(4, 0)

   (c) G(–3, 1)   (d) H(4, –2)

   (e) I(–3, –3)   (f) J(–21, 18)

   (g) K(–21, 37)   (h) L(23, –42)

   and list the new coordinates each time.

9. Rotate each of the points in question 8 by 90° **anticlockwise** about the origin :-

10. For each set of points describe the transformation :–

    (a) P(2, 2)   –>   P'(–2, –2)

    (b) Q(3, 1)   –>   Q'(1, –3)

    (c) R(–5, 2)   –>   R'(5, –2)

    (d) S(0, 2)   –>   S'(–2, 0)

    (e) T(–3, –2)   –>   T'(3, 2)

    (f) U(–4, –3)   –>   U'(–3, 4)

    (g) V(12, 23)   –>   V'(–23, 12)

    (h) W(a, –b)   –>   W'(b, a).

11. A triangle has vertices A(2, 1), B(4, 1), C(2, 3).

    (a) Transform ABC using a 180° rotation about the origin and state the coordinates of the vertices of the images A'B'C'.

    (b) Give ABC a 90° clockwise rotation about the origin and write down the coordinates of the vertex images. (*Use* A"B"C").

    (c) Under a 90° anticlockwise rotation write down the coordinates of the images of ABC. (*Use* A'''...).

12. For each shape below, state the coordinates of the vertices of the images under a :-

    (i) 180° rotation about the origin
    (ii) 90° clockwise rotation about the origin.

    (a) D(1, 1), E(3, 1), F(3, 3), G(1, 3)

    (b) H(–4, 1), I(–4, 3), J(0, 3), K(0, 1).

13. (a) A point is defined as P(6, 3).
        Give P a 180° rotation about the point (1, 2) and state coordinates of P'.

    (b) Give W(–1, 3) a 180° rotation about (2, 5) and state the coordinates of W'.

    (c) A triangle has vertices G(–2, 3), H(3, 4) and K(–4, –1).

        State the coordinates of the images of ΔGHK under a 90° anticlockwise rotation about the point (–1, –3).

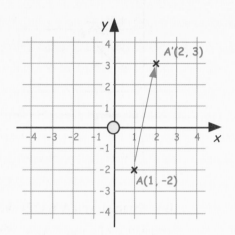 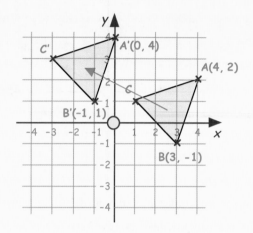
14.   State coordinates of C and C′ in the diagram.

15.   For each point below, state the image under a translation of $\begin{pmatrix} -1 \\ 3 \end{pmatrix}$:-

   (a)   D(1, 5)   (b)   E(1, 1)

   (c)   F(–2, 3)   (d)   G(–4, –1)

   (e)   H(0, 2)   (f)   I(4, –3).

16.   State the image of each point in question 15, under a translation of $\begin{pmatrix} -3 \\ -2 \end{pmatrix}$.

17.   For each point and its image describe the transformation in the form $\begin{pmatrix} x \\ y \end{pmatrix}$.

   (a)   M(0, 5)   –>   M′(4, 7)

   (b)   N(1, 3)   –>   N′(7, 2)

   (c)   P(–4, 2)   –>   P′(2, 3)

   (d)   Q(2, –3)   –>   Q′(3, 3)

   (e)   R(7, 1)   –>   R′(–2, –2)

   (f)   S(5, –3)   –>   S′(4, 1)

   (g)   T(–7, 11)   –>   origin

   (h)   U(0, –2)   –>   U′(11, –7).

18.   A triangle has vertices at D(2, 1), E(3, –1) and F(–1, 2).

   State the coordinates of the images of each of the vertices under a translation of :-

   (a) $\begin{pmatrix} 1 \\ 4 \end{pmatrix}$ (b) $\begin{pmatrix} 4 \\ 0 \end{pmatrix}$

   (c) $\begin{pmatrix} -3 \\ 2 \end{pmatrix}$ (d) $\begin{pmatrix} -4 \\ -5 \end{pmatrix}$.

19.   Parallelogram EFGH has vertices E(2, 0), F(2, 4), G(5, 1) and H(5, h).

   (a)   State the value of h.

   (b)   EFGH is reflected over the y-axis. State the coordinates of E′F′G′H′.

   (c)   E′F′G′H′ is given a translation of $\begin{pmatrix} -5 \\ 0 \end{pmatrix}$. State the coordinates of E″F″G″H″.

20.   A(0, 4), B(3, 3), C(1, 2), D(–2, 1) and E(–2, 2).

   These vertices are reflected over the x-axis and then under a translation of $\begin{pmatrix} -5 \\ -4 \end{pmatrix}$.

   State the the coordinates of the images of A, B, C, D and E.

- where a point, line or shape is projected away from or back towards a fixed point, *(usually the origin).*

Example 1 :- Under a dilatation of 2
P(2, 1) -> P'(4, 2).

(Notice *x* and *y* coordinate has been *multiplied by 2*).

Example 2 :- Under a dilatation of 3,
ABCD -> A'B'C'D'

(Notice each coordinate has been *multiplied by 3*).

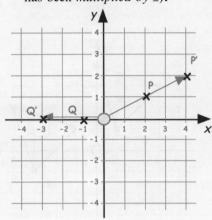

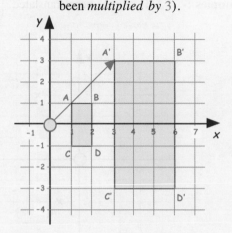

Under a dilatation of 3

Q(–1, 0) -> Q'(–3, 0).

If you started with A'B'C'D', under a dilatation of a third gives ABCD.

21. Write down the coordinates of the image of each point below under a dilatation of 2 :-

(a) A(2, 4)   (b) B(6, 4)

(c) C(–4, 0)   (d) D(16, –8)

(e) E(–6, –5)   (f) F(a, 4b).

22. Write down the image of each point in question 21 under a dilation of one half.

23. (a) Write down the coordinates of the image of $\triangle$GHI, under the dilation 3, where G(1, 1), H(3, 1) and I(2, –2).

(b) Write down the coordinates of the image of JKLM, under the dilatation 2, where J(2, 1), K(3, –1), L(–2, 1) and M(–1, 1).

(c) Write down the coordinates of the image of NOPQR, under the dilatation –2, where N(–2, –1), O(0, 0), P(2, 1), Q(3, 0), R(–2, 0).

Exercise 12·3   *Mixed exercise involving two transformations*

1. Write the coordinates of the image of each point below when rotated 180° about the origin **then** reflected over the *y*-axis :-

(a) A(4, 3)   (b) B(6, –2)

(c) C(–3, 2)   (d) D(–1, –5)

(e) E(0, –3)   (f) F(a, –b).

2. Write the coordinates of the image of each point below when rotated 90° clockwise about the origin **then** given a dilatation of 2 :-

(a) A(1, 1)   (b) B(–2, –1)

(c) C(5, –3)   (d) D(–4, 0)

(e) E(–2, 4)   (f) F(–a, –b).

3. Write the coordinates of the image of each point below under a translation of $\begin{pmatrix} -2 \\ 3 \end{pmatrix}$

then reflected over the *x*-axis :-

(a) A(3, 5)   (b) B(–2, 3)

(c) C(–6, –2)   (d) D(4, 0)

(e) E(2, –3)   (f) F(a, b).

4. Write the coordinates of the image of each set of vertices below when rotated 90° anti-clockwise about O **then** under a dilatation of 1·5 :-

(a) A(0, 4), B(4, 3), C(2, 0)

(b) D(–1, 0), E(–3, –1), F(–4, 2), G(–2, 3)

(c) H(2, 2), I(3, –1), J(0, –3), K(–2, –1), L(0, 1).

Remember Remember..... ?

1. Look at the coordinate diagram below.

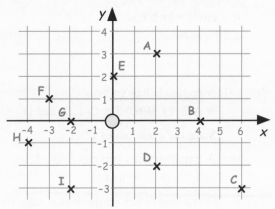

   (a) Write down the coordinates of all the points.

   (b) Write down the coordinates of the point(s)

      (i)   that lie on the *x*-axis
      (ii) that lie on the *y*-axis
      (iii) that have the same *y* coordinate.

2. Draw a large set of axis, (–7 to 7 on both scales). Plot each set of points, join them up and say what 2-dimensional shape each set makes.

   (a) A(–2, –1), B(–4, –3), C(–1, –6), D(1, –4)

   (b) E(2, –2), F(–2, –2), G(0, 3)

   (c) H(–1, 2), I(–3, –3), J(–7, –3), K(–5, 2)

   (d) M(–1, –3), N(0, 1), P(3, 1), Q(3, –2).

3. Shown is the point P(4, 3).

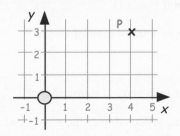

   State the coordinates of the image of P :-

   (a) if it is **reflected** over the *x*-axis

   (b) if it is **reflected** over the *y*-axis

4. A point is defined as (6, 2).

   State the coordinates of its image :-

   (a) under a **180° rotation** about the origin, O

   (b) under a **90° anti-clockwise** rotation about O

   (c) under a **dilatation of 1·5**.

5. Describe a transformation required to take each of these points onto its image point :-

   (a) M(1, 3)   ->   M′(3, 1)

   (b) N(5, 1)   ->   N′(5, –1)

   (c) P(–1, 3)   ->   P′(1, –3)

   (d) Q(1, –4)   ->   Q′(–1, 4)

   (e) R(0, 5)   ->   R′(5, 0)

   (f) S(6, –5)   ->   S′(4, 1)

   (g) T(–1, 9)   ->   origin

   (h) U(7, 3)   ->   U′(–3, 7).

6. Triangle ABC has vertices at (–1, 4), (3, 3) and (4, 0) as shown.

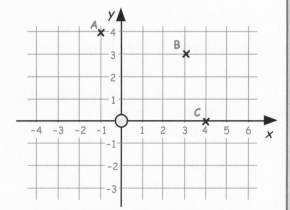

   State the coordinates of the images of A, B and C if the triangle is **reflected** over the :-
   (a) *y*-axis   (b) *x*-axis.

7. State the coordinates of the vertices of the images of ΔABC in Qu 6, when given a :-

   (a) **90° clockwise rotation** about the origin

   (b) **dilation** of **2**

   (c) **translation** of $\begin{pmatrix} -3 \\ -2 \end{pmatrix}$.

8. The point (6, 1) is given a **reflection** *and* a **rotation**. Its image is now (1, 6).

   (a) Describe two transformations used.

   (b) Describe *another* two transformations that could have been used.

   (c) Describe **one** transformation that could have been used to replace the two used.

1. Find :-
   (a) $\sqrt{121}$
   (b) $\sqrt{160\,000}$
   (c) 3^5
   (d) $(-2)^7$.

2. Write each of these using scientific notation :-
   (a) 34 000
   (b) 176 000 000
   (c) 2·05 million
   (d) 0·004
   (e) 0·000 004 12
   (f) 1720 millionths.

3. Write out each of the following numbers in "**normal**" number form :-
   (a) $8·3 \times 10^3$
   (b) $9·01 \times 10^{-2}$
   (c) $1·045 \times 10^7$
   (d) 7×10^{-4}
   (e) $\left(7·6 \times 10^{-4}\right) \times \left(9·8 \times 10^{11}\right)$.

4. A **light year** is the **distance** a particle of light would travel in 1 year. Its value is
   $$9·46 \times 10^{15} \text{ metres.}$$
   The Star, Bellea, is $2·1 \times 10^4$ light years away. How far away is Bellea (in metres) ?

5. Calculate the **circumference** of this circle with diameter 22 cm.

6.

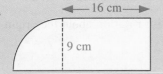

   Calculate the **perimeter** of this shape.

7. A 30 cm plastic ruler is bent into the shape of a semi-circle.
   Calculate the diameter of the semi-circle formed.

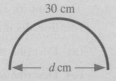

8. Calculate the **area** of this circle which has a 4·1 cm radius.

9. (a) A rectangle has vertices at A(3, 2), B(6, –1), C(1, 0) and D. State the coordinates of D.

   (b) A trapezium has vertices at D(–1, 0), E(0, 5), F(3, 5) and G.
   Given that G lies on the x axis, state the coordinates of G.

   (c) A parallelogram has vertices at I(–3, –1), J(–2, 3), K(2, –1) and L.
   (i) State the coordinates of L.
   (ii) State the coordinates of the point at which its diagonals intersect.

10. P is the point (4, 2).
    State the coordinates of the image of P when :-
    (a) reflected over the x-axis
    (b) reflected over the y-axis
    (c) given a dilation of 2·5
    (d) rotated 90° clockwise about the origin
    (e) rotated 90° anticlockwise about the point (–2, –1).
    (f) given a translation of $\begin{pmatrix} -3 \\ 2 \end{pmatrix}$.

11. A point Q is given a translation of $\begin{pmatrix} 1 \\ -2 \end{pmatrix}$.
    It is then reflected over the x-axis and finally given a 90° clockwise rotation about the origin. The coordinates of the image of Q is Q'(3, 7).
    Find the original point Q.

12. The point G(4, 0) is given a 270° rotation anti-clockwise about the point (1, –3), then reflected over the y-axis.
    State the coordinates of its image point G'.

13. There were exactly 29 874 spectators at the Irish League cup final.

Three boys gave rounded estimates as follows :-

    Ray says there were 30 000
    Tom says 29 900
    Jim says 29 880.

Whose answers are correct ? *Explain*.

14. Do the following and give your answers in standard form, correct to 2 significant figures :-

(a) $(1{\cdot}9 \times 10^6) \times (9{\cdot}7 \times 10^3)$

(b) $(8{\cdot}6 \times 10^8) \div (1{\cdot}7 \times 10^3)$.

15. Copy the diagram and fill in all the missing angles.

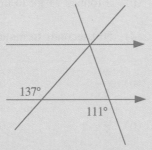

16. Fred works as a manager and earns £36 800 p.a. Three other companies offer him a higher wage.

    Company 1 offers $\frac{3}{16}$ more.

    Company 2 offers 12·5% increase.

    Company 3 offers a 0·13 increase.

Which company offers the highest wage ? (*Justify your answer*).

17. Justin pays £348 per month on his mortgage.

His payment was increased by 3% and six months later decreased by 5%.

"My monthly payment is then 2% less than the original £348 payment", said Justin.

Is there anything wrong with his statement ? (*Justify*).

18. Ali paid a 12% deposit on a £3400 car.

He then paid the rest in 24 equal payments. Ali ended up paying 20% more than the cash price.

How much was each monthly payment ?

19. Simplify fully :-

(a) $5(x + 4) - 2(2x + 7) - 3$

(b) $3p(4p - 5) - 2p(5 - 6p) - 2$.

20. Factorise fully :-

(a) $3t - 12$ (b) $2rt + 6r$

(c) $x^2 - 6x$ (d) $35k^3 - 14k^2$.

21. Copy the shape shown and complete it so that it has a rotational symmetry of order 4 about the red dot.

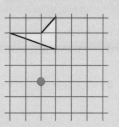

22. The width of a strip of metal needs to be 3·74 mm thick.

There is a 15 thousandth millimetre tolerance.

State the maximum acceptable width.

23. A line passes through (4, 1) and (6, 3).

Find the gradient of this line.

24. Solve :-

(a) $3(2x - 7) + 1 = 16$

(b) $\dfrac{2x - 3}{5} = 7$ (c) $\dfrac{2x}{5} - \dfrac{3}{4} = 1$.

25. A quarter of a circle has radius 4 cm.

Find the perimeter of this shape.

26. (a) A point P(3, 7) has its image P'(–3, –7). State two possible transformations.

(b) State the coordinates of the image of K if K(–4, 11) is rotated by 90° anticlockwise about the point (1, 6).

(c) P'(–3, –7) is found after reflecting the point P over the *x-axis* and then rotating it 270° anticlockwise about the point with coordinates (0, –3). State the coordinates of P.

1. Set down and find the following :-

   (a) $(23)^2$ (b) $8\overline{)5864}$ (c) $25 - 10 \times 2$ (d) $5000 - 297$

   (e) 415×300 (f) $15\,600 \div 600$ (g) 2^6 (h) $\dfrac{8 \times 15}{12 \times 6}$.

2. Set down and find :-

   (a) $53 \cdot 4 + 8 \cdot 956$ (b) $\begin{array}{r} 32 \\ \times\,24 \\ \hline \end{array}$ (c) $74 \div 5$ (d) $\dfrac{3 \times 6 \cdot 97}{100}$.

3. 58·56 litres of milk are poured equally into 8 buckets. How many litres must there be in each bucket ?

4. Change :-   (a) 48 m to km   (b) 2 tonnes 75 kg to kg

        (c) $\frac{4}{5}$ litre to ml   (d) 500 seconds to minutes and seconds .

5. Simplify :-   (a) $\dfrac{35}{105}$ (b) $\dfrac{49}{63}$ (c) $\dfrac{84}{91}$.

6. Find :-   (a) $5\frac{1}{2} - 3\frac{1}{2}$ (b) $\frac{4}{5} - \frac{2}{5}$ (c) $\frac{2}{3} \times 240$

        (d) $6 \times 2\frac{1}{2}$ (e) $4\frac{3}{4} - 1\frac{1}{2}$ (f) $\frac{3}{4}$ of $(12\frac{1}{2} + 11\frac{1}{2})$.

7. Find :-   (a) 20% of £12   (b) 15% of £4·40   (c) 90% of 600

        (d) 7% of £4   (e) 1% of 3200   (f) $12\frac{1}{2}$% of 240.

8. Sally saw a jacket costing £120. In a sale a 15% reduction was offered.

   Calculate the reduction and find what Sally would then pay for the jacket.

9. Find :-   (a) $29 - 43$ (b) $(-17) - 43$ (c) $(-39) + 18$

   (d) $(-24) - (-18)$ (e) $(-7) \times 11$ (f) $(-17) \times (-3)$ (g) $(-30)^2$

   (h) $63 \div (-9)$ (i) $(-115) \div (-5)$ (j) $\dfrac{(-4) \times (-9)}{-6}$ (k) $-\frac{1}{3} \times (-51)$.

10. Draw a set of coordinate axes and plot :- A(–7, –1), B(–3, 6) and C(5, 5).

    Find the 4th point (D) such that ABCD is a **rhombus**.

    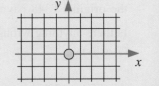

11. Write in 24 hour format :-

    (a) 20 to midnight   (b) 25 to 3 in the afternoon   (c) $\frac{1}{4}$ to 11 in the morning.

12. How long is it from :-   (a) 10·48 am to 1·15 pm   (b) 0855 to 1420 ?

13. Which of these were leap years :- (a) 2012   (b) 2006   (c) 1998 ?

Pythagoras

Pythagoras was a famous Greek Mathematician who discovered an amazing connection between the three sides of **any right angled triangle**.

This relationship, which connects the 3 sides, means it is possible to **CALCULATE** the length of one side of a right angled triangle as long as you know the lengths of the other two.

Look at this **right angled triangle** with sides 3 cm, 4 cm and 5 cm.

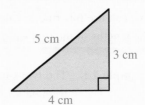

If you add the two smaller sides (3 cm and 4 cm) together, do you get the longer side (5 cm) ? – NO.

Can you see that
- $3^2 = 9$,
- $4^2 = 16$,
- $5^2 = 25$?

Can you also see that:- $3^2 + 4^2 = 9 + 16 = 25 = 5^2$?

> Pythagoras found that this connection between the three sides of a right angled triangle was true **for every right angled triangle**.

Introductory Exercise   (*A possible oral exercise*)

1.   The three sides of this right angled triangle are 6 cm, 8 cm and 10 cm.

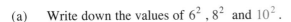

    (a)   Write down the values of 6^2, 8^2 and 10^2.

    (b)   Find the value of $6^2 + 8^2$.

    (c)   Check that $6^2 + 8^2 = 10^2$.

2.   The three sides of this right angled triangle are 9 cm, 12 cm and 15 cm.

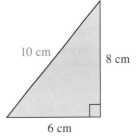

    (a)   Write down the values of 9^2, 12^2 and 15^2.

    (b)   Find the value of $9^2 + 12^2$.

    (c)   Check that $9^2 + 12^2 = 15^2$.

3.   The three sides of this right angled triangle are 5 cm, 12 cm and 13 cm.

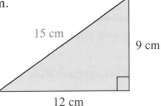

    (a)   Write down the values of 5^2, 12^2 and 13^2.

    (b)   Find the value of $5^2 + 12^2$.

    (c)   Check that $5^2 + 12^2 = 13^2$.

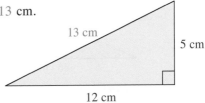

Pythagoras came up with a simple rule which shows the connection between the three sides of any right angled triangle.

The **longest** side of a right angled triangle is called the **HYPOTENUSE**.

If the three sides are a cm, b cm and c cm (the hypotenuse), then Pythagoras' Rule says :-

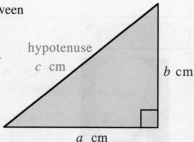

hypotenuse
c cm

b cm

a cm

$$=> \quad \boxed{c^2 = a^2 + b^2}$$

We can use this rule to calculate the length of the **hypotenuse** of a right angled triangle if we know the lengths of the two **smaller** sides.

Example 1 :- The two smaller sides of this right angled triangle are 12 centimetres and 16 centimetres.

To calculate the length of the hypotenuse, use **Pythagoras' Rule**.

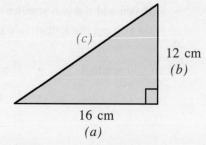

(c)

12 cm
(b)

16 cm
(a)

$$=> \quad c^2 = a^2 + b^2$$
$$=> \quad c^2 = 16^2 + 12^2$$
$$=> \quad c^2 = 256 + 144 = 400$$

use your "√" button on the calculator $\quad => \quad c = \sqrt{400} = \textbf{20 cm}.$

This is how you set down the working.

---

1. Use **Pythagoras' Rule** to calculate the length of the hypotenuse in this triangle :-

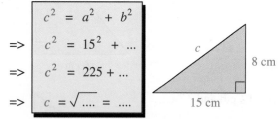

$$c^2 = a^2 + b^2$$
$$=> \quad c^2 = 15^2 + ...$$
$$=> \quad c^2 = 225 + ...$$
$$=> \quad c = \sqrt{....} = ...$$

c

8 cm

15 cm

Copy and complete the working.

2. Use **Pythagoras' Rule** to calculate the length of the hypotenuse in the right angled triangle shown below.

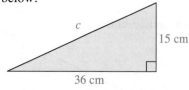

c

15 cm

36 cm

(*Show clearly your 4 lines of working*).

3. Use Pythagoras' Rule (referred to as **PYTHAGORAS' THEOREM**) to calculate the length of the hypotenuse in each of these 3 triangles :-

(a)

c

15 cm

20 cm

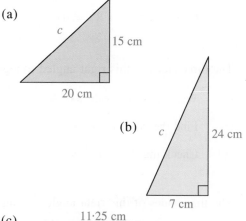

(b) c

24 cm

7 cm

(c)

11·25 cm

6 cm

c

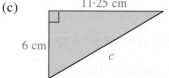

In most cases, the 3 sides are not exact values.

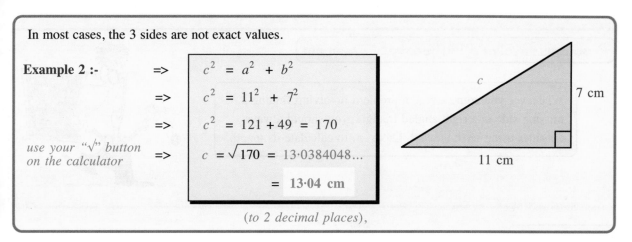

Example 2 :- => $c^2 = a^2 + b^2$

=> $c^2 = 11^2 + 7^2$

=> $c^2 = 121 + 49 = 170$

use your "√" button on the calculator => $c = \sqrt{170} = 13{\cdot}0384048...$

= **13·04 cm**

(to 2 decimal places),

(For the remainder of this exercise, give your answers correct to 2 decimal places).

4. Use **Pythagoras' Theorem** to calculate the length of the hypotenuse in this triangle.

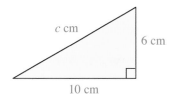

5. Use Pythagoras' Theorem to calculate the length of the hypotenuse in the right angled triangle shown .

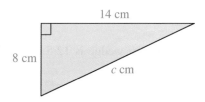

6. Calculate the length of the hypotenuse marked p cm.

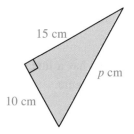

7. Calculate the length of the line marked q cm.

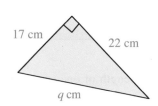

8. Calculate the length of the hypotenuse in this right angled triangle.

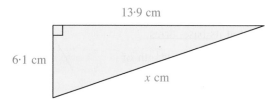

9. Sketch the following right angled triangles :-

Use **Pythagoras' Theorem** to calculate the length of the hypotenuse in each case.

(a)   (b)

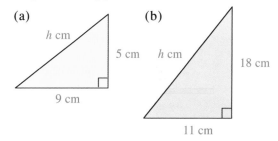

(c)   (d)

(e)   (f)

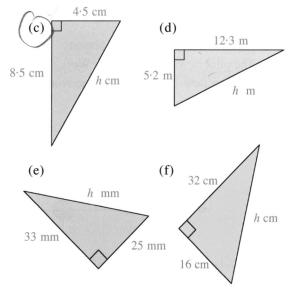

Problems involving Pythagoras' Theorem

Whenever you come across a problem involving finding a missing side in a right angled triangle, you should always consider using **Pythagoras' Theorem** to calculate its length.

(The triangles in these questions are right-angled).

1. A strong wire is used to support a pole while the cement, holding it at its base, dries.

    Calculate the length of the wire.

    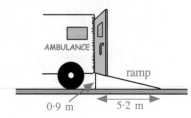
    wire   7·5 m   ←4 m→

2. A ramp is used to help push wheelchairs into the back of an ambulance.

    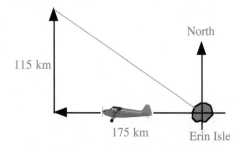
    AMBULANCE   ramp   0·9 m   5·2 m

    Calculate the length of the ramp.

3. A plane left from Erin Isle airport.
    The pilot flew 175 kilometres West.
    He then flew 115 kilometres due North.

    North   115 km   175 km   Erin Isle

    Calculate how far away the plane then was from Erin Isle.

4. A cable is used to help ferry supplies onto a yacht from the top of a nearby cliff.

    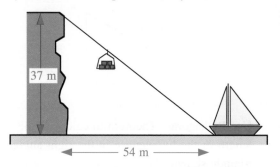
    37 m   54 m

    Calculate the length of the cable used.

5. This wooden door wedge is 12·5 cm long. and 3·1 cm high.

    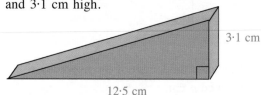
    3·1 cm   12·5 cm

    Calculate the length of the sloping face.

6. This trapezium shape has a line of symmetry shown dotted on the figure.

    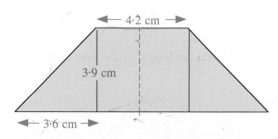
    ← 4·2 cm →   3·9 cm   ← 3·6 cm →

    Calculate the length of one of the sloping edges and hence calculate the **perimeter** of the trapezium.

7. A triangular corner unit (shown in yellow), is built to house a TV set.

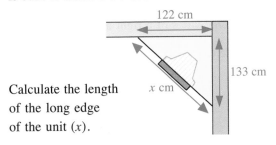

Calculate the length of the long edge of the unit (x).

8. A lawn in Edinburgh's Princes Street is in the shape of a rectangle 26 metres long by 14·5 metres wide.

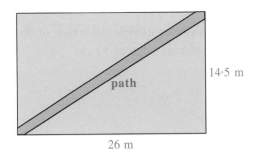

A path runs diagonally through the lawn.

Calculate the length of the path.

9.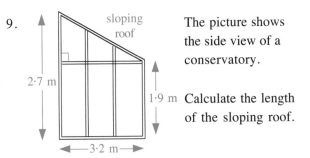

The picture shows the side view of a conservatory.

Calculate the length of the sloping roof.

10. The roof of a garage is in the shape of an isosceles triangle.

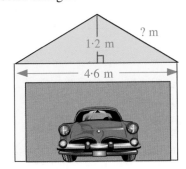

Calculate the length of one side of the sloping roof.

11. Rhombus PQRS has its 2 diagonals, PR and QS, crossing at its centre C.

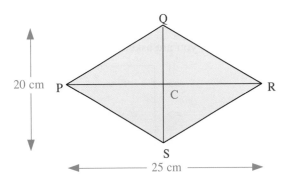

Calculate the **PERIMETER** of the rhombus.

12. Two wires are used to support a tree in danger of falling down after a recent storm.

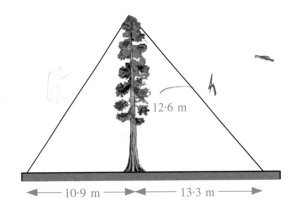

Calculate the **total** length of the support wires.

13. Calculate the **PERIMETER** of these 2 triangles.

(a)

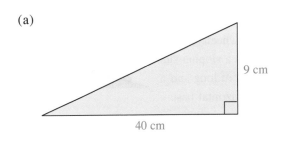

(b)

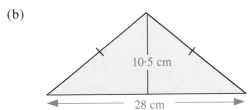

Calculating the Length of One of the Smaller Sides

You can use Pythagoras' Theorem to calculate one of the smaller sides of a right angled triangle.

This time, you are asked to find the length of the smaller side (a) :-

$$=> \quad a^2 = c^2 - b^2$$

$$=> \quad a^2 = 25^2 - 15^2$$

can you see why the "–" sign ?

$$=> \quad a^2 = 625 - 225 = 400$$

$$=> \quad a = \sqrt{400} = \textbf{20 cm}$$

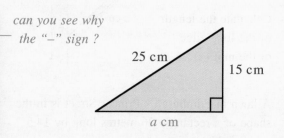

25 cm

15 cm

a cm

Exercise 13·3

1. Calculate the length of the side of this right angled triangle marked with a t.

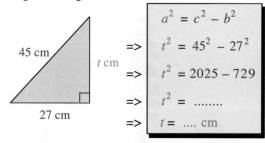

45 cm

t cm

27 cm

$$a^2 = c^2 - b^2$$
$$=> \quad t^2 = 45^2 - 27^2$$
$$=> \quad t^2 = 2025 - 729$$
$$=> \quad t^2 = \text{........}$$
$$=> \quad t = \text{.... cm}$$

2. Calculate the size of each of the smaller sides in the following right angled triangles.

(a)

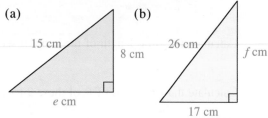

15 cm

8 cm

e cm

(b)

26 cm

f cm

17 cm

3. A wheelchair ramp has a sloping side 8·2 m long and a horizontal base 7·1 m long.

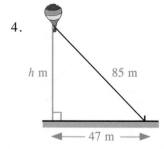

8·2 m

?

7·1 m

Calculate the height of the ramp.

4.

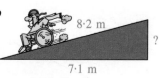

h m

85 m

47 m

A helium balloon is tethered by a rope to the ground as shown opposite.

Calculate the height of the balloon.

5. This isosceles triangle has a base of 96 cm and a sloping edge of 52 cm.

52 cm

H

96 cm

Calculate the **area** of the triangle.

6. Shown is the side view of a wooden bread tin.

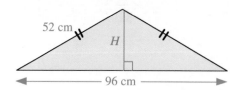

36 cm

32 cm

38 cm

x cm

Calculate the length (x) of the base of the bin.

7.

41 cm

40 cm

Calculate the **perimeter** of this right angled triangle.

8. Shown is a **right angled isosceles** triangle ABC.

Calculate the value of t.

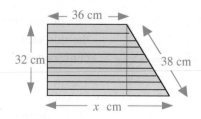

C

30 cm

t cm

A

t cm

B

Mixed Examples

In the following exercise, if you are asked to find :-

the hypotenuse   ->   use $c^2 = a^2 + b^2$.

a shorter side   ->   use $a^2 = c^2 - b^2$.

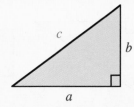

You must decide which formula you have to use.

Example 1 :-

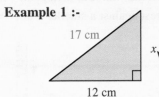

(here, you are looking for a short side)

$$x^2 = 17^2 - 12^2$$
$$x^2 = 289 - 144$$
$$x^2 = 145$$
$$x = \sqrt{145} = 12\cdot04 \text{ cm}$$

note

Example 2 :-

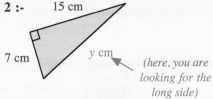

(here, you are looking for the long side)

$$y^2 = 15^2 + 7^2$$
$$y^2 = 225 + 49$$
$$y^2 = 274$$
$$y = \sqrt{274} = 16\cdot55 \text{ cm}$$

note

Exercise 13·4

1. Use the appropriate formula to find the value of x each time :-

(a)
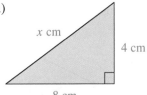

(b)
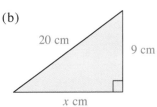

(c)
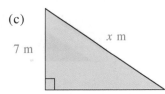

(d)
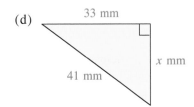

(e)

(f)
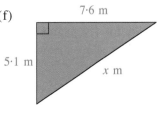

2. Andy was answering this question in a class test.

His working was set down as shown :-

Why should Andy have known that his answer **had** to be **wrong** ?

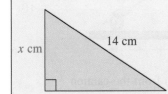

$$x^2 = 14^2 + 9^2$$
$$x^2 = 196 + 81$$
$$x^2 = 277$$
$$x = \sqrt{277} = 16\cdot6 \text{ cm}$$

3. **ONE** of the following two answers is known to be the **correct** value for y in this question.

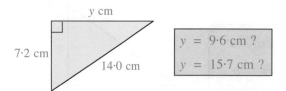

Without actually doing the calculation, say which one it must be and why the other is obviously wrong.

4.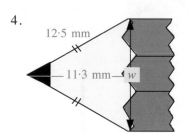

The tip of this pencil is in the shape of an isosceles triangle.

Calculate the width of the pencil (w).

5. This Scottish Flag is 2·35 metres long and 1·86 metres wide.

What length must each diagonal strip be?

6. A cannon ball was fired and flew in a straight line for 450 metres where it exploded 85 metres above the enemy lines.

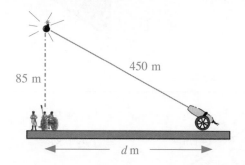

Calculate the distance (d m) from the cannon to the enemy soldiers.

7. This warning sign is in the shape of an **isosceles triangle**.

Calculate the height of the sign.

8. A ladder was leaning against a wall. It began to slide away from the wall, but it stopped when its base came to rest against a smaller wall.

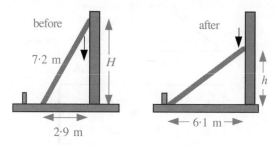

(a) Calculate the original height (H) of the top of the ladder above the ground.

(b) Calculate the new height (h) of the top of the ladder.

(c) By how many metres had the top of the ladder slipped ?

9. An orienteering competition was held over a triangular course.

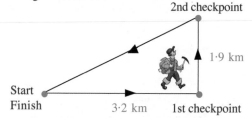

From the start, the participants walk East to the 1st checkpoint, North to the 2nd one and then race back to the finishing line.

Calculate the overall distance of the event.

10.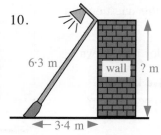

A lamp post fell over during a storm and came to rest with its top resting against the top of a wall.

Calculate the height of the wall.

Distances Between Coordinate Points

Consider the two coordinate points A(–3, –1) and B(5, 5).

They are plotted on the coordinate diagram opposite.

To **calculate** the distance from A to B :-

- draw in the 2 dotted lines to make a right angled triangle APB.

- write down the lengths of the two sides AP and BP.

- use Pythagoras' Theorem to calculate length of AB.

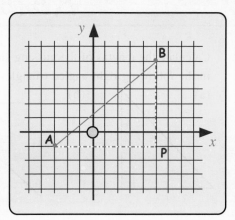

$$AB^2 = AP^2 + PB^2$$
$$AB^2 = 8^2 + 6^2$$
$$AB^2 = 64 + 36 = 100$$
$$AB = \sqrt{100} = \textbf{10 boxes}$$

Exercise 13·5

1. (a) Make a copy of this coordinate diagram, showing the 2 points P(1, –1) and Q(4, 3).

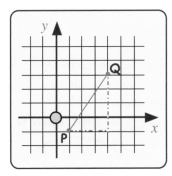

   (b) By drawing in the 2 dotted lines, create a right angled triangle and use it to calculate the length of the line PQ.

2. (a) Draw a new coordinate diagram and plot the 2 points M(–4, 2) and N(8, 7).

   (b) Create a right angle triangle in your figure and determine the length of the line MN.

3. Calculate the distance between the 2 points,
       R(–2, 0) and S(5, 4),
   giving your answer correct to 2 decimal places.

4. For each pair of points below, calculate the length of the line joining them, giving your answer to 2 decimal places each time.

   (a) F(2, –4) and G(–1, 5)

   (b) U(6, –2) and V(0, 4).

5. Terry thinks triangle AST below is isosceles.

   To prove it is, he has to find the lengths of the 2 lines AS and AT and show they are equal.

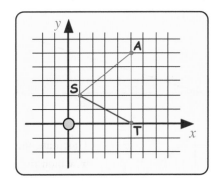

   (a) Write down the length of the line AT.

   (b) Calculate the length of the line AS.

   (c) Was Terry correct ?

6. Prove that triangle LMN is isosceles where
   L(–2, 2), M(6, 8) and N(4, –6).

Remember Remember..... ?

1. Calculate the lengths of the missing sides in the following right angled triangles :-

(a)
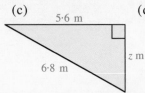
x cm
7 cm
7 cm

(b)
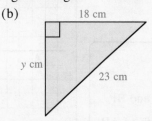
18 cm
y cm
23 cm

(c)
5·6 m
6·8 m
z m

(d)
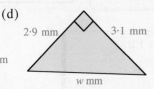
2·9 mm
3·1 mm
w mm

2. Shown is an isosceles triangle.

(a) Calculate the height of the triangle.

(b) Now calculate its **area**.

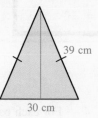
39 cm
30 cm

3. Calculate the **area** of the following rectangle :-

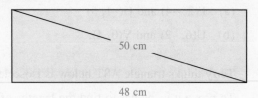
50 cm
48 cm

4. Calculate the **perimeter** of this right angled triangle :-

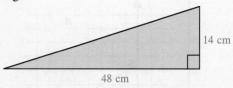
14 cm
48 cm

5.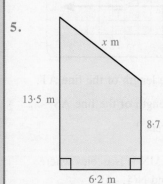
x m
13·5 m
8·7 m
6·2 m

Calculate the value of x, which indicates the length of the sloping side of this trapezium.

6. This shape consists of a rectangle with an isosceles triangle attached to its end.

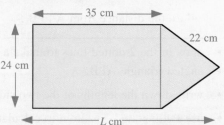
35 cm
22 cm
24 cm
L cm

(a) Calculate the total length (L) of the figure.

(b) Now calculate its area.

7. Shown are the points F(–5, –2) and G(4, 3).

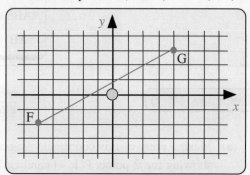
y
G
F
x

Draw a coordinate diagram, plot the two points and calculate the length of the line FG.

8. The circular cross-section of a water pipe linking two radiators in a classroom is shown with some water in it.
The radius of the circle, centre O, is 2 cm.

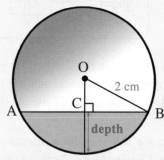
O
2 cm
A
C
B
depth

(a) What is the depth of the water when the pipe is half full ?

(b) Write down the distance OC, which shows how much the water dropped from half full to a depth of 1·4 cm.

(c) Calculate, to 1 decimal place, the width of the water surface (AB) when the depth of water is 1·4 centimetres.

Distance Travelled

Let us imagine being in a car travelling at 70 km/hr.

in 1 hour, you travel $1 \times 70 = 70$ km.

in 2 hours, you travel $2 \times 70 = 140$ km.

in 3 hours, you travel $3 \times 70 = 210$ km.

In other words :-   **Distance (travelled) = Speed × Time**   or, using letters :- $D = S \times T$

Example :-   A light aircraft flies at a speed of 240 m.p.h.

How far will it travel in $2\frac{1}{2}$ hours ?

You should also know the following :-

30 mins = 0·5 hr; 15 mins = 0·25 hr; 45 mins = 0·75 hr.

$D = S \times T$

$\Rightarrow D = 240 \times 2\cdot5$

$\Rightarrow D = 600$ miles

Exercise 14·1

1. Use the formula $D = S \times T$ to calculate how far is travelled each time :-

   (a) running at 12 km/hr for $1\frac{1}{2}$ hours.

   (b) flying at 400 km/hr for 2 hours.

   (c) walking at 6 km/hr for $2\frac{1}{2}$ hours.

   (d) strolling at 3·5 km/hr for $1\frac{1}{2}$ hours.

   (e) driving at 40 m.p.h. for $1\frac{1}{4}$ hours.

   (f) on a camel at 3·5 m.p.h. for 6 hours.

   (g) speed-boating at 24 m.p.h. for $1\frac{3}{4}$ hours.

   (h) in a truck cruising at 90 km/hr for $1\frac{1}{2}$ hrs.

2. How far did the following travel :-

   (a) a train, travelling for $2\frac{1}{2}$ hours at an average speed of 100 m.p.h. ?

   (b) a $\frac{3}{4}$ hour jog, at an average speed of 12 m.p.h. ?

   (c)   a riverboat sail lasting $2\frac{1}{4}$ hours at an average speed of 20 m.p.h. ?

2. (d) a helicopter flight for 15 minutes, at an average speed of 60 km/hr ?

   (e) a rocket ship journey of 8 hours 30 mins at an average speed of 2400 m.p.h. ?

3. What was the total distance travelled by each of the following :-

   (a) a satellite, orbiting at an average speed of 3600 m.p.h., for $\frac{1}{4}$ of an hour ?

   (b)  a motorboat, going at an average speed of 18 m.p.h., for quarter of an hour ?

   (c) a coach, travelling at an average speed of 44 m.p.h. for 2 hours 15 minutes ?

   (d) a train, travelling at an average speed of 120 km/hr for 45 minutes ($\frac{3}{4}$ hour) ?

   (e) an elephant, walking at an average speed of 8 km/hr for 2 hours 45 minutes ?

   (f) a yacht, sailing at an average speed of 16 km/hr for $1\frac{3}{4}$ hours ?

Speed - Calculation

I drove 150 miles, which took me 3 hours.

- in 3 hours, I travelled 150 miles.
- in 1 hour, I travelled $(150 \div 3) = 50$ miles.
- this means my speed was - 50 miles per hour.

(average speed)

In other words :- $\boxed{\text{Speed} = \text{Distance} \div \text{Time}}$

or, using letters :- $\boxed{S = \dfrac{D}{T}}$

Example :-

A train travels the 400 miles from Glasgow to London in 5 hours.

Calculate its (average) speed.

$$S = \frac{D}{T}$$
$$S = 400 \div 5$$
$$S = \boxed{80 \text{ m.p.h.}}$$

Time - Calculation

I drove 240 km at an average speed of 40 km/hr.

To travel 40 miles takes 1 hour,

=>   to travel 240 miles takes $240 \div 40 = 6$ hours.

In other words :- $\boxed{\text{Time} = \text{Distance} \div \text{Speed}}$

or, using letters :- $\boxed{T = \dfrac{D}{S}}$

Example :-

A coach travels the 260 miles from Edinburgh to Manchester at an average speed of 40 m.p.h.

How long will it take ?

$$T = \frac{D}{S}$$
$$T = 260 \div 40$$
$$T = 6.5 \text{ hrs}$$
$$= \boxed{6 \text{ hr } 30 \text{ mins}}$$

(note :- 6·5 hrs is NOT equal to 6 hr 5 mins or 6 hr 50 mins)

Exercise 14·2

1. Use the formula $S = \dfrac{D}{T}$ to find the average speed for these journeys :-

    (a) 200 miles travelled in 4 hours

    (b) 161 km travelled in 7 hours

    (c) 310 miles travelled in 5 hours.

2. Calculate the average speed for each of these journeys *(watch the units)* :-

    (a) 36 km travelled in 2 hours

    (b) 350 metres travelled in 5 minutes

    (c) 30 metres travelled in 6 seconds

    (d) 56 km travelled in 4 days.

3. Calculate the average speed of the following :-

    (a) A plane flies 2020 miles in 5 hours.

    (b) A lorry covers 252 kilometres in 6 hours.

    (c)  A train travels 30 km in $\frac{1}{2}$ hour.

    (d) A marathon runner runs 18 miles in $1\frac{1}{2}$ hrs.

    (e) A snail travels 204 cm in 3 hours.

4. Use the formula $T = \dfrac{D}{S}$ to calculate the time taken for each of these journeys :-

    (a) on a motorcycle, 480 km at 120 km/hr.

    (b) on a bus, 225 miles at 50 m.p.h.

    (c) in a race, 1800 m at 30 m/sec.

    (d) flying, 375 miles at 250 m.p.h.

5. Change these times into hours and minutes :-

    (a) $2\frac{1}{2}$ hours   (b) $5\frac{1}{4}$ hours

    (c) $3\frac{3}{4}$ hours   (d) 8·25 hours.

    > 1 hour 30 minutes is $1\frac{1}{2}$ or 1·5 hours.
    >
    > 4 hour 15 minutes is $4\frac{1}{4}$ or 4·25 hours.

6. Change the following times to both fractions of an hour and decimal form :-

    (a) 3 hours 30 mins   (b) 2 hours 15 mins

    (c) 5 hours 45 mins   (d) 0 hour 15 mins.

7. Calculate the time taken for these journeys :-

    (a) on a train, 100 km at 80 km/hr.

    (b) sailing, 25 miles at 20 m.p.h.

Time - Distance - Speed Problems

In the previous 2 exercises, you learned how to use three formulae
to calculate the **speed**, the **distance** or the **time** for a journey.

The triangle opposite shows a simple way of remembering how
to use each of the three formulae. *Try to memorise the diagram.*

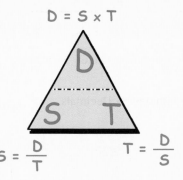

$$D = S \times T$$

$$S = \frac{D}{T} \qquad T = \frac{D}{S}$$

Example :-   David drove from his house to the coast,
a distance of 135 miles.

It took him 2 hrs 15 mins to do so.

Calculate David's average **speed**.

=>   From the triangle, we can see that $S = \dfrac{D}{T}$

=> $S = \dfrac{135}{2 \text{ hrs } 15 \text{ mins}} = \dfrac{135}{2\cdot25 \text{ hrs}} = \boxed{60 \text{ m.p.h.}}$

note

Exercise 14·3

1.   Calculate the missing quantity :-

(a)
Distance	Speed	Time
300 km	?	8 hours

(b)
Distance	Speed	Time
120 miles	40 mph	?

(c)
Distance	Speed	Time
?	29 mph	4 hours

(d)
Distance	Speed	Time
150 km	?	$2\frac{1}{2}$ hrs

(e)
Distance	Speed	Time
?	40 m/sec	$4\frac{1}{2}$ sec

(f)
Distance	Speed	Time
175 miles	100 mph	?

2.   Brian walked for half an hour and
covered a distance of 2700 m.

Calculate Brian's speed in :-

(a) metres/hour

(b) metres/minute.

3.   A plane flew 150 km at an
average speed of 300 km per hour.

For how long was it actually flying ?

4.   Paul and Paula towed their caravan and travelled
at an average speed of 42 km/hr.

The trip took $2\frac{1}{2}$ hours.

How far had they travelled ?

5.   A coach left Aberdeen at 1215 and arrived
at its destination at 1545.

If the coach travelled 210 miles, what was
its average speed ?

6.   A hill walker is crossing the valley at an average
speed of 8 km/hr.

How long will it take him to walk the whole
length of the valley which is 14 km long ?

7.   A satellite orbits the moon of a planet at
an average speed of 4800 km/hr.

It takes $2\frac{1}{4}$ hours to complete its orbit.

What is the length of the satellite's orbit ?

8.   It took old Mrs Broom 30 minutes
to walk the $1\frac{1}{2}$ miles to the post
office to collect her pension.

Now, with the aid of her electric
chair, she can do it in 15 mins.

(a) Calculate Mrs Broom's walking speed.

(b) How much **faster** does she travel in the
chair ?

In a previous exercise you learned :- $\frac{1}{2}$ hour = 0·5 hr, $\frac{1}{4}$ hour = 0·25 hr   and $\frac{3}{4}$ hour = 0·75 hr.

How would we enter **36 minutes** into our calculator as a decimal ?

Minutes => Decimals   =>

36 minutes is $\frac{36}{60}$ of an hour = 36 ÷ 60   = **0·6 hr.**

27 minutes is $\frac{27}{60}$ of an hour = 27 ÷ 60   = **0·45 hr.**

3 hr 40 mins is 3 + $\frac{40}{60}$ = 3 + (40 ÷ 60)   = **3·6666... hr.**

Simple rule :-   "To change minutes to a decimal of an hour => **divide by 60**".

Exercise 14·4

1.   You may use a calculator to change the following to decimals of an hour :-

(a)   48 minutes = $\frac{48}{60}$ hour (= 48 ÷ 60) = ... hr

(b) 18 minutes   (c) 6 minutes

(d) 54 minutes   (e) 24 minutes

(f) 39 minutes   (g) 21 minutes.

2.   Use your calculator to change these times to decimal form :- (*answers to 2 decimal places*).

(a) 10 minutes   (b) 17 minutes

(c) 20 minutes   (d) 52 minutes

(e) 50 minutes   (f) 70 minutes.

3.   Use your calculator to change the following times to decimal form :-

(a)   4 hours 12 minutes   = 4 + $\frac{12}{60}$

= 4 + (12 ÷ 60) = .. hr

(b) 3 hr 48 mins   (c) 4 hrs 36 mins

(d) 2 hrs 51 mins   (e) 2 hrs 57 mins

(f) 1 hr 12 mins   (g) 5 hrs 6 mins.

4.   A helicopter flies at 120 km/hr for 24 minutes. How far does it fly in that time ?
Show your working like this :-

$D = S \times T$ => $D = 120 \times (\frac{24}{60})$ (**not** 120 x 0·24)

=> $D = 120 \times 0·4$ (calculator)

$D = ...$ km

5.   Calculate the distances travelled here :-

(a)   A liner sailing at 15 mph for 36 minutes.

(b)   A cyclist travelling at 40 m.p.h. for 12 minutes.

(c)   A caravan pulled along at 30 km/hr for 21 minutes.

(d)   A jet plane flying at 450 mph for 20 minutes.

(e)   A hot air balloon travelling at 24 mph for 10 minutes.

6.   Bob and Ted set off at the same time.

•   Bob drives at 45 km/hr for 20 mins.

•   Ted drives at 60 km/hr for 12 mins.

Who travels the further, Bob or Ted, and by how much ?

7.   A train travels at 64 km/hr for 1 hour 24 mins. How far will it have travelled ?

Show your working as follows :-

$D = S \times T$ = 64 × (1 + $\frac{24}{60}$) calculator

D = 64 × (1·4)   (**not** 1·24)

D = ... km

8. Calculate the distance travelled each time :-

   (a) A cargo plane flies at 280 m.p.h. for 2 hours 36 minutes.

   (b) A lorry is driven at 70 mph for 1 hour 18 minutes.

9. A bus travels a distance of 35 kilometres in 42 minutes. Calculate its speed in km/hr.

   Show your working like this :-

   $$S = \frac{D}{T} \; = \; 35 \div (42 \text{ mins})$$
   $$= \; 35 \div \left(\tfrac{42}{60}\right) \qquad (\textbf{not } 35 \div (0\cdot42))$$
   $$= \; 35 \div 0\cdot7$$
   $$= \; .... \text{ km/hr} \qquad (\text{calculator})$$

10. Find the average speed each time here :-
    (*Give answers in m.p.h. or km/hr each time*).

    (a) A police car travels 14 miles in 12 mins.

    (b) A fire engine travels 10 kilometres in 6 minutes.

    (c) A jet covers 240 miles in 45 mins.

    (d) A hovercraft sails 42 miles in 36 mins.

    (e) A submarine covers 54 km in 1 hour 21 minutes.

    (f) A truck driver travels 56 miles in 48 minutes.

    (g) A space ship flies 18 600 miles in 3 hours 6 minutes.

    (h) A train travels 80 miles through the countryside in 1 hour 20 minutes.

Converting Decimal Times back to Hours and Minutes

In the last exercise you learned a simple rule for changing hours and minutes to decimal form.

Rule 1 :- "To change minutes to a decimal fraction => **divide by 60**".

If you have been using a calculator to find the time taken for a journey, it might appear as a decimal, like 0·35 hrs. There is an easy way of changing this to minutes.

Rule 2 :- "To change decimals back to a minutes => **multiply by 60**".

Examples :- Decimals to Minutes =>

$$0\cdot8 \text{ hr.} = (0\cdot8 \times 60) \text{ mins} = 48 \text{ minutes.}$$
$$0\cdot35 \text{ hr.} = (0\cdot35 \times 60) \text{ mins} = 21 \text{ minutes.}$$
$$2\cdot3 \text{ hr.} = \underline{2} + (0\cdot3 \times 60) \text{ mins} = 2 \text{ hr } 18 \text{ mins .}$$

Exercise 14·5

1. Change the following calculator display times *(in decimal form (of an hour))*, to minutes :-

   (a)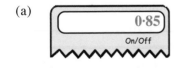

   (b)

   (c)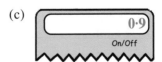

   (d)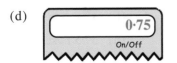

   (e)

   (f)

2. If you wish to change **3·9 hours** into hours and minutes :-

- Leave the hours as they are (**3 hours**)

- Multiply the 0·9 by 60 => (**... minutes**)

3. Use the same technique to change the following times to hours and minutes :-

(a)
$$3·2 \text{ hours } = 3 \text{ hours} + (0·2 \times 60) \text{ mins}$$
$$= 3 \text{ hours } ... \text{ minutes.}$$

(b) 5·5 hours   (c) 1·65 hours

(d) 2·8 hours   (e) 3·85 hours

(f) 4·7 hours   (g) 3·66666.. hrs

(h) 1·8333333 hours (i) 0·625 hours.

4. Write the following calculator (decimal) times in hours and minutes :-

(a)

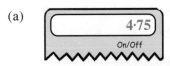

(b)

(c)

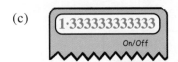

5. An ocean liner covers 66 miles at 20 mph.

(a) Calculate the time taken in hours.

$$(T = \frac{D}{S})$$ (*give answer as a decimal*).

(b) Change your answer to hours and mins.

6. A cyclist travelled 37·4 kilometres at an average speed of 22 km/hr.

(a) Calculate how long he took, (*as a decimal*).

(b) How long did he take in hours & minutes ?

7. Calculate the time taken (as a decimal) for each of the following, and then give your answer in hours and minutes :-

(a) A tank crosses 92 miles of desert at an average speed of 40 mph.

(b) A helicopter flies 18 kilometres at an average speed of 54 km/hr.

(c) A sports car races 28 miles at an average speed of 80 m.p.h.

(d) A canoeist paddles 13·5 miles at an average speed of 12 mph.

8. This map shows the 3 legs of an orienteering course. The average speed, as Bob covered the course, was 8 km/hr.

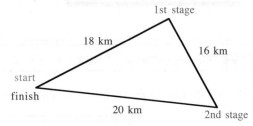

How long, in hours and minutes, should Bob take to walk between the :-

(a) start and 1st stage ?

(b) 1st and 2nd stages ?

(c) start and finish ?

9. Jill ran 490 metres in 70 seconds.

(a) What was her speed in metres per second ?

(b) Here is how to convert Jill's speed from metres per second to km/hr :-

- **step 1** Change the speed to metres per minute, then metres per hour

=> 7 m/sec   => 7 x 60 = 420 m/min

=> 420 x 60 => 25 200 metres/hour

- **step 2** Change the 25 200 metres to kilometres (÷ 1000)

=> 25 200 ÷ 1000 = ... km/hr

10. Change these speeds from m/sec to km/hr :-

(a) 8 m/sec   (b) 15 m/sec

(c) 200 m/sec   (d) 37·5 m/sec

(e) 0·5 m/sec   (f) 1000 m/sec.

Time - Distance (Speed) Graphs

The graph opposite shows an outward journey from **P → Q → R → S**, then a return home from **S → T**.

We can answer questions about the journey from the graph, including finding the **speed** at various stages.

Can you see that after an hour, a stop of half an hour was made at Q ?

Can you also see that since the line RS is **steeper** than the line PQ, the speed was **greater** for that part ?

We can calculate the **SPEED** at various stages as follows :-

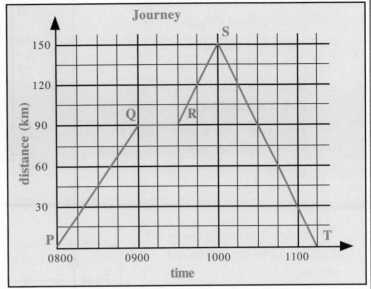

Journey

P to Q :-	Q to R :-	R to S :-	S back to T :-
Time = 1 hr	Time = $\frac{1}{2}$ hr	Time = $\frac{1}{2}$ hr	Time = $1\frac{1}{4}$ hr
Dist = 90 km	Dist = 0 km	Dist = 60 km	Dist = 150 km
$S = \frac{D}{T} = \frac{90}{1}$	$S = \frac{D}{T} = \frac{0}{0\cdot5}$	$S = \frac{D}{T} = \frac{60}{0\cdot5}$	$S = \frac{D}{T} = \frac{150}{1\cdot25}$
= 90 km/hr	= 0 km/hr	= 120 km/hr	= 120 km/hr

Exercise 14·6

1. Brian drove his mum off for a day's outing to Barnsby-on-Sea.

    They set out at 0900 along the motorway and stopped for a cup of tea, before finishing the rest of their trip along the A25 road.

    (a) How long was the first part of their journey along the motorway ?

    (b) How long did they stop for tea ?

    (c) When did they arrive in Barnsby ?

    (d) Calculate their speed :-

        (i)   on the motorway.

        (ii) between 1100 and 1200.

        (iii) along the A25.

    (e) Calculate their average speed between 9 am and 3 pm.

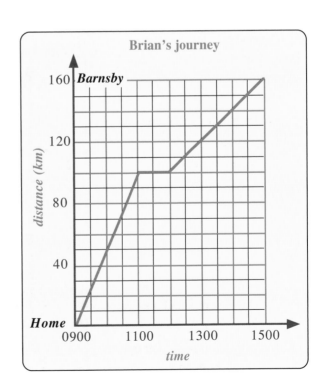

2. A helicopter flew from Struan to Bigly,
    dropped off supplies and returned to Struan.

    (a) For how long was the helicopter
         on the ground at Bigly ?

    (b) Calculate its speed for the
         outward flight to Bigly.

    (c) It hit a "head wind" on the way
         back. Calculate the return speed.

    (d) From your answers to (b) and (c),
         say whether the "head wind" slowed
         it down or helped it go faster.

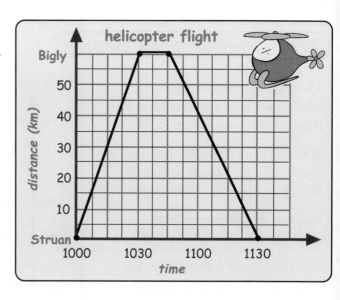

3. Gemma left Brioch Harbour in her
    dinghy at 10·00 am and set sail
    for Toule.

    Anton left Brioch at 10·30 am in
    his small motor launch.

    (a) Calculate Gemma's speed.

    (b) Calculate Anton's speed.

    (c) When did Anton's launch
         overtake Gemma's dinghy ?

    (d) How far away from **Toule**
         were they when Anton
         overtook Gemma ?

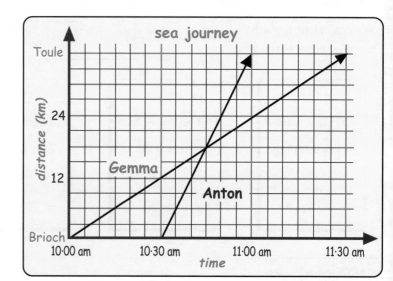

4. A goods train and a passenger
    train left 2 stations heading
    towards each other, one from
    London and one from Edinburgh.

    The goods train was the slower
    of the two.

    (a) Which line, A or B,
         represents the goods train's
         journey ? (*Explain why*).

    (b) Calculate the :-

         (i)   goods train's speed.

         (ii) passenger train's speed.

    (c) At what time did the two
         trains pass ?

    (d) At what time should train A
         reach London ?

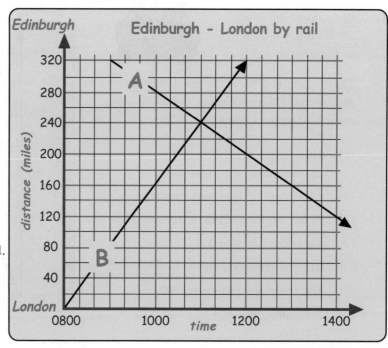

5. This diagram shows the journey of a pleasure boat on a Rhine cruise.

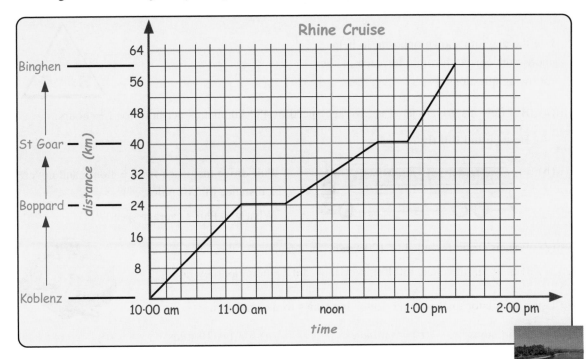

Rhine Cruise

(a)   Make a neat copy of this timetable and complete it for the pleasure boat's trip.

Koblenz	Boppard		St Goar		Binghen
depart	arrive	leave	arrive	leave	arrive
10·00 am —>	?	?	?	?	?

(b)   How many km is it from :-   (i)   Koblenz to Boppard   (ii)   St Goar to Binghen ?

(c)   Calculate the average speed of the boat :-

    (i)   from Koblenz to Boppard   (ii)   from Boppard to St Goar

    (iii)   from St Goar to Binghen   (iv)   from Koblenz to Binghen.

6.   Andrea left at 8·00 am and drove her coach from Inverness to Stirling, 150 miles away.

    She drove at an average speed of 40 miles per hour for the first 60 miles.

    Andrea stopped for 15 minutes for petrol and a break.

    She then set off again and reached Stirling at 11·15 am.

(a)   For how long was she driving before
    she stopped for her break ?

(b)   What was her average speed after
    her break ?

(c)   Copy and complete the graph
    for Andrea's journey.

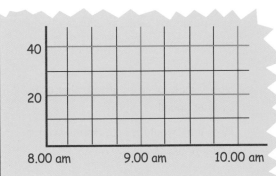

Remember Remember.....?

1. Use the diagram shown opposite to help choose the correct formula for each of the following questions :-

   (a) Bill flew his private jet at an average speed of 480 kilometres per hour for $1\frac{1}{2}$ hours.

   How far did Bill fly ?

   (b)  Phil drove his coach for $3\frac{1}{2}$ hours and covered a distance of 210 miles.

   What was Phil's average speed ?

   (c) Francis' train travelled at 120 km/hr on her journey through France.

   If the train travelled 150 km, how long did Francis' journey last ?

2. Use a calculator to change the following times to decimal form :-

   (a) 24 minutes   (b) 9 minutes   (c) 3 hrs 10 mins   (d) 2 hrs 51 mins.

3. Use a calculator to change the following to hours and minutes :-

   (a) 0·7 hour   (b) 0·35 hour   (c) 5·3 hours   (d) 1·65 hours.

4. (a) Alex took 18 minutes to cycle to his office, 3·6 miles away.

   What was Alex's average speed ?

   (b)  Steve's train travelled at an average speed of 64 km/hr.

   Mandy's train travelled at an average speed of 75 km/hr.

   If Steve's journey is 80 km long, and Mandy's is 100 km, whose trip took longer, and by how many minutes ?

5. Bob cycled to his friend Ted's house.

   When the rain came on, Ted's dad ran Bob home.

   (a) At what time did Bob leave his house ?

   (b) How far is Ted house from Bob's ?

   (c) What was Bob's average cycling speed ?

   (d) How long did Bob stay at Ted's ?

   (e) How long did it take Bob to get home ?

   (f) What was the average speed on the journey home ?

   (g) Bob's walking speed is half that of his cycling speed.

   How long would it take Bob to walk to Ted's house ?

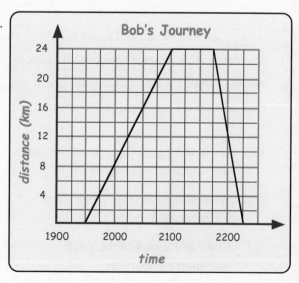

Chapter 15

Proportion

Proportional Division - Sharing in a Given Ratio

Example :-

Rosie and Jim share a prize of £2700 in a ratio of 5 : 4.

How much money will each get ?

Step 1	Since the ratio is 5 : 4, there are (5 + 4) = 9 shares
Step 2	Each share is worth (£2700 ÷ 9) = £300
Step 3	Rosie gets 5 shares (5 × £300) = **£1500**
	Jim gets 4 shares (4 × £300) = **£1200**

(*Check that the total for Rosie and Jim is £2700*).

Exercise 15·1

1. Share £455 between Lennie and Jean in the ratio 2 : 5.

   Copy and complete :-

   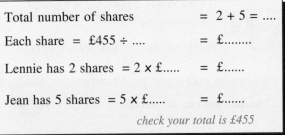

   Total number of shares   = 2 + 5 = ...

   Each share = £455 ÷ ....   = £........

   Lennie has 2 shares = 2 × £.....   = £......

   Jean has 5 shares = 5 × £.....   = £......

   check your total is £455

2. Show similar working for each of the following and work out :-

   (a) Share £10 000 between Ken and Kath in the ratio 1 : 4.

   (b) Share £120 between Dan and Dean in the ratio 3 : 5.

   (c) Share £7200 between Mark and Mary in the ratio 7 : 2.

   (d) Share £880 between Fred and Jess in the ratio 5 : 6.

   (e) Share £4000 between Will and Anne in the ratio 11 : 9.

   (f) Share £50 between Pete and Pat in the ratio 13 : 12.

   (g) Share £250 between Bushra and Mo in the ratio 23 : 27.

3. Joe (aged 6) and Lesley (aged 9) are left £300 000 in their Papa's will. The money is to be shared between them in the ratio of their ages.

   How much will Joe get ?

4. Mavis and Donna are in the final of an omelette making competition. They will share the £90 prize money in the ratio of how many omelettes they make in five minutes.

   Mavis makes 18. Donna makes 12.

   How much more prize money than Donna did Mavis win ?

5. Share :-

   (a) £56 between Flo, Jan and Mel in the ratio 1 : 2 : 4.

   (b) £3000 between Pat, Fran and Jed in the ratio 2 : 3 : 5.

   (c) 400 stamps between Bert, Tom and Ken in the ratio 4 : 6 : 10.

6. A fish stall was set up in a market. The ratio of haddock : cod : salmon on sale was 8 : 5 : 2.

   If there were 200 cod altogether, how many fish in total were on sale ?

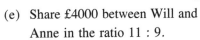
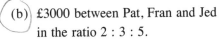

Basic Unitary Proportion

You can work out how many miles your car gets to a litre of petrol by looking
at how many miles you travel and how much fuel you use on the journey.

Example :- Dave drove to Blackpool, covering a distance of 189 kilometres.

He used 13·5 litres of petrol on the journey.

How many kilometres to the litre is he getting from his car ?

> —> **DIVIDE** => 13·5 litres —> 189 km
>
> 1 litre —> 189 ÷ 13·5 = **14 km** (*by calculator*)
>
> (Rate =) **14 kilometres per litre**

Exercise 15·2

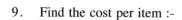

1. A taxi covered 270 km on 20 litres of diesel.

   Calculate how many km to the litre it got.

2. 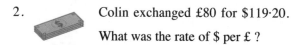 Colin exchanged £80 for $119·20.

   What was the rate of $ per £ ?

3. An 8 kg sack of potatoes costs £4.

   What is the weight per £ ?

4. A pack of 24 ice lollies cost me £30.

   What is the cost for one ?

5. 18 boxes of matches are emptied on to a table.
   There are now 756 matches on the table.

   If every box has the same number of
   matches, how many are in each box ?

6. It took 5 bin lorries to move 10·75
   tonnes of rubbish.

   Find the rate of tonnes per bin lorry.

7. When I parked my car in Glasgow Airport car
   park for 7 hours, it cost me £16·45.

   Calculate the rate per hour.

8. 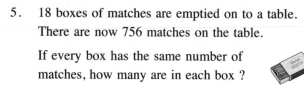 During April, Hamish was cycling
   around the islands to raise money
   for charity.
   In that month, he travelled 975 km.

   How many kilometres on average did
   he cycle each day ?

9. Find the cost per item :-

   (a) 20 truffles costing £45·60.

   (b) 8 ties costing £103·92.

   (c) 12 pet mice costing £5·76.

   (d) 25 jars of gherkins costing £65.

   (e) 30 cups of tea costing £14·40.

10. It cost Sandy £3195 for 9 football
    season tickets.

    Work out the rate per season ticket.

11. £60 can be exchanged for 69 euros

    Calculate the rate of euro/£.

12. Jenny's heart beat 760 times over a
    ten minute period.

    What was her bpm (*beat per minute*) ?

13. Ailsa and Debbie put their cars into different
    garages for an annual service.

    Ailsa's garage charged £114
    for 3 hours work, whereas Debbie
    paid £154 for 4 hours work at hers.

    Who got the better deal ?

14. Bruce works 7 hours as a delivery man
    and earns £58·10.

    Jean works at the market for
    6 hours and earns £50·70.

    (a) Calculate Bruce's rate of pay. (*£'s/hour*)

    (b) Calculate Jean's rate of pay. (*£'s/hour*)

    (c) Who has the lower rate of pay ?

Direct Proportion

Two quantities, (for example, the **number** of DVD's sold and their **total** cost), are said to be in **direct proportion**, if : -

"*... when you double the number of DVD's you double the cost.*"

Example :-

The cost of 6 DVD's is £75.

Find the cost of 11 of these DVD's.

DVD'S		Cost
6	—>	£75
1	—>	£75 ÷ 6 = £12·50
11	—>	11 × £12·50
		= **£137·50**

(Note :- Always find the cost or value of 1 item first.)

Exercise 15·3

1. The cost of 8 scientific calculators is £37·60. What do 5 of these calculators cost ?

2. Before going on holiday, I changed £380 into euros, receiving 425·60 euros for my money. My friend, Beth changed her £75 spending money into Euros at the same exchange rate. How many euros did she get ?

3. A man can tile an area of 600 cm² in 4 minutes.

   He works for 10 minutes tiling.

   What area does he tile ?

4. A machine for making board tacks can produce 560 tacks every 7 seconds.

   How many board tacks will it make in one minute ?

5. A potato picker can pick 40 potatoes in 25 seconds.

   Working at the same rate, how many potatoes can he pick in an hour ?

6. Nine pastries cost £8·01.

   What will ten cost ?

7. Which of the following shows that the two quantities are in **direct proportion** ?

   (a) 5 scones cost £1·90. Six cost £2·28.

   (b) 9 pens cost 72p. Five cost 35p.

   (c) 3 DVD's for £34·20. 4 DVD's for £45·50.

   (d) A box of 20 vitamin tablets for £0·50. A box of 30 tablets for 75p.

8. A box of 500 pencils are on sale for £10. How much is it for 300 ?

9. 200 litres of oil costs £60. Find the cost of 150 litres.

10. 80 metres of fencing costs £128. How much would it cost for 130 metres ?

11. 40 trucks can remove 2600 tonnes of rubble in a day.

    How much rubble could 15 trucks remove in a day ?

12. The cost of painting is directly proportional to the **area** being painted.

    A wall 12 metres by 3 metres costs £54 to paint.

    How much would it cost for a wall 18 metres by 4 metres ?

The table below shows the cost of packets of "Rolos".

No. of Pkts	1	2	3	4	5	6
Cost (p)	50	100	150	200	250	300

We can represent each pair as a set of coordinates.
    (1, 50), (2, 100), (3, 150), (4, 200), etc...

Can you see that all of the points lie on a
straight line, passing through the **origin** ?

This is true for any two quantities which
 are in **DIRECT PROPORTION**.

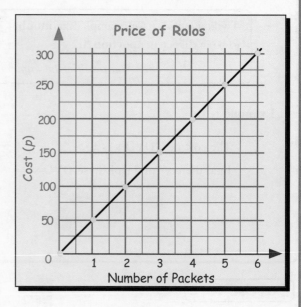

Price of Rolos

1.   (a)   Copy and complete the table.

     (b)   Using the same scales as in
           the above graph, plot the
           points (1, 25), (2, ?), ...

No. of Buns	1	2	3	4	5	6
Cost (p)	25	50				

     (c)   Join the points with a straight line

     (d)   Does the line pass through the origin ?

     (e)   Explain why the line **must** pass through the origin.

2.   (a)   Copy and complete this table.

     (b)   Use an appropriate scale to
           plot the points (1, 45), (2, ...), etc.

Hours worked	1	2	3	4	5	6
Pay (£)	45	90				

     (c)   Join the points with a straight line.

     (d)   Does the line pass through the origin ?

3.   (a)   Copy and complete this table for the time taken to be served in a work's canteen.

     (b)   Using a scale of 2 boxes to represent
           3 workers on the horizontal axis and
           2 boxes to represent 18 seconds on
           the vertical axis, plot the points
           and draw a line through them.

No. Workers	3	6	9	12	15	18
Time (seconds)	27	54	81			

     (c)   How long should it take to serve :-   (i)   24 workers   (ii)   19 workers ?

4. (a) Draw a set of coordinate axes and using an appropriate scale, plot the points indicated in the table below.

x	1	2	3	4
y	4	8	12	16

Remember the simple check from CfE Level 3 ?
Divide each pair of values ....
$(4 \div 1)$, $(8 \div 2)$, $(12 \div 3)$, $(16 \div 4)$
If you **always** obtain the **same value**, then they are in **direct proportion**.
If even **one** of the values differs from the rest, they are **NOT** in **direct proportion**.

(b) Are y and x in direct proportion in this example ?

5. A holiday company claims the cost, £C, of its flights is **proportional** to the distance, D km, travelled by the aircraft.

(a) Examine the graph. Do you agree with the holiday company's claim ?

(b) Find a formula for C in terms of D.

(c) Calculate the cost of a 1500 km flight.

(d) Calculate how far this holiday company will fly you for £620.

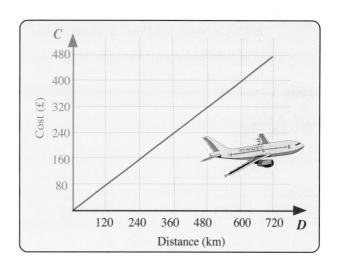

6. Which **three** of the following tables indicate examples of direct proportion ?

(a)
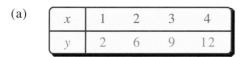

x	1	2	3	4
y	2	6	9	12

(b)

x	1	2	3	4
y	4	8	16	32

(c)

m	1	2	3	4
P	3	6	9	12

(d)
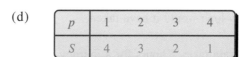

p	1	2	3	4
S	4	3	2	1

(e)
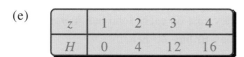

z	1	2	3	4
H	0	4	12	16

(f)

d	1	2	3	4
T	15	30	45	60

(g)
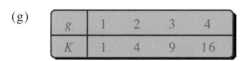

g	1	2	3	4
K	1	4	9	16

(h)

e	5	10	15	20
W	1	2	3	4

7. For each of your three answers to question 6, verify they are in direct proportion by plotting the points and showing a line can be drawn through these points and the origin.

8. **Hard :-** It takes 4 men 12 hours to manage the gardens in a large estate.

(a) If you were asked to find how long it would have taken 3 men to do the same work, would this be a **direct** proportion question ?

(b) Calculate how long you think it would take 3 men working at the same rate.

Indirect (or Inverse) Proportion

Direct Proportion means - the **more** of a quantity you buy, the **more** it will cost.

Indirect Proportion - again two quantities, but this time ....
as one quantity **increases** the other **decreases**.

For example ..... the **faster** you travel in a car, the **less** time it takes for the journey.

Example :-

It takes 8 hours for 3 men to paint a fence.

How long will it take 4 men to paint it if they worked at the same pace ?

Obviously less time !

MEN		HOURS	
3	–>	8	note
1	–>	3 × 8 = 24 (*man hours*)	
4	–>	24 ÷ 4	
		note	= **6 hours**

*More men working on the job take **less** time, as expected !*

Exercise 15·5

1. It takes 5 men 12 hours to wash a fleet of buses.

   If 6 men were to do the job, how long would it take ?

2. It took 6 women 8 hours to decorate their store for Christmas.

   If only 5 women had been doing this, how long would it have taken ?

3. A train takes 7 hours for a journey at an average speed of 90 km/hr.

   At what speed would the train have to travel to cover the same journey in 5 hours ?

4. A group of five hill climbers take enough food to last a 12 day trip.

   Another seven climbers join the group, but they do not bring food.

   How many days will the food now last this larger group ?

5. Jade has enough bugs to feed her 10 pet spiders for 3 weeks.

   She loses 4 of the spiders.

   How long will the food now last ?

6. A town's planning department reckoned that it would take 60 men 2 years to erect a new school building.

   If the building has to be ready in 18 months, how many **more** men will have to be employed ?

7. A truck takes 3 hours to complete a journey travelling at an average speed of 40 km/hr.

   At what speed will the truck have to travel on average if it is to cover the journey in 4 hours ?

8. If they cost 6p each, John has **just** enough money to buy 40 pencils.

   With the same money, how many could he buy if they only cost 5p each ?

9. It took 6 pupils 40 minutes to stock the school library.

   If 8 pupils had done the job, how much **quicker** would it have been done ?

10. Thirty hens have enough feed to last 6 days.

    If 10 hens escape, how much **longer** will the feed last those remaining ?

1. Mr Thomas promised his twin daughters a share of his £77 lottery win, depending on how they scored in their graphics test.

   • Hazel scored 80%
   • Ina got 60%

   This meant dad's money was split 80 : 60.

   (a)   Write this ratio in its **simplest** form.

   (b)   How much did Ina get ?

2. A butcher had to sell off meat which was reaching its sell by date.

   He had a range of pork : lamb : beef steak cuts for sale in the ratio 12 : 5 : 3.

   If there were 160 cuts of meat altogether, how many were cuts of lamb ?

3. A cheetah can cover 140 metres in 5 seconds.

   What is that speed in metres per second ?

4. 12 880 Korean Won can be exchanged for £8.

   Calculate the rate of Won to the £.

5.    Nine "99's" cost £11·25.

   What is the cost of six ?

6. A box of 50 vitamin D^5 tablets are selling for £2·25 in Wunderdrug.

   Chemsurf have them priced at £4·40 for 100.

   Which shop offers the better deal ?

7. If they cost 40p each, John has **just** enough money to buy 10 toffee apples.

   With the same money, how many could he buy if the price rose to 50p each ?

8. It took 6 hours for 8 cement finishers to lay the founds for a car showroom.

   How much **quicker** would it have taken 12 workers to do the same job ?

9. Which of the following tables indicate examples of direct proportion ?

   (a)

a	1	2	3	4
B	7	14	21	28

   (b)

d	1	2	3	4
C	2	8	14	20

   (c)

h	2	4	6	8
J	4	16	36	64

   (d)

n	3	5	7	9
M	15	25	35	45

   (e)

p	5	8	11	14
Q	15	24	33	52

   (f)

r	2	6	18	54
S	81	27	9	3

   (g)

v	800	400	200	100
W	160	80	40	20

   (h)

x	30	60	90	120
y	20	10	5	2·5

1. Calculate the values of *x* and *y* in these right angled triangles :-

    (a)   (b)

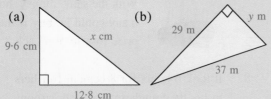

2. Shown is an isosceles triangle ABC.

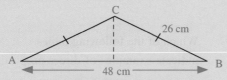

    Calculate its **AREA**.

3. Calculate the total length (*L*) of this shape :-

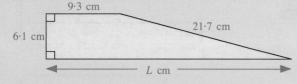

4. A circular gold necklace has a gold quadrilateral inset as shown. If the gold costs £23 per centimetre calculate the cost of the necklace.

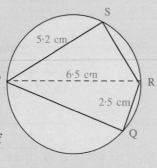

5. Plot the two points G(−4, 7) and H(6, −1) on a coordinate diagram and calculate the length of the line GH, correct to 2 decimal places.

6. (a) Write 3 hours and 24 minutes as hours in decimal form.

    (b) Write 2·35 hours out fully in hours and minutes.

    (c) How many seconds are in :-

        (i) a day   (ii) a year ?

7. (a) A satellite took 2 hours and 48 minutes to complete one full orbit.

        If it was travelling at 24 000 km/hr, calculate the length of one orbit.

    (b) How long would it take a plane to travel 810 miles at a speed of 360 m.p.h. ?

8. Baz drove a 340 mile journey on a motorway. He started at 3.25 pm and arrived at 8.05 pm. Did he break the 70 mph speed limit ?

9. Sally bought 6 identical blouses for £72. How much would it have cost for 5 ?

10. A packet of 12 biscuits cost £1·04. The 18 biscuit pack costs £1·60.

    Which is the better value for money ? (*Justify your answer*).

11. (a) Alex exchanged £474 for 72 524·16 Yen. How many Yen would he get for £600 ?

    (b) Zara got 39 467 Baht for her £870. How many Baht would she get for £990 ?

    (c) Which countries did Alex and Zara visit ?

12. Which of these tables, if any, indicate direct proportion. *Explain your answers*.

    (a)

x	1	2	3	4
y	6	12	20	32

    (b)

p	2	4	6	8
k	7·5	15	22·5	30

13. Copy and complete the diagram filling in all missing angles.

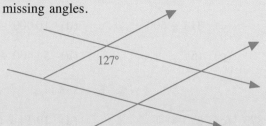

127°

14. A spaceship travels for eight days at an average speed of $9 \cdot 5 \times 10^4$ km/hr.

(a) Find the distance travelled by the spaceship.

(b) If the speed is increased by 20%, how much quicker, to the nearest hour, will the ship travel the same distance.

15. Harry has a gross income of £18 600 and a net income of £14 755.

He paid income tax of £2418 and he paid 6% of his gross wage for superannuation.

His only other deduction was N.I. (National Insurance).

Calculate his N.I. payment.

16. Copy and complete the shape shown so that the **red** dotted lines are lines of symmetry.

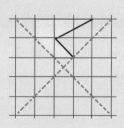

17. The line AB has equation $y = 3x + 1$.

(a) State the gradient and the y-intercept of the line AB.

(b) Draw a pair of axes and sketch the line $y = 3x + 1$, showing all the line's important points and features.

18. Solve for x :-

(a) $\frac{1}{4}x - 3 = 7$ (b) $\frac{3x-1}{6} + \frac{1}{4} = 3$.

19. A red square of side 30 cm has a quarter circle removed (in blue).

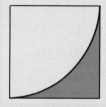

(a) Find the area of the red section.

(b) Find the perimeter of the blue quarter circle.

20. A kite has vertices A(3, 3), B(0, 3), C(−3, −3) and D(3, 0).

Find the coordinates of the images of the vertices under a rotation of 180° about the point (−2, 2).

21. A right angled triangle is as shown below.

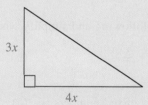

$3x$

$4x$

Find, in terms of x, the perimeter.

22. In a jar there are 1p, 2p and 5p coins in a 9 : 4 : 1 ratio.

There are sixty 2p coins in the jar.

How much money is in the jar ?

23. Evan exchanged £450 for 535·50€.
Donnie received 854·10€ for £730.
Fran got an exchange rate of 1·18 euros to £.

Who got the best exchange rate ?
(*Justify your answer with calculation*).

24. There are 10 containers on a ship.
There are 100 palettes in a container.
There are 100 boxes in a palette.
There are 1000 packets in a box.
There are 100 sweets in a packet.
One sweet sells for 10p.

How many ships are needed to transport £1 billion worth of sweets ?

1. Set down and find :-

   (a) $(41)^2$ (b) $5173 \div 7$ (c) 314×600 (d) $10\,000 - 927$

   (e) $9\,\overline{)12\,132}$ (f) $19 - 5 \times 3$ (g) $(5)^4$ (h) $54\,400 \div 80.$

2. Set down and find :-

   (a) $\begin{array}{r} 19{\cdot}73 \\ \times\,7 \\ \hline \end{array}$ (b) $49 + 16{\cdot}78 + 0{\cdot}873$ (c) $8\,\overline{)190{\cdot}4}$ (d) $19{\cdot}14 \times 600$

   (e) $828 \div 600$ (f) $35 - 14{\cdot}247$ (g) $0{\cdot}8 \times 0{\cdot}8$ (h) $7{\cdot}38 \div 3000.$

3. Find :-   (a) $\frac{5}{9}$ of 504   (b) $\frac{7}{8}$ of £10·40   (c) $\frac{5}{6}$ of £9.

4. Simplify :-

   (a) $\frac{65}{85}$ (b) $\frac{32}{56}$ (c) $\frac{17}{51}$ (d) $\frac{66}{121}$.

5. Do the following and simplify where possible :-

   (a) $\frac{2}{5} + \frac{3}{4}$ (b) $5\frac{1}{4} + 2\frac{2}{3}$ (c) $\frac{5}{8} \times \frac{12}{13}$ (d) $4\frac{2}{5} - 1\frac{3}{4}$.

6. Write as mixed numbers :-   (a) $\frac{21}{9}$ (b) $\frac{47}{7}$ (c) $\frac{103}{8}$.

7. Express as a fraction :-   (a) $87\frac{1}{2}\%$ (b) 36% (c) $6\frac{1}{4}\%$.

8. Find :-   (a) 40% of £170   (b) 5% of £12   (c) 75% of 1040

   (d) $33\frac{1}{3}\%$ of 264   (e) 7% of 500   (f) $17\frac{1}{2}\%$ of 240.

9. (a) Of the 45 dogs in the kennels, 27 are male. What percentage are male ?

   (b) Having bought a games machine for £240, I sold it later for £192.
   Express my loss as a percentage of the cost price.

10. Find :-

    (a) $34 - 76$ (b) $(-79) + 36$ (c) $(-34) - 26$ (d) $(-16) - (-18)$

    (e) $(-13)^2$ (f) $(-8) \times (-6) \div (-4)$ (g) $\frac{(-12) - 6}{(-3) - 3}$ (h) $15 - 4 \times (-3)$

    (i) $17 \div (-2)$ (j) $(-1005) + 995$ (k) $-4(-5 - (-9))$ (l) $\frac{5 - (-7)}{(2) - (-2)}$.

11. (a) Today is the 24th May. How many days till my mum's birthday on July 6th ?

    (b) Today is September 8th. My parent's anniversary was 3 weeks ago. What was that date ?

12. (a) Convert a speed of 20 metres per second to kilometres per hour.

    (b) Convert a speed of 180 km/hr to metres per second.

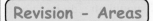

Revision - Areas

The formulae for calculating the **areas** of quadrilaterals, circles and triangles should already be known :-

SQUARE

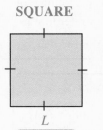

L

Area = L^2

RECTANGLE

B

L

Area = $L \times B$

RHOMBUS

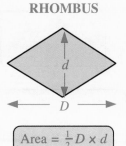

d

D

Area = $\frac{1}{2}D \times d$

KITE

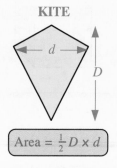

d

D

Area = $\frac{1}{2}D \times d$

PARALLELOGRAM

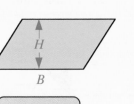

H

B

Area = $B \times H$

TRIANGLE

H

B

Area = $\frac{1}{2}B \times H$

CIRCLE

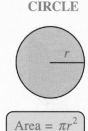

r

Area = πr^2

TRAPEZIUM

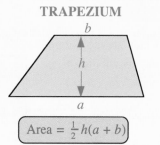

b

h

a

Area = $\frac{1}{2}h(a + b)$

Exercise 16·1

1. Use the appropriate formula from the above to calculate the **areas** of the following figures :-

(a)

6 cm

13 cm

(b)

5 cm

(c)

15 cm

(d)

8 cm

17 cm

(e)

8 m

20 m

(f)

11 mm

14 mm

(g)

14 cm

30 cm

(h)

12 cm

25 cm

2. Calculate the **area** of each figure by splitting it into shapes whose areas you can find easily :-

(a)

9 cm

10 cm

7 cm

16 cm

(b)

12 cm

6 cm

7 cm

4 cm   4 cm

(c)

9 cm

5 cm

8 cm

(d)

11 cm

15 cm   7 cm

(e)

20 cm

6 cm

(f)

12 cm

6 cm   20 cm

The formulae for calculating the **volume** and **surface area** of a cube and cuboid should already be known.

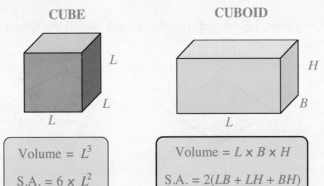

CUBE

Volume = L^3

S.A. = $6 \times L^2$

CUBOID

Volume = $L \times B \times H$

S.A. = $2(LB + LH + BH)$

CAPACITY

When you talk about the volume of a **liquid** quantity, you refer to it as its **CAPACITY**.

NOTE

1 cm^3 = 1 millilitre (ml)

1000 ml = 1 **litre**

Exercise 16·2

1. Calculate the volume of this cuboid in cubic cm, (cm^3).

7 cm
5 cm
10 cm

2. The volume of this shallow block is 126 cm^3.

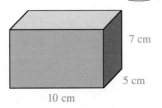

h cm
6 cm
7 cm

Calculate its height (h cm).

3. (a) Calculate the volume of this box in cm^3.

30 cm
25 cm
50 cm

(b) How many millilitres of liquid will it hold ?

(c) What is its **capacity** in litres ?

4. How many litres of water will this box hold when it is only **half** full ?

20 cm
15 cm
25 cm

5. This metal tank holds 67·2 litres when full.

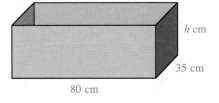

h cm
35 cm
80 cm

(a) How many millilitres is this ?

(b) Calculate the height, h cm, of the tank.

6. (a) Calculate the volume of this tank in cm^3.

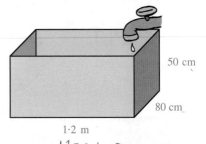

50 cm
80 cm
1·2 m
1200 cm

(b) When the tap is opened fully, water flows in at the rate of 6 litres per minute.

How long before the tank overflows ?

7. This tank is built to hold 1350 litres of oil.

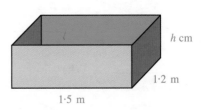

h cm
1·2 m
1·5 m

Calculate the height of the tank.

8. Shown is a cube with each of its sides 1 metre, or 100 cm long.

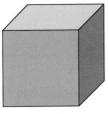

1 metre = 100 cm

(a) Calculate its volume in cubic metres (m^3).

(b) Now, calculate its volume in cm^3. (100 × 100 × ...).

(c) Hence, copy and complete the statement :-

$$1\,m^3 = \text{..........}\ cm^3.$$

9. A cube measures 200 cm by 200 cm by 200 cm.

(a) Calculate its volume in cm^3.

(b) Now write down its volume in m^3.

10. Calculate the volume of this concrete block in both cubic centimetres and cubic metres.

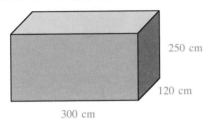

250 cm

120 cm

300 cm

11. This "podium" is created using concrete.

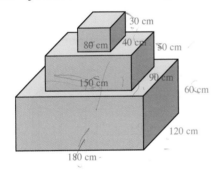

30 cm
80 cm   40 cm   50 cm
150 cm   90 cm
                60 cm
                120 cm
180 cm

(a) Calculate the total volume, in cm^3.

(b) How many cubic **metres** of concrete were used to make the podium ?

12. Look at this cuboid.

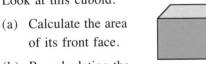

6 cm
5 cm
10 cm

(a) Calculate the area of its front face.

(b) By calculating the area of each of its other 5 faces, write down the **total surface area** of the cuboid.

13. This cuboid measures 15 cm by 12 cm by 8 cm.

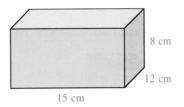

8 cm
12 cm
15 cm

Calculate its total surface area, in cm^2.

14. Use the formula :-

$$S.A. = 2(LB + LH + BH),$$

to calculate the surface area of this cuboid.

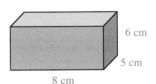

6 cm
5 cm
8 cm

15.

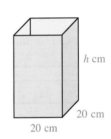

12 cm
10 cm
25 cm

This metal box is made from aluminium sheeting.

The sheeting costs 3·2p per cm^2 to produce.

(a) Calculate the total surface area.

(b) Calculate the cost of the aluminium sheeting needed to make it.

16. An open topped metal container is to be manufactured to hold exactly **12 litres** of oil.

h cm
20 cm
20 cm

(a) Calculate the height of the metal box.

(b) Calculate the area of sheet metal which would be required to make the (open topped) container.

17. From a rectangular piece of card measuring 30 cm by 40 cm, four squares of side 5 cm are removed from the corners.

The remaining piece is then folded and glued to make the shallow tray shown.

Calculate both the volume and the surface area of the tray.

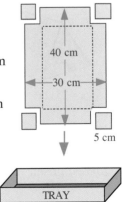

40 cm
30 cm
5 cm

TRAY

Prisms

A **PRISM** is any solid shape with two parallel **congruent** faces (or ends) generally in the shape of polygons.

Examples :-

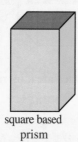
square based
prism

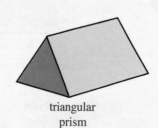
triangular
prism

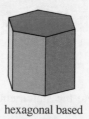
hexagonal based
prism

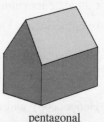
pentagonal
prism

The **RED** face is the one that runs right through the shape, (top to bottom, left to right or front to back).

Volume of a Prism

It is very easy to calculate the volume of a prism, as long as you know the **area** of the **congruent** face.

> **VOLUME** (prism) = **Area** (of end face) × **length**
> **or**
> **VOLUME** (prism) = **Area** (of base) × **height**

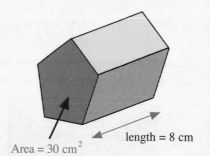

Area = 30 cm^2

length = 8 cm

For this pentagonal prism,

$$
\begin{aligned}
\text{Volume} &= \text{Area} \times \text{length} \\
&= 30 \text{ cm}^2 \times 8 \text{ cm} \\
&= \boxed{240 \text{ cm}^3}
\end{aligned}
$$

* The usual formula is :- $\boxed{V = A \times h}$

Exercise 16·3

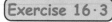

1. The area of the top of this
   square based prism is 24 cm^2.
   Its height is 6 cm.

   Calculate its **volume**.

Area = 24 cm^2
6 cm

2.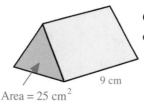
   9 cm
   Area = 25 cm^2

   Calculate the volume
   of this triangular prism.

3. Calculate the volume
   of this hexagonal
   based prism.

Area = 80 cm^2
15 cm

4. The volume of this
   prism is 144 cm^3.

   Calculate the height
   of the prism.

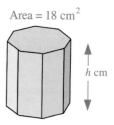
Area = 18 cm^2
h cm

5.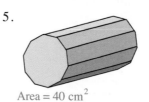
   Area = 40 cm^2

   The volume of this
   prism is 1040 cm^3.

   Calculate the length
   of the prism.

6. The volume of this square
   based prism is 432 cm^3.

   Calculate the length of
   each **side** of its base.

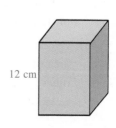
12 cm

7. This is a (right angled) triangular prism.

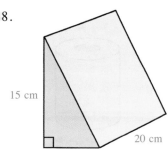

   (a) Calculate the **area** of the pink triangular face.

   (b) Now calculate the **volume** of the prism.

8.

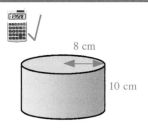

Calculate the volume of this prism in a similar way.

9. The yellow face of this prism is an isosceles triangle.

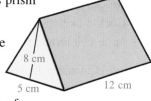

   The base of the triangle is 5 cm and its height is 8 cm.

   (a) Calculate the **area** of the yellow triangular face.

   (b) Now calculate the **volume** of the prism.

10. The volume of this prism is 510 cm³.

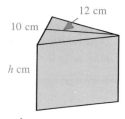

   The isosceles triangle on top has base 10 cm and height 12 cm.

   Calculate the height of the prism.

A Special Prism - The Cylinder

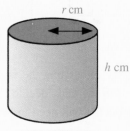

If the common face of a prism is a **CIRCLE**, then the prism is called a **CYLINDER**, and there is a special formula for calculating its volume.

Volume = **Area** (of base) × **height**   => $V = \pi r^2 h$

CYLINDER

Example :-   Calculate the volume of this cylindrical tin can.

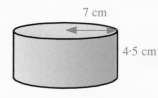

$$V = \pi r^2 h$$
$$V = 3{\cdot}14 \times 7 \times 7 \times 4{\cdot}5$$
$$V = \boxed{692{\cdot}37 \ \text{cm}^3}$$

Exercise 16·4

1. Calculate the **volume** of this cylinder with base radius 8 cm and height 10 cm.

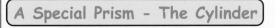

2.

Calculate the volume of this cylinder.

3. The **diameter** of the base of this cylinder is 12 cm.

   (a) Write down its radius.

   (b) Calculate its volume.

4. These two cylindrical cans are to be filled with soup. Which one will hold more ?

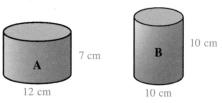

5. This hot water tank has base diameter 60 cm. It is 80 cm tall.

   How many **litres** of water will it hold when full.

   (*Find volume in ml first*).

6. Brocks cook up their
   Cock-a-Leekie soup in a
   large cylindrical pot.

   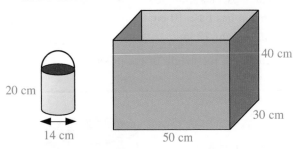

   50 cm

   40 cm

   (a) Calculate the volume
       of soup if the pot is full.

   (b) Each tin holds $\frac{1}{2}$ litre.

   BROCKS

   How many tins can be
   filled from the pot ?

7. A cylindrical bucket is used to fill a rectangular
   tank with hot water.

   40 cm

   20 cm

   30 cm

   14 cm   50 cm

   By calculating the volume of both the bucket
   and the tank, decide how many times the
   bucket will need to be used to fill the tank.

8. This section of pipe forms part of a sewer.

   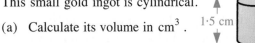

   9 cm

   1·5 metres

   How many litres of water will it hold ?

9. This small gold ingot is cylindrical.

   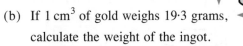

   1·5 cm

   1 cm

   (a) Calculate its volume in cm^3 .

   (b) If 1 cm^3 of gold weighs 19·3 grams,
       calculate the weight of the ingot.

   (c) If gold is valued at £18·40 per gram,
       determine the value of the gold ingot.

10. This trough is used to feed cattle with grain.

    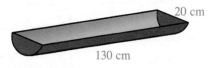

    20 cm

    130 cm

    It is in the shape of a half-cylinder.

    Calculate the volume of grain it can hold.

    (Hint - *find the volume of the whole cylinder*).

11. This piece of gutter is 3·5 metres long.

    10 cm

    3·5 m

    If caps are fitted on the ends, how much water
    will the gutter hold when full ? (*in litres*).

12. This toilet roll has a
    hollow cardboard
    tube in its middle.

    Calculate the volume of
    the actual toilet paper
    surrounding the tube.

    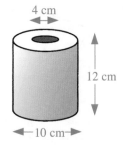

    4 cm

    12 cm

    10 cm

13. This metal block has 4 identical cylindrical holes
    drilled out of it as shown.

    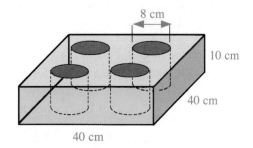

    8 cm

    10 cm

    40 cm

    40 cm

    The **diameter** of each circle is 8 cm.

    (a) Calculate the volume of one of the holes.

    (b) Calculate the volume of the metal block
        remaining after the holes have been drilled.

14. George uses wooden beading as an edging
    round the skirting of his newly laid floor.

    The ends are quarter circles,
    with a radius of 1·5 cm.

    Calculate the volume
    of a piece of beading
    which is 2 metres long.

    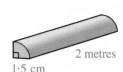

    2 metres

    1·5 cm

15. Timmy has a cube of plasticine of side 4 cm.

    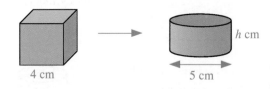

    h cm

    4 cm   5 cm

    He rolls it into a cylinder as shown with a base
    diameter of 5 cm.

    Calculate the **height** (h) of the cylinder formed.

A **PYRAMID** is any solid shape with a polygon as its base and triangular sides with a common vertex.

Examples :-

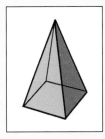

square based
pyramid

pentagonal based
pyramid

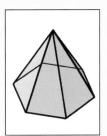

hexagonal based
pyramid

circular based
pyramid

Volume of a Pyramid

It is possible to calculate the volume of a pyramid,
as long as you know the **area** of the base.

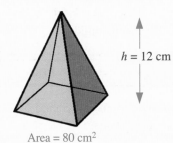

$h = 12$ cm

VOLUME (pyramid) = $\frac{1}{3}$ × **Area** (of base) × **height**

$$V = \frac{1}{3}Ah$$

Area = 80 cm^2

For this square based pyramid,

$$
\begin{aligned}
\text{Volume} &= \frac{1}{3} \times \text{Area} \times \text{height} \\
&= \frac{1}{3} \times 80 \text{ cm}^2 \times 12 \text{ cm} \\
&= \frac{1}{3} \times 960 \text{ cm}^3 = 320 \text{ cm}^3
\end{aligned}
$$

Exercise 16·5

1. The area of the base of this
   square based pyramid is 13 cm^2.
   Its height is 9 cm.
   Calculate its **volume**.

   9 cm

   Area = 13 cm^2

4. The base of this pyramid
   is a square with each
   side 7 cm.
   It is 12 cm tall.
   Calculate its volume.

   12 cm

   7 cm

2.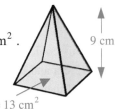

   7·5 cm

   Area = 20 cm^2

   Calculate the volume of this
   triangular based pyramid.

5. Shown are two cartons used to hold popcorn.

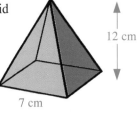

   15 cm

   15 cm

   12 cm

   12 cm

   20 cm

   16 cm

3. Calculate the volume
   of this hexagonal
   based pyramid.

   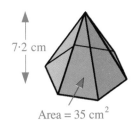

   7·2 cm

   Area = 35 cm^2

   How much **more** does the big one hold than
   the small one ?

 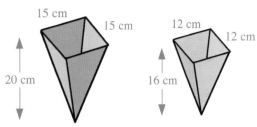

6. The base of this pyramid is an **equilateral triangle** with its sides 6 cm long.

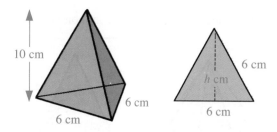

(a) Use Pythagoras' Theorem to calculate the height (h cm) of the equilateral triangle.

(b) Now calculate the area of the triangular base and use this to find the volume of the pyramid.

Special Case - The Cone

A **Circular Based** Pyramid is simply called a **CONE**.

The formula for its volume is :-

$$V = \tfrac{1}{3}\pi r^2 h$$

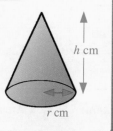

7. The radius of the base of this cone is 5 cm and its height is 9 cm.

Copy and complete :-

Volume $= \tfrac{1}{3}\pi r^2 h$

$\Rightarrow V = 3\cdot14 \times 5 \times 5 \times 9 \div 3$

$\Rightarrow V = \text{..........} \text{ cm}^3$

8. Calculate the volumes of these cones :-

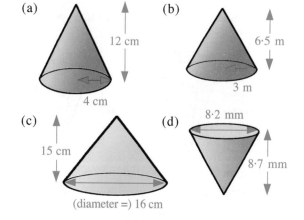

(a) 12 cm, 4 cm

(b) 6·5 m, 3 m

(c) 15 cm, (diameter =) 16 cm

(d) 8·2 mm, 8·7 mm

9. The **volume** of this cone is 400 cm³.

(a) Calculate the **area** of its base.

(b) Now calculate the height (h cm) of the cone.

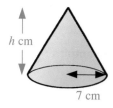

h cm

7 cm

10.

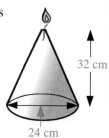

5·4 m

4·8 m

A farmer uses this conical container to hold grain for his cattle.

Calculate the weight of grain in the full container, if $1\,\text{m}^3$ of grain weighs 750 kilograms.

11. This glass conical oil lamp has a base **diameter** of 24 cm and is 32 cm tall.

How many litres of oil will the lamp hold when full ?

32 cm

24 cm

12.

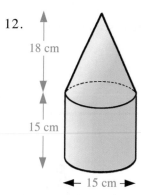

18 cm

15 cm

15 cm

This shape consists of a conical tower on top of a cylindrical base.

By calculating the volume of base and top, determine the volume of the whole shape.

13. This conical paper cup has a top diameter of 12 cm and is 16 cm tall. It was filled with water and then some of the water was poured out.

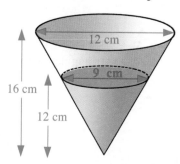

12 cm

9 cm

16 cm

12 cm

(a) Calculate the volume of water in the paper cup when it was full.

(b) Calculate the volume of water poured out.

Curved Surface Area of a Cylinder

The top of a cylinder is a circle and its area is easily found. ($A = \pi r^2$).

The **curved** bit is more difficult :-

Imagine the "label" of a tin of soup cut and opened out to reveal - a **rectangle**.

- The "breadth" of the rectangle this time is h cm.

- The "length" is in fact the **circumference** of the top circle => $L = \pi D$ *(can you see this ?)*

=> This means that the **curved surface area** is given by :- $C.S.A. = \pi D h$

=> (nearly there !) - Since $D = 2 \times r$, => $\boxed{C.S.A. = 2\pi r h}$ is the formula used.

Example :- Find the curved surface area of this cylinder :-

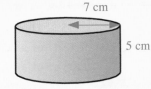

$$C.S.A. = 2\pi r h$$
$$=> C.S.A. = 2 \times 3 \cdot 14 \times 7 \times 5$$
$$=> C.S.A. = 219 \cdot 8 \text{ cm}^2$$

Exercise 16·6

1. Calculate the **C.S.A.** of this cylinder with base radius 8 cm and height 10 cm.

2. 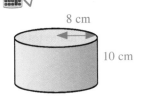 Calculate the **C.S.A.** of this cylinder.

3. The **diameter** of the base of this cylinder is 40 cm.

    (a) Write down its radius.

    (b) Calculate its C.S.A.

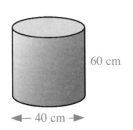

4.  This cylinder has top radius 10 cm and height 16 cm.

    (a) Calculate the area of the **top** surface.

    (b) Calculate the **C.S.A.** of the cylinder.

    (c) Now calculate the **Total Surface Area** of the cylinder. (*Top, bottom and curved bit*).

5. Which of these two cylinders has the larger **total surface area (T.S.A.)** ?

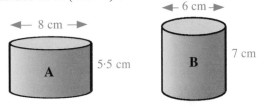

6. This **open topped** can is made out of aluminium sheeting.

    Calculate the area of aluminium sheeting needed to make it.

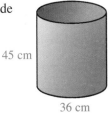

7. A paddling pool is made out of rigid plastic.

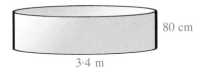

    Calculate the total area of plastic required.

8. (Hard) This is the label off a tin of soup.

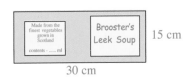

    Calculate the **volume** of the tin of soup.

Volume of a Sphere

The correct name for a "ball" shape is a **SPHERE**.

The volume* of a sphere is given by :- $V = \frac{4}{3}\pi r^3$

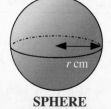

SPHERE

Example :- Calculate the volume of this football which has a **diameter** of 30 cm.

30 cm

$D = 30$ cm $\Rightarrow r = 15$ cm

$V = \frac{4}{3}\pi r^3$ note

$V = 4 \times 3{\cdot}14 \times 15 \times 15 \times 15 \div 3$

$V = \boxed{14\,130 \text{ cm}^3}$

* It is not possible to prove this is the correct formula until you have met a mathematical topic called Integral Calculus.

Exercise 16·7

1. Calculate the volume of the sphere shown with radius 12 cm.

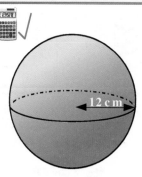

12 cm

2.  Calculate the volume of this golf ball which has a **diameter** of 40 mm.

3. This box is **tightly packed** with 3 tennis balls.

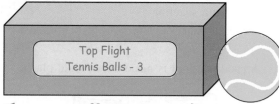

Top Flight
Tennis Balls - 3

30 cm

Calculate the volume of 1 tennis ball.

4. The diameter of this **hemi-spherical** bowl is 50 cm.

   (a) Calculate its volume.

   (b) How many litres of water would it hold when full ?

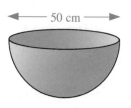

50 cm

5. This hot water tank consists of a hemi-sphere on top of a cylinder.

   The diameter of both the cylinder and hemi-sphere is 60 cm and the cylinder is 50 cm tall.

   Calculate the **total** volume.

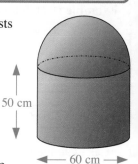

50 cm

60 cm

6.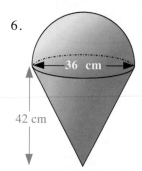

   36 cm

   42 cm

   This large metal shape is used to advertise Monty's Ice-Cream Shop.

   It consists of a hemi-sphere on top of a cone.

   Calculate the volume of the metal shape.

7. A stainless steel ashtray is made by drilling out a hemi-sphere from a square based cuboid.

   The diameter of the hemi-sphere is 8 cm.

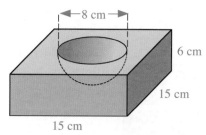

8 cm

6 cm

15 cm

15 cm

   (a) Calculate the volume of the ashtray.

   (b) Calculate the weight of the ashtray given 1 cm³ of stainless steel weighs 8·03 grams.

1. For the cuboid shown below, calculate its

   (a) volume

   (b) surface area.

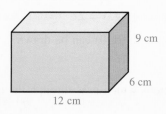

9 cm

6 cm

12 cm

2.

   30 cm

   80 cm

   1·2 m

   How many **litres** will this tank hold when full?

3. Calculate the volume of each of these prisms :-

   (a) Area = 55 cm²

   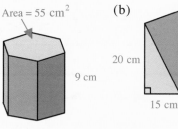

   9 cm

   (b)

   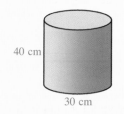

   25 cm

   20 cm

   30 cm

   15 cm

4. Calculate the volume of this tank, in cm³ and write down its **capacity** in litres.

   40 cm

   30 cm

5. When this pipe is filled with oil, it holds 5 litres.

   10 cm

   ? cm

   (a) How many millilitres is this ?

   (b) Calculate what the pipe length must be.

6. Calculate the volume of each of these pyramids.

   (a)

   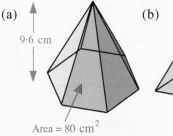

   9·6 cm

   Area = 80 cm²

   (b)

   11 cm

   9 cm

   9 cm

7.  Calculate the volume of this cone.

   15 cm

   6 cm

8. This shape is formed from a cone and a cylinder.

   Calculate its volume.

   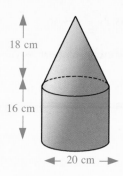

   18 cm

   16 cm

   20 cm

9. 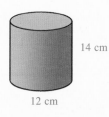 For the wooden cylinder shown, calculate :-

   14 cm

   12 cm

   (a) the area of the top

   (b) the curved surface area

   (c) the total surface area.

10. 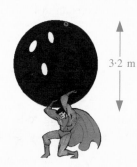 This statue is used to advertise "Townend Bowling Club".

    3·2 m

    Calculate the volume of the sphere used in the sign.

11. Calculate the **capacity** (in litres), of this bowl.

    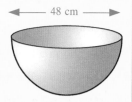

    48 cm

12. 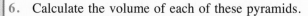 This shape consists of a cone on top of a cylinder on top of a hemi-sphere.

    13 cm

    10 cm

    24 cm

    Calculate the **total** volume of the shape.

Simple Patterns of the form $y = mx$

A **linear equation** through the **origin** has the form $y = mx$. (e.g. $y = 2x$, $y = 21x$, $y = \frac{1}{4}x$)

A table of values can be drawn up and a straight line through $(0, 0)$ can be drawn.

Other letters (**variables**) can be used.

(e.g. $A = 3t$, $P = 7n$, $H = \frac{1}{4}d$ are all linear equations which pass through the origin).

Linear equations can be found to represent simple patterns.

Example :- Squares can be produced by welding four 1 metre metal rods together.

| 1 square | 2 squares | 3 squares | 4 squares |
| 4 lengths | 8 lengths | 12 lengths | 16 lengths |

the pattern continues ...

A table of values can be drawn up to show this pattern.

No. of Squares (S)	1	2	3	4	5	6
No. of Lengths (L)	4	8	12	16	?	?

We need to **derive** a formula to determine larger numbers of squares or lengths.

4   4   4   (*very important)

Since the rise (or **increment**) is constant, (4), this tells us that the pattern is **linear**, (*the 4 times table*).

The **number of Lengths** is 4 × the **number of Squares**.   The formulae is $\boxed{L = 4S}$

Exercise 17·1

1. Look at this pattern of triangles using rods.

| 1 triangle | 2 triangles | 3 triangles |
| 3 lengths | 6 lengths | 9 lengths |

(a) Form a table similar to the one above.

(b) What is the **increment** ? (*the rise*).

(c) Derive a formula. (L = ...)

(d) Use your formula to determine how many lengths are needed for **50 triangles**.

(e) How many triangles can you make from **72 lengths** ?

2. Repeat question 1 for this pattern :-

| 1 hexagon | 2 hexagons | 3 hexagons |
| 6 lengths | ... lengths | ... lengths |

Derive a formula from each of these tables.

3. (a)

x	1	2	3	4
y	5	10	15	20

$y = ..$

(b) Find y when $x = 8$.

(c) Find x when $y = 75$.

4. (a)

p	1	2	3	4
T	17	34	51	68

$T = ..$

(b) Find T when $p = 10$.

(c) Find p when $T = 340$.

5. (a)

z	3	4	5	6
W	1·5	2	2·5	3

$W = ..$

(b) Find W when $z = 40$.

(c) Find z when $W = 30$.

Most **linear** equations take the form $y = mx + c$.
(A straight line which does **not** pass through the origin).

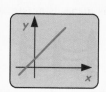

These linear equations can also be derived from many patterns.

Example :-   A pattern has been made using 1 metre lengths of wood to make these shapes.

1 square   2 squares   3 squares
4 lengths   7 lengths   10 lengths

S	1	2	3	4
L	4	7	10	13

Notice the **increment** is constant (**3**) - this means that the pattern must be linear. (*Try the 3 times table.*)

But, $3 \times 1 \neq 4$, $3 \times 2 \neq 7$, $3 \times 3 \neq 10$, ...   etc...

This time, a **correction value** must be found.

Look at ($S = 2$.) $3 \times 2 = 6$ (we find that we need to **add 1** to obtain the 7).

To find the number of lengths needed,
multiply the S-value by 3, then add 1.
(We can check this by substitution - using our table.)

Formula is $L = 3S + 1$

1. Look at this pattern of shapes.

1 triangle   2 triangles   3 triangles   4 triangles
3 lengths   5 lengths   ... lengths   ... lengths

(a) Form a table similar to the one above.

(b) What is the **increment** ?

(c) **Derive** a formula to show this pattern.

$$(L = ...)$$

(d) Use your formula to determine how many lengths are needed for **10 triangles**.

(e) How many triangles can you make from **61 lengths** ?

2. Repeat question 1 for each of these patterns :-

(i)

1 pentagon   2 pentagons   3 pentagons

(ii)

1 hexagon   2 hexagons   3 hexagons

3. Look at the tile pattern below.

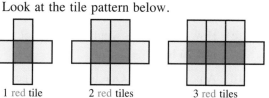

1 red tile   2 red tiles   3 red tiles
4 blue tiles   6 blue tiles   ... blue tiles

(a) Form a table using *R* (**red** tiles) and *B* (**blue** tiles).

(b) **Derive** a formula to show this pattern.

(c) Use your formula to find how many **blue** tiles you need if you have **10 red** tiles.

(d) Use your formula to find how many **red** tiles you need if you have **40 blue tiles**.

4. Look at this pattern of tiles.

1 red tile   2 red tiles   3 red tiles
8 blue tiles   10 blue tiles   ... blue tiles

(a) Derive a formula to show this pattern.

(b) How many **blue** tiles would you need if you had **20 red tiles** ?

(c) How many **red** tiles would you need if you had **36 blue tiles** ?

5. A fence is made using strips of wire and posts.

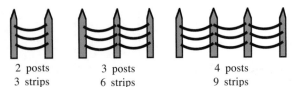

| 2 posts | 3 posts | 4 posts |
| 3 strips | 6 strips | 9 strips |

(a) Derive a formula for S in terms of P.

(*Note : This time the correction value has to be subtracted*).

(b) How many strips of wire would you need if you had **10 posts** ?

(c) How many posts would you need if you had **57 strips** of wire ?

6. Each bar on this fence is 2 metres long.

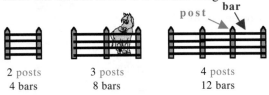

post   bar

| 2 posts | 3 posts | 4 posts |
| 4 bars | 8 bars | 12 bars |

(a) Derive a formula using B in terms of P.

(b) How many bars would you need if you had **20 posts** ?

(c) How many posts would you need if you had **76 bars** ?

(d) A post costs £1. One bar costs 20 pence.

How much would it cost for a fence **50 metres long** ?

7. A chemistry model set has spheres and links to build molecule models.
The pattern below shows how the model was made.

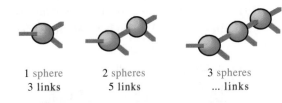

| 1 sphere | 2 spheres | 3 spheres |
| 3 links | 5 links | ... links |

(a) Derive a formula for L in terms of S.

(b) How many links would I need if I had **11 spheres** ?

(c) How many spheres would I need to build a molecule model with **171 links** ?

8. A liquid is heated at a constant rate.
The time, t, (*in minutes*) and temperature T, (*in °C*) are shown in the table.

t	1	2	3	4
T	2·6	8·3	14	19·7

$T = ...$

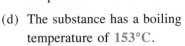
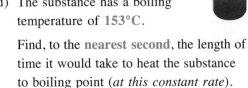

(a) Derive a formula for T in terms of t.

(b) What would the temperature be after **17 minutes** ?

(c) How many minutes would it take for the temperature to reach **82·4°C** ?

(d) The substance has a boiling temperature of **153°C**.

Find, to the **nearest second**, the length of time it would take to heat the substance to boiling point (*at this constant rate*).

9. (a) Derive a formula from the table below.

p	2	3	4	5
G	42	50	58	66

$G = ...$

(b) Find G, when $p = 18$

(c) Find p, when $G = 298$.

10. (a) Derive a formula from the table below.

a	10	11	12	13
H	87	96	105	114

$H = ...$

(b) Find H when $a = 100$.

(c) Find a, when $H = 51$.

11. (a) **Carefully**, derive a formula from the table.

q	1	2	3	4
V	5·1	4	2·9	1·8

(b) Find V, when $q = -23·5$.

(c) Find q, when $V = -5·9$.

12. (a) **Carefully**, derive a formula from the table.

g	2	4	6	8
t	6	10	14	18

(b) Find t, when $g = 15$.

(c) Find g, when $t = 82$.

Number patterns can also produce formulae which are **not linear**.

Example :-   The pattern of counters below form what are referred to as *Square Numbers.*

   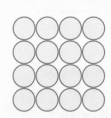 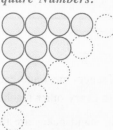

This pattern is formed by :-   **multiplying the term number by itself.**

(e.g. the 9th pattern = 9 × 9 = 81, the 15th pattern = 15 × 15 = 225).

A square number's n^{th} pattern *(n × n)* is written as n^2 .

Exercise 17·3

1.   Look at this pattern of bricks.   ▭ – 1st pattern

  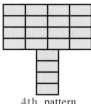

2nd pattern   3rd pattern   4th pattern

(a) How many bricks are in pattern number :-
(i) 5   (ii) 6   (iii) 7   (iv) 9 ?

(b) Copy and complete :-

"The nth pattern is $n^2 + ...$"

2.   Look at the pattern using square tiles :-

1st pattern   2nd pattern   3rd pattern   4th pattern

(a) Can you see that in :-

Pattern 1 : $3^2 - 1^2 = 9 - 1 = 8$

Pattern 2 : $4^2 - 2^2 = 16 - 4 = 12$?

(b) Use the method in part (a) to find how
many tiles are in pattern number :-

(i) 3   (ii) 4   (iii) 5   (iv) 6.

(c) Write the nth pattern. (**hint** : $(n+2)^2 - ...^2$),
and simplify.

3.   This pattern shows what is called the set of
triangular numbers :-

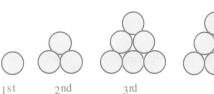

1st   2nd   3rd   4th
pattern   pattern   pattern   pattern

(a) How many dots are needed for pattern :-
(i) 5   (ii) 6   (iii) 7   (iv) 8 ?

(b) Write down each of these values :-

$\frac{1}{2}(1 \times 2)$, $\frac{1}{2}(2 \times 3)$, $\frac{1}{2}(3 \times ...)$,   ...

(c) What do you notice ?

(d) Copy and complete :-

"The nth pattern is $\frac{1}{2}(n \times ...)$"

4.   (a) Write down the first 6 **triangular numbers**.

(b) Show by drawing four diagrams that :-
"adding two consecutive **triangular
numbers** gives a **square number**".

Hint :-
$(3 + 6)$

(c) Which two consecutive triangular numbers
add together to give the square number :-

(i)   64   (ii)   100   (iii)   144 ?

Solving a tricky problem sometimes involves investigating a similar, but easier, one first.

Exercise 17·4

1. Twelve teachers meet and each teacher shakes hands with every other teacher.

   How many handshakes are there altogether ?

   (Hint :–   Start with 2 teachers, then 3 teachers, then 4, then 5, and try to find an expression for the nth pattern. Then solve for n = 12.)

2. Can you see that the grid shown has **14 squares** ?
   (1 big, 4 medium and 9 small).

   How many squares are on a chessboard ? (An 8 × 8 grid).

3. There are 18 points equally spaced on the circumference of a circle as shown.

   Each point is joined to every other point by a straight line.

   How many lines will there be ?
   (Hint :– try for 4 dots, 5 dots, 6, etc)

4. A **polygon** is a **many–sided** closed shape.

   Diagonals are the lines which join (*non-touching*) corners.

   20 sided polygon

   How many diagonals would there be in an icosagon ? (*a twenty sided shape*).

5. Imagine you tear a piece of paper in half and place one piece on top of the other.

   You repeat the tearing putting the 4 pieces on top of each other.

   (a) If you could repeat this process making **30 tears**, stacking each time, how many pieces of paper would be there be in the stack ?

   (b) If each piece of paper is **0·05 mm** thick, how many *kilometres* high is the stack ?

More Difficult Patterns

Exercise 17·5

1. The difference between the squares of any two consecutive whole numbers can be found by using this pattern :-

   > 1st term : $2^2 - 1^2 = 3 = 2 + 1$
   >
   > 2nd term : $3^2 - 2^2 = 5 = 3 + 2$
   >
   > 3rd term : $4^2 - 3^2 = 7 = 4 + 3$

   (a) Find the :-

      (i)   fifteenth term

      (ii) thirtieth term.

   (b) Write an expression for the nth term.

2. The sum of the numbers 1 to 10 can be found using the method below :-

   > Let - $S_{10} = 1 + 2 + 3 + ... + 10$
   >
   > Reverse the sum - $S_{10} = 10 + 9 + 8 + ... + 1$
   >
   > Now add in pairs - $2S_{10} = 11 + 11 + 11 + ... + 11$
   >
   > This can be thought of as - $2S_{10} = 10 \times 11$
   >
   > Which leads us to - $S_{10} = \dfrac{10 \times 11}{2} = 55.$

   (a) Use this method to find the sum from :-

      (i)   1 to 100   (ii) 1 to 1000.

   (b) Find a general expression for the sum :-

   $$1 + 2 + 3 + ... + n.$$

3. Look at the number pattern below :-

   > $1^3 + 1 = (1 + 1)(1^2 - 1 + 1)$
   >
   > $2^3 + 1 = (2 + 1)(2^2 - 2 + 1)$
   >
   > $3^3 + 1 = (3 + 1)(3^2 - 3 + 1)$

   (a) Write an expression for :-

      (i) $5^3 + 1$ (ii) $8^3 + 1.$

   (b) Write an expression for $n^3 + 1.$

4. A pattern of numbers is found as follows :-

$3 + 2 - 1$	1st term
$6 + 3 - 3$	2nd term
$9 + 4 - 5$	3rd term
....	
....	

(a) Write down the next 2 terms in this pattern.

(b) Write an expression for the *n*th term in this pattern and express it in its simplest form.

5. The sequence of odd numbers starting with 3 is

$$3, \ 5, \ 7, \ 9, \ 11, \ ......$$

Consecutive numbers from this sequence can be added using the following pattern :-

$3 + 5 + 7 + 9$	$= \mathbf{4 \times 6}$
$3 + 5 + 7 + 9 + 11$	$= \mathbf{5 \times 7}$
$3 + 5 + 7 + 9 + 11 + 13$	$= \mathbf{6 \times 8}$

(a) Express $3 + 5 + ... + 25$ in the same way.

(b) The first *n* numbers in this sequence are added.

   Find a formula for the total.

6. The following number pattern can be used to sum consecutive square whole numbers.

$$1^2 + 2^2 = \frac{2 \times 3 \times 5}{6}$$

$$1^2 + 2^2 + 3^2 = \frac{3 \times 4 \times 7}{6}$$

$$1^2 + 2^2 + 3^2 + 4^2 = \frac{4 \times 5 \times 9}{6}$$

(a) Express $1^2 + 2^2 + 3^2 + ... + 10^2$ in the same way.

(b) Express $1^2 + 2^2 + 3^2 + ... + n^2$ in the same way.

7. The sequence of multiples of 5 is ......

$$5, \ 10, \ 15, \ 20, \ 25, \ ....$$

Consecutive numbers from this sequence can be added using the following pattern :-

$5 + 10 + 15 + 20$	$= 2{\cdot}5 \times 4 \times 5$
$5 + 10 + 15 + 20 + 25$	$= 2{\cdot}5 \times 5 \times 6$
$5 + 10 + 15 + 20 + 25 + 30$	$= 2{\cdot}5 \times 6 \times 7$

(a) Express $5 + 10 + 15 + ... + 50$ in the same way.

(b) The first *n* numbers in the sequence are added. Find a formula for the total.

8.

1, 3, 5, 7, ...

The **first** odd number can be expressed as

$$1 = 1^2 - 0^2.$$

The **second** odd number can be expressed as

$$3 = 2^2 - 1^2.$$

The **third** odd number can be expressed as

$$5 = 3^2 - 2^2.$$

(a) Express the **fourth** odd number in this form.

(b) Express the number 19 in this form.

(c) Write down a formula for the nth odd number and simplify this expression.

(d) **Prove** that the product of two consecutive odd numbers is always odd.

   (*even numbers –> 2n, odd numbers –> 2n + 1*).

9. Coloured beads are arranged as shown.

1st Pattern   2nd Pattern   3rd Pattern

A quick way of finding a number in this sequence is as follows :-

1st Pattern	$(2 \times 3) - 1 = 5$
2nd Pattern	$(3 \times 4) - 1 = 11$
3rd Pattern	$(4 \times 5) - 1 = 19$

(a) Find the number which the 20th pattern in the sequence produces.

(b) Find, in its simplest form, an expression for the nth pattern in this sequence.

Remember Remember..... ?

1. Look at the pattern of shapes below :-

1 pentagon   2 pentagons   3 pentagons
5 lines   10 lines   ... lines

(a) Copy and complete the table.

Pentagons	1	2	3	4
Lines	5	10	...	...

(b) What is the **increment** ? (*the rise*)

(c) Derive a formula for L in terms of P.

(d) Use your formula to determine how many lines are needed for 40 pentagons.

(e) How many pentagons can you make from 75 lines ?

2. (a) Derive a formula from the table below.

h	1	2	3	4
B	1·5	3	4·5	6

$B = ...$

(b) Find B, when $h = 14$.

(c) Find h, when $B = 63$.

3. Look at this pattern.

1 rectangle   2 rectangles   3 rectangles   4 rectangles
4 lines   7 lines   10 lines   ... lines

(a) Form a table of values.
    (Use L - lines and R - rectangles)

(b) Derive a formula to show this pattern.

(c) Use your formula to determine how many lines you need to make **20 rectangles**.

(d) How many rectangles can you make with **121 lines** ?

4. (a) Derive a formula from the table below.

P	1	2	3	4
T	8	11	14	17

$T = ...$

(b) Find T, when $P = 41$.

(c) Find P, when $T = 41$.

5. (a) Derive a formula from the table below.

S	5	6	7	8
K	16	17	18	19

(b) Find K, when $S = 19$.

(c) Find S, when $K = 90$.

6. (a) Derive a formula from the table below.
    (**note** :- it is **NOT** $M = 6G + ...$)

G	2	4	6	8
M	1	7	13	19

(b) Find M, when $G = 20$.

(c) Find G, when $M = 328$.

7. (a) Derive a formula from the table below.

d	10	20	30	40
V	4	9	14	19

(b) Find V, when $d = 41$. (*Careful*)

(c) Find d, when $V = 197$.

8. The nth term of a pattern is :- $(2n-1)^2 + 1$.
Find the first 5 terms of this pattern.

9. Each **small** block below is 1 cm^3.

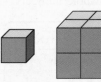 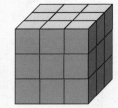

(a) How many small cubes would you need to make the **sixth** shape in the pattern ?

(b) What is the **volume** of the tenth shape ?

(c) Write an expression for the number of small cubes needed to make the nth shape.

(d) Write the length of a cube made up from eight million small centimetre cubes.

Angles formed Inside Circles - Isosceles Triangles

Any line joining two points on the circumference of a circle is call a **chord**.

A **diameter** is a special chord.

If the two points, A and B, are joined by a chord **AB**, then the triangle formed must be an **isosceles** triangle.

∠OAB = ∠OBA

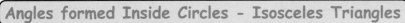

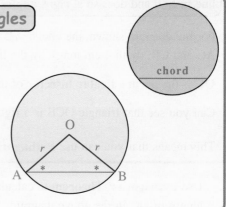

Exercise 18·1

1. Calculate the sizes of the angles in triangle OAB shown opposite.

2. Find the missing angles in each of these :-

(a) 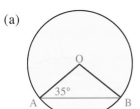   (b) 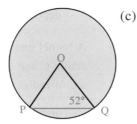   (c) 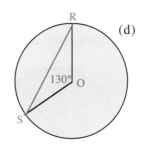   (d)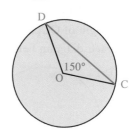

3. Use a coin to sketch each of these circles and fill in all the missing angles :-

(a) 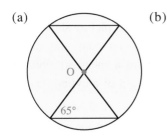   (b) 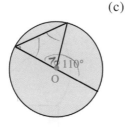   (c) 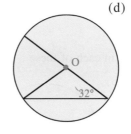   (d)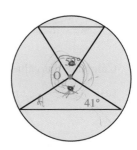

(e) 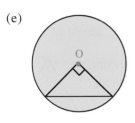   (f) 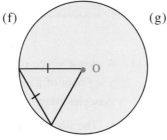   (g) 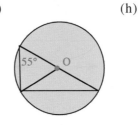   (h)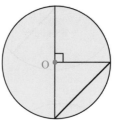

(i) 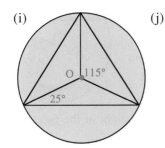   (j)    (k) 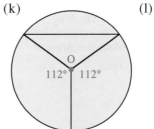   (l)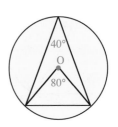

A **perpendicular bisector** is a line which cuts another line **in half** and does so at **right angles** to the first line.

For the diagram shown, the **chord AB** is now cut into two parts AC and CB, (both 4 cm long), by the line OC.

OC is the **perpendicular bisector** of the chord AB.

Can you see that triangle OCB is a right angled triangle ?

This means that you can use **Pythagoras' Theorem** to find the length of OC.

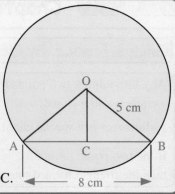

4. Use **Pythagoras' Theorem** to calculate the length of OC in the above diagram.

Copy and complete :-

$$OC^2 = OB^2 - CB^2$$
$$OC^2 = 5^2 - 4^2$$
etc.

5. Use Pythagoras' Theorem to calculate the length of OC, to the nearest millimetre, in each diagram below :-

(a)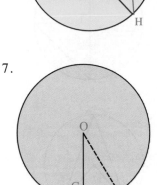

(b)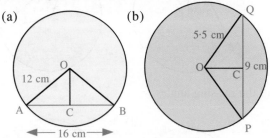

6. Calculate the value of x in each of these :-

(a)

(b)

7.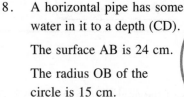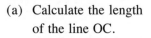

In this circle, chord PQ is 10 cm and the line OC is 12 cm long.

Calculate the **area** of the circle.

8. A horizontal pipe has some water in it to a depth (CD).

The surface AB is 24 cm.

The radius OB of the circle is 15 cm.

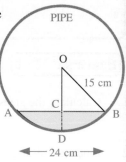

(a) Calculate the length of the line OC.

(b) Now write down the depth of the water CD.

9. A tunnel entrance has centre C and a circular arc of radius 8 metres.

Calculate the height of the tunnel entrance.

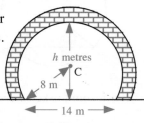

10.

The picture shows a glass lamp, consisting of part of a spherical globe on top of a cylindrical base.

(a) Calculate the length of the red line.

(b) Calculate the total height of the lamp.

11. A clown's face is drawn using a segment of a circle, with an isosceles triangular hat.

• The Radius = 26 cm
• Line OC = 10 cm
• Side TB = 40 cm

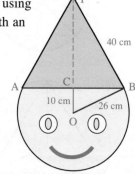

(a) Calculate the length of the base AB of triangle ATB.

(b) Calculate the total height of the face and hat.

Angles in a Semi-Circle

The diagram shows a semi-circle with diameter AB and a 3rd point
C drawn somewhere on the circumference of the semi-circle.

Two chords, AC and BC are drawn to create triangle ABC.

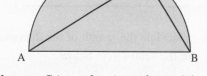

If you measure the size of ∠ACB, it **always turns out to be 90°**, (*as long as C is on the circumference*) !

Every triangle in a semi-circle, formed like this, with the diameter as base, is a right angled triangle.

Exercise 18·2

1. Calculate the values of a, b, c, d and e in each of the following :-

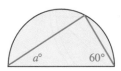 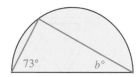 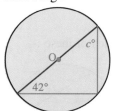 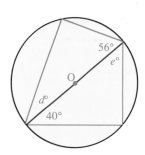

2. Sketch each of the following (*a coin might help*) and fill in all the missing angles :-

(a) 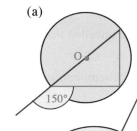 (b) 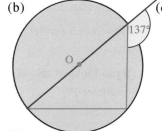 (c) 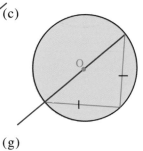 (d)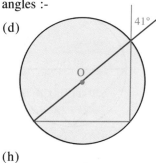

(e) 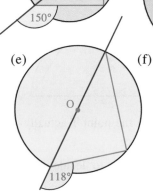 (f) 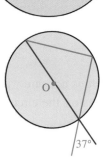 (g) 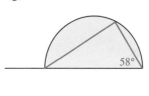 (h)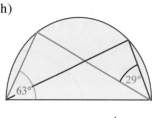

(i) 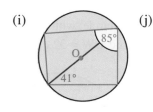 (j) 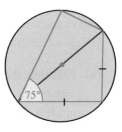 (k)  (l)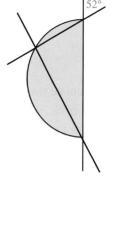

(m) 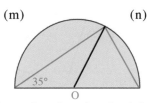 (n) 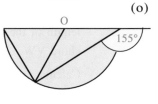 (o)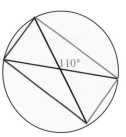

(*remember - isosceles triangles*)

3. Calculate the length of the diameter AB shown
   in the semi-circle below.

   Copy and complete :-

   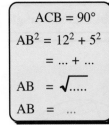

   ACB = 90°
   $AB^2 = 12^2 + 5^2$
      = ... + ...
   AB = √.....
   AB = ...

   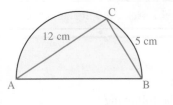

4. Calculate the value of x for each of these :-

   (a)   (b)

   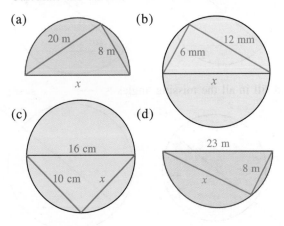

   (c)   (d)

   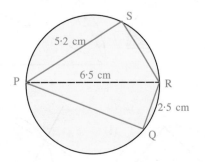

5. Calculate the **perimeter** of quadrilateral PQRS,
   where PR is a diameter of the circle.

   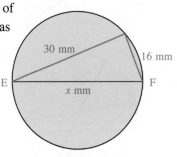

6. Calculate the **area** of
   this circle, which has
   EF as its diameter.

   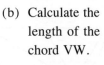

7. An entrance to a tunnel, through which water
   flows, is in the shape of a semi-circle.

   Two wooden beams are used to support it while
   work is being carried out on the tunnel.

   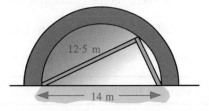

   Calculate the length of the smaller beam.

8. A semi-circular swimming pool has a diameter
   of 20 metres.

   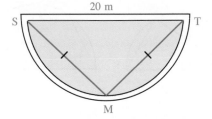

   Lucy swims from T to M, then from M to S.
   Josh walks directly from T to S.

   How much further has Lucy travelled than Josh ?

9. Ryan looks at this sketch of a semi-circle with
   diameter PQ.

   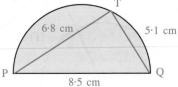

   He is not sure whether the point T actually
   lies **on** the circumference.

   Use **Pythagoras' Theorem** to decide if T lies on
   the circumference or not.

10. The **circumference** of this circle, with diameter
    UV, is **125·6 cm**, and chord UW = 32 cm.

    (a) Calculate the
        size of the
        circle's diameter.

    (b) Calculate the
        length of the
        chord VW.

    (c) Calculate the total area
        of the **pink** segments.

    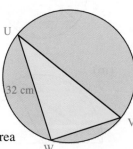

Tangents to a Circle

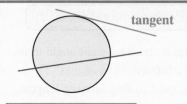

tangent

A **tangent** is a line which, even if extended, would only
ever touch a circle **at one point.**

Only the **red** line shown opposite is a **tangent.**

A Special Property

The diagram shows a tangent, AB, meeting the circle at point B.

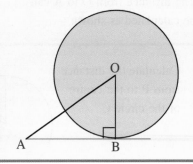

If we draw a radius (OB) to this point of contact B, it is found
that the radius and the tangent are **at right angles.** (∠ABO = 90°)

Exercise 18·3

1. PA is a tangent to this circle, meeting it at the
   point A.

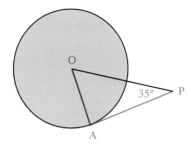

(a) What is the size of ∠PAO ?

(b) Write down the size of ∠POA.

2. Write down the values of *a, b, ... g.*

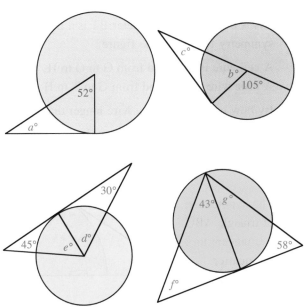

3. Sketch the following, (*a coin might help*), and
   fill in the sizes of all the missing angles.

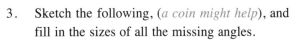

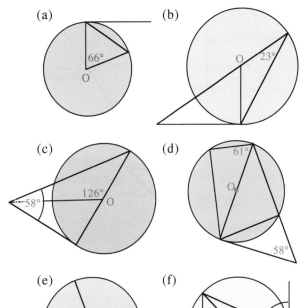

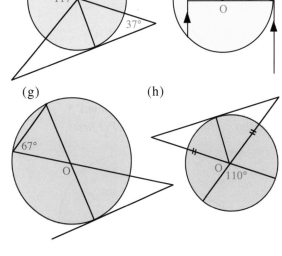

Again, because right angle triangles
are formed, **Pythagoras' Theorem** can
be used to find missing lengths.

$$OA^2 = 24^2 + 10^2$$
$$OA^2 = 576 + 100$$
$$OA^2 = 676$$
$$OA = \sqrt{676} = 26 \text{ mm}$$

The distance from O to A can
be calculated as shown :-

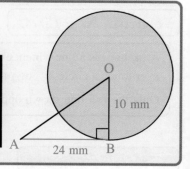

4. Calculate the distance
   from P to the centre
   of the circle C.

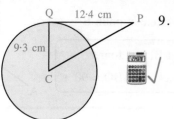

5. Determine the lengths of the **red** lines.

   (a)   (b)

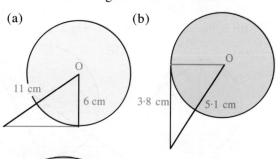

6.   Calculate the
                                      area of this
                                      circle.

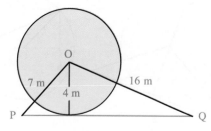

7. Determine the length of the tangent PQ.

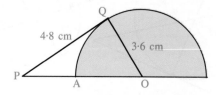

8. Determine the length of the line PA.
   (*Hint :- find the length of PO first*).

9. BA is a diameter of this semi-circle and is
   extended to point S.
   ST is a tangent meeting the semi-circle at the
   point T.

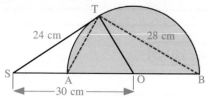

   (a) Calculate the size of radius OT.

   (b) Now find the length of the chord AT.

10. The diagram shows a wheel, centre O, with a
    radius of 6·5 centimetres.

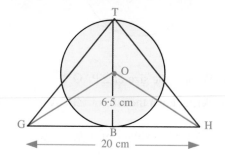

    GH is a tangent and diameter BT is a line of
    symmetry for the whole figure.

    A **red** wire is stretched from G to O to H.
    A **blue** wire is stretched from G to T to H.

    By how much is the blue wire longer than
    the red one ?

11. Triangle ABC is right angled
    at C.
    The hypotenuse, AB,
    of triangle ABC
    is a tangent to
    the quarter
    circle at T.

    Calculate the **perimeter** of triangle ABC.

The Tangent Kite

From any point P, outside a circle, it is possible to draw 2 tangents PA and PB to the circle.

By symmetry, these 2 tangents are **equal** in length.

Can you see that **OA = OB** and **PA = PB** ?

=> Quadrilateral OAPB must be a **KITE**.

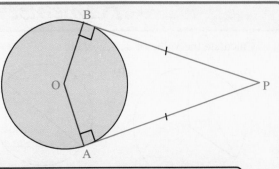

=> When a kite is formed from tangents, it is referred to as a **TANGENT KITE**, and this kite has the special property that its 2 equal angles are both **right angles** (90°).

Special Property of Tangent Kite

Since ∠OAP = ∠OBP = 90°, this means that =>   ∠AOB + ∠APB = 180°

Exercise 18·4

1. Look at the tangent kite at the top of the page.
   If ∠APB = 55°, calculate the size of ∠AOB.

2. Make a neat sketch of this tangent kite.

   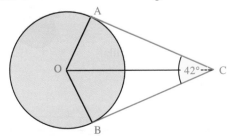

   Given that ∠ACB = 42°, calculate the sizes of all the missing angles.

3. Write down the values of a, b, c and d.

   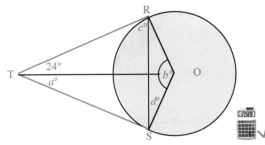

4. The radius, OG, of this circle is 11 cm long.

   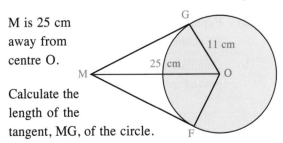

   M is 25 cm away from centre O.

   Calculate the length of the tangent, MG, of the circle.

5. P is a point, 39 cm away from the centre O of this circle. The tangent PN is 36 cm long.

   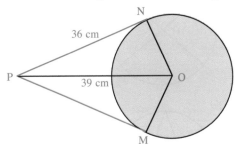

   Calculate the **area** of the circle with centre O.

6. Diameter PQ = 20 cm and QC = 18 cm.

   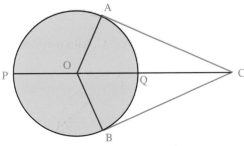

   (a) Use the above information to write down the size of   (i) the radius   (ii) the line OC.

   (b) Calculate the length of the tangent AC.

7. The **circumference** of this circle is 60 cm and the distance from O to X is 23 cm.

   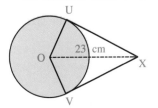

   Calculate the length of the **perimeter** of the tangent kite OUXV.

   (*Find the radius first !*)

1. Calculate the value of a, b, c, d etc ......

(a)
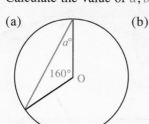

(b)
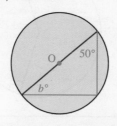

(c) (d)
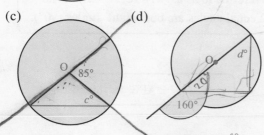

(e) (f)
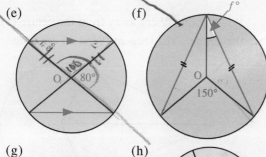

(g) (h)
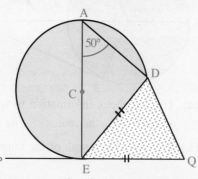

2. Shown is a circle, centre C, with diameter AE.

PQ is a tangent to the circle, meeting it at E.

Δ EDQ is isosceles with ED = EQ.

Given that $\angle$ EAD = 50°, calculate the size

of $\angle$ DQE.

(*Explain clearly how you obtained your answer*).

3. Calculate the value of x for each of these :-

(a) (b)
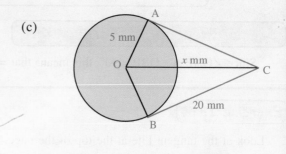

(c)

4. A new style of park bench is designed.

The base is a cylindrical log with part of it removed.

The seat is a rectangular piece of pine wood.

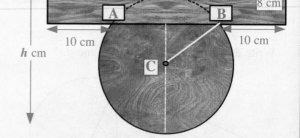

The top has a rectangular end face measuring 50 centimetres by 8 centimetres.

The radius of the (part) circle is 25 centimetres.

(a) Explain why the line AB is 30 centimetres long.

(b) Calculate the height of the bench from the ground to the top of the wooden seat.

1. Calculate (i) the **volume** and (ii) the **surface area** of both shapes below :-

(a)

(b)

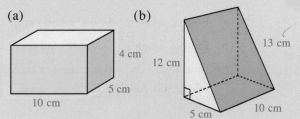

4 cm
12 cm
13 cm
5 cm
10 cm
5 cm
10 cm

2.

30 cm
12 cm

(a) Calculate the **volume** of this cylinder.

(b) How many litres of water would it hold when full ?

3. A wax sphere has a 20 cm diameter. If the wax was melted down and a cube formed from the same amount of wax, find to the nearest millimetre, the side length of the cube.

4. Derive a **formula** from each of the tables below.

(a)

A	1	2	3	4
B	2	4	6	8

$B = ...$

(b)

T	1	2	3	4
P	3	7	11	15

$P = ...$

(c)

x	1	2	3	4
y	4	5	6	7

$y = ...$

(d)

k	1	2	3	4
Q	4·1	4·6	5·1	5·6

$Q = ...$

5. Derive a **formula** from the table below :-

M	1	2	3	4
R	4	9	14	19

$R = ...$

(a) Find R, when $M = 30$.

(b) Find M, when $R = 89$.

6. The sequence of even numbers starting with 2 is   2, 4, 6, 8, 10, ...

Consecutive numbers from this sequence can be added using the following pattern :-

$$
\begin{array}{rcl}
2 + 4 + 6 & = & 3 \times 4 \\
2 + 4 + 6 + 8 & = & 4 \times 5 \\
2 + 4 + 6 + 8 + 10 & = & 5 \times 6
\end{array}
$$

(a) Express $2 + 4 + ... + 20$ in the same way.

(b) The first n numbers in this sequence are added. $(2 + 4 + 6 + ...)$

Determine a *formula* for the total.

7. Copy each diagram and fill in all the missing angles :-

(a)   (b)

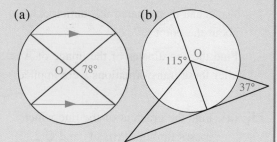

O   78°
115°   O
37°

8. Calculate the value of x.

Give your answer to 2 significant figures.

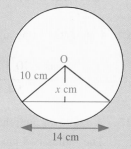

O
10 cm
x cm
14 cm

9. (a) Calculate the **radius** of the circle shown.

(b) Calculate the **circumference** of this circle.

(c) Calculate the **area** of the circle.

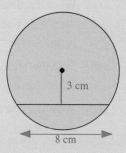

O
3 cm
8 cm

10. A car leaves Ayton at 11 am
and drives at an average
speed of 70 km/hr to
Beeton, 140 km away.

At noon, a train travels
from Ayton to Beeton at
an average speed of
100 km/hr.

Which will arrive first and by how many
minutes (*to the nearest minute*) ?

11. Last year, Peter earned £17 600.
After a pay rise, he gets £18 450 this year.

What was his percentage pay rise ?
(*Answer to 2 significant figures*).

12. The point A(73, 61) is reflected over the
x-axis and then rotated 90° anticlockwise
about the point (17, 6).

Find the coordinates of the image of A
after these transformations were applied.

13. (a) Find the gradient of the line which
passes through P(0, –1) and Q(2, 7).

(b) Write down the equation of the line.

14. Calculate to one significant figure :-

$$\frac{\left(3 \cdot 6 \times 10^7\right) \times \left(7 \cdot 2 \times 10^2\right)}{5 \cdot 4 \times 10^8}.$$

15. A **sector** of a circle is as shown.
The radius is 8 cm.

(a) What fraction of
the whole circle
is this sector ?

(b) Find the area of the
original circle.

(c) What do you think the
area of the sector might be ?

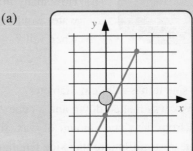

8 cm

36°

16. Find :-

(a) $6x \times 3x \times x$ (b) $12p^2 q \div 4pq$

(c) $8 - 4 \times 2$ (d) $-6t - (-2t) + (-4t)$.

17. A formula is defined as

$$s = ut + \tfrac{1}{2}at^2 .$$

(a) Find *s*, when $u = 0$, $a = 2$ and $t = 3$.

(b) Find *u*, when $s = 30$, $t = 5$ and $a = 2$.

(c) Investigate and write a short sentence on
where this formula would be used.

18. Calculate the **reflex** angle between the
hands of a clock at 1730 hrs.

19. Find the equation for each of the 3 lines
indicated below :-

(a)

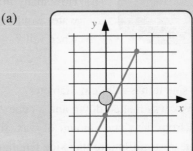

(b) passing through (–3, 4) and (0, –6)

(c) a vertical line passing through (0, 4).

20. Factorise fully :-

(a) $16ab^2 - 12ab$ (b) $9k^2 p - 6kp + 12k$.

21. Solve for *x* :-

(a) $12 - (5 - x) \geq 7$

(b) $3(x - 7) + 4 < \dfrac{5x + 1}{3}$

(c) $3x^2 - 75 = 0$.

22. Prove that the triangle below is **not** a
right angled triangle.

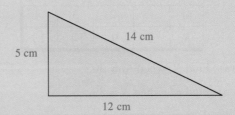

14 cm

5 cm

12 cm

1. Set down and find the following :-

   (a) $(40)^3$

   (b) $7 \overline{)6251}$

   (c) $54 - 19 \times 3$

   (d) $2000 - 1891$

   (e) 208×50

   (f) $86\,000 \div 500$

   (g) 3^5

   (h) $\dfrac{9 \times 15}{27 \times 5}$.

2. Set down and find :-

   (a) $68 \cdot 2 + 1 \cdot 824$

   (b) $\begin{array}{r} 262 \\ \times\,18 \\ \hline \end{array}$

   (c) $126 \div 4$

   (d) $\dfrac{4 \times 56 \cdot 65}{2000}$.

3. A 5 ml spoon is used to dispense 2 litres of medicine. How many spoonfuls can be dispensed ?

4. Change :-

   (a) $6 \cdot 3$ m to km

   (b) $216 \cdot 8$ mm to cm

   (c) $\frac{3}{8}$ litre to millilitres

   (d) 700 seconds to minutes and seconds.

5. Simplify :-

   (a) $\dfrac{27}{81}$

   (b) $\dfrac{42}{105}$

   (c) $\dfrac{15}{570}$.

6. Find :-

   (a) $5\frac{3}{4} - 3\frac{1}{2}$

   (b) $\frac{2}{5} - \frac{1}{10}$

   (c) $\frac{4}{5} \times 160$

   (d) $8 \times 3\frac{1}{2}$

   (e) $5\frac{3}{4} - 1\frac{1}{8}$

   (f) $\frac{3}{4}$ of $(8\frac{1}{2} + 1\frac{1}{2})$.

7. Find :-

   (a) 10% of £45

   (b) 15% of £6·40

   (c) 80% of 2000

   (d) 8% of £5

   (e) $1\frac{1}{2}$% of 8000

   (f) $12\frac{1}{2}$% of 6400.

8. Find :-

   (a) $56 - 87$

   (b) $(-15) - 33$

   (c) $(-37) + 19$

   (d) $(-54) - (-35)$

   (e) $(-6) \times 13$

   (f) $(-15) \times (-5)$

   (g) $(-30)^2$

   (h) $81 \div (-9)$

   (i) $(-225) \div (-5)$

   (j) $\dfrac{(-3) \times (-15)}{-5}$

   (k) $-\frac{1}{3} \times (-57)$.

9. Draw a neat set of coordinate axes and plot :- A(–2, 3), B(5, 5) and C(0, –2). Find the 4th point (D) such that ABCD is a **parallelogram**.

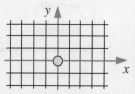

10. Write in 24 hour format :-

    (a) 5 to midnight

    (b) quarter past six in the evening

    (c) $\frac{1}{4}$ to 10 in the morning.

11. How long is it from :-

    (a) 8·37 am to 3·13 pm

    (b) 0323 to 1302 ?

12. A jet flies at 450 km/hr for 3 hours and 20 minutes. How far has the jet travelled ?

13. The diameter of a circular garden is 20 metres. Calculate the area of the garden.

14.

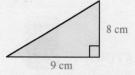

   8 cm

   9 cm

   A right angled triangle has smaller sides of length 8 cm and 9 cm.

   Find to the **nearest whole number**, the length of the longest side.

Trigonometry - an Introduction

Trigonometry is one topic in mathematics that helps you calculate the **size** of an **unknown side** in a right angled triangle. (**Pythagoras' Theorem** is another).

It can also help calculate the **size** of an **unknown angle** in a right angled triangle.

Look at the following 3 right angled triangles.   They all have **TWO** things in common.

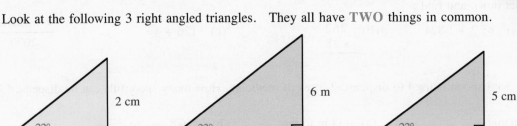

- They all have an angle in common (*in this case 22°*).
- When you divide the vertical side by the horizontal side in each case, you obtain the same answer.

$$\frac{2}{5} = 0\cdot4, \qquad \frac{6}{15} = 0\cdot4, \qquad \frac{5}{12\cdot5} = 0\cdot4.$$

For every Right Angled Triangle (*with an angle of 22°*), it is always true that when you divide the **vertical side** of the triangle by the **horizontal side**, you get an answer of $0\cdot4$.

This number, $0\cdot4$ has a special name here - It is called the "**TANGENT of 22°**" or "**tan 22°**" for short.

The Tangent (and the Naming of the Sides in a Right Angled Triangle)

Instead of **vertical** and **horizontal**, we use 3 names
to describe the sides of a right angled triangle :-

hypotenuse	- the **longest** side
opposite	- directly **across from** the angle
adjacent	- right **next to** the angle

The **Tangent** is defined as follows :-

$$=> \qquad \textbf{Tangent of angle A} = \frac{\text{opposite}}{\text{adjacent}}$$

$$\text{or} \qquad \boxed{\tan A = \frac{\text{opp}}{\text{adj}}} \qquad \text{for short.}$$

From the above triangles we saw :- $\tan 22° = \frac{2}{5} = 0\cdot4$, $\tan 22° = \frac{6}{15} = 0\cdot4$, $\tan 22° = \frac{5}{12\cdot5} = 0\cdot4$.

Note :-   Every angle from 0° to 90° has its own tangent value.

These values can be found using a **SCIENTIFIC CALCULATOR**.

1. Use the **tangent** (or tan) button on a scientific calculator to find the following tangents and give your answer correct to **3 decimal places** :-

    (a) tan 23°   (b) tan 47°   (c) tan 54°   (d) tan 85°

    (e) tan 55°   (f) tan 16°   (g) tan 4°   (h) tan 64°

    (i) tan 83°   (j) tan 45°   (k) tan 65·3°   (l) tan 3·5°.

2. Check with your calculator that tan 22° really is 0·40 (to 2 decimal places).

3. Look at this right angled triangle with $\angle G = 58°$.

    (a) What is the length of the "**opposite**" side ?

    (b) What is the length of the "**adjacent**" side ?

    (c) Divide :- (**opposite ÷ adjacent**) to get => tan 58°.

    (d) Look up tan 58° on your calculator
         to check you get the same answer.

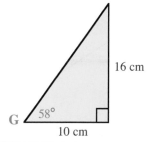

16 cm

G 58°

10 cm

Using Trigonometry to Calculate the Opposite Side

You can use your calculator, along with **tangents**, to quickly calculate the length of the **opposite** side of a right angled triangle as long as you already know the **angle** and the **adjacent side**.

Example :-

The right angled triangle shown has angle P = 25° and adjacent side = 8 cm.

Calculate the length of the **opposite side**.

$$\tan P = \frac{opp}{adj}$$

=> $\tan 25° = \frac{x}{8}$

=> $0·466... = \frac{x}{8}$

=> $x = 8 \times 0·466... = 3·7304.....$

=> $x = 3·7$ cm (*to 1 decimal place*)

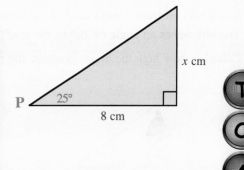

P 25°   8 cm   x cm

T
O
A

---

1. Make a sketch of this right angled triangle and use the method shown above to calculate the size of the **opposite** side.

$$\tan C = \frac{opp}{adj}$$

=> $\tan 65° = \frac{x}{15}$

=> $x = ... \times \tan 65°$

=> $x = ... $ cm   (*to 1 decimal place*)

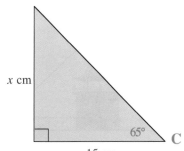

x cm

65° C

15 cm

2. Sketch each of these right angled triangles and use **tangents** to calculate the length of the opposite side (x cm) in each case, to 1 decimal place :-

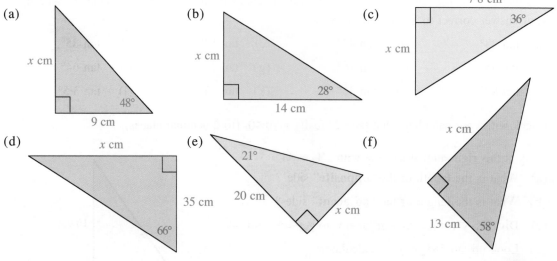

(a) x cm 48° 9 cm

(b) x cm 28° 14 cm

(c) 7·8 cm 36° x cm

(d) x cm 66°

(e) 21° 35 cm 20 cm x cm

(f) x cm 13 cm 58°

3. From a point 80 metres away from the foot of the pagoda, the angle of elevation of the top is measured as 35°.

Calculate the height of the pagoda.

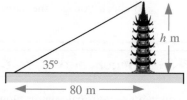

h m 35° 80 m

4.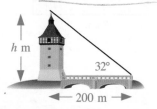

h m 18° 25 metres

The angle of elevation of the top of a tree from a point 25 metres from its foot is 18°.

Calculate the height of the tree.

5. A hill runs up from a main road to the house at the top. The hill makes an angle of 20° to the road.

Calculate how high the house is above the road.

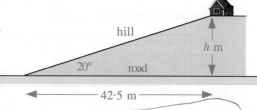

hill h m 20° road 42·5 m

6.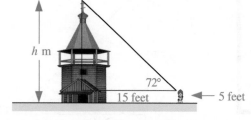

h m 32° 200 m

From the far end of a bridge, the angle of elevation of a belfry is 32°.

If it is 200 metres from the far end of the bridge to the foot of the belfry, how high is the belfry ?

7. From the top of a cliff, a small boat is observed at an angle of depression of 19°.

If the boat is 120 metres from the foot of the cliff, find the height of the cliff.

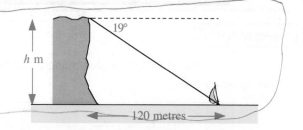

19° h m 120 metres

8. h m 72° 15 feet 5 feet

A girl, whose eyes are 5 feet above ground-level, is attempting to measure the height of this tower.

She is standing 15 feet from the tower looking to the top at an angle of 72° to the horizontal.

How high is the tower ?

Calculating an Angle using the Tangent

Qu. Imagine you already know that **tan A = 0·9**.

How can you work backwards to find the size of ∠A ?

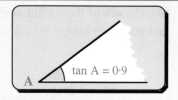

tan A = 0·9

Ans. You press **two** buttons (shift) (tan) along with **0·9** and the answer **42** appears.

(In some calculators it is (2nd) (tan) and in others it is (Inv) (tan))

* check with your teacher

Example :-

The right angled triangle shown has sides AB = 8 cm and BC = 5 cm.

Calculate the size of angle BAC.

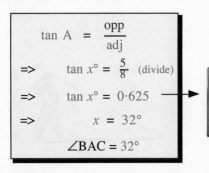

tan A = $\frac{\text{opp}}{\text{adj}}$

=> tan x° = $\frac{5}{8}$ (divide)

=> tan x° = 0·625

=> x = 32°

∠BAC = 32°

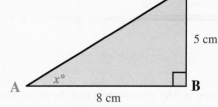

PRESS your 2 buttons NOW

C

5 cm

A x°

8 cm

B

T

O

A

Exercise 19·3

1. Check which buttons you need to press on **YOUR** calculator and find the sizes of the angles A, B, C ..... to the nearest degree :-

   (a) tan A = 0·466   (b) tan B = 1·483

   (c) tan C = 0·249   (d) tan D = 0·105

   (e) tan E = 1   (f) tan F = 0·781

   (g) tan G = $\frac{2}{5}$ (h) tan H = $\frac{3}{14}$

   (i) tan I = $\frac{9}{4}$ (j) tan J = $\frac{23}{2}$.

2. Make a sketch of this right angled triangle and use the method shown above to calculate the size of ∠RPQ, to 1 decimal place.

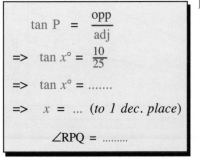

tan P = $\frac{\text{opp}}{\text{adj}}$

=> tan x° = $\frac{10}{25}$

=> tan x° = ...

=> x = ... (to 1 dec. place)

∠RPQ = ...

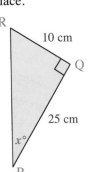

R

10 cm

Q

25 cm

x°

P

3. Do the same for the following triangles. Calculate the sizes of angles y° and z° (*to 1 decimal place*).

   (a)

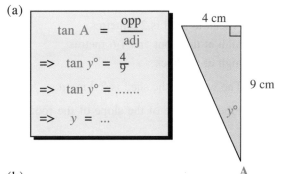

tan A = $\frac{\text{opp}}{\text{adj}}$

=> tan y° = $\frac{4}{9}$

=> tan y° = ...

=> y = ...

4 cm

9 cm

y°

A

   (b)

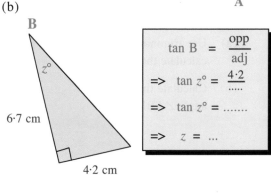

B

z°

6·7 cm

4·2 cm

tan B = $\frac{\text{opp}}{\text{adj}}$

=> tan z° = $\frac{4·2}{.....}$

=> tan z° = ...

=> z = ...

4. Sketch each of these right angled triangles and use **tangent** to calculate the size of angles $a, b, ... f,$ and give each correct to 1 decimal place :-

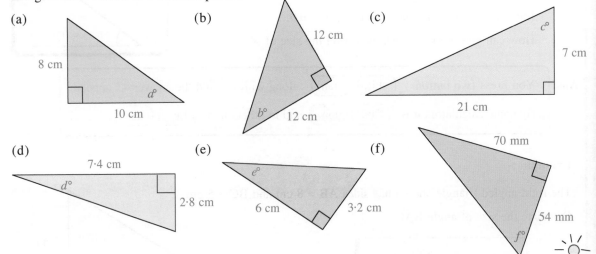

(a)

8 cm
10 cm
$d°$

(b)

12 cm
12 cm
$b°$

(c)

$c°$
7 cm
21 cm

(d)

7·4 cm
$d°$
2·8 cm

(e)

$e°$
6 cm
3·2 cm

(f)

70 mm
54 mm
$f°$

5. Winston is 185 centimetres tall. In the sunshine he casts a shadow on the ground 300 centimetres long.

Find the angle of elevation $(x°)$ of the sun.

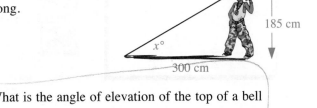

185 cm
$x°$
300 cm

6.

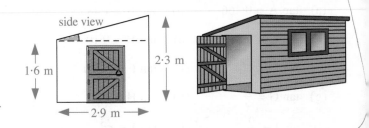

100 ft
$x°$
35 ft

What is the angle of elevation of the top of a bell tower 100 feet high, from a point on level ground 35 feet from the base of the tower ?

7. A lean-to shed is 2·3 metres high at the front and 1·6 metres high at the back.

The width of the shed is 2·9 metres.

Find the angle of the slope of the roof.

side view

1·6 m
2·3 m
2·9 m

8. Triangle ADC is right angled at C.

(a) Use trigonometry to calculate the size of ∠BDC.

(b) Calculate the size of angle ∠ABD.

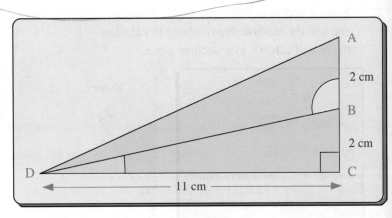

A
2 cm
B
2 cm
D
C
11 cm

The Sine Ratio

In a similar way to the tangent ratio, where you worked with the opposite and the adjacent sides of a right angled triangle, there is another trig ratio, called the **Sine Ratio** where you again work with 2 sides, – this time, the **opposite** and the **hypotenuse**.

For every given angle (A) in a right angled triangle, the **sine of A°** (or **sin A°** for short) is defined as :-

$$\Rightarrow \quad \text{Sine of angle A} = \frac{\text{opposite}}{\text{hypotenuse}}$$

or $\boxed{\text{Sin A} = \dfrac{\text{opp}}{\text{hyp}}}$ for short.

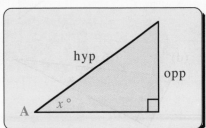

Example 1 :-

The right angled triangle below has

* angle Q = 25° and
* hypotenuse = 8 cm.

Calculate the length of the **opposite side**.

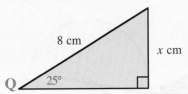

$$\sin Q = \frac{\text{opp}}{\text{hyp}}$$

$$\Rightarrow \quad \sin 25° = \frac{x}{8}$$

$$\Rightarrow \quad x = 8 \sin 25° = 3{\cdot}3809.....$$

$$\Rightarrow \quad x = 3{\cdot}4 \text{ cm } (\textit{to 1 dec. place})$$

Example 2 :-

The right angled triangle below has sides

$$BC = 5 \text{ cm and } AC = 8 \text{ cm}.$$

Calculate the size of **angle BAC**.

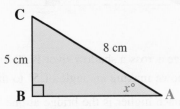

$$\sin A = \frac{\text{opp}}{\text{hyp}}$$

$$\Rightarrow \quad \sin x° = \frac{5}{8}$$

$$\Rightarrow \quad \sin x° = 0{\cdot}625 \rightarrow \boxed{\text{shift}}$$

$$\Rightarrow \quad x = 38{\cdot}7° \leftarrow \boxed{\text{sin}}$$

$$\angle BAC = 38{\cdot}7°$$

Exercise 19·4

1. Check which buttons you need to press on **YOUR** calculator, if you don't already know. Find the following :-

    (a) sin 50°   (b) sin 30°

    (c) sin 60°   (d) sin 84°

    (e) sin 7°   (f) sin 28·5°

    (g) sin 19·8°   (h) sin 72°

    (i) sin 89·9°   (j) sin 90°.

2. Use your calculator to determine the sizes of angles A, B, C, ... (*to 1 decimal place*).

    (a) $\sin A = \frac{2}{5}$ (b) $\sin B = \frac{3}{14}$

    (c) $\sin C = \frac{4}{9}$ (d) $\sin D = \frac{24}{25}$

    (e) $\sin E = \frac{1}{8}$ (f) $\sin F = \frac{2}{11}$

    (g) $\sin G = \frac{17}{34}$ (h) $\sin H = \frac{1}{4}$

    (i) $\sin I = \frac{2 \cdot 5}{7 \cdot 5}$ (j) $\sin J = \frac{6 \cdot 4}{10 \cdot 9}$.

3. Sketch each of these right angled triangles and use **sine** to calculate the length of the opposite side (x cm) in each case, (*to 1 decimal place*) :-

(a)
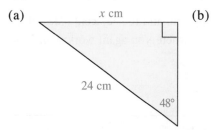
x cm
24 cm
48°

(b)
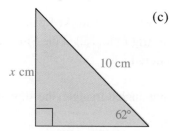
x cm
10 cm
62°

(c)
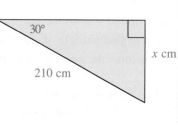
30°
210 cm
x cm

(d)
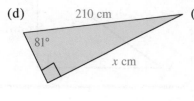
210 cm
81°
x cm

(e)
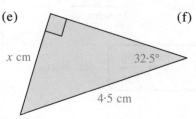
x cm
32·5°
4·5 cm

(f)
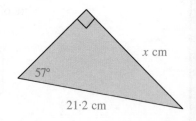
x cm
57°
21·2 cm

4.
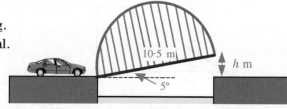
3·5 m
h m
30°

A plank is 3·5 metres long, and lies at an angle of 30° to the ground.

It is just touching the top of a wall.

Calculate the height (h metres) of this wall.

5. A bridge across a shallow river is 10·5 metres long.
It is shown making an angle of 5° to the horizontal.

How much higher is the bridge at one end than it is at the other at this stage ?

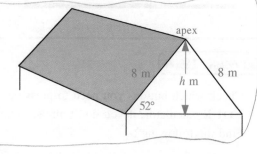
10·5 m
h m
5°

6.
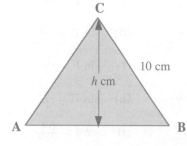
h km
4·8 km
18·5°

An aeroplane takes off in a straight line at an angle of 18·5° to the horizontal and flies for 4·8 km on this path.

What height is the plane at that point ?

7. The angle of slope of a roof is 52°.

If the sloping part is 8 metres long, how high is the apex above the foot of the roof ?

apex
8 m
h m
8 m
52°

8.
C
10 cm
h cm
A   B

Triangle ABC is an **equilateral** triangle of side 10 cm.

(a) Write down the size of ∠BAC.

(b) Calculate its height (h cm), **using trigonometry**.

(c) Now check your answer using **Pythagoras' Theorem**.

9. Sketch each of these right angled triangles and use **sine** to calculate the size of angles $a, b, c.....f$.
   (*Answer correct to 1 decimal place*).

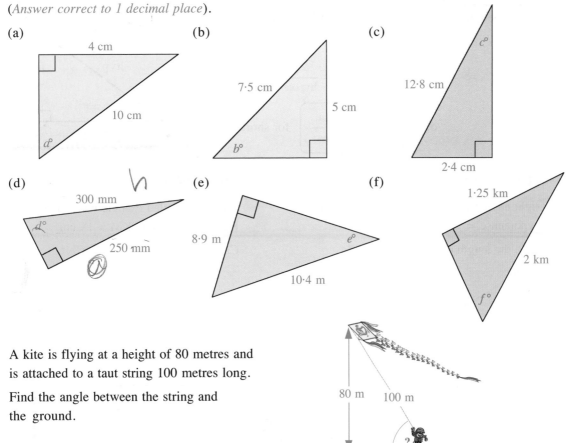

(a)
4 cm
10 cm
$a°$

(b)
7·5 cm
5 cm
$b°$

(c)
$c°$
12·8 cm
2·4 cm

(d)
300 mm
$d°$
250 mm

(e)
8·9 m
$e°$
10·4 m

(f)
1·25 km
2 km
$f°$

10. A kite is flying at a height of 80 metres and is attached to a taut string 100 metres long.

    Find the angle between the string and the ground.

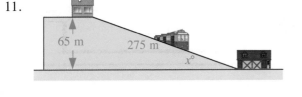

80 m   100 m   ?

11.

65 m   275 m $x°$

A funicular railway is 275 metres long and the difference between the height from the top to the bottom is 65 metres.

Find the angle of inclination between the railway and the ground.

12. The hand-rail of a staircase is 12 metres long. Its lower end is 1·4 metres above ground and its upper end 4·6 metres above ground.

    Find the angle between the hand-rail and the horizontal.
    (*Draw a sketch to show the required angle*).

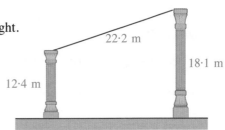

12 m   4·6 m   1·4 m

13. Two vertical columns are 12·4 metres and 18·1 metres in height. A wire, stretched from top to top, is 22·2 metres long.

    Find the angle of the slope of the wire.
    (*Draw a sketch to show the required angle*).

22·2 m   18·1 m   12·4 m

For every given angle (A) in a right angled triangle, the **cosine of A°** (or **cos A°** for short) is defined as :-

=> Cosine of angle A = $\dfrac{\text{adjacent}}{\text{hypotenuse}}$

or $\boxed{\text{Cos A} = \dfrac{\text{adj}}{\text{hyp}}}$ for short.

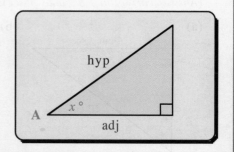

Example 1 :-

The right angled triangle below has angle M = 18° and hypotenuse = 9 cm.

Calculate the length of the **adjacent side**.

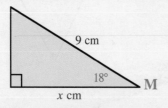

$\cos M = \dfrac{\text{adj}}{\text{hyp}}$

=> $\cos 18° = \dfrac{x}{9}$

=> $x = 9 \cos 18° = 8\cdot559.....$

=> $x = 8\cdot6$ cm (*to 1 decimal place*)

Example 2 :-

The right angled triangle below has sides KL = 14·5 cm and KM = 18 cm.

Calculate the size of **angle MKL**.

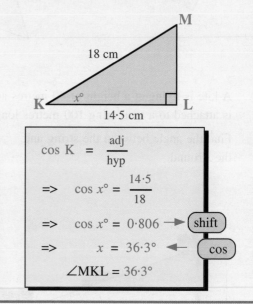

$\cos K = \dfrac{\text{adj}}{\text{hyp}}$

=> $\cos x° = \dfrac{14\cdot5}{18}$

=> $\cos x° = 0\cdot806$ → shift

=> $x = 36\cdot3°$ ← cos

∠MKL = 36·3°

Exercise 19·5

1. Check which buttons you need to press on **YOUR** calculator, if you don't already know. Find the following :-

   (a) cos 40°   (b) cos 80°

   (c) cos 60°   (d) cos 30°

   (e) cos 5°   (f) cos 52·5°.

2. Use your calculator to determine the sizes of angles A, B, C, ...

   (a) $\cos A = \frac{4}{5}$ (b) $\cos B = \frac{5}{14}$

   (c) $\cos C = \frac{1}{9}$ (d) $\cos D = \frac{21}{25}$

   (e) $\cos E = \frac{2}{11}$ (f) $\cos F = \frac{7}{8}$.

3. Sketch each of these right angled triangles and use **cosine** to calculate the length of the adjacent side (x cm) in each case.

   (*to 1 decimal place*) :-

   (a)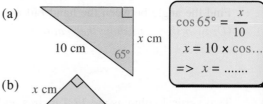

   $\cos 65° = \dfrac{x}{10}$

   $x = 10 \times \cos...$

   => $x = ...$

   (b)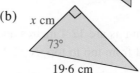

   (c)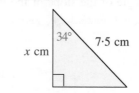

4. The diagonal of this rectangle ABCD is 25 centimetres long.

Calculate the length of the side DC.

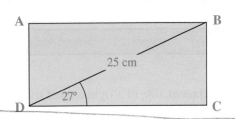

5.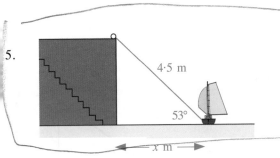

A yacht is moored to the quay wall by a rope 4·5 metres long. When the rope is taut, it makes an angle of 53° with the surface of the sea.

How far is the yacht from the quay wall ?

6. This umbrella has a cord joining the end of the handle to one of the "prongs" of the cover.

Calculate the length of the handle shown (x).

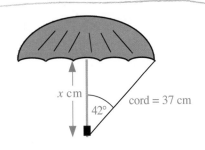

7.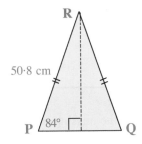

Triangle PQR is isosceles with

- side PR = 50·8 cm.
- ∠RPQ is 84°.

Calculate the length of side PQ.

8. A new floodlight has to be held in place overnight to enable its concrete base to dry. It is secured by two strong metal wires. The longer wire is 39 metres in length and is attached to the ground 30 metres from the base of the floodlight.

Calculate the angle this wire makes with the ground.

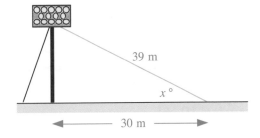

9.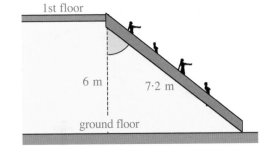

An escalator connects the 1st floor to the ground floor 6 metres below.

(a) If the escalator is 7·2 metres long, calculate the size of the angle between the escalator and the vertical.

(b) Write down the size of the angle between the escalator and the ground floor.

10. Triangle KLM is **isosceles** with sides ML = 240 mm and MK = 74 mm.

Calculate the size of angle MKL.

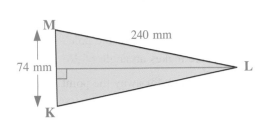

A Mixture of Tangents, Sines and Cosines - Trickier Examples

Finding :-

      1. the **adjacent** side of a right angled triangle using **tan**.

      2. the **hypotenuse** of a right angled triangle using **sin**.

      3. the **hypotenuse** of a right angled triangle using **cos**.

Example 1 :-

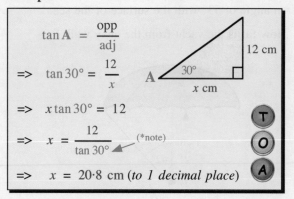

$$\tan A = \frac{opp}{adj}$$

$$=> \quad \tan 30° = \frac{12}{x}$$

$$=> \quad x \tan 30° = 12$$

$$=> \quad x = \frac{12}{\tan 30°} \quad \text{(*note)}$$

$$=> \quad x = 20\!\cdot\!8 \text{ cm } (\textit{to 1 decimal place})$$

Example 2 :-

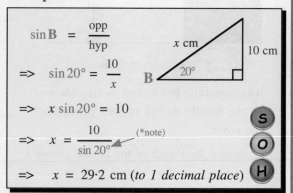

$$\sin B = \frac{opp}{hyp}$$

$$=> \quad \sin 20° = \frac{10}{x}$$

$$=> \quad x \sin 20° = 10$$

$$=> \quad x = \frac{10}{\sin 20°} \quad \text{(*note)}$$

$$=> \quad x = 29\!\cdot\!2 \text{ cm } (\textit{to 1 decimal place})$$

Example 3 :-

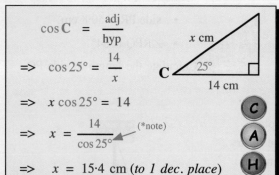

$$\cos C = \frac{adj}{hyp}$$

$$=> \quad \cos 25° = \frac{14}{x}$$

$$=> \quad x \cos 25° = 14$$

$$=> \quad x = \frac{14}{\cos 25°} \quad \text{(*note)}$$

$$=> \quad x = 15\!\cdot\!4 \text{ cm } (\textit{to 1 dec. place})$$

* note :-

When the missing length, (the x), appears on the **bottom** of the fraction, you end up "swapping" it with the *sin*, *tan* or *cos*.

Exercise 19·6

1.   Use **tangent** to calculate the length of the **adjacent side** in each case, (*to 1 decimal place*) :-

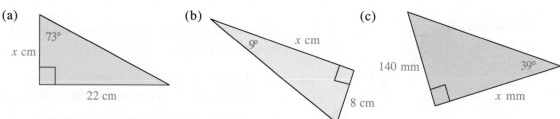

(a) 73° x cm   22 cm

(b) 9° x cm 8 cm

(c) 140 mm 39° x mm

2.   Use **tangent** in this question.

The 5·9 metre telephone pole has a support cable attached from its top to a point on the ground, along from the base of the pole.

The cable makes an angle of 36° with the ground.

Calculate how far away the point is from the pole.

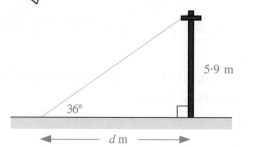

5·9 m

36°

d m

3. Use **sin** to calculate the length of the **hypotenuse** in each case, (*to 1 decimal place*) :-

(a)
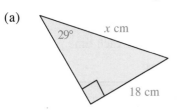

(b)
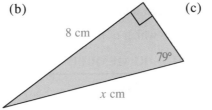

(c)
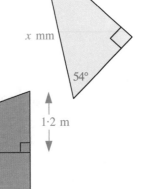

4. Use **sin** in this question.

The angle between the sloping roof on this house and the horizontal is 23°.

From the ceiling of the room to the top of the roof is 1·2 metres.

What is the length of the sloping roof ?

5. Use **cos** to calculate the length of the **hypotenuse** in each case, (*to 1 decimal place*) :-

(a)
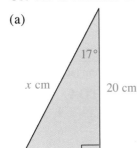

(b)
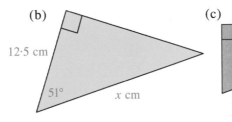

(c)
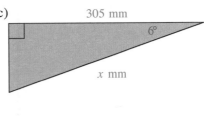

6. Use **cos** in this question.

A pencil lies with its end just resting against a book.

The point of the pencil sits on a table 14·5 cm from the binding of the book.

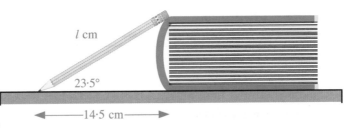

If the angle between the pencil and the table top is 23·5°, calculate the length of the pencil.

7.
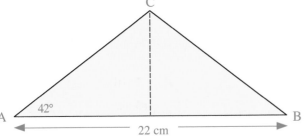

Shown is an **isosceles** triangle with

- ∠BAC = 42°
- base AB = 22 cm.

Calculate the **perimeter** of triangle ABC.

8. PQRS is a trapezium with

- ∠QPS and ∠RSP = 90°
- ∠PQR = 125°
- PS = 8·4 cm

Calculate the length of the sloping line QR.

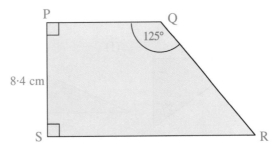

SOHCAHTOA

Up till now in this chapter you have been told which ratio to use **sin - cos - tan**.

Now, **YOU** have to decide which of the three ratios you must use each time.

REMEMBER - REMEMBER - REMEMBER

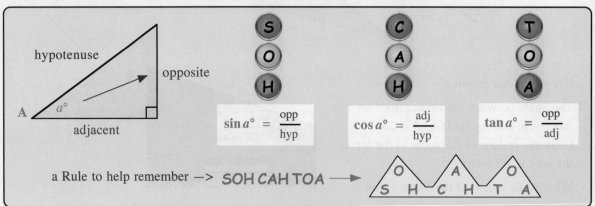

$$\sin a° = \frac{opp}{hyp}$$

$$\cos a° = \frac{adj}{hyp}$$

$$\tan a° = \frac{opp}{adj}$$

a Rule to help remember —> SOH CAH TOA

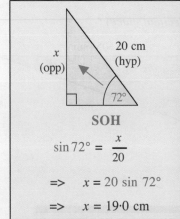

SOH

$$\sin 72° = \frac{x}{20}$$

$$=> \quad x = 20 \sin 72°$$

$$=> \quad x = 19.0 \text{ cm}$$

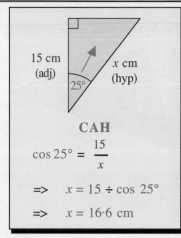

CAH

$$\cos 25° = \frac{15}{x}$$

$$=> \quad x = 15 \div \cos 25°$$

$$=> \quad x = 16.6 \text{ cm}$$

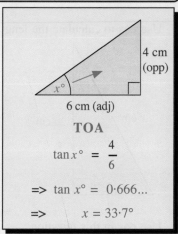

TOA

$$\tan x° = \frac{4}{6}$$

$$=> \tan x° = 0.666...$$

$$=> \quad x = 33.7°$$

Exercise 19·7

1. Choose your ratio from **SOHCAHTOA** to find the value of x in each case, (*to 1 decimal place*).

2. Choose the correct ratio to find the size of angle $x°$ in each case, (*to 1 decimal place*).

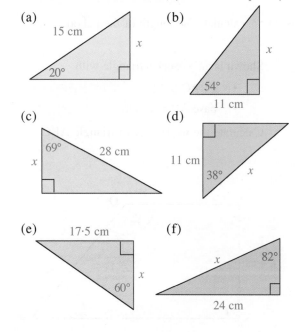

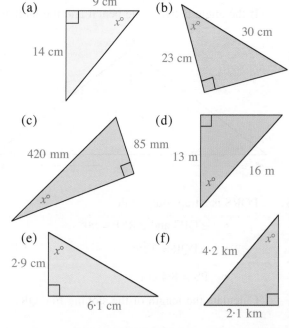

3. The angle of elevation from the ground to the top of an apartment block is 42·5°. The angle is measured at a point 43 metres from the block.

Calculate the height, h metres, of the apartment block, correct to 1 decimal place.

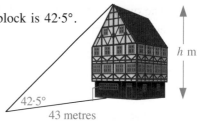

42·5°
43 metres

4.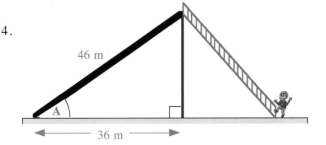

46 m

A

36 m

A park has a new slide 46 metres long. The foot of the slide is 36 metres from the metal support pole.

Calculate the size of the angle (**A**), between the slide and the ground.

5. At low tide, passengers have to disembark from the ship, up a gangway, to the dockside.

The water level is 17 feet below the top edge of the dockside and the gangway is at an angle of 22° to the water.

Calculate the length of the gangway.

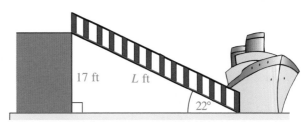

17 ft L ft

22°

6.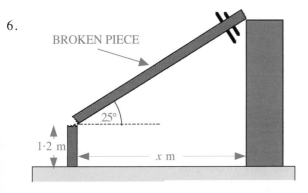

BROKEN PIECE

25°

1·2 m

x m

A telegraph pole was 9 metres in height before it snapped during a storm and toppled over.

The top of the pole came to rest on a wall as shown.

(a) Use the information in the diagram to write down the length of the broken piece.

(b) Now calculate how far the base of the pole was from the wall.

7. In a school hall, the stage is lit by a spotlight fixed to a wall.

The spotlight is 4·62 metres up the wall and is set to shine on a spot on the stage at a downward angle of 70°, as shown.

Calculate the length of the beam of light.

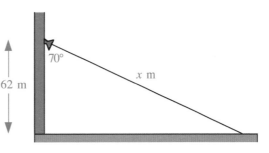

70°

x m

4·62 m

8.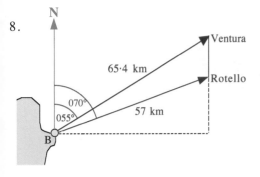

N

Ventura

65·4 km

Rotello

070°
055°

57 km

B

Two ships, the Ventura and the Rotello, set sail from Barlow Harbour.

- the Ventura sails for 65·4 km on a bearing of 055°.
- the Rotello sails for 57 km on a bearing of 070°.

At that point, the Ventura was directly North of the Rotello.

How far apart were the two ships ?

9. The owners of Kingston Hall Manor erected an accessible entrance ramp at the main front entrance.

Local building regulations stated that ramps had to be built at an angle of not more than 13·8° to the horizontal ground.

A side view of the ramp which was actually erected is shown.

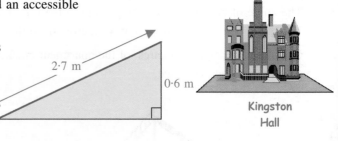

2·7 m

0·6 m

Kingston Hall

Did this ramp satisfy the local building regulations ?

10.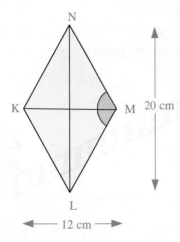

N

K   M   20 cm

L

← 12 cm →

KLMN is a rhombus.

Its diagonals LN and KM are 20 centimetres and 12 centimetres long respectively.

Calculate the size of the shaded angle NML.

11. The figure shows a square PQRS with a right angled triangle APS attached.

AS = 12 centimetres, ∠SAP = 60°.

Calculate the **area** of square PQRS.

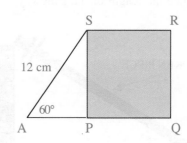

S   R

12 cm

60°

A   P   Q

12.

14·9 m

75°

← x m →

A taxi is parked next to a cable supporting the car park floodlights.

This cable makes an angle of 75° with the ground.

The height from the ground to the lights is 14·9 metres.

How far away is the foot of the cable from the base of the floodlight pole ?

13. The design of a wheel for a wheelbarrow is shown. The safety requirements state that angle (x) must be greater than 35°.

Part of this design has its measurements as shown.

Do these measurements satisfy the safety requirements ?

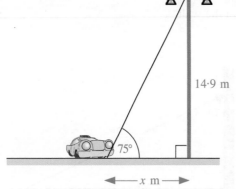

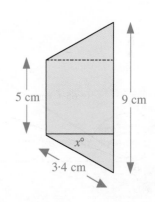

5 cm

9 cm

x°

3·4 cm

1. Calculate the value of x in each case, to 1 decimal place :-

(a)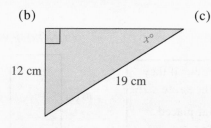

15 cm

45°

x cm

(b)

12 cm

19 cm

$x°$

(c)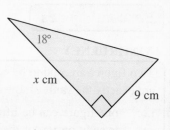

18°

x cm

9 cm

In Questions **2, 3 and 4**, it will be of some help to draw an appropriate diagram.

2. A 15 metre ladder, resting against a wall, is secured 6·5 metres from the foot of the wall.

Calculate the angle the ladder makes with the ground.

3. A boy who is 1·2 metres tall flies a kite on a string of length 36 metres.

The string of the kite makes an angle of 62° with the horizontal.

What is the **height** of the kite above the ground ?

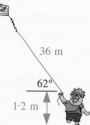

36 m

62°

1·2 m

4.

22°

1262 m

1140 m

Two mountains are 1140 metres and 1262 metres high.

A man, standing on the peak of the lower one looks up through an angle of elevation of 22° to see the summit of the higher peak.

Calculate the horizontal distance between the peaks.

5. A camera is placed at the top of a 90 metre skyscraper.

Two cars are viewed from the camera with angles of depression of 31° and 47°.

(a) How far is each car from the base of the tower ?

(b) How far apart are the cars, (*to 2 sig. figs.*) ?

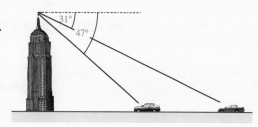

31°

47°

6. A ship leaves harbour and travels 25 kilometres due South and then 18 kilometres due West.

On what **bearing** must it travel to return to harbour ? (*to the nearest degree*).

N

25 km

18 km

7. A glass has a **radius** of 4·5 centimetres.

The red straw in the glass makes an angle of 72° with the base and protrudes 4 centimetres above the rim of the glass.

How long is the straw ?

4 cm

72°

radius 4·5 cm

Similar Figures

CONGRUENCY

Two figures are said to be **congruent** if they are exactly the **same shape** and the **same size**.

i.e.   one figure can be lifted and placed exactly on top of the other.

CONGRUENT

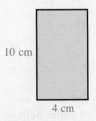

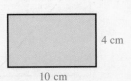

same shape - rectangles

same size - both 10 cm by 4 cm

SIMILARITY

Two figures are said to be **similar** if they are basically the **same shape**, with one being an **enlargement** or a **reduction** of the other.

The two **similar** shapes will have :-

- their **corresponding angles equal**
- their **corresponding sides in the same ratio**
  (*the same scale factor*)

SIMILAR

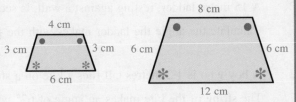

both trapezia - corresponding angles equal

scale factor :- $\dfrac{12}{6} = \dfrac{8}{4} = \dfrac{6}{3} = 2$

Example 1 :-

These two shapes are **similar**.

(a)   Calculate the (**enlargement**) scale factor.

(b)   Calculate the length of the side marked x.

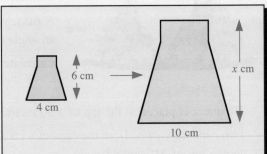

Solution

(a) $S.F. = \dfrac{10}{4} = 2\cdot5$

(b) $x = 6 \times 2\cdot5 = $ **15 cm**

Example 2 :-

The two cars shown are **similar**, one car being a model of the other.

(a)   Calculate the (**reduction**) scale factor.

(b)   Calculate the height (x) of the model car.

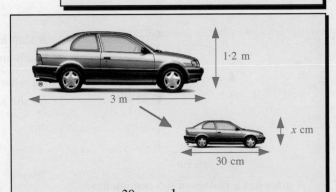

Solution

(a) $S.F. = \dfrac{30}{300} = \dfrac{1}{10}$ or $0\cdot1$

(b) $=> x = 0\cdot1 \times 1\cdot2 = 0\cdot12$ m $= $ **12 cm**

1. Look at the following ten shapes.

   Match them up in **congruent** pairs.

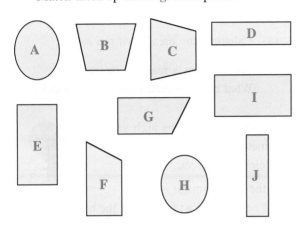

2. Prove that the two objects in each question below are similar. (*Hint - check the ratios*)

   (a)

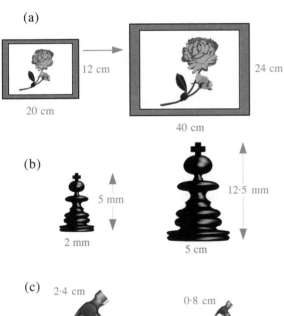

   12 cm 24 cm

   20 cm 40 cm

   (b)

   5 mm 12·5 mm

   2 mm 5 cm

   (c) 2·4 cm 0·8 cm

   10 cm

   30 cm

   (d) 16 mm 12 mm

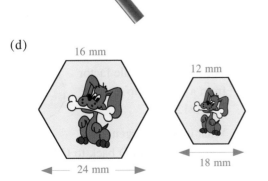

   24 mm 18 mm

3. Which of the quadrilaterals B, C, D, E **might** be and which **cannot** be similar to figure **A** ? (*Justify your answer*).

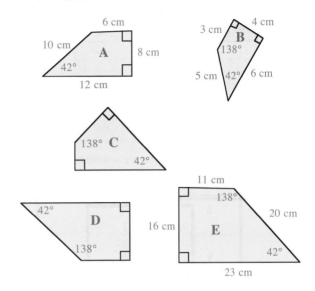

4. Each of these pairs of figures are **similar**.

   (i) Find the **scale factor** for each.

   (ii) Calculate the missing lengths.

   (a) 5 cm ◄ 9 cm ► ◄ ? cm ► 10 cm

   (b) 22 mm ? mm

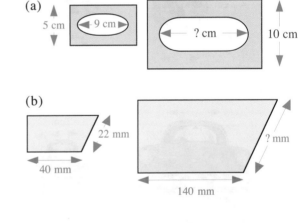

   40 mm 140 mm

   (c) 0·3 m ? m

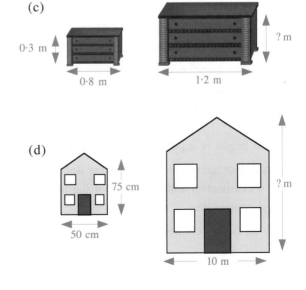

   0·8 m 1·2 m

   (d) 75 cm ? m

   50 cm 10 m

5. For each pair of similar shapes, find the scale factor and the missing measurement.

(a)
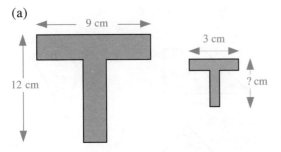

(b) These two rectangles are **similar**.

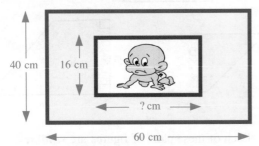

(c)
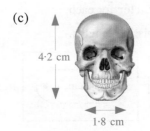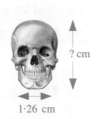

(d)
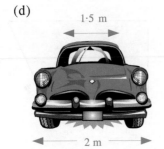

6. An aircraft has a length of 24 metres and a wing-span of 32 metres.

A scaled model is to be made with a wing span of 12 centimetres.

Calculate the length of the model.

7. The height of a porch door is 1·8 metres.

In a photograph, the height of the door is 0·6 centimetres and the height of the house 2·4 centimetres.

What is the **real** height of the house ?

8. A cruise ship is 240 metres long and 40 metres broad at its widest point.

A model of the ship is to be made which is 30 centimetres long.

(a) Calculate the breadth of the model.

(b) The ship has a mast 12 metres high. What height would it be on the model ?

9. A pagoda, 15 metres high and 9 metres wide, appears on a television screen.

If the screen image is 5·4 centimetres wide, what is the height of the pagoda on the TV screen ?

10. A photograph 10 cm high and 8 cm wide is enlarged to give a print 14 cm wide.

What is the height of the enlarged print ?

11. The 3 prints of this mouse are similar.

(a) Calculate the length of the middle mouse.

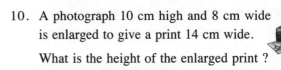

(b) Calculate the height of the largest mouse.

(c) If the tail of the smallest mouse is 30 mm, calculate the lengths of the tails of the other mice.

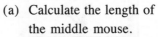

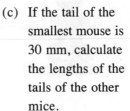
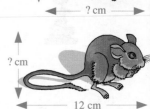

12. (a) The **enlargement** scale factor from a shape A to a shape B is $\frac{8}{5}$.

What must the **reduction** scale factor be from B back to A ?

(b) The **reduction** scale factor from a shape C to a shape D is 0·125.

What is the **enlargement** scale factor from D back to C ?

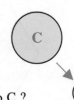

Similar Triangles

Triangles are special.

> If pairs of corresponding angles are equal,
>
> => ratios of corresponding sides are equal.
>
> => triangles are similar.

> If ratio of pairs of corresponding sides are equal,
>
> => corresponding angles are equal.
>
> => triangles are similar.

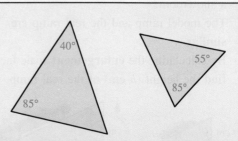

The triangles above are **equiangular** (both have angles 85°, 40° and 55°).

The triangles are **similar**.

Their corresponding sides must be in the same ratio.

Example :-

Shelf brackets are made in two sizes. They are **similar right angled triangles**.
By calculating the **enlargement** scale factor first, find the length of the edge marked x.

Solution :-

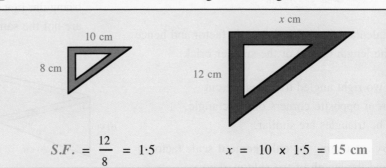

$$S.F. = \frac{12}{8} = 1{\cdot}5 \qquad x = 10 \times 1{\cdot}5 = \boxed{15 \text{ cm}}$$

Exercise 20·2

1. Which of these pairs of triangles are **similar** ?

(a)

(b)

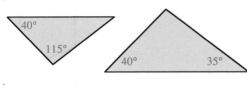

(c)

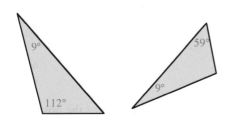

2. Arrange the sides in order of size to help you calculate which pairs of triangles have their corresponding sides in proportion and hence are **similar**. (Units are in centimetres).

(a)

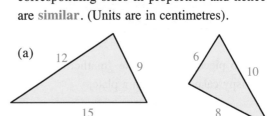

(b)

(c)

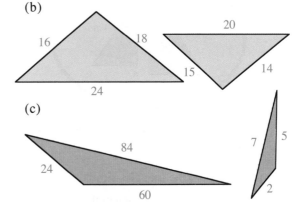

3. A model is made of a car on a ramp in a showroom.
The model ramp and the real ramp are **similar**.
By calculating the **enlargement** scale factor, find the height (h cm) of the real ramp.

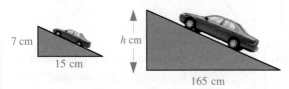

4. A triangular monoblocking slab comes in two sizes. The bricks are **similar** in shape.

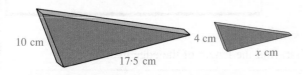

Calculate the **reduction** scale factor and hence the length (x cm) of the smaller brick.

5. Two right angled triangles are cut from opposite corners of a rectangle. The triangles are similar.

By calculating the **enlargement** scale factor, find the length of the side marked x.

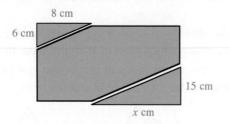

6. Two pieces of chocolate "mathematical" crispy cake are laid on a plate.

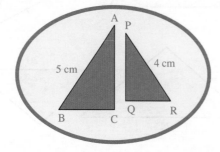

The angles at C and Q are right angled and
$\angle ABC = \angle PRQ$.

(a) Why are the triangles similar ?

(b) If BC = 2 cm, calculate QR.

7. A young boy buys a plastic traffic sign to go at a road junction on his play mat. Sketches of his plastic traffic sign and the real traffic sign are shown below.

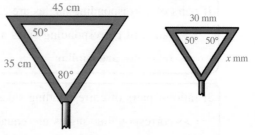

(a) Prove that the triangles are **similar**.

(b) Calculate the size of the side marked x.

8. A bottle of medicine is sitting on a shelf in the bathroom.

The shelf is supported by two right angled triangular brackets, shown in yellow, which are not the same size.

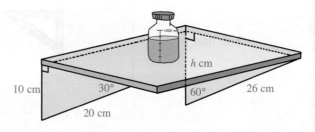

(a) Are the triangular supports **similar** ? Justify your answer.

(b) Calculate the height of the larger bracket h.

9. The figure below shows an American Football goal and its shadow.
Each post casts a shadow 18 metres long.
The part of the post below the crossbar is 3 metres high and casts a shadow 8 metres long.

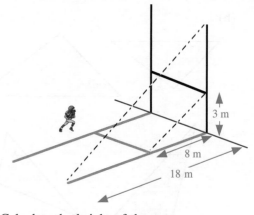

Calculate the height of the posts.

Example 1 :-

In the figure, QR is parallel to ST.

All units are centimetres.

(a)   Prove that ΔPQR is similar to ΔPST.

(b)   Calculate the value of *x*.

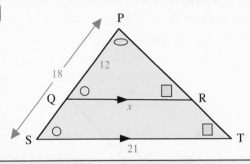

(a)   As QR is parallel to ST :-

∠PQR = ∠PST ○ corresponding angles (*F shape*)

∠PRQ = ∠PTS □ corresponding angles (*F shape*)

∠QPR = ∠SPT ○ common angle

=> Triangles are **equiangular** and so are **similar**.

(b)   *SF* (reduction) = $\frac{12}{18}$ $\left(=\frac{2}{3}\right)$

$x = \frac{12}{18} \times 21 = \boxed{14}$ (or $\frac{2}{3} \times 21 = 14$)

Example 2 :-

Calculate the value of *p* in this figure.

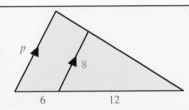

SF (enlargement) = $\frac{18}{12}$ NOT $\frac{12}{6}$

=> $p = \frac{18}{12} \times 8 = \boxed{12}$

Exercise 20·3

1.   For each triangle, calculate :-

(i)   the **enlargement** or **reduction** scale factor.

(ii)   the length of the side marked *x*.

(All units are in centimetres)

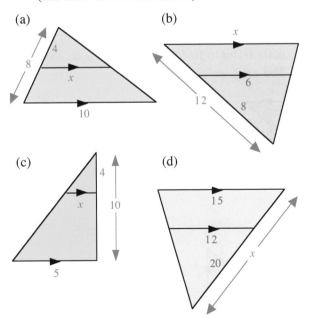

(a)

(b)

(c)

(d)

2.   The map below shows the motorway routes from the town of Appleby (A) to Dunsport (D) and Ealing (E) along with the two minor roads BC and DE which link the motorways.

The minor roads are parallel to each other.

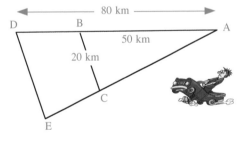

(a) Prove that ΔABC is **similar** to ΔADE.

(b) Calculate the length of the minor road linking Dunsport and Ealing.

(c) If the motorway linking Appleby with Ealing is 96 km in length, calculate :-

(i)   how far it is from Appleby to Corby (C).

(ii)   the distance from Corby to Dunsport via Ealing.

3. The neighbourhood watch volunteers in the town of Fintry have nicknamed themselves "The Fintry Volunteers" (**F–V**) and have adopted the emblem shown below.

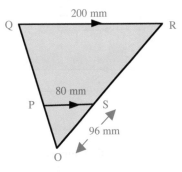

Calculate the length of :-

(a) OR

(b) SR.

4. (a) For the figure below, explain why the triangles are similar.

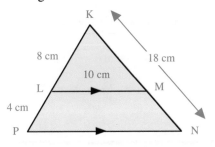

(b) Calculate the length of :-

(i) PN

(ii) KM.

5. The McCaig family want to convert the roof space in their villa into a spare bedroom.

The roof space with some measurements are shown below.

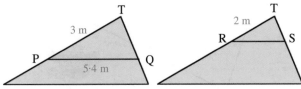

The position, PQ, of the wooden beam must be altered to position RS, as shown.

The wooden beam must always be parallel to the floor.

Calculate the length of the wooden beam in its new position RS.

6. Calculate the values of v, w, x and y in the figures below.

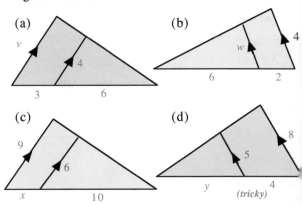

7. (a) **Copy** the figure below and carefully mark in the equal angles.

(*It has been done for you this time !*)

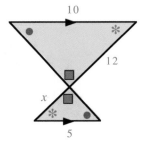

(b) Use the appropriate pair of corresponding sides (here ✳ and ●) to find the **reduction** (or enlargement) scale factor.

$$\frac{5}{10} = ...$$

(c) Now use this scale factor to find x.

$$x = \frac{1}{2} \times ..... = ...$$

8. Sketch each of the following triangles, mark in equal angles and use the **reduction/enlargement** scale factor to find the letters a, b, c, d, x and y. The units are centimetres.

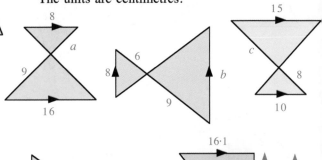

Similar Areas

The two figures shown are similar.
The **red** one shows a 3 by 2 grid.
The **blue** shows a 9 by 6 grid.
The **linear** scale factor is 3.
But the **area** scale factor is 9. (6 boxes —> 54 boxes)

Area = 6 boxes

Area = 54 boxes

> The **AREA** scale factor = the **LINEAR** scale factor "**SQUARED**". 3^2 = 9 shown above.

Example :-

The two pictures of the little girl are similar.

(a) Calculate the **linear scale factor**.

(b) Calculate the **area scale factor**.

(c) Calculate the **area** of the larger picture.

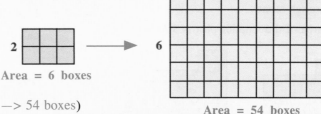

Area 25 cm²

9 cm

18 cm

(a) Linear $S.F.$ = $\dfrac{18}{9}$ = 2

(b) Area $S.F.$ = 2^2 = 4

(c) Area large picture = 4 × 25 = 100 cm²

Exercise 20·4

1. In the figure below, AM is parallel to BN.
   QA = 2 cm, AB = 2 cm and BN = 4 cm.

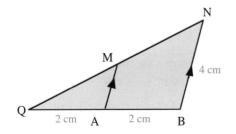

N

M

4 cm

Q

2 cm A 2 cm B

(a) Calculate the length of AM.

(b) State the **area** scale factor (enlargement) from ΔQAM to ΔQBN.

2. These billboards are similar.

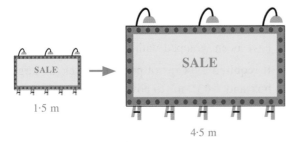

SALE

SALE

1·5 m

4·5 m

Calculate the **area** scale factor.

3. These two oval place mats are similar.

Area = 280 cm²

20 cm

50 cm

Calculate the **area** of the larger one.

4. The butterflies are also similar. Calculate the **area** covered by the larger butterfly's wings.

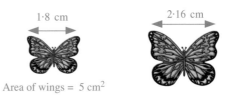

1·8 cm

2·16 cm

Area of wings = 5 cm²

5. The two chocolate box tops are similar. The area of the smaller top is **250 cm²**.

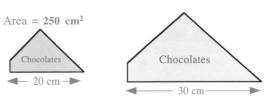

Area = 250 cm²

Chocolates

Chocolates

20 cm

30 cm

What is the **area** of the larger one ?

6. Two similar plots of land are to be covered with rough stones.

The area of the smaller plot is **990 m²**.

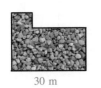 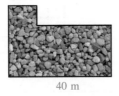

30 m   40 m

Calculate the **area** of the larger one.

7. Both oval mouse mats shown are similar.

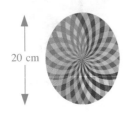

20 cm   10 cm

The smaller mouse mat is **half** the length of the larger one, but is **NOT** half its area.

What is the area of the smaller mouse mat if the larger one is **240 cm²** in area ?

8. The portable 20 inch tall TV screen is **similar** to the 30 inch tall Plasma TV.

30 in   20 in

If the area of the Plasma TV screen is **1170 square inches**, calculate the area of the portable TV screen.

9. Shown are two framed photographs of a bridge.

The picture on the right is a **reduction** of the larger one on the left.

Area = 850 cm²

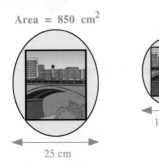

15 cm

25 cm

What is the **area** of the smaller photograph ?

10. Shape Q is an **enlargement** of shape P.

If the area of shape Q is **45 mm²**, calculate the area of shape P.

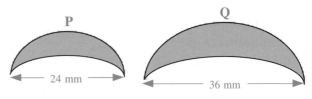

P   Q

24 mm   36 mm

11. The two "L–Shapes" are **similar**.

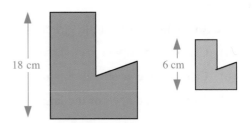

18 cm   6 cm

If the large one has an area of **270 cm²**, calculate the area of the smaller.

12. (a) In the figure below, why is ΔABC **similar** to ΔADE ?

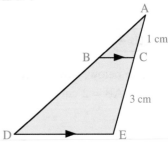

A

1 cm

B   C

3 cm

D   E

(b) Write down the **linear** scale factor from ΔABC to ΔADE.

(c) If BC = 0·8 cm, find the length of DE.

(d) What is the scale factor of the **reduction in area** from ΔADE to ΔABC ?

(e) The area of ΔADE is **6·4 cm²**.
Calculate the area of ΔABC.

13. **Tricky :-**

Two boxes are mathematically **similar** and both have been wrapped with birthday paper.

It required **1·84 m²** of paper to cover the larger box and **1·035 m²** to cover the small box.

If the large box is **36 cm** high, what is the height of the small one ?

 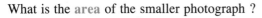

Similar Volumes

The three cubes shown are **similar**.

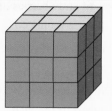

A cube of side 1 cm
Volume = **1 cm³**.

This cube is a **2** times (*linear*)
enlargement of the first one.

Its volume is 8 boxes - a
volume enlargement of **8** times.

(2 "cubed") or 2³.

This cube is a **3** times (*linear*)
enlargement of the first one.

Its volume is 27 boxes - a
volume enlargement of **27** times.

(3 "cubed") or 3³.

> The **VOLUME** scale factor = the **LINEAR** scale factor "**CUBED**". 2³ = 8 shown above.

Example :-

Two Martini glasses are **similar** in shape.

The smaller one is 6 cm high and
holds 44 ml of juice.

If the other glass is 12 cm in height,
how much juice will it hold ?

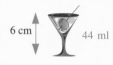

> **Linear** scale factor = 12 ÷ 6 = **2**
>
> **Volume** scale factor = 2³ = **8**
>
> **Volume** of juice in large glass = 8 x 44 = **352 ml**

Exercise 20·5

1. These two cans of lime
   juice are **similar**.

   Calculate the volume
   of the larger can if
   the volume of the
   smaller one is 64 cm³.

2. The two mugs shown below are **similar**.
   One is plastic from a child's tea set, the
   other a normal kitchen mug.

   If the smaller one is 2·6 cm high and holds
   30 ml of tea, how many ml of tea will the
   larger mug hold ?

3. A tub of fresh ice-cream is 16 cm in height and
   holds 2560 ml of ice-cream.
   A **similar** tub is 8 cm in height.

   How much will the smaller tub hold ?

4. The footballs shown below are **similar** to each
   other. The larger 20 cm diameter ball is for
   outside use, the other with diameter 10 cm is
   for playing within the house.

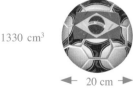

   If the large ball has a volume of 1330 cm³,
   what is the volume of the small one ?

5. Two sizes of strawberries and ice cream are on sale at a tennis competition.

One is **similar** to the other.

The cost depends on the **volume** of strawberries and ice cream in the dish.

The smaller one above costs £2.

What will the bigger one cost ?

8 cm

12 cm

6. The diagram shows two bottles of Grape & Redcurrant Juice.

The two bottles are **similar** and the cost of the juice depends only on the volume of liquid in the bottle.

10 cm

14 cm

If the small one costs £2·50, what should the large one cost ?

7. The picture below shows two saucepans which are mathematically **similar**.

20 cm   25 cm

(a) Find the height of the smaller saucepan if the height of the larger saucepan is 15 cm ?

(b) The volume of the large pan is 3·75 litres. Calculate the volume of the small one.

8. The weight of a memorial which stands outside the town hall is 54 tonnes.

A new memorial, **similar** to this one, is to be built in the cenotaph.

It is to be made of the same stone but is to be only **two thirds** of the height of the original.

What will the new memorial weigh ?

9. Shown are two tubes of toothpaste.

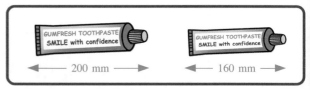

GUMFRESH TOOTHPASTE
SMILE with confidence

GUMFRESH TOOTHPASTE
SMILE with confidence

200 mm   160 mm

If the tubes are mathematically **similar** and the price of the toothpaste depends only on the the volume of toothpaste in the tube, what will be the cost of the small tube when the large one costs £2·50 ?

10. Shown are three **similar** Popcorn Boxes.

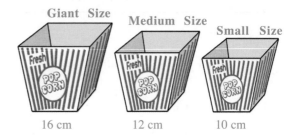

Giant Size   Medium Size   Small Size

16 cm   12 cm   10 cm

(a) Find the **reduction** linear scale factor from

(i) Giant to Medium

(ii) Medium to Small.

(b) The Giant box needs **1600 cm²** of cardboard to make it.

How much will the Medium Size box need ?

(c) The Medium Size holds **1080 cm³** of Sweet Popcorn.

How much will the Small Size hold ?

11. Two boxes of soap powder are **similar**.

When full, the small one weighs 160 grams and the large one, 540 grams.

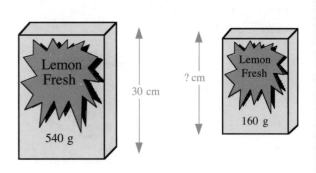

Lemon Fresh

30 cm

? cm

Lemon Fresh

160 g

540 g

If the large box is 30 centimetres in height, what is the height of the small box ?

1. Prove that the two crests shown opposite are **similar**.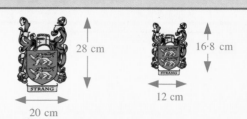

2.  A gent's and a boy's shirt and tie sets are **similar**.

    (a) Find the scale factor, (*small to big*).

    (b) Calculate the length of the gent's shirt.

3. A sponge cake is baked in two sizes, both **similar**.

    The larger cake has a 27 cm base and is 12 cm deep.

    Calculate the depth of the smaller cake which has an 18 cm base.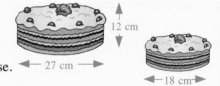

4. 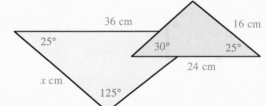   (a) Explain why these two triangles are **similar**.

    (b) Calculate the size of the side marked *x*.

5. Calculate the values of *a* and *b* in the two triangles shown opposite.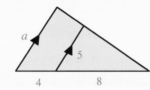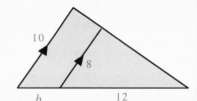

6. The two "number 5's" are **similar**.

    If the large one has a surface area of **75 cm²**, calculate the **surface area** of the smaller one.

7. The picture opposite shows two wine glasses which are mathematically **similar**.

    (a) Find the height of the small glass if the height of the large glass is 18 cm ?

    (b) The small glass can hold 125 ml of wine when full.

    Calculate how much the large glass can hold when it is full.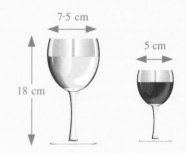

8. Two cartons of soup, one large, one small, are **similar**.

    The height of the large carton is 20 cm, compared to the small one's height of 16 cm.
    The cost of the carton of soup depends only on the volume of soup in the carton.

    If the large one costs £2·50, what should the small one cost ?

What is a Fraction ?

A fraction consists of 2 parts.

$$\frac{3}{5}$$ ← the numerator
← the denominator

It may be possible to simplify a fraction by dividing top and bottom by a particular number.

$$\frac{9}{12} \text{ becomes } \frac{9}{12} {\div 3 \atop \div 3} = \frac{3}{4}$$

Mixed Fractions

A fraction, like, $\frac{23}{4}$, where the numerator is bigger than the denominator is a "top-heavy" fraction.

A number consisting of "whole" part and a "fraction" part, like $1\frac{2}{3}$, is called a mixed fraction.

Example 1 :- Changing a top-heavy fraction to a mixed fraction :-

note *

=> $\frac{23}{4}$ means $(23 \div 4) = 5$ (remainder 3) $= 5\frac{3}{4}$

Example 2 :- Changing a mixed fraction back to a top-heavy fraction :-

=> To change $6\frac{2}{3}$ into "thirds"

- **Step 1** - multiply the 6 by the 3
- **Step 2** - now add on the 2 (thirds).

$6 \times 3 = 18 + 2 = 20$ => $\frac{20}{3}$

Exercise 21·1

1. Copy and complete the following :-

   (a) $\frac{17}{2}$ means $17 \div 2$ => $2\overline{)17} = 8\frac{?}{2}$.

   (b) $\frac{29}{6}$ means $29 \div 6$ => $6\overline{)29} = 4\frac{?}{6}$.

   (c) $\frac{17}{9}$ means $17 \div ...$ => $...$ $= ...$

2. In a similar way, change the following top-heavy fractions to mixed numbers :-

   (a) $\frac{10}{3}$ (b) $\frac{19}{4}$ (c) $\frac{31}{6}$

   (d) $\frac{11}{2}$ (e) $\frac{37}{5}$ (f) $\frac{51}{8}$.

3. (a) Five girls decide to share 13 bars of tablet evenly. What will each girl receive, (*as a mixed number*) ?

   (b) 23 kg of onions are packed evenly into 6 bags. What weight of onions goes into each bag ?

   (c) A container holds 27 litres of water. An equal quantity of water is poured into 5 cups such that each holds the same amount. How much water will be in each cup ?

4. Copy and complete :-

   $\frac{26}{6} = 26 \div 6 = 4\frac{2}{6} = 4\frac{?}{3}$ (<— simplified).

5. Change each of the following to mixed numbers and simplify where possible :-

   (a) $\frac{21}{6}$ (b) $\frac{14}{4}$ (c) $\frac{26}{8}$

   (d) $\frac{42}{10}$ (e) $\frac{21}{9}$ (f) $\frac{30}{8}$.

6. This diagram represents $2\frac{3}{4}$ pies.

   (a) How many "$\frac{1}{4}$" pie slices do you get from 1 pie ?

   (b) How many "$\frac{1}{4}$" pie slices do you get from 2 pies ?

   (c) How many "$\frac{1}{4}$" pie slices do you get from $2\frac{3}{4}$ pies ?

7. These pizzas have been cut into "thirds".

   (a) From the 3 whole pizzas, you get ... thirds ?

   (b) From the $\frac{2}{3}$ pizza, you get ..... thirds ?

   (c) How many thirds is this altogether ?

   (d) Write this as $3\frac{2}{3} = \frac{?}{3}$.

8. Copy and complete :-

   $4\frac{3}{5} = ((4 \times 5) + 3)$ "fifths" $= 23$ "fifths" $= \frac{?}{5}$.

9. Copy and complete :–

   (a) $3\frac{2}{3} = ...$ (b) $5\frac{3}{7} = ...$ (c) $6\frac{4}{5} = ...$

10. Change each of the following mixed numbers to top heavy fractions :-

   (a) $2\frac{1}{2}$ (b) $3\frac{3}{4}$ (c) $10\frac{3}{5}$

   (d) $6\frac{1}{8}$ (e) $9\frac{2}{3}$ (f) $2\frac{7}{10}$.

11. How many $\frac{1}{2}$ pizza slices can I get from :-

   (a) 3 pizzas   (b) 7 pizzas

   (c) $4\frac{1}{2}$ pizzas (d) $9\frac{1}{2}$ pizzas ?

12. How many $\frac{1}{3}$ litre glasses can be filled from :-

   (a) 2 litres   (b) $2\frac{2}{3}$ litres   (c) $4\frac{1}{3}$ litres ?

13. How many $\frac{1}{4}$ kg bags can be filled from :-

   (a) 5 kg   (b) $2\frac{1}{4}$ kg   (c) $3\frac{3}{4}$ kg ?

14. To add $3\frac{3}{5} + 2\frac{4}{5}$ you change them to "$\frac{1}{5}$'s".

   Copy and complete :-

$$3\frac{3}{5} + 2\frac{4}{5}$$
$$= \frac{?}{5} + \frac{?}{5}$$
$$= \frac{?}{5}\quad = 6\frac{?}{5}.$$

Simple Rule :–   You can only add (or subtract) two fractions if :-

=> THEY HAVE THE SAME DENOMINATOR.

Example 1 :-

$$\frac{2}{9} + \frac{5}{9}$$
$$= \frac{7}{9}$$

Example 2 :-

$$\frac{5}{8} - \frac{3}{8}$$
$$= \frac{2}{8}$$
$$= \frac{1}{4}$$

Example 3 :-

$$3\frac{3}{5} + 2\frac{4}{5}$$
$$= 5\frac{7}{5}$$
$$= 6\frac{2}{5}$$

Example 4 :-

$$4\frac{5}{6} - 1\frac{1}{6}$$
$$= 3\frac{4}{6}$$
$$= 3\frac{2}{3}$$

Exercise 21·2

1. Copy and complete the following :-

   (a) $\frac{1}{5} + \frac{3}{5}$
     $= \frac{?}{5}$

   (b) $\frac{7}{9} - \frac{5}{9}$
     $= \frac{?}{9}$

   (c) $\frac{9}{10} - \frac{3}{10}$
     $= \frac{?}{10} = \frac{?}{5}$

   (d) $\frac{3}{16} + \frac{3}{16}$
     $= \frac{?}{16} = \frac{?}{8}$.

2. Copy the following and simplify :-

(a) $\frac{5}{7} + \frac{4}{7}$ (b) $\frac{1}{9} + \frac{7}{9}$ (c) $\frac{5}{8} - \frac{3}{8}$

(d) $\frac{3}{5} + \frac{3}{5}$ (e) $\frac{9}{11} - \frac{4}{11}$ (f) $\frac{3}{10} + \frac{1}{10}$.

3. Copy the following and simplify :-

(a) $4\frac{1}{2} + 2\frac{1}{2}$ (b) $7\frac{3}{4} - 3\frac{1}{4}$ (c) $5\frac{1}{3} + 1\frac{1}{3}$

(d) $3\frac{7}{9} + 2\frac{4}{9}$ (e) $9\frac{3}{4} - 5\frac{1}{4}$ (f) $3\frac{2}{7} + 8\frac{3}{7}$.

4. Of the $\frac{7}{10}$ km to her school, Davida had walked $\frac{3}{10}$ km. How much further had she to go ?

5. Hat sizes go up in $\frac{1}{8}$'s of an inch at a time.

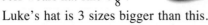

Jeff wears hat size $6\frac{7}{8}$.

Luke's hat is 3 sizes bigger than this.

What is Luke's hat size ?

6. Nick mixes $5\frac{4}{5}$ kg of sand with $3\frac{3}{5}$ kg of cement.

What is the total weight of the mixture ?

7. (a) A piece of rope was $6\frac{5}{8}$ metres long.

A piece measuring $3\frac{3}{8}$ metres was cut off.

What length of rope remained ?

(b) 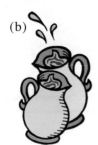 2 jugs of water were poured into an empty basin.

The first jug held $2\frac{3}{4}$ litres and the second held $1\frac{3}{4}$ litres.

How much water was in the basin in total ?

(c) Of the $9\frac{5}{7}$ kilometres from her house to the shops, Jan has cycled $2\frac{2}{7}$ km.

How much further has Jan to cycle to reach the shops ?

7. (d) Steve ate $\frac{3}{8}$ of a pie, Harry ate $\frac{3}{8}$ and Mandy ate $\frac{1}{8}$.

How much had they eaten altogether ?

(e)  Lizzie weighed $41\frac{4}{5}$ kilograms.

She went on a diet and lost $3\frac{3}{5}$ kilograms.

What is Lizzie's new weight ?

8. A table was $5\frac{7}{10}$ feet long by $2\frac{3}{10}$ feet wide.

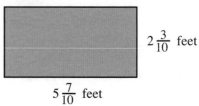

$2\frac{3}{10}$ feet

$5\frac{7}{10}$ feet

(a) By how much is the length bigger than the breadth ?

(b) Calculate the **perimeter** of the table top.

9. A lorry weighs $4\frac{5}{8}$ tonnes.

Crates are loaded onto the lorry.

TeeJay Publishers Ltd.

Unladen weight - $4\frac{5}{8}$ tonnes

$\frac{3}{8}$ tonne

Each crate weighs $\frac{3}{8}$ tonne.

What is the total weight of the lorry carrying a load with :-

(a) 1 crate   (b) 2 crates   (c) 3 crates ?

10. Look at the picture of the hammer.

Calculate the length of the rubber handle.

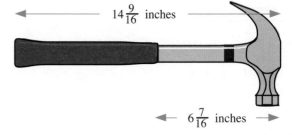

$14\frac{9}{16}$ inches

$6\frac{7}{16}$ inches

Adding and Subtracting Fractions (Harder Examples)

Remember the Golden Rule :-   The denominators MUST be the same if you wish to add or subtract.

Question :-   What do we do if the denominators are not the same ?

Answer :-   Change each fraction so that they DO HAVE THE SAME denominator.

Example 1 :- Find :- $\frac{2}{3} + \frac{1}{2}$.   –   note :-   this does not add to give the answer $\frac{3}{5}$ ✗

- the denominators 3 and 2 are not the same.

=>   what is the l.c.m. (lowest common multiple) of 3 and 2 ? —> answer is 6.

=>   we must change the $\frac{2}{3}$ and the $\frac{1}{2}$ into $\frac{1}{6}$'s.

$$\frac{2}{3} + \frac{1}{2}$$
note $\rightarrow$ $$\frac{4}{6} + \frac{3}{6}$$ $\leftarrow$ note
$$= \frac{7}{6} = 1\frac{1}{6}$$

$(\frac{2}{3} = \frac{?}{6})$ —> ? = 4

$(\frac{1}{2} = \frac{?}{6})$ —> ? = 3

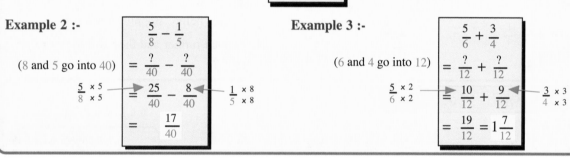

Example 2 :-

(8 and 5 go into 40)

$$\frac{5}{8} - \frac{1}{5}$$
$$= \frac{?}{40} - \frac{?}{40}$$
$\frac{5}{8} \times \frac{\times 5}{\times 5}$ → $= \frac{25}{40} - \frac{8}{40}$ ← $\frac{1}{5} \times \frac{\times 8}{\times 8}$
$$= \frac{17}{40}$$

Example 3 :-

(6 and 4 go into 12)

$$\frac{5}{6} + \frac{3}{4}$$
$$= \frac{?}{12} + \frac{?}{12}$$
$\frac{5}{6} \times \frac{\times 2}{\times 2}$ → $= \frac{10}{12} + \frac{9}{12}$ ← $\frac{3}{4} \times \frac{\times 3}{\times 3}$
$$= \frac{19}{12} = 1\frac{7}{12}$$

Exercise 21·3

1.   Copy and complete the following :-

(a) $\frac{3}{4} + \frac{1}{3}$

$= \frac{9}{12} + \frac{?}{12}$

$= \frac{?}{12} = 1\frac{?}{12}$

(b) $\frac{4}{5} - \frac{2}{3}$

$= \frac{?}{15} - \frac{?}{15}$

$= \frac{?}{15}$

(c) $\frac{7}{8} - \frac{3}{4}$

$= \frac{?}{8} - \frac{?}{8}$

$= \frac{?}{8}$

(d) $\frac{6}{7} + \frac{2}{3}$

$= \frac{?}{21} + \frac{?}{21}$

$= \frac{?}{21} = 1\frac{?}{21}$.

2.   Simplify the following :-

(a) $\frac{2}{5} + \frac{1}{3}$

(b) $\frac{1}{2} - \frac{1}{4}$

(c) $\frac{3}{4} + \frac{2}{3}$

(d) $\frac{3}{5} + \frac{1}{4}$

(e) $\frac{5}{6} - \frac{1}{2}$

(f) $\frac{7}{8} - \frac{2}{3}$

(g) $\frac{3}{10} + \frac{4}{5}$

(h) $\frac{5}{9} - \frac{1}{2}$.

3.   Show all your working here :-

(a) $\frac{1}{4} + \frac{1}{3} + \frac{1}{2}$

(b) $\frac{7}{8} - \frac{1}{2} - \frac{1}{4}$

(c) $\frac{1}{3} + \frac{4}{5} - \frac{1}{2}$

(d) $\frac{3}{4} + \frac{1}{5} - \frac{1}{3}$.

Mixed Fractions

One way of solving mixed fraction problems is to deal with the **whole numbers first** – then the fractions.

Example 4 :-

$$3\tfrac{3}{4} + 2\tfrac{2}{3}$$
$$= 5(\tfrac{3}{4} + \tfrac{2}{3})$$
$$= 5(\tfrac{9}{12} + \tfrac{8}{12})$$
$$= 5\tfrac{17}{12} = 6\tfrac{5}{12}$$

Example 5 :-

$$6\tfrac{5}{8} - 4\tfrac{1}{3}$$
$$= 2(\tfrac{5}{8} - \tfrac{1}{3})$$
$$= 2(\tfrac{15}{24} - \tfrac{8}{24})$$
$$= 2\tfrac{7}{24}$$

Example 6 :-

$$3\tfrac{3}{5} + \tfrac{5}{6}$$
$$= 3(\tfrac{3}{5} + \tfrac{5}{6})$$
$$= 3(\tfrac{18}{30} + \tfrac{25}{30})$$
$$= 3\tfrac{43}{30} = 4\tfrac{13}{30}$$

4. Copy and complete the following :-

(a) $5\tfrac{2}{3} + 3\tfrac{1}{2}$ (b) $4\tfrac{3}{4} - 1\tfrac{2}{3}$

(c) $7\tfrac{5}{8} - 3\tfrac{1}{4}$ (d) $5\tfrac{1}{2} + 3\tfrac{4}{5}$

(e) $3\tfrac{5}{6} - 1\tfrac{3}{5}$ (f) $2\tfrac{1}{3} + 1\tfrac{3}{8}$

(g) $5\tfrac{5}{9} + 1\tfrac{1}{2}$ (h) $6\tfrac{9}{10} - 2\tfrac{3}{4}$.

6. Use the above method to find :-

(a) $3 - 1\tfrac{1}{3}$ (b) $7 - 2\tfrac{7}{9}$

7. From a 6 metre length of cable, the engineer cut off a piece which was $3\tfrac{3}{8}$ metres long.

What was the length of the piece of cable remaining ?

5. Copy and complete the following :-

(a) $7 - 3\tfrac{1}{4}$
$$= 4 - \tfrac{1}{4}$$
$$= 3\tfrac{?}{4}$$

(b) $6 - 1\tfrac{3}{5}$
$$= 5 - \tfrac{3}{5}$$
$$= 4\tfrac{?}{5}.$$

8. It is exactly 12 miles from Brum to Dyer.

Davie and Bob left Brum and jogged for $7\tfrac{3}{5}$ kilometres before stopping for a rest.

How much further had they still to jog to get to Dyer ?

A Problem with Subtraction   What is $4\tfrac{1}{3} - 1\tfrac{3}{5}$?

- **Step 1 –** Subtract whole numbers first —> $3(\tfrac{1}{3} - \tfrac{3}{5})$

- **Step 2 –** Change both fractions to $\tfrac{1}{15}$'s => $3(\tfrac{5}{15} - \tfrac{9}{15})$

  (* **you cannot take** $\tfrac{9}{15}$ **from** $\tfrac{5}{15}$ **!!!!** *)

- **Step 3 –** Take 1 whole number from the 3 and write it as $\tfrac{15}{15}$ (= 1)

  —> $\qquad\qquad 3(\tfrac{5}{15} - \tfrac{9}{15})$

  becomes $\qquad 2 + \tfrac{15}{15} + (\tfrac{5}{15} - \tfrac{9}{15}) = 2 + \tfrac{20}{15} - \tfrac{9}{15}$
  $$= 2\tfrac{11}{15}.$$

One More Example :-

$$6\tfrac{1}{4} - 1\tfrac{2}{3}$$
$$= 5(\tfrac{1}{4} - \tfrac{2}{3})$$
$$= 5(\tfrac{3}{12} - \tfrac{8}{12})$$
$$= 4 + \tfrac{12}{12} + (\tfrac{3}{12} - \tfrac{8}{12})$$
$$= 4\tfrac{7}{12}$$

change 1 (of the 5) to $\tfrac{12}{12}$

9. Copy and complete the following :-

(a) $5\tfrac{2}{5} - 1\tfrac{1}{2}$
$$= 4(\tfrac{2}{5} - \tfrac{1}{2})$$
$$= 4(\tfrac{4}{10} - \tfrac{5}{10})$$
$$= 3 + \tfrac{10}{10} + (\tfrac{4}{10} - \tfrac{5}{10})$$
$$= 3\tfrac{?}{10}$$

(b) $4\tfrac{3}{8} - 2\tfrac{3}{5}$
$$= 2(\tfrac{3}{8} - \tfrac{3}{5})$$
$$= 2(\tfrac{15}{40} - \tfrac{?}{40})$$
$$= 1 + \tfrac{?}{40} + (\tfrac{15}{40} - \tfrac{?}{40})$$
$$= 1\tfrac{?}{40}.$$

10. Show all your working here :-

(a) $4\tfrac{1}{5} - 1\tfrac{1}{2}$ (b) $6\tfrac{3}{5} - 1\tfrac{5}{6}$

(c) $4\tfrac{1}{4} - 2\tfrac{1}{2}$ (d) $6\tfrac{3}{8} - 4\tfrac{3}{4}$

(e) $10\tfrac{1}{3} - 7\tfrac{1}{2}$ (f) $6\tfrac{1}{7} - 1\tfrac{1}{2}$

(g) $8\tfrac{1}{3} - 3\tfrac{7}{10}$ (h) $8\tfrac{1}{6} - 5\tfrac{2}{5}$.

Multiplying Fractions

The rule for multiplying two basic fractions is very simple.

To multiply $\frac{3}{5} \times \frac{4}{7}$ —> multiply the numerators
—> multiply the denominators —> $\frac{3}{5} \times \frac{4}{7} = \frac{3 \times 4}{5 \times 7} = \frac{12}{35}$

Example 1 :-

$$\frac{3}{4} \times \frac{3}{5}$$
$$= \frac{3 \times 3}{4 \times 5}$$
$$= \frac{9}{20}$$

Example 2 :-

$$\frac{4}{5} \times \frac{5}{6}$$
$$= \frac{20}{30} \left(\frac{\div 10}{\div 10} \right)$$
$$= \frac{2}{3} \ (simplified)$$

Example 3 :-

$$\frac{8}{9} \times \frac{3}{4}$$
$$= \frac{24}{36} \left(\frac{\div 12}{\div 12} \right)$$
$$= \frac{2}{3}$$

Exercise 21·4

1. Copy each of the following and complete :-

(a) $\frac{2}{3} \times \frac{4}{5}$

$= \frac{2 \times 4}{3 \times 5}$

$= \frac{?}{15}$

(b) $\frac{5}{6} \times \frac{1}{3}$

$= \frac{5 \times 1}{6 \times 3}$

$= \frac{?}{?}$.

2. Multiply the following fractions and simplify (where possible) :-

(a) $\frac{2}{5} \times \frac{2}{3}$

(b) $\frac{5}{6} \times \frac{3}{5}$

(c) $\frac{3}{7} \times \frac{4}{9}$

(d) $\frac{3}{10} \times \frac{5}{6}$.

2. (e) $\frac{3}{8} \times \frac{4}{5}$ (f) $\frac{7}{12} \times \frac{4}{7}$

(g) $\frac{11}{16} \times \frac{2}{5}$ (h) $\frac{2}{9} \times \frac{9}{10}$.

3. Calculate the **area** of a rectangular sheet of metal measuring $\frac{5}{6}$ metre by $\frac{3}{8}$ metre.

4. I spent $\frac{3}{4}$ of my pocket money in a shop. Of that, $\frac{2}{5}$ of it went on comics.

What fraction of my money was spent on comics ? (i.e $\frac{2}{5} \times \frac{3}{4}$)

Dealing with Mixed Fractions :- $(4\frac{3}{4} \times 1\frac{1}{3})$

Simple Rule :– You **MUST CHANGE** any mixed fraction into a **top-heavy fractions**

Example 4 :-

$$4\frac{3}{4} \times 1\frac{1}{3}$$
$$= \frac{19}{4} \times \frac{4}{3}$$
$$= \frac{76}{12}$$
$$= \frac{19}{3} = 6\frac{1}{3}$$

5. Copy and complete the following :-

(a) $1\frac{1}{2} \times 2\frac{1}{3}$

$= \frac{3}{2} \times \frac{7}{3}$

$= \frac{21}{6}$

$= 3\frac{?}{6} \ = 3\frac{?}{?}$

(b) $5\frac{2}{3} \times 1\frac{1}{4}$

$= \frac{17}{3} \times \frac{5}{4}$

$= \frac{85}{12}$

$= 7\frac{?}{?}$

6. Do the following in the same way :-

(a) $2\frac{1}{3} \times 2\frac{1}{2}$ (b) $4\frac{1}{5} \times 2\frac{1}{2}$.

6. (c) $5\frac{1}{3} \times 3\frac{3}{4}$ (d) $1\frac{2}{7} \times 4\frac{2}{3}$

(e) $6\frac{1}{4} \times 1\frac{3}{5}$ (f) $2\frac{5}{6} \times 5\frac{1}{2}$

(g) $1\frac{3}{10} \times 4\frac{1}{3}$ (h) $1\frac{1}{2} \times 7\frac{2}{5}$

(i) $3\frac{2}{3} \times 1\frac{3}{4}$ (j) $5\frac{1}{2} \times 4\frac{4}{5}$

(k) $10\frac{1}{2} \times \frac{6}{7}$ (l) $6\frac{1}{2} \times \frac{4}{5}$.

Remember Remember.....?

1. Change to a mixed number :-   (a) $\frac{29}{5}$ (b) $\frac{46}{8}$ (c) $\frac{76}{10}$.

2. Re-write as a top-heavy fraction :-   (a) $5\frac{2}{3}$ (b) $6\frac{3}{5}$ (c) $10\frac{7}{9}$.

3. How many $\frac{1}{3}$ pizza slices can by sold from $4\frac{2}{3}$ pizzas ?

4. Copy and complete :-

     (a) $\frac{5}{7} + \frac{1}{7}$ (b) $\frac{3}{4} - \frac{1}{2}$ (c) $\frac{5}{8} - \frac{1}{8}$ (d) $2\frac{2}{5} + 3\frac{4}{5}$

     (e) $\frac{5}{6} - \frac{1}{4}$ (f) $4\frac{4}{5} + 1\frac{2}{3}$ (g) $5\frac{7}{8} - 2\frac{3}{5}$ (h) $3\frac{1}{2} - 1\frac{2}{3}$.

5. Copy and complete :-

     (a) $\frac{1}{2} \times \frac{3}{5}$ (b) $\frac{7}{9} \times \frac{2}{3}$ (c) $\frac{3}{7} \times \frac{21}{9}$ (d) $\frac{5}{11} \times \frac{33}{35}$

     (e) $\frac{1}{2} \times 4\frac{1}{2}$ (f) $\frac{1}{3} \times 6\frac{2}{3}$ (g) $3\frac{1}{2} \times 1\frac{1}{5}$ (h) $6\frac{3}{4} \times 1\frac{7}{9}$.

6. Before going on his diet, Antonio weighed $14\frac{1}{2}$ stones.

     He lost $3\frac{3}{4}$ stones on his diet.

     What did Antonio then weigh ?

7. 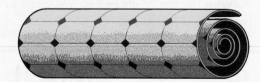 A 1 metre length of this linoleum weighs $3\frac{3}{5}$ kg.

     What will the weight of a $2\frac{3}{4}$ metre length be ?

8. An empty wooden crate weighs $3\frac{3}{8}$ kg.

     It holds 6 bags of ready mix cement.

     Each bag weighs $2\frac{3}{4}$ kg.

     Calculate the total weight of the crate and the 6 bags.

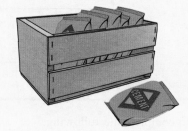

9.

$3\frac{1}{5}$ m

$3\frac{3}{4}$ m

     The length of this rectangular lawn is $3\frac{1}{5}$ m.

     Its breadth is $3\frac{3}{4}$ m.

     How many packets of feeding will be needed to cover it if one packet covers 4 square metres ?

10. Find :- $\frac{2}{3} \times \frac{3}{4} \times \frac{4}{5} \times \frac{5}{6} \times \frac{6}{7} \times \frac{7}{8} \times \frac{8}{9} \times \frac{9}{10}$.   *(This should only take about 10 seconds !).*

1. Calculate the values of *x* and *y* in the following right angled triangles.

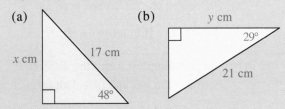

(a)   (b)

2. Calculate the value of *s* and *t* in the following right angled triangles.

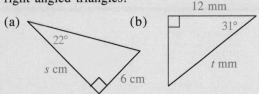

(a)   (b)

3. Calculate the size of the angles marked *c* and *d* in the following right angled triangles.

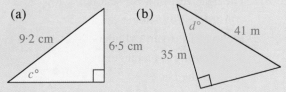

(a)   (b)

4. Shown is a trapezium ABCD with a line of symmetry (shown dotted).

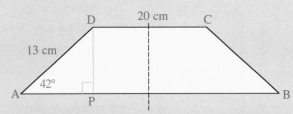

By considering right angled △APD, calculate the length of the line AP, and hence determine the **perimeter** of the trapezium.

5. The breadth and height of a poster is 48 cm by 36 cm.

A *similar* postcard is made from the poster.
The postcard has a 12 cm breadth.

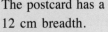

Calculate the height of the postcard.

6. The picture below shows two antique vases which are mathematically **similar**.

(a) Find the height of the small vase if the height of the large vase is 30 cm ?

(b) The small vase can hold 1·2 litres of water when full.

   Calculate how much water the large vase can hold when it is full.

7. These ladybirds are also **similar**.

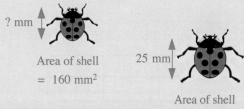

? mm

Area of shell = 160 mm²

25 mm

Area of shell = 250 mm²

Calculate the **length** of the smaller ladybird's shell.

8. Find :-

(a) $\frac{2}{3} + \frac{3}{5}$ (b) $4\frac{1}{2} - 1\frac{2}{3}$

(c) $\frac{3}{4} \times \frac{8}{9}$ (d) $4\frac{1}{3} \times 3\frac{3}{4}$

9. A rectangular field has dimensions as shown.

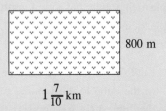

800 m

$1\frac{7}{10}$ km

(a) Calculate the **area** of the field.

(b) Calculate the **perimeter** of the field.

10. A right angled triangle has dimensions as shown below.

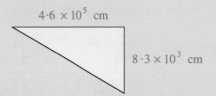

$4 \cdot 6 \times 10^5$ cm

$8 \cdot 3 \times 10^3$ cm

Find the **area** of this triangle in scientific notation, to one significant figure.

11. A cylinder has a volume of 9420 cm^3.

The diameter of the the cylinder is 20 cm.

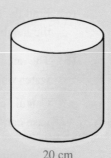

20 cm

(a) Calculate the height of this cylinder.

(b) Calculate the surface area of this cylinder.

12. (a) Derive a formula from the table below.

x	−1	0	1	2
y	−2	1	4	7

(b) Find y, when $x = 25$

(c) Find x, when $y = 73$.

13. A quadrilateral defined on a Cartesian coordinate grid has vertices A(3, 0), B(4, −3), C(−2, −3) and D(1, 0).

(a) Calculate the area of this quadrilateral.

(b) Calculate the obtuse angle ADC.

14. A plasticine cube has side length $2x$.
A plasticine cuboid has length $4x$ a breadth of x and a height of x.

(a) Find the ratio of the volume of the cube to the volume of the cuboid (in its simplest form).

(b) Find, in its simplest form, the ratios of their surface areas.

15. A sequence is defined as $1, \frac{1}{2}, \frac{1}{3}, \frac{1}{4}, \frac{1}{5}, \ldots\ldots$

(a) Prove that the difference between the 9th and 10th terms is $\frac{1}{90}$.

(b) Find, in simplest form, the difference between the nth and $(n + 1)$th terms.

16. Two right angled triangles are joined together to form the shape shown in the diagram.

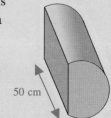

A

15 cm

D

8 cm

25°

B   C

Find the length of the line AD.

17. The head rest of a car seat is constructed by slicing off a section of a foam cylinder and securing a rectangular plate to the back.

The end face is shown below with centre C.

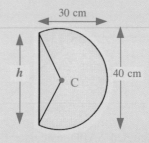

50 cm

30 cm

h 40 cm

C

The diameter of the foam cylinder is 40 cm.

Calculate the height, h, (in cm) of the flat section **and** find the area of metal plate required.

18. A pattern can be formed such that any three consecutive numbers can have a value of one.

3, 4, 5 -	$4^2 - 3 \times 5 = 1$
4, 5, 6 -	$5^2 - 4 \times 6 = 1$
5, 6, 7 -	$6^2 - 5 \times 7 = 1$

(a) Continue this pattern for 7, 8, 9.

(b) Prove that any three consecutive numbers will equal one when using this pattern.
(Hint - use x, $x + 1$, $x + 2$).

1. Set down and find :-

   (a) 176
        × 27

   (b) 6 ⟌ 3522

   (c) 12 × 781

   (d) 1234
        × 9

   (e) 42 × 500

   (f) 800 × 4000

   (g) 50 200 ÷ 500

   (h) 10 000 − 5768.

2. The temperature of a liquid which was −12°C is raised by 23°C. What is the temperature now ?

3. Set down and find :-

   (a) 126 ÷ 9

   (b) 7·8 − 8·912

   (c) 50 − 4·567

   (d) 68 ÷ 40

   (e) 0·0012 × 300

   (f) 23·769
        × 4

   (g) 18·1 − 1·12 × 10

   (h) 3 ⟌ 15·15.

4. Find :-

   (a) $\frac{2}{7}$ of 840

   (b) $\frac{4}{5}$ of £72

   (c) $\frac{3}{8}$ of 3200

   (d) $\frac{11}{40}$ of 360.

5. Find :-

   (a) $\frac{2}{3} + \frac{1}{6}$

   (b) $8 - 3\frac{2}{7}$

   (c) $5 \times 4\frac{2}{5}$

   (d) $\frac{1}{4}$ of $\frac{1}{4}$.

6. Sasha had £360, but spent $\frac{5}{6}$ of this money on DVD's and $\frac{2}{3}$ of the remainder on CD's.

   How much money did he have left ?

7. A function is given as $f(x) = x^2 + 2x - 6$.   (a) Find $f(3)$ (b) Find $f(\frac{1}{2})$.

8. Find :-   (a) 10% of £8·90

   (b) 60% of £8

   (c) 7% of £321·00

   (d) 15% of £85

   (e) $33\frac{1}{3}$% of £129

   (f) $2\frac{1}{2}$% of £1600.

9. Dave buys a car valued at £8000. His car **depreciates** at a rate of 25% per year.

   How much will his car be worth after 3 years ?

10. Find :-

    (a) $(-8) + 7$

    (b) $(-23) - 31$

    (c) $37 + (-11)$

    (d) $34 - (-26)$

    (e) $(-87) - (-39)$

    (f) $(-8) \times 12$

    (g) $(-11)^2$

    (h) $72 \div (-8)$

    (i) $(-8) \times (-3)^2$

    (j) $\frac{(-4) \times 15 \times (-5)}{25 \times (-3)}$

    (k) $-1((-2) - (-3))$

    (l) $(-90) \div (-6)$.

11. The rate of exchange today is | 1€ = 70p. |

    (a) How many euros can I get for £343 ?

    (b) How many pounds can I get for 300€ ?

12. Today is 4th May. My birthday was 5 weeks ago. On what date was my birthday ?

13. The end face of a **circular** hose holder has a **radius** of 15 centimetres.

    Calculate the **circumference** of this face.

 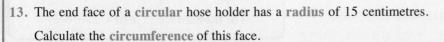

Statistics - a Definition

Statistics is the branch of Mathematics which analyses information and data gleaned from surveys, questionnaires or reports. Its purpose is to present this information in a more understandable form, either graphically or in some numeric format.

"Average" and "Spread"

Imagine we had a set of numbers to analyse - for example, the ages of those on a Sunday School trip to the beach.

2, 6, 6, 7, 7, 7, 7, 8, 8, 8, 10, 10, 11, 13, 55.

There are basically two "numerical" aspects you might wish to look at.

- The **AVERAGE** age - this is a measure of where the "**centre**" of the group lies.

- The **SPREAD** of ages - this gives you an idea of what "**range**" of ages there are.

Averages - Mean, Median and Mode   Revision of CfE Level 3 work.

You have already learned how to calculate an **average** of a set of values - namely, the **mean**.

You will now learn that there are two further measures of **average**, called the **median** and the **mode**.

MEAN - "**Add**" all the data together and "**divide**" by the number of pieces of data.

$$\frac{2 + 6 + 6 + 7 + \quad .... + 13 + 55}{15} = \boxed{11}$$

MEDIAN - The "**middle**" number, (*as long as the numbers are in "order"*).

2, 6, 6, 7, 7, 7, 7, 8, 8, 8, 10, 10, 11, 13, 55.

median = 8

MODE - The number that occurs "**most**".

2, 6, 6, 7, 7, 7, 7, 8, 8, 8, 10, 10, 11, 13, 55.

mode = 7

Exercise 22·1

1. Calculate the **mean** for each set of data :-

   (a) 2, 3, 4, 5, 6, 7, 8, 9, 10

   (b) 8, 9, 12, 13, 13, 18, 22, 25

   (c) 21, 22, 24, 27, 27, 29

   (d) 0·3, 0·5, 0·6, 0·7, 0·8, 0·9, 1·1

   (e) 121, 123, 123, 126, 136, 181

   (f) 25, 35, 19, 33, 45, 17, 35, 23, 25, 7

   (g) 6, –2, 8, –13, 5, 11, –17, 2.

2. Find the **median** for each set of data :-
   (*Remember to put the numbers in order first*)

   (a) 6, 9, 5, 3, 2, 7, 3, 10, 8

   (b) 41, 51, 44, 16, 57, 39, 45

   (c) 2·7, 3·3, 2·4, 3·5, 2·1, 2·8, 3·3

   (d) 122, 133, 76, 184, 155, 130, 168.

   If there is not a single middle number :-
   take the **mean of the middle two numbers**.

   Example :-   2, 2, 4, 5, 6, 7, 8, 10

   The **median** is (5 + 6) ÷ 2 = 5·5

3. Find the **median** for each of the following :-

(a) 14, 21, 17, 18, 22, 17

(b) 9, 13, 15, 31, 7, 35, 25, 17, 21, 19

(c) 111, 107, 108, 106, 104, 107, 103, 110

(d) 0·6, 0·7, 0·1, 1·0, 1·6, 0·9, 0·2, 0·3

(e) −6, −6, −3, −1, 1, 3, 5, 10

(f) 2, $2\frac{1}{2}$, $2\frac{1}{2}$, $4\frac{1}{2}$, $5\frac{1}{2}$, $5\frac{1}{2}$, $5\frac{1}{2}$, 7.

4. Find the **mode** for each set of data :-

(a) 2, 3, 4, 5, 6, 7, 8, 8, 9

(b) 21, 32, 23, 64, 21, 23, 41, 20, 23

(c) 1·4, 1·8, 2·0, 1·1, 1·8, 5·7, 2·5

(d) 2, 0, 2, 0, 2, 0, 2, 0, 2, 0, 2

(e) 1131, 1210, 1113, 1124, 1021, 1120, 1124

(f) $\frac{3}{4}$, $\frac{1}{4}$, $\frac{2}{3}$, $\frac{1}{2}$, $\frac{3}{4}$, $\frac{4}{5}$, $\frac{1}{4}$, $\frac{3}{4}$.

A Measure of Spread - The Range

The **RANGE** is a mathematical tool used to measure how widely spread a set of numbers are.

=> **Range = Highest score – Lowest score**

Example :- For the set of numbers :-   3, 3, 4, 6, 7, 7, 8, 11, 13, 13,

=> **Range = 13 – 3 = 10**

---

5. Calculate the **range** for each set of data in :-

(a) question 3   (b) question 4.

6. Look at this data set :-

5, 7, 2, 9, 10, 2, 3, 4, 57

(a) Find the **range**.

(b) Find the **mean**, **median** and **mode**.

(c) Which average is best suited here ?

(d) Explain why you think the other two averages are less suitable.

7. Calculate the **mean**, **median**, **mode** and **range** for each set of data below :-

(a) 2, 3, 3, 3, 5, 9, 17

(b) 6·7, 3·3, 5·4, 5·4, 6·1, 5·4, 4·8

(c) 307, 106, 293, 314, 307, 299

(d) 40, 42, 33, 51, 65, 46, 37, 40

(e) 65, 65, 63, 64, 67, 66, 67, 67

(f) 13 000, 10 000, 15 000, 10 000, 19 000

(g) −5, −2, 7, 15, −8, −5, 0, 7, −5, 6.

8. The weights of six women are shown :-

45 kg, 55 kg, 68 kg, 45 kg, 52 kg, 54 kg.

(a) Find the **range** of their weights.

(b) Calculate the **mode** and **median** weights.

(c) Choose which is the better average of the two and explain why.

9. Rory buys 10 Easter Eggs.

The number of chocolates in each is listed below :-

| 8, | 7, | 9, | 6, | 8, |
| 7, | 8, | 11, | 5, | 9 |

(a) Calculate the **mean**, **median** and **mode**.

(b) How many eggs have **less** than the **mean** number of chocolates ?

10. (a) Calculate the **mean** and the **range** of the first ten **prime** numbers.

(b) Calculate the **mean** and the **range** of the first ten **square** numbers.

(c) Find the **median** of the first 100 **square** numbers.

11. The heights of six boys are shown opposite.

    Bob says, " the average height is 1·23 m."

    Bill says, " the average height is 1·57 m."

    Ben says, " the average height is 1·47 m"

    (a) Explain why, technically, all three could be correct.

    (b) Which of the three would be least likely to be used ?

1·56 m   1·59 m
1·23 m
1·58 m   1·63 m
          1·23 m

12.

    The mean weight of two tyres is 12 kilograms.

    If one of the tyres weighs 13·5 kg, what must the weight of the other tyre be ?

13. The mean age of five children is 13 years old.
    Four of the children's ages are 10, 10, 12 and 16.

    What is the age of the fifth child ?

14.

    When a family of seven visit gran, their mean age is 22.

    When gran is included in the group, the mean age of the eight then goes up to 29.

    How old must gran be ?

15.

    Billy owns a corner sweet shop and buys in 10 jars of lollies.

    He discovers that the jars contain the following number of lollies :-

    59, 61, 57, 60, 58, 59, 58, 58, 61, 59.

    (a) Is the statement on the jar correct ? (*explain*).

    (b) An eleventh jar is examined. How many lollies would need to be in that jar in order for the sweet manufacturer's claim to **then** be 100% accurate ?

lollies
average
contents 60

16. Ten people threw 3 darts at a dartboard and recorded their scores.
    The mean for the the first nine was 33.
    The 10th contestant pushed the mean score up to 39.

    What must the woman have scored with her three darts ?

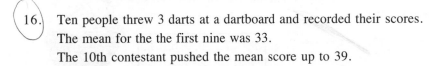

17.

    On a putting green, the mean score for the 4 children for a round was 54.
    The mean score of the 3 adults with them was 61.

    Calculate the mean score of all 7 in the group.

18. Freddy's dad said he would buy him a new bike if he could get a
    mean score of at least 75% for his **six** science tests.

    In his first **five** tests Freddy scored : 72%, 69%, 83%, 65% and 60%.

    Can Freddy possibly do well enough to get the bike ? (Explain !!)

Mean, Median and Mode from a Frequency Table

When you are given a frequency table, you will find that adding a third column helps you to find the total number of items and hence the **mean**.

This table shows the number of make-up items found in the purses of a group of women.

No. of items x	Freq f	f × x
1	8	1 × 8 = 8
2	2	2 × 2 = 4
3	1	3 × 1 = 3
4	4	4 × 4 = 16
5	1	5 × 1 = 5
TOTALS	**16**	**36**

Total purses   Total items

=> Mean number of items = $\frac{36}{16}$ = **2·25**

=> Mode is the no. of items which occur most = **1**

=> Median is the middle no. of items (*between the 8th and 9th*) = **1·5**

the 8th is a 1 and the ninth is a 2.

=> median = $\frac{1+2}{2}$

1. This table shows the results from a group of third year pupils who were asked how many textbooks they carried to school one day.

   (a) **Copy** and complete the table.

   (b) How many pupils were asked ?

   (c) How many textbooks in total were there ?

   (d) Calculate the **mean** number of textbooks.

   (e) What is the **modal** number of books ? (*the mode*).

   (f) What is the **median** ?

No. of books x	Freq f	f × x
0	2	0 × 2 = 0
1	6	1 × 6 = ...
2	11	2 × .. = ...
3	7	.. × .. = ...
4	4	.. × .. = ...
	30	...

2.

No. of passes x	Freq f	f × x
2	3	
3	7	
4	9	
5	4	
6	2	
...		...

The table shows the number of National 5 passes gained by a group of 4th year pupils.

   (a) **Copy** and complete the frequency table.

   (b) Find the total number of pupils.

   (c) Find the total number of National 5 passes.

   (d) Calculate the **mean** number of passes.

   (e) What is the **modal** number of passes ?

   (f) What is the **median** ?

3. (a) **Copy** and complete each of the following tables, add a **third** column and calculate the **mean**.

    (b) For each table, calculate the **mode** and the **median**.

(i)

No. of passengers x	Freq f
2	5
3	12
4	7
5	2
6	4

(ii)

No. of teams x	Freq f
2	1
4	9
6	2
8	6
10	1
12	1

(iii)

No. of coins x	Freq f
3	3
4	6
5	2
6	7
7	0
8	1
9	0
10	1

4. Look at the tables in question 3.

    Table (i) has **range** $(6 - 2) = 4$.

    Find the **range** for 3 (ii) and 3 (iii).

5. A group of people was each asked 10 questions in a quiz.

    Two points were given for a correct answer.

    (a) How many people took part in the quiz ?

    (b) Find the **range** of scores.

    (c) Find the **mean** score for the group.

    (d) Find the **median** from this table.

    (e) Write down the **modal** score.

Test score x	Freq f
8	2
10	3
12	9
14	6
16	5

6. A group of 18 year old boys was asked how old they were when they went out on their first date.

    The results are shown in this bar graph.

    (a) Make up a frequency table from the information in the bar graph.

    (b) Calculate the :-

        (i) **mode**

        (ii) **range**

        (iii) **mean**

        (iv) **median**.

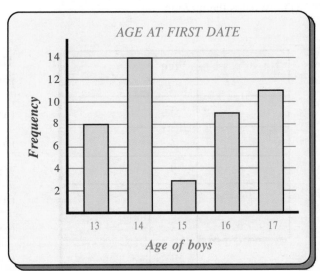

AGE AT FIRST DATE

Cumulative Frequency

It is sometimes handy to show a table which "**totals up**" the frequencies "as you go along", (*to accumulate the frequencies*).

Example :- A group of rail passengers was asked to note how many £1 coins they had in their pockets.

The *22 in the Cumulative Frequency simply tells you that 22 passengers had "**3 or fewer** £1 coins".

No. of £1 coins x	Freq f	Cumulative Frequency
1	5	5
2	7	12 (5 + 7)
3	10	* 22 (12 + 10)
4	8	30 (22 + 8)
5	1	31 (30 + 1)
	31	

Total £1 coins

It is quite easy to find the **median** from the **Cumulative Frequency** column.

There were **31** passengers - the median must be the **16th** passenger.

=> Since 12 passengers had 2 or fewer coins and 22 had 3 or fewer => the **median** is 3 coins.

Exercise 22·3

1. A school recorded the number of new absences of First Year pupils, (*due to a flu epidemic*), over a 7 week period.

   The results are shown in the frequency table.

   (a) **Copy** and complete the table.

   (b) How many new absences **in total** were there over the 7 week period ?

   (c) How many new absences had there been altogether by the end of week 5 ?

   (d) During which week was the infection at its worst ?

Week	Frequency (new cases)	Cumulative Freq (total so far)
1	5	5
2	10	15
3	12	...
4	25	...
5	17	...
6	8	...
7	3	...

2. For each frequency table :-   • add a **cumulative frequency** column   • find the **median**.

(a)

TV's	Frequency
2	1
3	10
4	16
5	7
6	3
7	2
8	1

(b)

Shots	Frequency
3	2
4	6
5	8
6	20
7	42
8	14
9	8

(c)

Age	Frequency
5	4
10	2
15	7
20	11
25	19
30	7
35	1

3. Shown are the ages of a group of teenagers at a youth club :-

   16, 19, 15, 17, 16, 18, 19, 15, 20, 15, 17, 17, 19, 16, 18, 16, 15, 17, 17, 19, 15, 15, 18, 19, 16.

   (a) Draw up a frequency table (*using tally marks if it helps*) to show all the ages.

   (b) Add on a 3rd column, ($f \times x$), to calculate the **mean** age.

   (c) Add on a 4th column, (*cumulative frequency*), and from it, calculate the **median** age.

1. Calculate the **mean**, **median**, **mode** and **range** :-

    (a) 9, 10, 10, 10, 12, 16, 24

    (b) 8·7, 5·3, 7·4, 7·4, 8·1, 7·4, 6·8, 8·9

    (c) 208, 107, 392, 115, 302, 208

    (d) 40, 42, 33, 42, 65, 42, 37, 40, 50, 60

    (e) –12, –9, –2, 3, –1, 4, 5, 8, –9, 3

    (f) 10, $5\frac{1}{2}$, $2\frac{1}{2}$, $4\frac{1}{2}$, $5\frac{1}{2}$, $2\frac{1}{2}$, $5\frac{1}{2}$, 4.

2.  The mean price of two vacuum cleaners is £99·95.

    If one of the vacuums costs £89·55 what must the other one cost ?

3. The **mean** number of chocolates I counted in the first 3 of my Easter eggs was 18.

    After opening the 4th Egg, I discovered that the mean for all 4 was then 22.

    How many chocolates were in that last egg ?

4.  A sweet factory claims that the average number of imperials in one of their jars is 120.

    A number of jars were opened for inspection and the number of imperials found in these jars were :-

    124,   117,   117,   125,   128,

    107,   116,   117,   121,   118.

    (a) Did the factory find its claim to be true ? (*Justify your answer*).

    (b) An eleventh jar was opened.

    How many imperials would need to be in that jar so that the factory's claim could be said to be true?

5. The frequency table below shows the cost of a tin of NICE Beans in various shops in and around Aberdeen.

Cost of 1 Tin x	Freq f	$f \times x$
31p	4	
32p	7	
33p	10	
34p	6	
35p	3	

Total shops   Total cost

    (a) What is the **modal** cost (the mode) ?

    (b) What is the **median** cost ?

    (c) State the **range**.

    (d) **Copy** the table and complete the 3rd column to help determine the **mean** cost.

6. (a) Add a third column ($f \times x$), on to the frequency table below to help you calculate the **mean** mark in a History test out of 50.

mark	Frequency
20	5
25	2
30	6
35	4
40	8
45	4
50	1

    (b) Add on a 4th column, (*cumulative frequency*) and from it, calculate the **median** mark.

Bar Charts & Line Graphs

Data can be represented in many different ways, so that information can be more easily understood.

The **Comparative Bar Graph** below shows the gender of three second year classes.

This **Comparative Line Graph** shows the sales of two car companies.

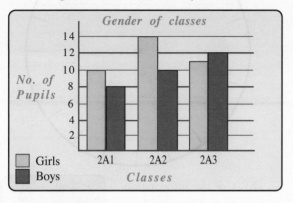

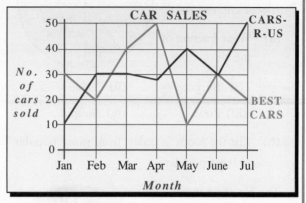

There are 8 boys in 2A1.
There are 18 pupils altogether in 2A1.

Best Cars sold 20 cars in February.
Cars-R-Us sold 10 cars in January.

Exercise 23·1

1. Look at the bar graph directly above.

   (a) How many boys are there in 2A2 ?

   (b) How many girls are there in 2A3 ?

   (c) How many pupils are there in 2A3 ?

   (d) How many **more** girls than boys are there in total in all three classes ?

2. Construct a **Comparative Bar Graph** showing the gender of the three First Year classes listed below.

	1A1	1A2	1A3
Boys	10	16	11
Girls	14	7	13

3. Construct a **Comparative Bar Graph** showing the number of medals won in an inter-schools competition.

	Swimming	Athletics	Gymnastics
Clyde High	5	4	3
Ayr High	2	4	3
Oban High	3	2	4

4. Look at the line graph above.

   (a) How many cars did **Cars-R-Us** sell in :-

      (i) March   (ii) May   (iii) July ?

   (b) **Estimate** how many cars were sold in April by **Cars-R-Us.**

   (c) How many cars were sold by **Best Cars** from January to July **inclusive** ?

5. Construct a **Comparative Line Graph** showing these two companies' house sales.

	Jan	Feb	Mar	Apr	May
Scot Homes	10	40	30	50	55
Brit Estates	5	20	35	35	50

6. Construct a **Comparative Line Graph** showing the average rainfall (in mm) in the three towns.

	May	June	July	Aug	Sept
Ayton	100	40	10	30	50
Beeton	80	60	20	20	25
Ceeton	45	35	30	25	35

1. The pie chart shows the results of a class survey into *favourite school canteen food*.

   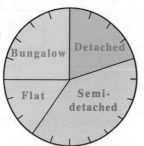

   (a) What fraction of the class chose :-

      (i) Burger ($\frac{?}{10}$)   (ii) Salad

      (iii) Pizza   (iv) Soup ?

   (b) List the foods in order, from **most** popular to **least** popular.

2. The pie chart shows the results of a year-group analysis into hair colour.

   (a) What percentage of the year-group had :-

      (i) dark brown

      (ii) light brown

      (iii) blonde hair ?

   (b) If 300 pupils were in the year-group, **how many** of them :-

      (i) had blonde hair ?

      (ii) did **not** have black hair ?

3. This pie chart shows the type of houses the people at a political meeting live in.

   (a) What percentage of the people live in a :-

      (i) bungalow   (ii) semi-detached

      (iii) flat   (iv) detached villa ?

   (b) There are 500 people at the meeting. **How many** people live in a :-

      (i) flat   (ii) semi-detached ?

4. (a) Copy or trace the blank pie chart below.

   COPY

   (b) Use the information from this table to complete your blank pie chart.

Football	-	50%
Rugby	-	20%
Tennis	-	5%
Hockey	-	15%
Netball	-	10%

   Copy or trace the blank pie chart above to help you draw pie-charts to represent the following :-

5. In a bowl of minestrone soup, the ingredients were as follows :-

   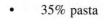

   • 35% pasta
   • 40% carrots
   • 15% tomato
   • the rest was celery.

   Draw a **pie chart** to show the information above.

6. The information below shows the most popular pets in third year at Greenby High school.

   • 40% owned dogs.
   • 30% owned cats.
   • of the others, half owned fish and the other half owned mice.

   Draw a **pie chart** to show this information.

7. Of the 40 000 people at a football match, 20 000 of them were season ticket holders, 10 000 of them were tickets sales, 6000 of them were juvenile ticket holders and the rest held concessionary tickets.

   Draw a **pie chart** to show this information.

The table of data shows the number of different types of footwear bought from *Sandy's Shoe Shop* one day.

When drawing a pie chart, it is sometimes easier to add columns to the table for calculations.

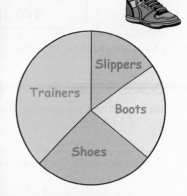

Type of Footwear	No. Sold
Trainers	34
Shoes	24
Boots	18
Slippers	14

Type of Footwear	Number	Fraction	Angle
Trainers	34	$\frac{34}{90}$	$\frac{34}{90} \times 360 = 136°$
Shoes	24	$\frac{24}{90}$	$\frac{24}{90} \times 360 = 96°$
Boots	18	$\frac{18}{90}$	$\frac{18}{90} \times 360 = 72°$
Slippers	14	$\frac{14}{90}$	$\frac{14}{90} \times 360 = 56°$
TOTAL	**90**	**1**	**360°**

Step 1 :- **add** all the "numbers" together to get a total (**in this case - 90**).

Step 2 :- express each "number" as a **fraction** of this total. (e.g. $\frac{34}{90}$).

Step 3 :- find this **fraction of 360°** each time (e.g. $\frac{34}{90} \times 360 = 136°$).

Step 4 :- draw the pie chart showing these angles using a **protractor**.

1. (a) **Copy** and **complete** the table which shows the favourite type of pizza chosen by a group of 180 people.

    (b) Construct a pie chart using compasses, a protractor and the table information.

Type of Pizza	Number	Fraction	Angle
Hawaiian	20	$\frac{20}{180}$	$\frac{20}{180} \times 360 = 40°$
Four Seasons	90	$\frac{90}{180}$	$\frac{90}{180} \times 360 = \ldots°$
Americano	10	$\frac{}{180}$	$\frac{}{180} \times 360 = \ldots°$
Hot & Spicy	60	$\frac{}{180}$	$\frac{}{180} \times 360 = \ldots°$
TOTAL	**180**	**1**	**360°**

2. The table shows the favourite T.V. programmes of a group of women.

    (a) **Copy** and **complete** the table.

    (b) Construct an accurate pie chart showing this information.

Programme	Number	Fraction	Angle
Comedy	5	$\frac{5}{45}$	$\frac{5}{45} \times 360 = 40°$
Soap	20	$\frac{20}{45}$	....
Sport	18	$\frac{}{45}$	....
Educational	2	.....	....
TOTAL	**45**	**1**	**360°**

3. (a) Copy and complete the table showing the hair colour of a class of S3 pupils.

Hair colour	Number	Fraction	Angle
Brown	10	$\frac{10}{30}$	$\frac{10}{30} \times 360 = ...°$
Black	12		$\times 360 = ...°$
Blonde	7		$\times 360 = ...°$
Red	1		$\times 360 = ...°$
TOTAL	**30**		.....°

(b) Construct an accurate **pie chart** showing this information.

4. Copy each of the following tables, add new columns to show what calculations you are performing, then construct an accurate **pie chart** to represent the information.

(a)

Super Hero	Number
Rat-Man	36
Chat-Woman	20
Sider-Man	4
Souper-Man	12
TOTAL	72 ....

(b)

Favourite Sport	Number
Football	20
Tennis	8
Snooker	5
Netball	3
TOTAL	36 ...

(c)

Height (cm)	Number
150 - 154	400
155 - 159	240
160 - 164	70
165 - 169	10
TOTAL	720 ....

5. The four main blood groups are **A, B, AB** and **O**.

This table shows the results of the fourth year biology students who tested their individual blood groups.

(a) **Copy** and **complete** the table below :-
(*add any columns you might need to help you make a pie chart*)

Blood Group	Tally Mark	Number
A		
B		
AB		
O		

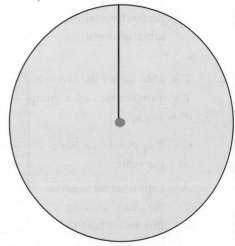

(b) Construct an accurate pie chart for this information.
(*Copy or trace the pie chart shown*).

Remember Remember..... ?

1. Use this table to construct a **Comparative Bar Graph** showing the sex of a group of pupils in three senior Maths classes.

	5M1	5M2	5M3
Boys	12	14	11
Girls	14	8	13

2. Use this table to construct a **Comparative Line Graph** to show the sales of TV sets in 2 television shops last week.

	Wed	Thu	Fri	Sat	Sun
Commet	6	8	4	12	10
Dixies	4	6	10	11	12

3. In a survey in a fish market, 540 people were asked which method they preferred to cook a piece of haddock.

   The results are shown in the pie chart.

   (a) What angle at the centre is taken up by grilling the fish ?

   (b) How many people preferred the haddock :-
   (i) done in the oven   (ii) fried ?

   (c) How many preferred to have their haddock grilled ?

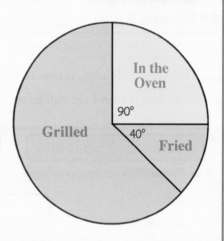

4. (a) **Copy** and complete the table showing how a group of third year pupils travel to school.

   (b) Construct a **pie chart** to represent the information shown.

Transport	No.	Fraction	Angle
Bus	20	$\frac{20}{60}$	$\frac{20}{60} \times 360 = ...°$
Train	14		$\times 360 = ...°$
Walk	24		$\times 360 = ...°$
Taxi	2		$\times 360 = ...°$
TOTAL	...		360°

5. *Revision*

   Joyce went online to find the prices of quality inkjet printers.
   She found 20 sites which had a printer she could afford and was in stock.

   Here are the prices she found :-

   £123   £138   £144   £170   £160   £150   £170   £158   £144   £157

   £150   £166   £123   £144   £155   £160   £133   £172   £151   £144

   (a) Construct an **ordered stem-and-leaf diagram**, including a key.

   (b) What is the modal price of the printers ?

   (c) Determine the median price.

Probability

The **Probability** of "something" happening is simply the **likelihood** or **chance** of it happening.

Examples :-   What is the **probability** that :-

if today is Monday, then tomorrow will be Wednesday ?	(impossible)
it will rain **every day** in June ?	(unlikely)
if I toss a coin, it will land heads ?	(even chance)
if I toss 8 coins, at least one will be tails ?	(likely)
if I put my hand in a fire, I will get burned ?	(certain)

Exercise 24·1   - (Oral exercise)

For each statement below, say whether the probability of it happening is :-

impossible - unlikely - evens (50-50) - likely - certain.

1.   If today is Monday, yesterday was Thursday.

2.   The next person I see will be male.

3.   No trains will be on time tomorrow.

4.   There will be snow in January.

5.   I will win the lottery jackpot this week.

6.   I will have a birthday this year.

7.   Christmas will be in November next year.

8.   I will blink today.

Calculating Probability

The **Probability** of an event happening simply means "what **fraction** of the time it will happen".

It is defined as :-

$$\text{Probability} = \frac{\text{number of favourable outcomes}}{\text{number of possible outcomes}}$$

Example :-   This bag contains 8 **blue** balls and 4 **red** balls.

If I choose a ball at random without looking, what is the **probability** that I will pick a **red** ball ?

$$\text{Probability of red} = P(\text{red}) = \frac{\text{number of red balls}}{\text{total number of balls}} = \frac{4}{12} = \frac{1}{3}$$

Exercise 24·2

1.   A bag contains 6 black balls and 12 white balls.

   If a ball is picked at random, what is the **probability** that it will be **black** ?

   (*Use the notation :-* $P(\textbf{black}) = ...$)

2.   A bag has 3 red sweets, 6 green sweets and 9 blue sweets.
   If a sweet is picked at random, what is the probability that the sweet will be :-

   (a)   **red**   (b)   **green**

   (c)   **blue**   (d)   **orange** ?

3.   A dice numbered from 1 to 6, is rolled.

   (a)   What is the probability that the dice will end up showing the number 5 on top ?
   (i.e. $P(5) = ...$)

   (b)   Find :-

   (i) $P(3)$ (ii) $P(\text{odd})$

   (iii) $P(8)$ (iv) $P(\text{smaller than 2})$.

4. A **duodecagon** (12 sided) spinner is spun and its number is noted.

Find :-

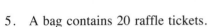

(a) *P*(less than 4)

(b) *P*(multiple of 3)

(c) *P*(prime)

(d) *P*(factor of 12).

5. A bag contains 20 raffle tickets.

Four tickets win a cuddly toy, two tickets win £10 and the rest are losing tickets. If you buy a single ticket, find the following probabilities :-

(a) *P*(win a toy)   (b) *P*(losing ticket)

(c) *P*(win £10)   (d) *P*(**not** win £10).

6. A garage forecourt has the following colours of cars :-

12 blue, 8 green, 6 silver,
4 white,   3 black, 2 red,
1 yellow.

Find the following probabilities :-

(a) *P*(blue)   (b) *P*(green)

(c) *P*(silver)   (d) *P*(white)

(e) *P*(black)   (f) *P*(red)

(g) *P*(yellow)   (h) *P*(red or blue)

(i) *P*(**not** red or blue).

7. In a word game, letters are chosen at random from the word :-

Find :-

(a) *P*(A)   (b) *P*(R)

(c) *P*(vowel)   (d) *P*(consonant).

8. The probability of an event happening is calculated to be $\frac{3}{7}$.

What is the probability the event will **not** happen ?

9. Three coins are tossed at the same time.

(a) Make a neat list of all the possibilities.

(HHH, HHT, HTH etc....).

(b) Find :–   (i) *P*(all heads)   (ii) *P*(2 tails).

10. One dart is thrown at a dartboard, numbered 1 – 20.

If the dart actually lands on the board, find :-

(a) *P*(16)   (b) *P*(over 12)

(c) *P*(even)   (d) *P*(prime).

11. Look at the two bags shown.

How many **more** green balls do I have to put into bag 2 so that each bag has the same probability of picking, at random, a **green** ball ?

bag 1

bag 2

12. The weathermen reckon that the probability it will rain in Perth tomorrow is 0·25.

What is the probability it will **not** rain in Perth ?

13. After counting the number of boys and girls in a 3rd year group, the teacher says the following :-

"If I chose a name at random, from this group, the probability it will be a male is $\frac{3}{5}$ " .

The teacher knows there are 60 in the group.

How many boys and how many girls are there ?

14. A pack of cards consists of 52 cards. There are 13 spades, 13 clubs, 13 hearts and 13 diamonds.

Each suit has :- Ace, 2, 3, 4, 5, 6, 7, 8, 9, 10, Jack, Queen and King.

If I shuffle the cards and look at the top one, what are the following probabilities :-

(a) *P*(a red card)   (b) *P*(a spade)

(c) *P*(an Ace)   (d) *P*(King of Hearts)

(e) *P*(a face card)   (*Jack, Queen or King*).

15. I roll **two** six-sided dice and add the 2 numbers.

Make a list of all 36 possible pairings like this :-

(1, 1), (1, 2), (1, 3).......... (5, 6), (6, 6).

Calculate the following probabilities :-

(a) *P*(total = 3)   (b) *P*(total = 7)

(c) *P*(total = 12)   (d) *P*(1st no. > 2nd no.).

16. Felix bought 9 raffle tickets from a book containing 55 tickets.

    Sheena bought 11 tickets from a 61 ticket book.

    (a) Write Felix's chances as a fraction. (9/...)

    (b) Write Sheena's chances as a fraction.

    (c) Change both fractions to a decimal, then to a percentage.

    (d) Compare both percentages and decide who has the better chance of winning.

17. It is calculated that Celia has a 2 in 17 chance of achieving her target weight at a weight-watchers' class.

    Daria has a 9 in 49 chance.

    Who has the better chance of reaching their target weight ? (*Justify your answer*).

18. The weather forecast predicts there is a 6 in 38 chance of rain.

    There is also a 5 in 32 chance of snow.

    Which is more likely ?
    (*Justify your answer*).

19. Three strikers have scored the following goals :-

    Rivaldo - 3 goals in 7 matches
    Jonson - 2 goals in 5 matches
    Erikton - 5 goals in 12 matches.

    Who has the best chance of scoring the most goals over the next ten matches ?
    (*Justify your answer*).

Remember Remember..... ?

1. For each statement below, say whether the probability of it happening is :-

   impossible - unlikely - evens - likely - certain.

   (a) If today is Sunday, yesterday was Tuesday.

   (b) The next person I see will be female.

   (c) I will score 100% in a difficult Maths test.

2. There are 52 cards in a deck. If I choose one without looking, what is the probability it will **not** be a face card ?
   (*King, Queen or Jack*).

3. An eight sided dice is thrown. Find :-

   (a) P(3)

   (b) P(even)

   (c) P(prime)

   (d) P(ten).

4. The probability of an event not happening is calculated as 0·45.

   What is the probability of the event happening ?

5. A box contains some red and blue marbles. There are a total of thirty marbles and there is a 40% probability of picking a red at random.

   (a) How many blue marbles are in the box ?

   (b) How many red marbles do I need to add to the box so that there is an evens chance of picking a red at random ?

6. There are 49 balls in the lottery. The following balls were drawn :-

   2, 12, 23, 37 and 45.

   For the remaining balls, find :-

   (a) P(3)   (b) P(12)

   (c) P(odd)   (d) P(>40).

7. Two boxes have green and red balls.

   Box 1 : 13 green and 6 red balls
   Box 2 : 11 green and 5 red balls.

   Which box would you choose so that you would have a better chance of picking out a red ball ?

   (*Justify your answer*).

1. Calculate the mean, median, mode and range for each of the following sets of data :-

   (a) 8, 8, 11, 13, 14, 15, 21

   (b) –10, –7, –1, 0, –1, 3, 6, 7, –1, 3

   (c) 2, $3\frac{1}{2}$, 4, $7\frac{1}{2}$, 11, 11, $13\frac{1}{2}$, 9.

2. Four boys have a mean age of 14.
   Three of the boys are aged 10, 11 and 16.

   What is the age of the fourth boy ?

3. The frequency table below recorded the number of marks in a class test.

mark (x)	Frequency (f)
20	4
25	3
30	4
35	6
40	7
45	5
50	1

   (a) How many pupils sat the test ?

   (b) What was the range of marks ?

   (c) Add a third column ($f \times x$) and calculate the mean mark.

   (d) Calculate the median mark.

4. The number of coins in the pockets of a third year class are counted and recorded.

9	0	4	6	5	3	1
6	7	7	0	0	1	2
3	5	6	6	2	1	7
5	0	4	3	0	8	1

   (a) Construct an ordered stem and leaf graph to show this information.

   (b) Find the modal number of coins.

   (c) How many pupils are in the class ?

   (d) Find the mean number of coins.

5. The table shows the number of men and women who passed their driving test first time with ROY's School of Motoring, over a 6 week period.

Week	1	2	3	4	5	6
Men	4	6	8	5	2	3
Women	6	9	10	7	1	5

   Show the above statistics in a neatly labelled **Comparative Bar Graph**.

6. The table shows the number of hours four part-time female workers were employed last week.

Name	Hours	Fraction	Angle
Julie	24	$\frac{24}{...}$	$\frac{24}{...}$ x .. = ..
Mandy	20		
Norma	16		
Li Ming	30		
TOTAL	...		....

   (a) Copy and complete the above table.

   (b) Now draw a neat labelled **pie-chart** to represent the above information.

7. A ten sided dice is thrown.
   Write down :-

   (a) P(10)   (b) P(odd)

   (c) P(square)   (d) P(prime).

8. Balls in a bag are numbered from 10 to 20.
   Alf picks, at random, balls 11, 15 and 16.

   If the balls are not returned to the bag what is the probability of Alf picking a prime number on the next pick ?

9. Andie plays a maths game.
   It has been calculated she has a 3 in 11 chance of beating her last score and a 0·5 chance of equalling her score.

   What is the probability of her scoring below her last score ?

1.■ Round to **2 significant figures** :-

   (a)   13·782   (b)   0·06749   (c)   23 496.

2.■ Evaluate :-   (a) $7·21 + 3·8 \times 4$

   (b) $7·3 - 5·05 \div 5$ (c) $8·4 \div (6·1 - 1·1)$.

3.■ Find :-

   (a) $(-4) + 11$ (b) $-3p^2 - 7p^2$

   (c) $-5 - (-9)$ (d) $-4d - (-4d)$

   (e) $(-6) \times (-5p)$ (f) $24 \div (-6)$

   (g) $(-7ab)^2$ (h) $24st \div (-4s)$.

4.■ Calculate the values of a, b and c.

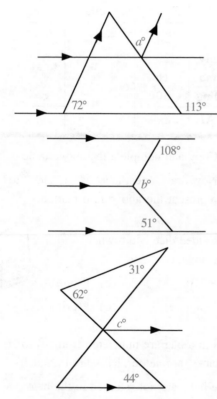

5.■ Find without a calculator :-

   (a)   15% of \$52   (b) $2\frac{1}{2}$% of 360

   (c)   90% of 120 ml   (d) $66\frac{2}{3}$% of £3000.

6.■ A shopkeeper buys 3 dozen Easter eggs for £64·80 altogether. He sells them at £2·25 each.

Calculate his actual total profit and express this as a percentage of the cost price.

7.■ Mrs Ritchie sees a new cooker in a shop window priced £290.

 £290 + VAT

As she is a senior citizen, the shopkeeper offers her a 10% discount on any cooker.

She asks the shopkeeper if he would mind adding the 20% V.A.T. after her discount is taken off as it would be cheaper for her.

The shopkeeper tells her it would be better if the V.A.T. was added first, and then the 10% discount was applied.

Who is correct, giving reasons for your answer ?

8.■ Simplify :-

   (a) $2(3 - 2x) + 3x - 6$

   (b) $-4(1 - 3x) - 2(3x - 1)$.

9.■ Factorise fully :-

   (a) $4a^2 - 6a$ (b) $24x^2y - 40y^2$.

10.■ Sketch these figures on squared paper.

Rotate each by 180° clockwise around the **pink** dot.

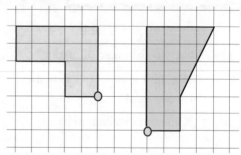

11.■ What **order** of rotational symmetry has a :-

   (a)   parallelogram   (b)   regular hexagon ?

12.■ Write down the maximum and minimum values given by these tolerances :-

   (a) $(70 \pm 4·5)$ cm   (b) $(8·99 \pm 0·02)$ km.

13.■ Put the following into tolerance form :-

   (a)   min = 0·23 m   (b)   min = 0·053 m

           max = 0·27 m   max = 0·069 m.

14.■ Using the exchange rate of .....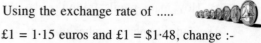

£1 = 1·15 euros and £1 = \$1·48, change :-

   (a)   £260 into euros   (b)   \$444 into £'s.

15. This jet ski can be paid for by making a 15% deposit of the cash price, followed by 30 equal monthly payments of £150.

£4200 Cash

How much **dearer** is this than the cash price ?

16. Charles has a **gross income** of £32 500.

He pays income tax of £4700, N.I. £2300 and 6% of his gross wage on Superannuation.

(a) Calculate his annual **take home** pay.

(b) Calculate his **monthly** take home pay.

17. Water is leaking from a barrel at a steady rate.

Every hour, the volume is read and here are the results :-

Time (*t*) hrs	0	1	2	3	4	5
Vol (*V*) litres	850	830	810	790	770	750

(a) Find a formula for V in terms of t.

$$V = \ldots\ldots$$

(b) The 850 litre reading was taken at midday on Monday.
At what time and on what day will the barrel finally be empty ?

18. Look at the pattern for expanding brackets which are "cubed" :-

$$(4 + 5)^3 = 4^3 + 3 \times (4)^2 \times (5) + 3 \times (4) \times (5)^2 + 5^3$$

$$(5 + 6)^3 = 5^3 + 3 \times (5)^2 \times (6) + 3 \times (5) \times (6)^2 + 6^3$$

$$(6 + 7)^3 = 6^3 + 3 \times (6)^2 \times (7) + 3 \times (6) \times (7)^2 + 7^3$$

(a) Write down a similar expression for $(10 + 11)^3$.

(b) Write down an expression for $(x + 1)^3$ and simplify it.

(c) Hence, rewrite the following expression **in its factorised form** :-

$$a^3 + 3a^2b + 3ab^2 + b^3.$$

19. Solve these equations showing **ALL** working :-

(a) $6x - 3 = 30$ (b) $3(2x + 4) = 42$

(c) $9x - 2 = 4x + 23$

(d) $10 - 8(1 - x) = 18$

(e) $10x - 2(3x + 6) = x$

(f) $\dfrac{3x}{2} - \dfrac{x}{5} = 3$ (g) $\dfrac{3}{4}x - \dfrac{1}{3} = \dfrac{1}{2}$

(h) $\dfrac{3}{5}x - \dfrac{2}{3} = \dfrac{1}{2}x + \dfrac{3}{4}$

(i) $\dfrac{x-1}{4} - \dfrac{2x+1}{3} = 1$

(j) $\dfrac{12}{x} + \dfrac{2}{3} = 2$ (k) $\dfrac{x+1}{2} - \dfrac{x-1}{3} = 2$.

20. Solve these **inequalities** :-

(a) $2(4x + 5) - 3(2x + 1) < 19$

(b) $-2x > 12$ (c) $-3x \le -15$

(d) $8 - 3(x - 2) \ge 5$ (e) $\dfrac{1}{3}x - 1 < 5$.

21. George has 5 packets of TOFFY chews and another 5 chews.

Lesley has 2 packets of TOFFY chews and another 35 chews.

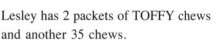

Given that George has less sweets than Lesley, what can you say about the number of chews in a single packet of TOFFY's ?

22. Write in scientific notation :-

(a) 185 000   (b) 0·0037.

23. Write out fully :-

(a) $1·78 \times 10^8$ (b) 6×10^{-4} .

24. Calculate :-

(a) $(2·7 \times 10^5) \times (3·1 \times 10^{-2})$

(b) $(1·225 \times 10^{11}) \div (4·5 \times 10^{-6})$.

25. A bee weighs approximately $1·98 \times 10^{-4}$ kg. An eagle is 93 times heavier.

Calculate the weight of the eagle in scientific notation.

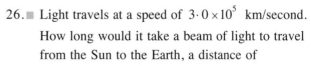

26. Light travels at a speed of $3·0 \times 10^5$ km/second. How long would it take a beam of light to travel from the Sun to the Earth, a distance of

$$1·476 \times 10^8 \text{ km ?}$$

Answer in minutes and seconds.

27. ■ Calculate the **perimeter** of this shape :-

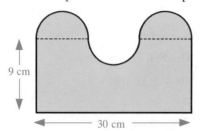

30 cm

9 cm

28. ■ Calculate the **area** of this shape :-

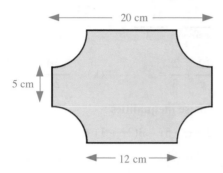

20 cm

5 cm

12 cm

29. ■ Calculate the **diameters** of these circles :-

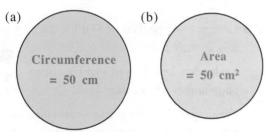

(a) Circumference = 50 cm

(b) Area = 50 cm²

30. ■ Draw a set of *x*–*y* axes and plot the points

A(1, 2), B(5, 2) and C(5, 4).

Find the coordinates of the image of triangle ABC after it is :-

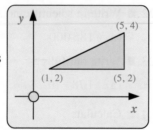

(1, 2) (5, 2) (5, 4)

(a) reflected over the *y*-axis.

(b) rotated 180° clockwise around the origin.

(c) moved under a translation of $\begin{pmatrix} -6 \\ -2 \end{pmatrix}$.

31. ■ A man walked from point A on a river bank to tree T, then from the tree he rejoined the river bank at B.

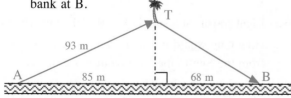

T

93 m

A   85 m   68 m   B

Calculate the distance from T to B.

32. ■ A clown's face consists of an isosceles triangle PQR on top of a segment of a circle.

The diameter of the circle is 20 centimetres.

The base of the triangle is 16 centimetres and its sloping sides are 17 centimetres long.

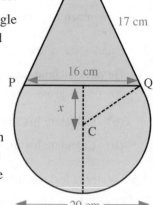

R

17 cm

16 cm

P   Q

x   C

20 cm

(a) Calculate *x*, the distance in centimetres from the centre of the circle to the base of the triangle.

(b) Calculate the total height of the figure.

33. ■ A plane flew at 720 km/hr for 2 hrs 24 minutes. How **far** did it travel ?

34. ■ A train covers 248 km in 2 hrs 40 minutes. What is its average **speed** ?

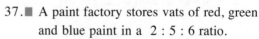

35. ■ At an average speed of 80 km/hr, **how long** will it take (in hours and minutes) to cover a distance of 288 km ?

36. ■ A king shares his wealth amongst his three sons in the ratio of their ages.

George is 16, Fred is 24 and Cyril is 28.

How much of his fortune, which amounted to £340 000, should each son receive ?

37. ■ A paint factory stores vats of red, green and blue paint in a 2 : 5 : 6 ratio.

(a) If there are 12 vats of red paint, how many vats of blue paint are there ?

(b) There are a total of 65 vats in the factory. How many vats of green are there ?

38. ■

8 taps having the same rate of flow, fill a tank in 27 minutes.

If two taps go out of order, how long will the remaining taps take to fill the tank?

39. ■ Calculate the volumes of these shapes :-

(a)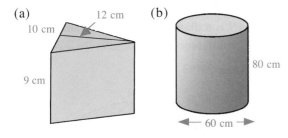
12 cm
10 cm
9 cm

(b)
80 cm
← 60 cm →

(c)
$V = \frac{1}{3}\pi r^2 h$
12 cm
4 cm

(d)
← 50 cm →
$V = \frac{4}{3}\pi r^3$ for sphere

40. ■ (a) Calculate the **curved surface area** of a cylinder with base diameter 14 cm and height 12 cm.
12 cm

(b) Now calculate the **total area** of **all** its surfaces.
14 cm

41. ■ A cylindrical tin of lemonade is 16 centimetres in height and 7·5 centimetres in diameter.

A new cylindrical tin holds the same volume but has a reduced height of 10 centimetres.

Calculate the diameter of the new tin, to one decimal place.

42. ■ A rectangular tank, whose base measures 30 cm by 20 cm, is half full of water. 300 spherical ball bearings, each of diameter 2 cm, are dropped into the tank.

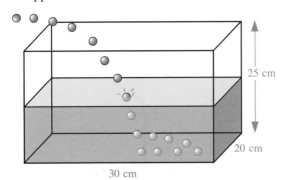
25 cm
20 cm
30 cm

(a) Find the volume of one of the ball bearings.

(b) By how many centimetres did the water level rise within the tank after the ball bearings were added ? (*Answer to the nearest 0·1 cm*).

43. ■ A wooden toy box is prism-shaped as shown.

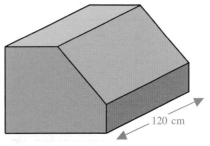
120 cm

The side part of the box (the cross section) is shown below.
40 cm
65 cm
30 cm
80 cm

(a) Calculate the area of this cross section.

(b) Calculate the volume of the box, (a prism), in cubic centimetres.

44. ■ Find the equations of these lines :-

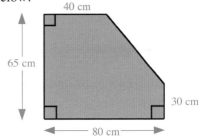

A
$m = -4$
(0,−3)

B
(8, 7)
(0, 3)

C
(3, 8)
(0,−4)

D
(0, 3)
(6, 0)

45. The diagram shows the line through the points A and B.

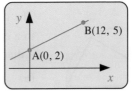
B(12, 5)
A(0, 2)

The point P($2p, p$) lies on the line AB.

Find the equation of the line and the value of p.

46. ■ This graph shows the pressure (*P*) in a boiler, (*t*) minutes after the burner is turned off.

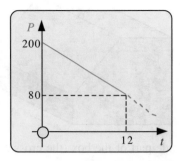

(a) Construct a formula connecting *P* and *t*.
$$(P = ...).$$

(b) What is the pressure after 7 minutes ?

(c) After how many minutes will the pressure drop to **zero** ?

47. ■ Calculate the size of angles *a*, *b* and *c*.

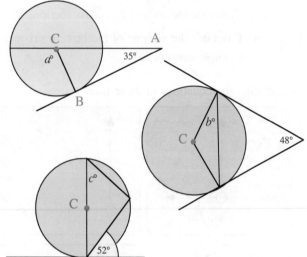

48. ■ Given that radius = 25 cm and AB = 48 cm, calculate the length of the line MT.

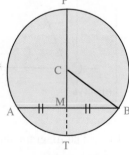

49. ■

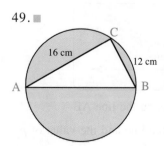

The triangle ABC is placed in a circle so that AB forms a diameter.

(a) Calculate the length of the circle's radius.

(b) Calculate the total pink area.

50. ■ AB is a tangent to the circle, centre O, meeting the circle at point N.

MN is a diameter and P is a point on the circumference of the circle.

Angle MPO = 62°.

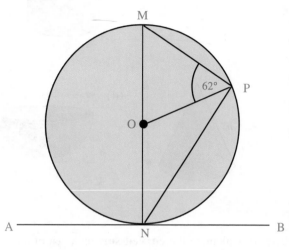

Calculate the size of ∠PNM. (*Explain fully*).

51. ■ A wooden beam, PQ, is 6·5 metres long.

It balances on top of a 1 metre high vertical pillar at M.

When Q is on the ground, P is 1·3 metres above the ground.

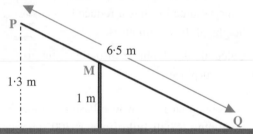

When P falls to the ground, Q rises.

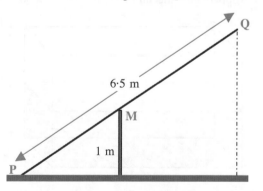

By calculating the length of PM, find how far Q is above the ground.

52. Shape Q is an enlargement of shape P.

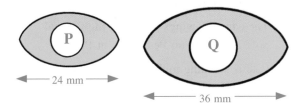

24 mm

36 mm

If the area of shape Q is 108 mm², calculate the area of shape P.

53. ■ Two cocktail glasses are mathematically similar in shape.

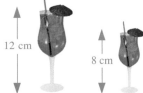

The smaller one is 8 centimetres high and holds 20 ml of liqueur.

12 cm   8 cm

The larger one is 12 centimetres high.

What volume of liqueur will the larger one hold ?

54. ■ Find :-

(a) $\frac{1}{2} + \frac{3}{4}$

(b) $\frac{2}{3} - \frac{1}{6}$

(c) $\frac{7}{8} - \frac{2}{5}$

(d) $4\frac{1}{2} + 5\frac{1}{4}$

(e) $2\frac{2}{5} + 3\frac{2}{3}$

(f) $8\frac{5}{6} - 3\frac{1}{3}$

(g) $5\frac{1}{3} - 2\frac{3}{4}$

(h) $7 - 4\frac{3}{10}$.

55. ■ Find :-

(a) $\frac{5}{8} \times \frac{4}{7}$

(b) $\frac{3}{5} \times \frac{6}{11}$

(c) $1\frac{1}{2} \times 2\frac{1}{6}$

(d) $3\frac{1}{5} \times 2\frac{1}{2}$

(e) $\frac{3}{4}(4\frac{1}{3} - 1\frac{2}{5})$

(f) $\frac{2}{3}$ of $(1\frac{3}{16} - \frac{1}{4})$.

56. ■ The table shows the number of coins each of 20 boys had in their pockets during a maths lesson.

(a) Copy the frequency table.

(b) What is the modal value ?

(c) What is the median value ?

(d) What is the range of coins ?

(e) Add a third column and calculate the mean.

No. of coins (x)	Freq (f)
5	2
6	7
7	3
8	5
9	1
10	1
11	0
12	1

57. Find the mean, median, mode and range of the numbers :-

5, 6, 2, 2, 1, 7, 9, 3, 4, 2, 3.

58. The mean age of a group of eight girls was 15. One more girl joined the group and the mean age became 14.

How old was the ninth girl ?

59. The pie-chart shows a survey indicating the proportion of readers of 4 of Scotland's daily newspapers.

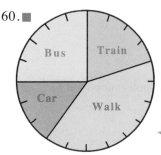

Express 36°
Record ? °
Herald 72°
108°
Sun

(a) What is the size of the angle representing Record readers ?

(b) If 1500 people took part in the survey, how many of them indicated that they read the Herald ?

60. ■

Bus   Train
Car   Walk

The pie chart illustrates the results of a 300 pupil survey into finding the most common mode of transport to school.

(a) What percentage of pupils walk to school ?

(b) How many pupils in the survey of 300 do not walk to school ?

(c) If you were to construct the pie chart, how many degrees would you need to represent the central angle for transport by car ?

61. ■ Two dice each numbered 1 to 6 are thrown.

Find the probability of throwing a **total** of more than 10.

62. ■ Jo's school sells 1350 raffle tickets. She buys 15 tickets.

Her church sells 2000 raffle tickets She buys 25 tickets.

Which raffle gives a better chance of winning ?

(*Justify your answer with working*).

63. ■ Alice was told that the probability of her choosing a lemon gum, her favourite, from a packet of fruit gums was 0·3. When she counted, she discovered there were 9 lemon gums in the packet.

How many gums were there in the packet altogether ?

64. ■ Calculate the value of *x* in these right angled triangles.

(a)
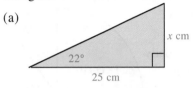

(b)
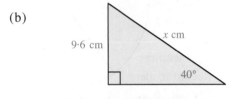

(c)
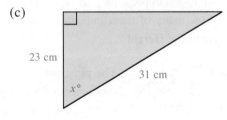

65. ■ Shown is a telegraph pole, supported by 2 wires.

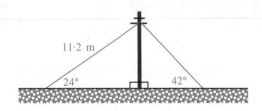

Calculate the length of the smaller wire.

66. ■ A ship set off on a bearing which after it had travelled 135 km, took it 25 km North of Port Talbert.

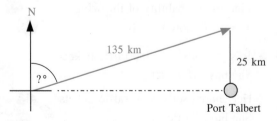

Calculate the size of the bearing on which it must have sailed.

67. ■ A CCTV camera is mounted on top of a 12 metre tall pole based at B.

The camera swings 45° from the vertical pole and picks up Pete at point P.

Pete is standing midway between the pole and another man Mike at point M.

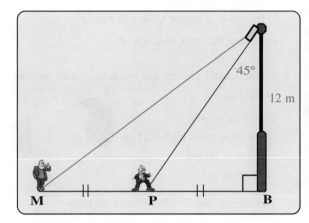

Through how many **more** degrees must the camera swing to pick up Mike ?

68. ■ Shown is a sketch of two hills, joined by a cable car.
The heights of the hills are 195 m and 480 m, and the length of the cable car run is 1·2 km.
For such an incline, a cable car system is deemed unsafe if the angle between the cable and the horizontal is more than 16°.

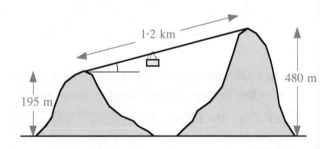

Is the cable car system in this case safe ?

69. ■ Construct an ordered stem-and-leaf diagram showing the ages of the people at grandad's 60th birthday party.

21	32	60	58	45	37
12	25	53	19	25	42
51	38	39	47	33	22
17	49	36	30	28	45

1. a 5·54 b 0·16 c 11·07 d 10·00
2. a 7·7 b 1200000
   c 11 d 60000000
3. a 2 b 4
4. a 400 b 18000000
5. £24
6. a £975 b £95
7. a 360 b 1380000
   c 400 d 690
8. a 11 b 16
9. a -14 b 27 c -1 d -32
   e 9 f -57·3... g 64 h -1
10. a 12 b 24 c 6 d 120
11. a 5 b 6 c 240 d 7
12. a 41, 43, 47
   b 91, 97, 101, 103, 107, 109
13. a $2 \times 3 \times 7$ b $2 \times 2 \times 5 \times 5$
   c $2 \times 2 \times 3 \times 3$ d $2 \times 2 \times 2 \times 2 \times 2 \times 2$
14. a 36 b 900 c 27
   d 256 e 7 f 200
15. a 0·5 b 0·6 c 0·13 d 0·09
16. a 50% b 40% c 75% d 66·666%
17. £680
18. 525
19. a $^7/_2$ b $^{11}/_3$ c $^{47}/_6$ d $^{77}/_6$
20. a $6^3/_4$ b $16^1/_2$ c $34^3/_5$ d $607^7/_8$
21. a $^5/_6$ b $5^3/_8$ c $5^2/_{15}$ d $^{10}/_{21}$
22. a 5·5 b 12
23. Yes (should have been £3·60)
24. 75 mins
25. Can (only 80p/100ml - bottle 90p/100 ml)
26. £216
27. £1757
28. a 65 mph b 60 km c 2 hrs 15 mins
29. 300 mph
30. a 35 cm²   b 15 m²
31. 439·6 cm
32. 1256 cm²
33. 54 litres
34. 55 cm²
35. a 151, 142   b 30, 42
   c 21, 34
36. $H = 6d + 9$
37. a $7x - 3y$ b q
   c $20ab$ d $4c$
38. a $6x - 12$ b $6m^2 - 4mn$
   c $-12x + 20y$ d $2g - g^2$
39. a $6t + 18s$ b $4k + 1$
   c $31 - 3h$ d -12
40. a 14 b 55 c 24 d 1
41. a 9 b 4·5 c 4 d 2·75
   e -8 f 8 g 2 h 44
42. a $x > 6$ b $x > 6$ c $x \geq 4$ d $x \leq 45$
43. a $10a + 4b + cd$ b 71
44. a   b

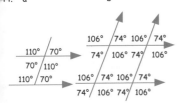

---

c   d

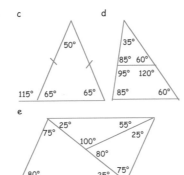

e

45. a 180° b 270° c 090° d 045°
46. a SW b NW
47. 230°
48. 160 m
49. 80 cm
50. 1 cm = 14 km
51. a A(-3, 4)   b D(3, -2)
   c C(5, 2)
52. a Yes b No c Yes
   d Yes e Yes f Yes
53. a 30 b 2 c 3·5 d 8
54. Median
55. a £170 b £50 c £45 d £32·50
56. 88
57. a $^{150}/_{360}, {}^5/_{12}$ b 75
58.

1	12468
2	33445789
3	45
4	0255778
5	012223789
6	2358

Key 2│3 = 23

59. $^6/_{15} = {}^2/_5$
60. 15
61. a $3, ^1/_3$ b $4, ^1/_4$ c $6, ^1/_6$ d $2, ^1/_2$
62. a   b

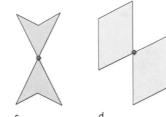

c   d

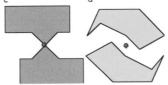

Exercise 1·1 - page 6

1. a 1 b 1 c 2 d 4
2. a 3 b 3 c 4 d 3
   e 3 f 4 g 2 h 7
   i 2 j 7 k 6 l 2
3. a 50 b 500 c 6000 d 20000
   e 4000 f 5000 g 2 h 0·4
   i 0·8 j 0·002 k 0·02 l 4000000
   m 0·0008 n 80
4. a 810 b 7100 c 31000 d 180000
   e 46 f 20 g 7·2 h 0·34
   i 0·0037   j 90
5. a 5840 b 25100 c 73900 d 482000
   e 15·8 f 12·8 g 0·287 h 0·294
   i 0·00168   j 0·0500
6. 14700 - 15000   7. £460 8. £72·23

Exercise 1·2 - page 7

1. a 7000 b 50000 c 800000 d 30000
   e 5000 f 80000 g 500000 h 210000
   i 50 j 10 k 2000 l 40
   m 150000000   n 1000 o 500
2. a 1000 b 190 c 45000 d 9500
   e 50000 f 380000 g 1200000 h 200
   i 540 j 292000 k 0·3 l 50
3. a 2300 b 220000 c 400
   d 17 e 0 f 25
   g 201 h 10 i 14
4. a 6000   b 30
5. a £2157000   b £20900000
6. Check all answers using a calculator

Exercise 1·3 - page 8

1. a 70 b 26 c 100
   d 70 e 196 f 5
2. a 10 b 5 c 19·5
   d 6 e 30 f 32
   g 23 h 29 i 1
3. a 60 b 25 c 450
   d 2 e 11 f 24
4. a $4 + (8 \times 2) = 20$ b $37 - (7 \times 5) = 2$
   c $(20 + 28) \div 2 = 24$ d $(30 + 50) \div (8 \times 5) = 2$
   e $(25 + 50) \div (28 - 3) = 3$
   f $4 + 9 \times 4 - (8 + 5) = 27$
5. a 140 b 12 c 180
   d 60 e 60 f 80
   g 150 h 9 i 10

Exercise 1·4 - page 9

1. a -1 b -18 c 4 d -45
   e -17 f -13 g -33 h 12
   i -10 j 5 k 210 l -610
2. a $13x$ b $-5x$ c $7a$ d $6y$
   e $-8b$ f $9e$ g $-10m$ h $2x$
   i x j $-c$ k $-21w$ l $4a + 5b$
3. a -3 b -3 c -8 d 16
   e 9 f -10 g 2 h -10
4. a 8 b 20 c 2 d -6
   e 1 f 0 g $8x$ h $11x$
   i x j $-8x$ k $5x$ l 0
5. a -3 b -1 c 2 d -4
   e 1 f -5 g 5 h -4

6.   a −9   b −35   c −9   d 0
    e −10a   f 21y   g −6x²   h −10
    i −10x   j −2p   k −5   l −28
    m −48   n −10   o 70   p 200
    q 5   r 10   s 40   t 4
    u 12a²   v 49   w 64   x 24
7.   a 0   b 3   c 29   d −10
    e 27   f 104   g 117   h 5
    i −21   j 0

Remember Remember Ch 1 - page 10

1.   a 60   b 400   c 5000   d 50000
    e 4   f 0·4   g 0·05   h 7000000
    i 0·0004   j 50
2.   a 710   b 7100   c 51000   d 270000
    e 58   f 70   g 8·2   h 0·45
    i 0·0017   j 40
3.   a 6940   b 34100   c 63000   d 731000
    e 13·8   f 13·3   g 0·400   h 0·294
    i 0·00178   j 0·0378
4.   a 7000   b 50000   c 1000000
    d 100000   e 40   f 3000
    g 80000000   h 3000   i 10000
5.   a 1010   b 210   c 31000   d 30000
    e 360000   f 57000
    g 60000000   h 2   i 20
    j £120000
6.   a 1   b 28   c 33
    d 29   e 0   f 0
7.   a −8x   b −12p   c −14n   d −g
    e −y   f 3a + b   g 2w   h 40x
    i 6m   j −6x²
8.   a −42   b −30a   c −27y   d −20x²
    e −10x   f −10   g 54k²   h 25
    i −32   j 128
9.   a 2   b 1   c −9   d −1
    e 6   f −2   g 2   h 3
    i 0   j −1   k 8   l −7
    m 20   n −8   o 18   p 66
    q 56   r −19
10.   a 39   b 25

┌─────────────────────────────────┐
│ Answers to Chapter 2 Page 11 │
└─────────────────────────────────┘

Exercise 2·1 - page 11

1.   a 58°   b 134°   c 111°   d 49°
    e 50°   f 112°   g 41°   h 77°
    i 52°   j 105°   k 19·5°   l 90°
2.   m 119°   n 77°   o 37°   p 50°
    q 74°   r 50°   s 71°   t 111°
    u 47°   v 120°   w 66°   x 19°
3.   a   b

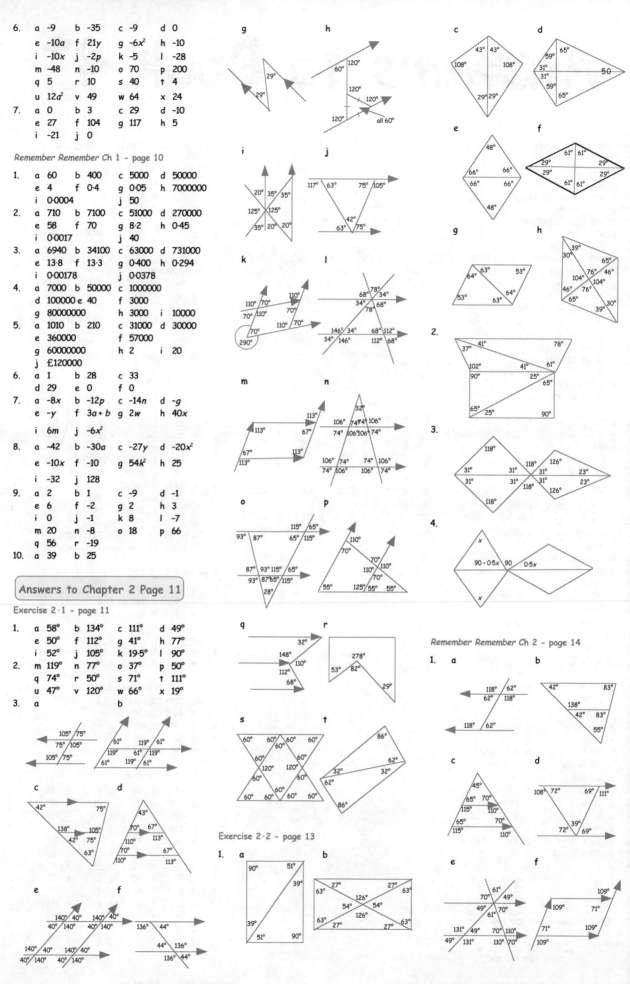

Exercise 2·2 - page 13

Remember Remember Ch 2 - page 14

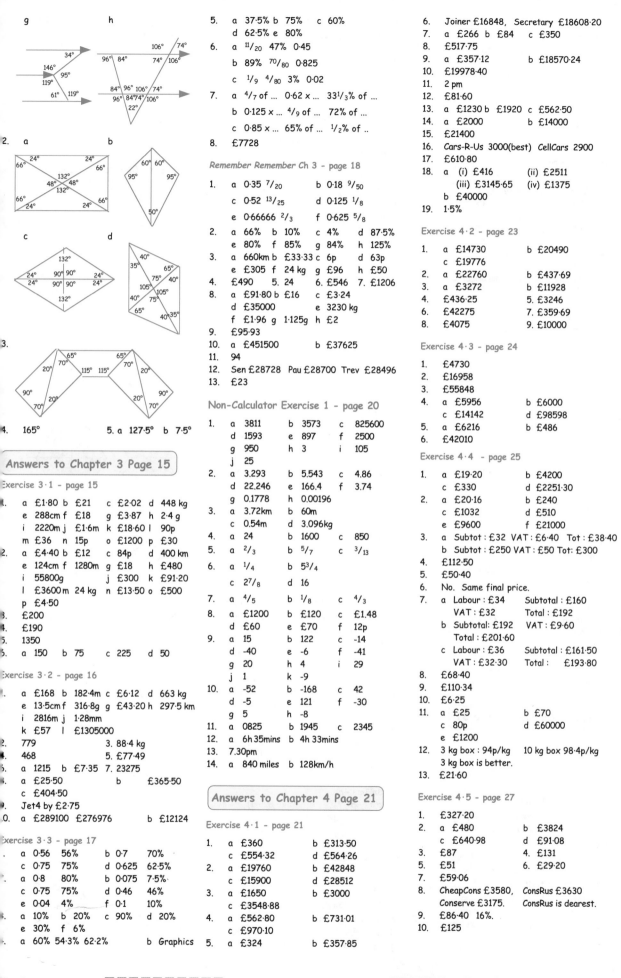

g   h

2. a   b

c   d

3.

4. 165°   5. a 127·5° b 7·5°

Exercise 3·1 - page 15

1. a £1·80 b £21   c £2·02 d 448 kg
   e 288cm f £18   g £3·87 h 2·4 g
   i 2220m j £1·6m k £18·60 l 90p
   m £36 n 15p o £1200 p £30
2. a £4·40 b £12   c 84p   d 400 km
   e 124cm f 1280m g £18 h £480
   i 55800g   j £300 k £91·20
   l £3600 m 24 kg n £13·50 o £500
   p £4·50
3. £200
4. £190
5. 1350
6. a 150 b 75   c 225 d 50

Exercise 3·2 - page 16

1. a £168 b 182·4m c £6·12 d 663 kg
   e 13·5cm f 316·8g g £43·20 h 297·5 km
   i 2816m j 1·28mm
   k £57 l £1305000
2. 779   3. 88·4 kg
4. 468   5. £77·49
6. a 1215 b £7·35 7. 23275
8. a £25·50   b   £365·50
   c £404·50
9. Jet4 by £2·75
10. a £289100 £276976   b £12124

Exercise 3·3 - page 17

1. a 0·56   56%   b 0·7   70%
   c 0·75   75%   d 0·625 62·5%
2. a 0·8   80%   b 0·075 7·5%
   c 0·75   75%   d 0·46   46%
   e 0·04   4%   f 0·1   10%
3. a 10% b 20% c 90% d 20%
   e 30% f 6%
4. a 60% 54·3% 62·2%   b Graphics

5. a 37·5% b 75%   c 60%
   d 62·5% e 80%
6. a $^{11}/_{20}$ 47% 0·45
   b 89% $^{70}/_{80}$ 0·825
   c $^1/_9$ $^4/_{80}$ 3% 0·02
7. a $^4/_7$ of ... 0·62 × ... 33$^1/_3$% of ...
   b 0·125 × ... $^4/_9$ of ... 72% of ...
   c 0·85 × ... 65% of ... $^1/_2$% of ..
8. £7728

Remember Remember Ch 3 - page 18

1. a 0·35 $^7/_{20}$ b 0·18 $^9/_{50}$
   c 0·52 $^{13}/_{25}$ d 0·125 $^1/_8$
   e 0·66666 $^2/_3$ f 0·625 $^5/_8$
2. a 66% b 10%   c 4%   d 87·5%
   e 80% f 85%   g 84% h 125%
3. a 660km b £33·33 c 6p   d 63p
   e £305 f 24 kg g £96 h £50
4. £490   5. 24   6. £546 7. £1206
8. a £91·80 b £16   c £3·24
   d £35000   e 3230 kg
   f £1·96 g 1·125g h £2
9. £95·93
10. a £451500   b £37625
11. 94
12. Sen £28728 Pau £28700 Trev £28496
13. £23

Non-Calculator Exercise 1 - page 20

1. a 3811   b 3573   c 825600
   d 1593   e 897   f 2500
   g 950   h 3   i 105
   j 25
2. a 3·293 b 5·543 c 4·86
   d 22·246 e 166·4 f 3·74
   g 0·1778 h 0·00196
3. a 3·72km b 60m
   c 0·54m   d 3·096kg
4. a 24   b 1600   c 850
5. a $^2/_3$ b $^5/_7$ c $^3/_{13}$
6. a $^1/_4$ b 5$^3/_4$
   c 2$^7/_8$ d 16
7. a $^4/_5$ b $^1/_8$ c $^4/_3$
8. a £1200 b £120   c £1·48
   d £60   e £70   f 12p
9. a 15   b 122   c -14
   d -40   e -6   f -41
   g 20   h 4   i 29
   j 1   k -9
10. a -52   b -168   c 42
    d -5   e 121   f -30
    g 5   h -8
11. a 0825 b 1945   c 2345
12. a 6h 35mins b 4h 33mins
13. 7.30pm
14. a 840 miles b 128km/h

Exercise 4·1 - page 21

1. a £360   b £313·50
   c £554·32   d £564·26
2. a £19760   b £42848
   c £15900   d £28512
3. a £1650   b £3000
   c £3548·88
4. a £562·80   b £731·01
   c £970·10
5. a £324   b £357·85

6. Joiner £16848, Secretary £18608·20
7. a £266 b £84   c £350
8. £517·75
9. a £357·12   b £18570·24
10. £19978·40
11. 2 pm
12. £81·60
13. a £1230 b £1920 c £562·50
14. a £2000   b £14000
15. £21400
16. Cars-R-Us 3000(best) CellCars 2900
17. £610·80
18. a (i) £416   (ii) £2511
       (iii) £3145·65 (iv) £1375
    b £40000
19. 1·5%

Exercise 4·2 - page 23

1. a £14730   b £20490
   c £19776
2. a £22760   b £437·69
3. a £3272   b £11928
4. £436·25   5. £3246
6. £42275   7. £359·69
8. £4075   9. £10000

Exercise 4·3 - page 24

1. £4730
2. £16958
3. £55848
4. a £5956   b £6000
   c £14142   d £98598
5. a £6216   b £486
6. £42010

Exercise 4·4 - page 25

1. a £19·20   b £4200
   c £330   d £2251·30
2. a £20·16   b £240
   c £1032   d £510
   e £9600   f £21000
3. a Subtot : £32 VAT : £6·40 Tot : £38·40
   b Subtot : £250 VAT : £50 Tot: £300
4. £112·50
5. £50·40
6. No. Same final price.
7. a Labour : £34   Subtotal : £160
      VAT : £32   Total : £192
   b Subtotal: £192   VAT : £9·60
      Total : £201·60
   c Labour : £36   Subtotal : £161·50
      VAT : £32·30   Total :   £193·80
8. £68·40
9. £110·34
10. £6·25
11. a £25   b £70
    c 80p   d £60000
    e £1200
12. 3 kg box : 94p/kg 10 kg box 98·4p/kg
    3 kg box is better.
13. £21·60

Exercise 4·5 - page 27

1. £327·20
2. a £480   b £3824
   c £640·98   d £91·08
3. £87   4. £131
5. £51   6. £29·20
7. £59·06
8. CheapCons £3580, ConsRus £3630
   Conserve £3175.   ConsRus is dearest.
9. £86·40 16%.
10. £125

Exercise 4·6 - page 28

1. £18·60
2. a £32　　　b £13·30
3. £66·80
4. a £72·70　　b £74·48
5. £90000
6. a £6·10　　b £11·40
   c £7·70
7. a £38·70　　b £12·20
   c £31·75

Exercise 4·7 - page 29

1. a 46€　　　　b 201·25€
   c 1380€　　　d 9775€
   e 51750€　　f 230000€
2. a 138€　　　b £327·75€
3. a £1020　　b £202·20
   c £480·40　d £572·80
   e £450000　f £1·20
4. a £176　　　b 18200€
   c 91000€　　d same price
5. £120
6. 552€
7. a 2511 yen　　b 1108·8 peso
   c 18562·5 rupees　d $666
   e £80　　　f £39
   g £58　　　h £420
   i £10950　　j £1690
8. £20
9. £925
10. $28
11. $1406
12. a 100440 yen　　b 1513·60 peso

Remember Remember Ch 4 - page 30

1. a £21632　　b £12540
   c £32520·80
2. a £2340　　b £540
3. £248·40
4. £7
5. a £5850　　b £17850
6. 5·5%
7. £18850
8. a £25478　　b £489·96
9. £46523·08
10. a £3780　　b £14982
    c £76098
11. a £15·36　　b £223·20
12. £665·40
13. £59·50
14. £56·88
15. a 517·50€　　b £648·50
    c $5920

Answers to Chapter 5 Page 31

Exercise 5·1 - page 31

1. a $12m$　b $2p$　c $14x$
   d $2b + 7c$　e $2v$　f $10g - 3r$
   g $a^2 - h^2$　h 0
2. a $15c$　b $18u$　c t^2
   d $6p^2$　e $9s^2$　f $6ky$
   g $21c$　h $20u$　i $54a^2$
   j $42v^2$　k $3h^2$　l $48n^3$
   m $15p^2$　n $64w^2$　o $8k^3$
   p $27f^3$　q $4x^2y^2$　r $27k^3m^3$
   s $16m^4n^4$　t $16v^3w^3$
3. a $8xy$　b $15x^2y$　c $24xy^2$
   d $7xy^2$　e $2x^2y$　f $8x^3y$
   g $9xy^3$　h $3x^4y$　i $12x^2y^3$
   j $10x^2y^3$　k $6x^3y^2$　l $3x^3y^3$

Exercise 5·1 (continued)

m $16x^2y^2$　n $6x^3y^3$
o $24x^3y^2$　p $10x^4y^4$
4. a 12　　b 3　　c $2q$
   d $3g$　　e 2　　f $10n$
   g $4x$　　h $8a^2$　i $8ab$
   j $4ab$　　k $4a^2$　l $4a$
   m 4　　　n $3xy$

Exercise 5·2 - page 32

1. a $2b + 8$　　b $5a + 5$
   c $8d - 48$　d $9 - 9g$
   e $3m + 3n$　f $7c - 7t$
   g $33 + 11y$　h $30x - 150$
   i $18p + 3$　j $15 - 20q$
   k $88x - 56y$　l $ab + 7a$
   m $gh - 10g$　n $6x + x^2$
   o $3ek + 8gk$　p $40u^2 - 4uv$
   q $12a + 21b + 6$　r $9p + 9q - 36r$
   s $18 - 30f - 12g$　t $x^2 - xy - 9xz$
   u $-5a - 5$　v $-3x - x^2$
   w $-6g^2 + g$　x $-7xy + 11x^2$
2. a $2q + 11$　b $3e + 9$　c $5t + 22$
   d $6u + 5$　e $4p + 1$　f $3s - 2$
   g $10f + 8$　h $10h + 9$　i $k + 20$
   j $4z + 12$　k $50 + 7c$　l $14b + 14$
   m $17m - 9$　n $13w + 6$　o $19r - 8$
   p $6y - 1$　q $16a + 30p$　r $51g + 20h$
   s $30x - 30y$　t $150v + 10n$
   u $2q + 9$　v $4w - 24e$
   w $2x + 1$　x $22 - 2x$
3. a $7m + 10$　b $7b + 18$　c $11c + 26$
   d $6k + 6$　e $9g$　f $9a + 2$
   g $19 - 4p$　h $12 - 6u$　i $26y + 8$
   j $26t + 16$　k $38 - 2e$　l $21x + 7y$
4. a $3x + 1$　b $x + 2$　c $x + 3$
   d $5x - 2$　e $17x + 4$　f $2x + 30$
   g $3x + 21$　h $30x$　i $4x - 2$
   j $x^2 + 6x - 5$　k $x^2 - 2x - 5$
   l $8x^2 - 8x + 16$
5. a $1 - 2y$　b $12 - 6p$　c $9 - d$
   d $6h + 19$　e $20 - 9c$　f $2u + 10$
   g $10b - 21$　h $10 - 2n$　i $4m - 60$
   j $2x - 100$　k $5k - 22$　l $14w - 2$

Exercise 5·3 - page 33

1. a $5(a + b)$　b $2(x + 4y)$　c $2(3g + 2h)$
   d $p(q + r)$　e $c(d + 1)$　f $n(m + n)$
   g $v(w^2 + 1)$　h $3a(b + c)$　i $4(2x + 3y)$
   j $8(5b - 2a)$　k $4d(c - 2)$　l $3p(2 + 7p)$
2. a $5(a + 5)$　b $3(x + 4)$　c $9(p - 4)$
   d $11(v + w)$　e $6(p - q)$　f $10(c - 2h)$
   g $7(m - 4)$　h $12(n + 5)$　i $2(2x + 3y)$
   j $7(2u - 3v)$　k $5(4x - 5y)$　l $4(r - 8u)$
   m $3(3s + 8)$　n $11(2u - 1)$　o $8(3x - 7y)$
   p $6(3a + 2c)$
   d $a(a + 6)$　e $t(8 - t)$　f $c(c - 4)$
3. a $b(5 + c)$　b $x(7 - v)$　c $p(q + r)$
   g $4x(m + n)$　h $5a(d - 2e)$　i $17s(r - 1)$
   j $y(3y + 7)$　k $4x(3x - 5y)$　l $q(6q + 1)$
   m $2d(3 + 7d)$　n $a(1 - 13a)$　o $3y(y - 8c)$
   p $8n(3m + 4n)$
4. a $a(a + 4b - 7)$　b $x(8y - 8z + 1)$
   c $p^2(p + 1)$　d $4d(d^2 - 4)$　e $ac(a + c)$
   f $6rs(3s - 5)$　g $4x(2x - 3a)$　h $\frac{1}{5}h(g + j)$

Remember Remember Ch 5 - page 34

1. a $10a$　b $9a^2$　c 9　　d $3a$
   e $24x$　f g^2　g $32ab$　h $50p^2$
   i $4m^2n$　j $3xq^3$　k 20　　l $4x^2$
2. a $5a + 10$　b $-6x - 2$　c $9a + a^2$
   d $mn - m^2$　e $8 - 24r$　f $-5k^2 + 20$
   g $-6x^2 + 12xy$　h $-7p^3 + p^3q$

3. a $3x + 10$　b $y + 36$　c $16 - 3a$
   d $9w + 14$　e $18 - 8d$　f $3q + 2$
   g $5 - 5u$　h $2k + 6$　i $16m^2 - 2m$
4. a $x(9 + p)$　b $b(a - g)$　c $m(m + 3)$
   d $h(12 - h)$　e $5w(v - x)$　f $7k(r + 2p)$
   g $q(2q + 9)$　　　h $6x(2x - 3y)$
   i $8x(3x + 4a)$　　j $9a(4b - 5a)$
   k $y^2(y - 1)$　　　l $6q(q^2 - 7)$
   m $mn(n - m)$　　　n $8ab(2b + 5)$
   o $4tx^2(2a - 3)$　　p $\frac{1}{2}d(c + \frac{1}{2}ad)$

Answers to Chapter 6 Page ?

Exercise 6·1 - page 35

1. a 4　b 2　　c 0　　d 1
   e 1　f 3　　g 5　　h 6
   i 10　j 7　　k 9
2. a　　　　　b

c　　　　　d

e　　　　　f

g　　　　　h

i　　　　　j

k　　　　　l

3. a　　　　　b

c　　　　　d

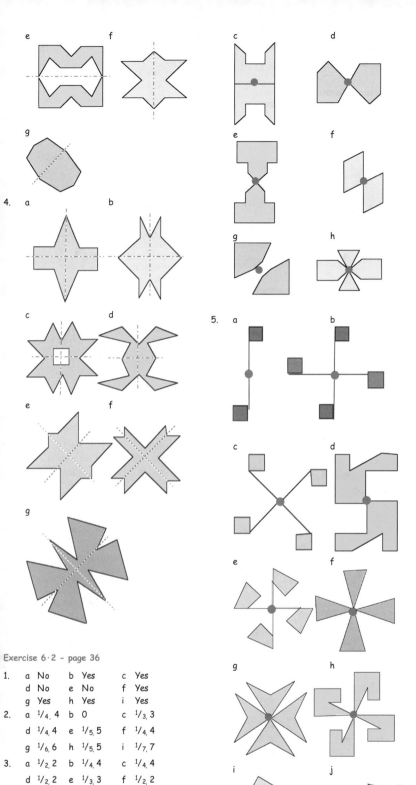

e   f

g

4. a   b

c   d

e   f

g

Exercise 6·2 - page 36

1. a No   b Yes   c Yes
    d No   e No   f Yes
    g Yes   h Yes   i Yes

2. a $1/4$, 4   b 0   c $1/3$, 3
    d $1/4$, 4   e $1/5$, 5 f $1/4$, 4
    g $1/6$, 6   h $1/5$, 5 i $1/7$, 7

3. a $1/2$, 2   b $1/4$, 4 c $1/4$, 4
    d $1/2$, 2   e $1/3$, 3 f $1/2$, 2
    g $1/8$, 8   h $1/8$, 8 i $1/10$, 10

4. a   b

c   d

e   f

g   h

i   j

Exercise 6·3 - page 38

1. Check diagrams
2. a c d e f h i j *"will tile the plane"*

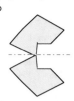

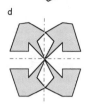

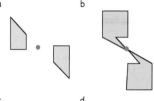

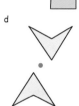

1.a 4 b   6 c   5 d   0
2.   a   b

c   d

3. a $1/5$, 5 b $1/16$, 16 c $1/4$, 4 d $1/2$, 2
4. a   b

c   d

5. a, c, d
6. a   b

Non-Calculator Exercise 2 - page 41

1. a 25606 b 627   c 124800 d 900
    e 343   f 5471 g 3   h 722
2. a 24.936   b 26.076
    c 92.62   d 10458
    e 0.19   f 0.721
    g 0.002   h 0.0076
3. a 105   b 240   c 720
4. a $4/7$ b $2/9$ c $1/4$ d $13/17$
5. a $2/3$ b $5\frac{1}{2}$ c $2\frac{1}{3}$ d $10\frac{2}{5}$
6. a $3/5$ b $12/25$ c $1/40$
7. a £120   b £150   c 9g
    d 30ml   e £96   f 99p
8. a 70%   b $33\frac{1}{3}$%
9. profit £1.20, % profit 40%
10. a 15   b -20   c -11   d 18
    e -7   f 48   g 40000 h -8
    i 9   j -5   k 6
11. a $x = -4$ b $x = 5$ c $x = 2$ d $x = 5$
12. a 2 h 42 mins   b 1 h 15mins
13. a 18mins   b 2 h 27mins
    c 1 h 40 mins

Exercise 7·1 - page 42

1. a 57 mm b 63 mm
2. a 19   21 mm   b 30   40 kg
   c 14   18 m   d 12   18 kg
   e 146   154 cm   f 73   77 mm
   g 340   360 km   h 105   135 mg
   i 80   120 ft   j 9·5   9·7 cm
   k 7·3   7·7 m   l 19·4 20 kg
   m 23·1 23·3 cm n 9·7   10·3 m
   o 29·5 30·5 ml p 84·5 85·5°c
   q 3·9   4·5 l   r 48·5 51·5 m
3. a 9·22 9·24 cm b 6·42 6·48 m
   c 18·20 18·30 km d 0·80 0·88 km
   e 10·18 10·28 kg f 24·54 24·60 °c
   g 4·96 5 g   h 3·145 3·149 g
   i 8·059 8·067 ml
4. a min 42 mm   max 48 mm
   b Reject 49 mm 50 mm 40 mm
5. a min 6·3 cm max 6·7 cm
   b No !
6. Accept 189 and 185 only
7. a 10·21 secs   b 10·25 secs
8. a 0·03 kg   b 0·04 kg
9. a Min 145 ml Max 155 ml
   b Yes OK !

Exercise 7·2 - page 43

1. 90 ± 10   2. 23 ± 3
3. a 19 ± 1   b 55 ± 5
   c 10·5 ± 0·5   d 130 ± 10
   e 4·5 ± 0·5   f 40 ± 3
   g 6·4 ± 0·2   h 10·3 ± 0·2
   i 1 ± 0·1   j 20·5 ± 0·3
   k 10 ± 0·2   l 800 ± 100
4. a 6·33 ± 0·01   b 8·07 ± 0·02
   c 0·26 ± 0·02   d 10·74 ± 0·03
   e 9·4 ± 0·02   f 0·07 ± 0·02
   g 1 ± 0·05   h 0·065 ± 0·003
5. a 6·5 ± 0·3   (i) too quiet   (ii) right
                  (iii) right   (iv) too loud
6. 32000 ± 2000
7. 106 ± 6   8. 40 ± 5
9. a £8 ± 0·20   b No
10. 56 ± 4
11. a 3·27 ± 0·03   b 3·29 & 3·3 ok
12. a 350 ± 10   b No
13. 18·75 ± 4·75
14. 35·5 ± 27·5 °C

Remember Remember Ch 7 - page 45

1. a 115 secs   b 135 secs
2. a 28   32 mm   b 70   80 m
   c 220   260 kg   d 1450 1750 m
   e 8·5   8·7 l   f 18·9 19·5 mg
   g 27·8 28·8 tonnes h 340 400 mph
   i 0·6   1 m
3. a 0·337 g   b 0·327 g
4. b & c acceptable
5. 54 ± 2 kg
6. a 65 ± 5   b 130 ± 2
   c 1600 ± 100   d 8·5 ± 0·1
   e 20 ± 0·3   f 0·75 ± 0·15
7. a 6·5 m   b 12·25 m

Exercise 8·1 - page 46

1. a $1/12$ b (i) Hill St   (ii) New St
2. a Sunny Hill $G = 1/8$ Dark Hill $G = 1/9$
   b Sunny Hill is steeper

---

3. 0·24, 0·20, 0·19, 0·16
4. a Ramp 1 $G = 2/9$ Ramp 2 $G = 5/19$
   b 0·22 and 0·26   c Ramp 2
5. $7/2$
6. Purple ladder/ladder on right
7. 4·63   8. 8m   9. 240m

Exercise 8·2 - page 48

1. 2
2. a $1/3$ b $3/4$
3. Blue = $3/5$ Red = $1/3$ Green = $1/5$
4. a 1   b $1/2$ c 4
5. a (i) (-2, -1)   (ii) (4, 3)   b $2/3$
6. a $1/4$ b 1
7. a 1   b $1/5$ c 2
   d $1/3$ e 4   f 1
8. $-1/2$ 9. a $-1/7$ b $-5/7$
10. a $m_{CD} = -2/3$ $m_{EF} = -1/8$ $m_{GH} = 0$
    b always 0
11. a $m_{PQ} = -5/2$ $m_{RS} = -5/2$ $m_{TV} = -5/2$
    b parallel lines have the same gradient
12. a (i) $1/2$ (ii) -2 (iii) 2   (iv) $-1/2$
    b $m_{EF} = 2$ $m_{FG} = -1/4$ $m_{GH} = 4$ $m_{EH} = -1/3$
    c this is not a parallelogram
      since opposite sides are NOT parallel
13. $m_{VT} = 7$ $m_{SU} = -1$
14. $m_{AB} = -1/5$ $m_{BC} = -1/5$
    since $m_{AB} = m_{BC}$ and B is common to both
    they lie on the straight line.

Exercise 8·3 - page 50

1. a
x	-1	0	1	2
y	3	0	3	6
   b see diagram   c m = 3
2. a (i)
x	-1	0	1	2
y	-4	0	4	8
   (ii) see diagram   (iii) m = 4
   b (i)
x	-1	0	1	2
y	-1	0	1	2
   (ii) see diagram   (iii) m = 1
   c (i)
x	-2	0	2	4
y	-1	0	1	2
   (ii) see diagram   (iii) m = $1/2$
   d (i)
x	-1	0	1	2
y	1	0	-1	-2
   (ii) see diagram   (iii) m = -1
3. a 6   b $1/5$ c -12   d 0·5
4. a
x	-1	0	1	2
y	-2	1	4	7
   b see diagram   c m = 3   d (0,1)
5. a (i)
x	-1	0	1	2
y	-5	-1	3	7
   (ii) see diagram   (iii) m = 4   (iv) (0,-1)
   b (i)
x	-1	0	1	2
y	5	3	1	-1
   (ii) see diagram   (iii) m = -2   (iv) (0, 3)
   c (i)
x	-2	0	2	4
y	2	3	4	5
   (ii) see diagram   (iii) m = $1/2$ (iv) (0, 3)
   d (i)
x	-1	0	1	2
y	-3	-4	-5	-6
   (ii) see diagram   (iii) m = -1   (iv) (0, -4)
6. a 5   b (0, 2)

Exercise 8·4 - page 51

1. a m = 3 (0, 2)   b m = 5   (0, -3)
   c m = 1 (0, 1)   d m = -2 (0, 5)
   e m = $1/2$(0, 2)   f m = $-1/3$(0, -1)

---

   g m = 0·5   (0, 9)   h m = -0·1(0, 2)
   i m = 2 (0, 4)   j m = -1 (0, 15)
2. (0 ,0)
3. a y = 2x + 3   b y = 4x - 2
   c y = 4x + 6   d y = -2x + 3
   e y = $1/3$x - 1   f y = 12x
4. a m = 2   b y = 2x + 4
5. a (i) m = $2/9$ (ii) (0,2) (iii) y = $2/9$x + 2
   b (i) m = 1   (ii) (0,0) (iii) y = x
   c (i) m = $1/9$ (ii) (0,3) (iii) y = $1/9$x + 3
   d (i) m = $-1/3$ (ii) (0,5) (iii) y = $-1/3$x + 5
   e (i) m = $4/5$ (ii) (0,-1) (iii) y = $4/5$x - 1
   f (i) m = -2   (ii) (0,-1) (iii) y = -2x - 1
6. a 2   b $1/4$ c y = $1/4$x + 2
7. a y = $5/4$x + 1   b y = $-1/6$x + 2
   c y = $1/2$x   d y = 4
8. a see diagram   b m = $1/2$
   c (0, 2)   d y = $1/2$x + 2
9. y = 5x + 30
10. graph 1 m = $5/2$ graph2   m = $4/5$
    graph 1 is steeper
11. a y = 2x - 2   b y = $3/5$x + 3
    c y = -x + 4   d y = $1/8$x - 1
12. a B   b C   c E
    d D   e A   f F
13. a y = x + 1   b y = $1/6$x + 5
    c y = -4x - 2   d y = 3x - 5
14. both have gradients of $3/2$ thus parallel.
15. $m_1 = 5/11$ $m_2 = 11/26$
    gradients different, so not parallel.
16. a y = 5x + 3   b y = -x - 6

Remember Remember Ch 8 - page 53

1. m = $3/12$ = $1/4$
2. skateboard, bike, car, ski-jump
   $1/2$, 0·3, 20%, 0·15
3. a m = $3/4$ b m = $1/2$
   c m = $-1/2$ d m = 0
4. a m = 1   b m = 0
   c m = -1   d m = infinity
5. a m = 2 (0,7)   b m = -1 (0,1)
   c m = $1/2$(0,2)   d m = $1/4$ (0,7)
   e m = 1 (0,-8)   f m = -2 (0,9)
   g m = $-1/5$ (0,-1) h m = $-1/3$(0,-1)
   i m = 0·2 (0,4)   j m = -0·9 (0,-9)
6. a y = 3x - 2   b y = -x + 7
   c y = -5x   d y = -1
   e x = -1
7. a grad $1/2$ intercept -1 y = $1/2$x - 1
   b grad $-1/3$ intercept 1 y = $-1/3$x + 1
8. y = x - 4
9. a y = 4x - 3   b y = $-1/2$x - 2
   c y = 2x - 3   d x = 7
   e y = -x + 2

Exercise 9·1 - page 55

1. a x = 2   b x = 0   c x = 12
   d x = 17   e x = 150   f x = -2
   g x = -14   h x = 5   i x = -1
   j x = 0   k x = -7   l x = -20
2. a x = 7   b a = 8   c b = 9
   d p = 1   e e = 1$1/2$ f c = 0
   g d = $1/2$ h y = 50   i r = 4$1/2$

j $q = 2\frac{3}{4}$ k $s = 5\frac{3}{5}$ l $t = 2\frac{6}{7}$
m $k = 3\frac{1}{2}$ n $n = \frac{4}{5}$ o $h = \frac{1}{4}$

3. a x = 4 b x = 5 c x = 6 d x = 2
e x = 4 f x = 3 g x = 7 h x = 1
i x = 8 j x = 11 k x = 3 l x = 10
m x = -1 n x = -1 o x = 4·5 p x = -4
q $x = 2\frac{1}{4}$ r $x = 4\frac{1}{2}$

4. a x = 3 b x = 7

5. a x = 3 b x = 5 c x = 4
d x = 7 e x = 5 f x = 6·5
g x = 7·5 h $x = 6\frac{1}{5}$ i x = 2·3

6. a x = 9 b x = 7 c x = 7
d x = 1·5 e x = 7·5 f x = 22
g x = 9 h x = -4 i x = 5·5

7. a x = 3 b x = 4 c x = 13
d x = 7 e x = 7 f x = 6·5
g x = 9 h x = 7 i x = -6

8. a x = 4 b x = 5 c x = 1
d x = 2 e x = 6 f x = 7
g x = 6 h x = 5 i x = -10

9. a x = 9 b x = 3 c x = 2
d x = 4 e x = 3 f x = 5
g x = 3 h x = 2 i x = 6
j x = 6

10. a 5x = x + 120 b x = 30

Exercise 9·2 - page 57

1. a x = 12 b x = 20
2. a x = 10 b x = 4 c x = 16
d x = 15 e x = 10 f x = 24
g x = 2 h x = 7·6 i $x = 8\frac{1}{3}$
j x = 8·5 k x = - 4 l $x = 1\frac{3}{5}$
m x = 18 n x = 40 o x = 24
p $x = -\frac{1}{6}$ q $x = -\frac{2}{5}$ r $x = 5\frac{5}{6}$

Exercise 9·3 - page 58

1. a x = 52 b $x = \frac{24}{7}$
2. a x = 18 b x = 13 c x = 15
d x = 5 e x = 13 f x = -18
g $x = -\frac{1}{2}$ h $x = 1\frac{2}{3}$ i x = 1
j x = 6 k $x = \frac{74}{11}$ l $x = -\frac{228}{17}$
m $x = \frac{16}{11}$ n x = 6 o $x = -\frac{5}{7}$
p x = 6 q $x = \frac{11}{3}$ r x = 15

Exercise 9·4 - page 59

1. a $x > 2$ b $y < -1$ c $p > 4$ d $t < 2$
e $v \geq 1$ f $g \leq -14$ g $d \geq 8$ h $e > 1$
i $q \geq 7$ j $k \leq 0$ k $b \leq -2$ l $m < -3$
2. a $x > 4$ b $y < 4$ c $m > 2$ d $p < -4$
e $b < -1$ f $n \leq 7$ g $k \geq -4$ h $u \leq -5·5$
3. a $x > 2$ b $a < 4$ c $b < 5$ d $c > -1$
e $d < 4$ f $e > 1$ g $g \leq -\frac{1}{2}$ h $h \geq 0$
i $k \leq \frac{1}{2}$ j $y \geq -3$ k $p \leq -5$ l $r < -14$
m $r > -2$ n $c > -\frac{3}{2}$ o $y \leq -4$ p $w \geq 30$
4. a 2 b 5 c 4 d 1
5. a 2 b 3 c 5 d 0
6. a $x < -4$ b $a > -2$ c $b > 6$ d $c < 5·5$
e $d > -6$ f $g < -1$ g $h \leq 5$ h $n \geq 13$
7. a $x > 3$ b $x < 5$ c $x > 8$ d $x \geq 1·5$
e $x \geq 4$ f $x \leq 3$ g $x \geq 7$ h $x \leq 0·5$
8. a $x > 4$ b $p > -3$ c $y \leq 0·1$ d $r \leq -4$
e $k < -4$ f $m \leq 6$ g $x \geq -4$ h $x > 0·2$
i $x \geq 2\frac{1}{4}$ j $x \geq -4$ k $x \geq 2·8$ l $x > -10$
m $x < 1$ n $x \leq 0$ o $x > 4·5$
9. a Proof b 150 ml
10. $10y + 15 \leq 245$ 23 books
11. $2·5x + 70 \geq 320$ 100 tickets
12. a 5d + 12, 12d + 5 b $5d + 12 < 12d + 5$ $d > 1$
c Over 1 day hire Taylors always cheaper

Remember Remember Ch 9 - page 61

1. a x = -5 b x = 1·5 c x = 5·5
d x = 7 e x = -2 f x = 4
g x = 8 h x = 15 i x = 10·5
j x = 3 k x = 2·5 l x = 6
2. a x = 12 b $x = 3\frac{1}{8}$ c x = -36
d $x = 5\frac{1}{5}$ e x = 13 f x = -2
g x = 3·5 h $x = \frac{16}{17}$ i $x = \frac{8}{7}$
j $x = \frac{6}{5}$ k $x = -\frac{82}{3}$ l $x = 4\frac{1}{5}$
3. a $a < 1$ b $b \geq 11$ c $c \leq -9$
d $d > 5·5$ e $e > -4$ f $f < 15$
g $g \geq 1·5$ h $h \leq 8$ i $i > 9$
j $j \geq -12$ k $k \geq \frac{1}{2}$ l $l \geq 1$
4. a $4x > 2·5x + 3$
b $x > 2$ (i) Electro (ii) Either (iii) Movie

Non-Calculator Exercise 3 - page 63

1. a 6575 b 837 c 360 d 27360
e 12500 f 6300000 g 880 h 7036
2. £2220
3. a 4·75 b 6·716 c 10·251 d 0·18
e 70 f 115·644 g 23·444 h 2·168
4. a 264 b 63 c 600
5. a $\frac{2}{3}$ b $\frac{8}{9}$ c $\frac{2}{3}$ d $\frac{1}{4}$
6. a $1\frac{1}{4}$ b $4\frac{3}{4}$ c 9 d $\frac{1}{4}$
7. 100 pupils
8. a £288 b £24 c £43·20
9. a £1·60 b £4·20 c 96p
d £9 e £75 f £30
10. £1632
11. a 7 b -29 c -17 d 40
e -60 f -45 g 121 h -5
i -45 j -6 k -18 l 35
12. 36°
13. 23rd May

Answers to Chapter 10 Page 64

Exercise 10·1 - page 64

1. a 16 b 36 c 64 d 100
e 121 f 144 g 1 h 900
i 1 j 25 k $\frac{1}{4}$ l $\frac{1}{16}$
m 64 n 729 o 1000 p -64
q -1 r 10000 s 1 t 64
u $\frac{1}{243}$
2. a 361 b 784 c 11025 d 4096
e 512 f 15625 g -729 h 2560000
i 2401 j 15625 k 10000000
l 59049 m 2187 n 7776 o 1
p 0 q 16384 r 20736 s 6561
t $\frac{1}{256}$ u 1048657
v 6723200000 w 10001 x 0
y 65293 z -77997

Exercise 10·2 - page 65

1. a 5 b 9 c 1 d 50
e 0·8 f 300 g 1100 h 8
2. a 2·65 b 5·29 c 8·31 d 10·25
e 22·36 f 44·72 g 10·11 h 316·23
3. a 5 b 8 c 7 d 10
e 15 f 28 g 110 h 400
4. a 3 b 3 c 5 d 4
e 9 f 2 g 3 h 2
i 5 j 8 k 3 l 11
m 10 n 5 o 0

Exercise 10·3 - page 66

1. $6·4 \times 10^3$
2. a $7·3 \times 10^1$ b $5·16 \times 10^2$
c $8·54 \times 10^3$ d $6·421 \times 10^3$
e $7·0 \times 10^3$ f $1·0 \times 10^4$
g $2·9 \times 10^4$ h $3·45 \times 10^4$
i 9×10^0 j $6·0 \times 10^1$
k $4·12 \times 10^5$ l $6·582 \times 10^5$
m $6·3 \times 10^2$ n $5·0 \times 10^6$
o $4·8 \times 10^6$ p $3·71 \times 10^6$
q $4·2 \times 10^7$ r $5·55 \times 10^7$
s $3·0 \times 10^8$ t $4·531 \times 10^8$
3. a 3000000 = $3·0 \times 10^6$
b 2500000 = $2·5 \times 10^6$
c 6290000 = $6·29 \times 10^6$
d 9500000 = $9·5 \times 10^6$
e 3600000 = $3·6 \times 10^6$
f 15500000 = $1·55 \times 10^7$
g 7632000 = $7·632 \times 10^6$
h 44250000 = $4·425 \times 10^7$
i 50750000 = $5·075 \times 10^7$
j £12400000 = £$1·24 \times 10^7$
k 285000 = $2·85 \times 10^5$
4. a $3·56 \times 10^1$ b $2·15 \times 10^0$
c $2·501 \times 10^2$ d $4·6255 \times 10^2$
e $6·4705 \times 10^3$ f $8·27001 \times 10^4$
g $2·000001 \times 10^5$ h $3·33333 \times 10^1$
5. a 230 b 6 410
c 800 000 d 77 300
e 9102 f 60 040
g 4,913,000 h 110 000
i 87 100 000 j 214 300
k 190 000 000 l 355 500
6. a 5 800 000 b 1 750 000 000
c 2 200 000 000 000
7. 773 000 litres 8. £4 250 000
9. 31 560 000 secs 10. 4 497 000 000
11. £8,105 12. 1,298,000,000
13. £24,300,000

Exercise 10·4 - page 68

1. a $5·0 \times 10^{-2}$ b $7·0 \times 10^{-3}$
c $9·0 \times 10^{-1}$ d $4·0 \times 10^{-4}$
e $6·0 \times 10^{-5}$ f $1·0 \times 10^{-6}$
g $4·3 \times 10^{-2}$ h $9·7 \times 10^{-3}$
i $3·5 \times 10^{-4}$ j $6·6 \times 10^{-5}$
k $1·47 \times 10^{-3}$ l $3·58 \times 10^{-1}$
m $2·49 \times 10^{-4}$ n $9·63 \times 10^{-6}$
o $3·0 \times 10^{-9}$ p $1·8 \times 10^{-11}$
2. a $1·2 \times 10^{-3}$ m b $2·4 \times 10^{-7}$ kg
c $9·9 \times 10^{-2}$ sec d $7·55 \times 10^{-7}$ mm
e $1·14 \times 10^{-4}$ years f $2·5 \times 10^{-3}$
3. a 0·0047 b 0·0034
c 0·005 d 0·000009
e 0·000801 f 0·003002
g 0·000004775 h 0·00006283
i 0·01111 j 0·005442
k 0·00000099 l 0·38874
4. 1g less
5. a 0·08 b 0·59
c 0·000814 d 0·001755
e 0·000005006 f 0·0000000000065
6. a 0·003 b 700 c 0·025 d 8200
e 48700 f 0·000603
g 0·000007123 h 385000
i 0·00002 j 700900000
7. a $6·0 \times 10^{-4}$ b $4·9 \times 10^1$
c $9·310 \times 10^3$ d $2·0 \times 10^{-2}$
e $3·0 \times 10^{-1}$ f $8·85 \times 10^5$
g $8·9 \times 10^{-2}$ h $1·95 \times 10^6$
i $5·5 \times 10^{-7}$ j $6·9 \times 10^7$

8. a $8{\cdot}295 \times 10^{4}$ $a = 8{\cdot}295$ $n = 4$
   b $2{\cdot}17 \times 10^{8}$ $a = 2{\cdot}17$ $n = 8$
   c $9{\cdot}0 \times 10^{-5}$ $a = 9{\cdot}0$ $n = -5$
   d $6{\cdot}27 \times 10^{5}$ $a = 6{\cdot}27$ $n = 5$
   e $4{\cdot}0 \times 10^{-1}$ $a = 4{\cdot}0$ $n = -1$
   f $1{\cdot}05 \times 10^{8}$ $a = 1{\cdot}05$ $n = 8$
   g $1{\cdot}365 \times 10^{4}$ $a = 1{\cdot}365$ $n = 4$
   h $1{\cdot}0 \times 10^{-6}$ $a = 1{\cdot}0$ $n = -6$
   i $1{\cdot}65 \times 10^{-5}$ $a = 1{\cdot}65$ $n = -5$
   j $9{\cdot}0 \times 10^{-3}$ $a = 9{\cdot}0$ $n = -3$
   k $8{\cdot}5 \times 10^{-5}$ $a = 8{\cdot}5$ $n = -5$
   l $4{\cdot}435 \times 10^{2}$ $a = 4{\cdot}435$ $n = 2$
   m (i) $2{\cdot}0 \times 10^{9}$ (ii) $3{\cdot}1 \times 10^{9}$
     (iii) $9{\cdot}6 \times 10^{10}$ (iv) $1{\cdot}75 \times 10^{10}$

Exercise 10·5 - page 70

1. a $2{\cdot}13 \times 10^{6}$ b $1{\cdot}782 \times 10^{9}$
   c $2{\cdot}769 \times 10^{6}$ d $1{\cdot}05 \times 10^{5}$
   e $1{\cdot}65 \times 10^{-3}$ f $1{\cdot}71 \times 10^{-6}$
   g $1{\cdot}71 \times 10^{-7}$ h $1{\cdot}628 \times 10^{-2}$
2. a $6{\cdot}44 \times 10^{2}$ b $4{\cdot}05 \times 10^{7}$
   c $1{\cdot}63 \times 10^{5}$ d $5{\cdot}11 \times 10^{1}$
   e $2{\cdot}36 \times 10^{-4}$ f $2{\cdot}67 \times 10^{-8}$
   g $7{\cdot}20 \times 10^{2}$ h $3{\cdot}04 \times 10^{8}$
3. a $5807 = 5{\cdot}807 \times 10^{3}$
   b $15500 = 1{\cdot}55 \times 10^{4}$
   c $9760 = 9{\cdot}76 \times 10^{3}$
   d $10{\cdot}043 = 1{\cdot}0043 \times 10^{1}$
   e $19{\cdot}25 = 1{\cdot}925 \times 10^{1}$
   f $800 = 8{\cdot}0 \times 10^{2}$
   g $54 = 5{\cdot}4 \times 10^{1}$
   h $0{\cdot}1462 = 1{\cdot}462 \times 10^{-1}$
4. a 2,540,000   b 0·0267
   c 5,280,000,000,000   d 6,250,000,000
   e 754,000,000,000,000,000
   f 233,000,000,000,000
5. $1{\cdot}578 \times 10^{8}$ seconds   6. £2·8 × 10⁶
7. £7·012 × 10⁷   8. $2{\cdot}03 \times 10^{-20}$ g
9. $6{\cdot}64 \times 10^{-15}$ 10. 8 mins 12 sec
11. 13 mins   12. $1{\cdot}786 \times 10^{25}$ stars
13. $7{\cdot}89 \times 10^{20}$ atoms   14. $2{\cdot}23 \times 10^{21}$ m/s
15. 1340 visitors   16. £101·47 per sec
17. $2{\cdot}39 \times 10^{5}$ miles

Remember Remember Ch 10 - page 72

1. a 512   b -125   c 70   d 0·04
2. a $8{\cdot}6 \times 10^{2}$ b $7{\cdot}21 \times 10^{3}$
   c $9{\cdot}52 \times 10^{4}$ d $1{\cdot}268 \times 10^{5}$
   e $1{\cdot}682 \times 10^{1}$ f $5{\cdot}24 \times 10^{6}$
   g $6{\cdot}0 \times 10^{6}$ h $2{\cdot}43 \times 10^{8}$
   i $5{\cdot}5 \times 10^{6}$ j $1{\cdot}75 \times 10^{6}$
3. $6{\cdot}23 \times 10^{-4}$
4 a $3{\cdot}6 \times 10^{-3}$ b $5{\cdot}21 \times 10^{-2}$
   c $7{\cdot}7 \times 10^{-5}$ d $8{\cdot}0 \times 10^{-4}$
   e $9{\cdot}89 \times 10^{-1}$ f $4{\cdot}2 \times 10^{-7}$
5. a 5900   b 808 000
   c 710   d 28 100
   e 4 000 000   f 3 200 000 000
   g 10 010 000   h 3 500 000 000 000
6. a 0·00058   b 0·099
   c 0·00062   d 0·23
   e 0·0000003   f 0·0004
7. a $4{\cdot}2 \times 10^{4}$ b $8{\cdot}01 \times 10^{-2}$
   c $1{\cdot}37 \times 10^{5}$ d $3{\cdot}4 \times 10^{-4}$
   e $6{\cdot}5 \times 10^{-6}$ f $9{\cdot}5 \times 10^{6}$
   g $3{\cdot}4 \times 10^{7}$ h $2{\cdot}0 \times 10^{-5}$

---

8. a 7 300 000   b 0·0049
   c 36 100   d 0·00008
   e 800 000 000   f 0·055
   g 303 000   h 0·42
9. a 6   b 8
10. a $5{\cdot}7 \times 10^{10}$ b $3{\cdot}1185 \times 10^{11}$
   c $1{\cdot}35 \times 10^{10}$ d $1{\cdot}7 \times 10^{11}$
   e $2{\cdot}9 \times 10^{13}$ f $1{\cdot}024 \times 10^{21}$
   g $2{\cdot}197 \times 10^{-12}$ h $3{\cdot}5 \times 10^{19}$
11. $8{\cdot}32 \times 10^{11}$ mm²
12. a $1{\cdot}08 \times 10^{12}$m   b $2{\cdot}59 \times 10^{13}$ m
   c $9{\cdot}45 \times 10^{15}$m
13. $1{\cdot}10 \times 10^{12}$ km³

> ### Answers to Chapter 11 Page 73

Exercise 11·1 - page 73

1. 25·12 cm
2. a 31·4 cm   b 37·68 cm   c 204·1 cm
   d 125·6 cm   e 1·57 cm   f 3·14 cm
3. a 188·4 cm   b 62·8 mm
   c 314 cm   d 172·7 cm
4. 62·8 cm
5. a 18·84 cm   b 3·14 cm
6. a 128·74 cm   b 9·42 m
7. 78·5 cm   8. 20·56 m   9. 25·7 m
10. 7·85 m
11. $A = 53$ cm $B = 53{\cdot}38$ cm B larger perim
12. a 13 m   b 71·4 mm
   c 278·5 m   d 65·7 cm
13. £59·10
14. £84·55

Exercise 11·2 - page 75

1. 7cm
2. a 157 cm b   11 m   c 1 mm   d 770 mm
3. a 50cm   b 123mm   c 2000m   d 0·1 km
4. a 25 cm   b 61·5 mm c 1000 m   d 0·05 km
5. 75 mm
6. 478 m
7. a 63·7 cm   b 2·5 cm   c 8·0 cm
   d (i) 2·9 cm (ii) 168·2 m
8. a 9·6 mm   b 6·28 cm   9. 607·2 cm

Exercise 11·3 - page 76

1. 50·24 cm²
2. a 78·5 cm²   b 283·4 mm²
3. a 2289·06 cm²   b 86·55 cm²
4. a 226·87 cm²   b 3·14 cm²
5. a 2826 cm² b   530·66 cm²
   c 3·80 m²   d 0·20 m²   e 0·20 m²
6. a 1225 cm²   b 961·625 cm²
   c 263·375 cm²
7. 3096 cm²
8. a 7850 cm²   b 0·785 km²
9. 25·12 m²   10. 92·52 m²   11. £110·39

Exercise 11·4 - page 78

1. a 10 cm
2. a 9 cm   b 3 m   c 13 cm   d 85 cm
3. 14·14 cm   4. 40 cm
5. a 77·5 cm   b 51 cm   6. 80 biscuits
7. circle would have diameter of 20·3 cm and
   square has length of 20 cm
8. 12 cm   9. 131·88 cm

Exercise 11·5 - page 79

1. a 226·08 cm²   b 47·5 m²
   c 19·625 cm²   d 0·196 m²
2 a (i) 129·12cm²   (ii) 46·56 cm

---

   b (i) 114·24 cm²   (ii) 44·56 cm
   c (i) 79·625 cm²   (ii) 41·85 cm
3. 1962·5 cm²
4. 383·08 cm
5. a 25·7 m   b 36·54 m
6. 95·54 cm
7. 82·24 cm
8. 117·81 cm

Remember Remember Ch 11 - page 80

1. a 37·68 cm b 34·54 cm
2. a 28·27 m   b 17·85 cm   c 362·8 m
3. a (i) 6·5 cm (ii) 1·5 km   b 52·5 mm
4. a 78·5 cm²   b 113·04 cm²
   c 628 cm²   d 0·785 cm²
5. a 706·5 cm²   b 415·27 cm
6. a 1·5 m   b 1 mm
7. 13·76 cm²
8. a (i) 33·55 cm   (ii) 1028 cm
   b (i) 58·875 cm²   (ii) 12·56 cm²
9. 14·13 cm²   10. 3·785 m²   11. 4·71 m²

> ### Answers to Chapter 12 Page 81

Exercise 12·1 - page 81

1. F(5, 3),   G(-3, 0),   H(-4, -2), I(0, 3),
   J(5, -3)   K(0, -2),   L(-2, -2),   M(3, -1)
2. a G   b I, K   c M   d H
   e J   f I&K, F&J and E&G
   g EIF, HLK   h L
3.

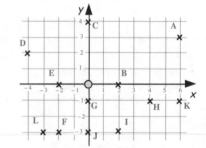

4. a square   b triangle
   c rectangle   d hexagon
   e pentagon   f octagon
5. a D(-4, -2)   b H(5, 0) or H(-1, -5)
   c L(-2, -1)   d various (0·5, any)
   e various (-1, 3)   f X(-3, -1)
6. Surprise !

Exercise 12·2 - page 83

1. ab Check diagram
   c A'(1, -1),   B'(1,-4),
     C'(3, -4),   D'(2, -3)
   d A"(-1, -1),   B"(-1, -4),
     C"(-3, -4),   D"(-2, -3)
2. a H(-1, -1)
   b E'(2, -2), F'(5, 1), G'(2, 4), H'(-1, 1)
   c E"(-2, -2), F"(-5, 1), G"(-2, 4), H"(1, 1)
3. a J'(-3, 2)
4. M'(-2, 0), L'(-2, -3), K'(-1, -4)
5. ab check diagram
   c P'(6, 5), Q'(3, -3), R'(8, -3)
6. a reflection over x -axis
   b reflection over y-axis
   c reflection over y-axis
   d reflection over y-axis
   e reflction over x-axis
   f reflection over y-axis
7. a D'(-3, -2)   b D'(2, -3)

8. a E'(-6, -1), E'(1, -6)
b F'(-4, 0) F'(0, -4)
c G'(3, -1) G'(1, 3)
d H'(-4, 2) H'(-2, -4)
e I'(3, 3) I'(3, -3)
f J'(21, -18) J'(18, 21)
g K'(21, -37) K'(37, 21)
h L'(-23, 42) L'(-42, -23)

9. a E'(1, 6) b F'(0, 4)
c G'(-1, -3) d H'(2, 4)
e I'(3, -3) f J'(-18, -21)
g K'(-37, -21) h L'(42, 23)

10. a 180° rotation about origin
b 90° clockwise rotation about origin
c 180° rotation about origin
d 90° anticlockwise rotation about origin
e 180° rotation about origin
f 90° clockwise rotation about origin
g 90° anticlockwise rotation about origin
h 90° anticlockwise rotation about origin

11. a A'(-2, -1), B'(-4, -1), C'(-2, -3)
b A''(1, -2), B''(1, -4), C''(3, -2)
c A'''(-1, 2), B'''(-1, 4), C'''(-3, 2)

12. a (i) D'(-1, -1), E'(-3, -1), F'(-3, -3), G'(-1, -3)
(ii) D''(1, -1), E''(1, -3), F''(3, -3), G''(3, -1)
b (i) H'(4, -1), I'(4, -3), J'(0, -3), K'(0, -1)
(ii) H''(1, 4), I''(3, 4), J''(3, 0), K''(1, 0)

13. a P'(-4, 1)
b W'(5, 7)
c G'(-7, -4), H'(-8, 1), K'(-3, -6)

14. C(1, 1), C'(-3, 3)

15. a D'(0, 8) b E'(0, 4)
c F'(-3, 6) d G'(-5, 2)
e H'(-1, 5) f I'(3, 0)

16. a D''(-2, 3) b E''(-2, -1)
c F''(-5, 1) d G''(-7, -3)
e H''(-3, 0) f I''(1, -5)

17. a $\begin{pmatrix}4\\2\end{pmatrix}$ b $\begin{pmatrix}6\\-1\end{pmatrix}$ c $\begin{pmatrix}6\\1\end{pmatrix}$ d $\begin{pmatrix}1\\6\end{pmatrix}$
e $\begin{pmatrix}-9\\-3\end{pmatrix}$ f $\begin{pmatrix}-1\\4\end{pmatrix}$ g $\begin{pmatrix}7\\-11\end{pmatrix}$ h $\begin{pmatrix}11\\-5\end{pmatrix}$

18. a D'(3, 5), E'(4, 3), F'(0, 6)
b D'(6, 1), E'(7, -1), F'(3, 2)
c D'(-1, 3), E'(0, 1), F'(-4, 4)
d D'(-2, -4), E'(-1, -6), F'(-5, -3)

19. a $h = -3$
b E'(-2, 0), F'(-2, 4), G'(-5, 1), H'(-5, -3)
c E''(-7, 0), F''(-7, 4), G''(-10, 1), H''(-10, -3)

20. A'(-5, -8), B'(-2, -7), C'(-4, -6), D'(-7, -5), E'(-7, -6)

21. a A(4, 8) b B(12, 8)
c C(-8, 0) d D(32, -16)
e E(-12, -10) f F(2a, 8b)

22. a A(1, 2) b B(3, 2)
c C(-2, 0) d D(8, -4)
e E(-3, -2·5) f F(a/2, 2b)

23. a G(3, 3), H(6, 3), I(6, -6)
b J(4, 2), K(6, -2), L(-4, 2), M(-2, 2)
c N'(4, 2), O'(0, 0), P'(-4, -2), Q'(-6, 0), R'(4, 0)

Exercise 12·3 - page 86

1. a A(4, -3) b B(6, 2)
c C(-3, -2) d D(-1, 5)
e E(0, -3) f F(a, b)

2. a A(2, -2) b B(-2, 4)
c C(-6, -10) d D(0, 8)
e E(8, 4) f F(-2b, 2a)

3. a A(1, -8) b B(-4, -6)
c C(-8, -1) d D(2, -3)
e E(0, 0) f F(a - 2, -b - 3)

4. a A(-6, 0), B(-4·5, 6), C(0, 3)
b D(0, -1·5), E(1·5, -4·5), F(-3, -6), G(-4·5, -6)
c H(-3, 3), I(1·5, 4·5), J(4·5, 0), K(1·5, -3), L(-1·5, 0)

Remember Remember Ch 12 - page 87

1. a A(2, 3), B(4, 0), C(6, -3), D(2, -2), E(0, 2), F(-3, 1), G(-2, 0), H-4, -1), I(-2, -3)
b (i) G, B (ii) E (iii) B&G and I&C

2. a rectangle b isosceles triangle
c parallelogram d kite

3. a P'(4, -3) b P'(-4, 3)

4. a (-6, -2) b (-2, 6)
c (9, 3)

5. a reflection over the line $y = x$
b reflection over the x-axis
c rotation of 180° around the origin
d rotation of 180° around the origin
e rotation of 90° clockwise around origin
f translation $\begin{pmatrix}-2\\6\end{pmatrix}$ g translation $\begin{pmatrix}1\\-9\end{pmatrix}$
h rotation of 90° anticlockwise aroung O

6. a A'(1, 4), B'(-3, 3), C'(-4, 0)
b A'(-1, -4), B'(3, -3), C'(4, 0)

7. a A'(4, 1), B'(3, -3), C'(0, -4)
b A'(-2, 8), B'(6, 6), C'(8, 0)
c A'(-4, 2), B'(0, 1), C'(1, -2)

8. Various answers here. e.g.
a reflect over y-axis and rotated 90° clockwise around the origin
b reflect over x-axis and rotated 90° anti-clockwise around the origin
c translation of $\begin{pmatrix}-5\\5\end{pmatrix}$ followed by a dilation scale factor 1.

Non-Calculator Exercise 4 - page 90

1. a 529 b 733 c 5 d 4703
e 124500 f 26 g 64 h $1^2/_3$

2. a 62·356 b 768 c 14·8 d 0·2091

3. 7·32 litres

4. a 0·048 b 2075 c 800 d 8 m 20 s

5. a $^1/_3$ b $^7/_9$ c $^{12}/_{13}$

6. a 2 b $^2/_5$ c 160
d 15 e $3^1/_4$ f 18

7. a £2·40 b £0·66 c £540
d £0·28 e 32 f 30

8. £18, £102

9. a -14 b -60 c -21 d -6
e -77 f 51 g 900 h -7
i 23 j -6 k 17

10. a see diagram b D(1, -2)

11. a 2340 b 1435 c 1045

12. a 2 hr 27 mins b 5 hr 25 mins

13. Only 2012 is a leap year.

Answers to Chapter 13 Page 91

Introductory Exercise - page 91

1. a 36, 64, 100 b 100 c check
2. a 81, 144, 225 b 225 c check
3. a 25, 144, 169 b 169 c check

Exercise 13·1 - page 92

1. 17 cm 2. 39 cm
3. a 25 cm b 25 cm c 12·75 cm
4. 11·66 cm 5. 16·12 cm
6. 18·03 cm 7. 27·80 cm
8. 15·18 cm
9. a 10·3 cm b 21·1 cm c 9·62 cm
d 13·35 m e 41·4 mm f 35·78cm

Exercise 13·2 - page 94

1. 8·5 m 2. 5·28 m 3. 209·4 km
4. 65·5 m 5. 12·9 cm
6. sloping edge 5·3 cm $p = 26·2$
7. 180·5 cm 8. 29·8 m 9. 3·3 m
10. 2·6 m 11. 64 cm 12. 35 m
13. a 90 cm b 63 cm

Exercise 13·3 - page 96

1. 36 cm 2. a 12·7 cm b 19·7 cm
3. 4·1 m 4. 70·8 m 5. 960 cm²
6. 56·5 cm 7. 90 cm 8. 21·2 cm

Exercise 13·4 - page 97

1. a 8·9 cm b 17·9 cm c 13·5 m
d 24·3 e 71·0 f 9·2 m
2. Hypotenuse is always the longest side
3. $y = 9·6$ is correct as y cannot be greater than the hypotenuse.
4. 10·6 mm 5. 3·00 m 6. 442 m
7. 42·7 cm
8. a 6·6m b 3·8 m c 2·8 m
9. 8·8 km 10. 5·3 m

Exercise 13·5 - page 99

1. a Diagram b 5 boxes
2. a see diagram b 13 boxes
3. 8·06 boxes
4. a 9·49 boxes b 8·49 boxes
5. a 5 boxes b 5 boxes c yes
6. MN = 14·14 LM = 10 LN = 10
since LM = LN —> triangle is isosceles.

Remember Remember Ch 13 - page 100

1. $x = 9·90$ cm $y = 14·3$ cm
$z = 3·86$ m $w = 4·24$ mm
2. a 36 cm b 540 cm²
3. 672 cm²
4. 112 cm
5. 7·84 m
6. a 53·4 cm b 1060·8 cm²
7. 10·3 boxes
8. a 2 cm b 0·6 cm c 3·8 cm

Answers to Chapter 14 Page 101

Exercise 14·1 - page 101

1. a 18 km b 800 km c 15 km
d 5·25 km e 50 miles f 21 miles
g 42 miles h 135 km
2. a 250 miles b 9 miles c 45 miles
d 15 km e 20400 miles
3. a 900 miles b 4·5 miles c 99 miles
d 90 km e 22 km f 28 km

Exercise 14·2 - page 102

1. a 50 mph b 23 km/h c 62 mph
2. a 18 km/h b 70 m/min c 5 m/sec
d 14 km/day
3. a 404 mph b 42 km/h c 60 km/h
d 12 mph e 68 cm/hour
4. a 4 hours b 4 hours 30 mins
c 60 sec d 1 hour 30 mins
5. a 2 hours 30 mins b 5 hours 15 mins
c 3 hours 45 mins d 8 hours 15 mins
6. a 3·5 hours b 2·25 hours
c 5·75 hours d 0·25 hours
7. a 1 hour 15 mins b 1 hour 15 mins

Exercise 14·3 - page 103

1. a 37·5 km/h b 3 hours c 116 miles
   d 60 km/h e 180 m f 1hour 45 mins
2. a 5400 m/h b 90 m/min
3. 30 mins   4. 105 km   5. 60 mph
6. 1 hr 45 mins
7. 10800 km
8. a 3 mph b 3 mph faster

Exercise 14·4 - page 104

1. a 0·8 hours b 0·3 hours c 0·1 hours
   d 0·9 hours e 0·4 hours f 0·65 hours
   g 0·35 hours
2. a 0·17 hours   b 0·28 hours
   c 0·33 hours   d 0·87 hours
   e 0·83 hours   f 1·17 hours
3. a 4·2 hours   b 3·8 hours
   c 4·6 hours   d 2·85 hours
   e 2·95 hours   f 1·2 hours
   g 5·1 hours
4. 48 km
5. a 9 miles   b 8 miles   c 10·5 km
   d 150 miles e 4 miles
6. Bob 15 km   Ted 12 km   Bob by 3 km
7. D = 89·6 km
8. a 728 miles b 91 miles
9. 50 km/h
10. a 70 mph   b 100 km/h c 320 mph
    d 70 mph   e 40 km/h f 70 mph
    g 6000 mph h 60 mph

Exercise 14·5 - page 105

1. a 51 min   b 36 min   c 54 min
   d 45 min   e 21 min   f 40 min
2. 3h 54 mins
3. a 3h 12 mins   b 5h 30 mins
   c 1h 39 mins   d 2h 48 mins
   e 3h 51 mins   f 4h 42 mins
   g 3h 40 mins   h 1h 50 mins
   i 37·5 mins
4. a 4 hours 45 mins b 3 hours 36 mins
   c 1 hour 20 mins
5. a 3·3 hours   b 3 hours 18 mins
6. a 1·7 hours   b 1 hour 42 mins
7. a 2·3 hours = 2 hours 18 mins
   b 0·33 hours = 20 mins
   c 0·35 hours = 21 mins
   d 1·125 hours = 1 hour 7 mins 30 secs
8. a 2 hours 15 mins b 2 hours
   c 6 hours 45 mins
9. a 7m/s   b 25·2km/h
10. a 28·8 km/h   b 54 km/h
    c 720 km/h   d 135 km/h
    e 1·8 km/h   f 3600 km/h

Exercise 14·6 - page 107

1. a 2 hours b 1 hour   c 1500
   d (i) 50 km/h (ii) 0   (iii) 20 km/h
   e 26·7 km/hr
2. a 15 mins b 120 km/h c 80 km/h
   d slowed him down
3. a 24 km/h b 72 km/h
   c 1045 am d 18 km
4. a A is the goods train - it is the less steep
      of the 2 lines.
   b (i) 40 mph   (ii) 80 mph
   c 1100   d 1700
5. Boppard arrive 11.00 am leave 11.30 am
   St Goar   arrive 12.30 pm leave 12.50 pm
   Binghen   arrive 1.20pm
   b (i) 24 km   (ii) 20 km
   c (i) 24 km/h   (ii) 16 km/h
      (iii) 40 km/h   (iv) 18 km/h
6. a 1 hour 30 mins b 60 mph
   c see diagram

Remember Remember Ch 14 - page 110

1. a 720 km   b 60 mph   c 1h 15 mins
2. a 0·4 h   b 0·15 h
   c 3·17 h   d 2·85 h
3. a 42 mins b 21 mins
   c 5h 18mins d 1h 39 mins
4. a 12 mph   b Mandy's by 5 mins
5. a 1930   b 24 km   c 16 km/h
   d 45 mins e 30 mins
   f 48km/h   g 3 hours

Answers to Chapter 15 Page 111

Exercise 15·1 - page 111

1. £130 £325
2. a £2000 £8000   b £45 £75
   c £5600 £1600   d £400 £480
   e £2200 £1800   f £26 £24
   g £115 £135
3. £120000
4. £18
5. a £8 £16 £32
   b £600 £900 £1500
   c 80 120 200
6. 600 fish

Exercise 15·2 - page 112

1. 13·5 km /litre 2. $1·49   3. 2 kg
4. £1·25   5. 42   6. 2·15 tonnes
7. £2·35   8. 32·5 km
9. a £2·28   b £12·99   c 48p
   d £2·60   e 48p
10. £355   11. 1·15   12. 76
13. Ailsa by 50p
14. a £8·30   b £8·45   c Bruce

Exercise 15·3 - page 113

1. £23·50   2. 84€   3. 1500 sq cm
4. 4800   5. 5760   6. £8·90
7. a and d   8. £6   9. £45
10. £208   11. 975 tonnes
12. £108

Exercise 15·4 - page 114

1. a 25 50 75 100 125 150
   b Graph
   c/d Straight line passing thro' origin
   e No Buns ... No Cost !
2. a 45 90 135 180 225 270
   b/c Straight line passing thro' origin
3. a 27 54 81 108 135 162
   b Straight line passing thro' origin
   c 216 secs 171 secs
4. a Straight line passing thro' origin
   b Yes
5. a Yes   b C = $^2/_3$D c £1000
   d 930 km
6. c, f and h
7. Three straight line graphs thro' origin
8. a no   b 16 hours

Exercise 15·5 - page 116

1. 10 hrs   2. 9·6 hrs   3. 126 km/hr
4. 5 days   5. 5 weeks 6. 20
7. 30 km/hr   8. 48   9. 10 mins
10. 3 days

Remember Remember Ch 15 - page 117

1. a 4:3   b £33
2. 40
3. 28 m/sec
4. 1610
5. £7·50
6. chemsurf

---

7. 8
8. 2 hrs
9. a, d and g

Non-Calculator Exercise 5 - page 120

1. a 1681   b 739   c 188 400 d 9073
   e 1348   f 4   g 625   h 680
2. a 138·11 b 66·653 c 23·8   d 11484
   e 1·38   f 20·753 g 0·64   h 0·00246
3. a 280   b £9·10 c £7·50
4. a $^{13}/_{17}$ b $^4/_7$ c $^1/_3$ d $^6/_{11}$
5. a $1^3/_{20}$ b $7^{11}/_{12}$ c $^{15}/_{26}$ d $2^{13}/_{20}$
6. a $2^1/_3$ b $6^5/_7$ c $12^7/_8$
7. a $^7/_8$ b $^9/_{25}$ c $^1/_{16}$
8. a £68   b £0·60   c 780
   d 88   e 35   f 42
9. a 60%   b 20%
10. a -42   b -43   c -60   d 2
    e 169   f -12   g 3   h 27
    i -8·5 j -10   k -16   l 3
11. a 43   b 18th August
12. a 72 km/hr   b 50 m/sec.

Answers to Chapter 16 Page 121

Exercise 16·1 - page 121

1. a 78 cm²   b 78.5 cm²
   c 22 5 cm²   d 68 cm²
   e 80 m²   f 77 mm²
   g 42 0 cm²   h 150 cm²
2. a 139 cm²   b 126 cm²
   c 58.5 cm²   d 91 cm²
   e 277 cm²   f 156 cm²

Exercise 16·2 - page 122

1. 350 cm³   2. 3 cm
3. a 37500 cm³ b 37500 ml c 37·5 litres
4. 3·75 litres
5. a 67200   b 24 cm
6. a 480000   b 80 mins
7. 75 cm
8. a 1 m³   b 1,000,000 cm³
   c 1 m³ = 1,000,000 cm³
9. a 8,000,000 cm³   b 8 m³
10. 9,000,000 cm³   =   9 m³
11. a 2,067,000 cm³   b 2·067 m³
12. a 60 cm²   b 280 cm²
13. 792 cm²   14. 236 cm²
15. a 1340 cm²   b £42.88
16. a 30 cm   b 2800 cm²
17. V= 3000 cm³ - surface area = 1100 cm²

Exercise 16·3 - page 124

1. 144 cm³   2. 225 cm³ 3. 1200 cm³
4. 8 cm   5. 26 cm   6. 6 cm
7. a 24 cm²   b 288 cm³
8. 1800 cm³   9. a 20 cm² b 240 cm³
10. 8·5 cm

Exercise 16·4 - page 125

1. 2009·6 cm³   2. 1271·7 cm³
3. a 6 cm   b 2034.72 cm³
4. A = 791·28 cm³ , B = 785 cm³ => A
5. 226080 cm³ = 226·08 litres
6. a 62800 cm³ = 62·8 litres   b 125 tins
7. Tank = 60000 cm³ = 60 litres
   Bucket = 3077·2 cm³ = 3·0772 litres
   It needs to be filled 20 times
8. 9·54 litres

a 1·1775 cm³ b 22·73 g c £418·15
0. 20410 cm³   11. 13·74 litres
2. 791·28 cm³
3. a 502·4 cm³ b 13990·4 cm³
4. 353·25 cm³   15. 3·26 cm

Exercise 16·5 - page 127

. 39 cm³   2. 50 cm³   3. 84 cm³
. 196 cm³   5. 732 cm³
. a 5·2 cm b 52 cm³
. 235·5 cm³
. a 200·96 cm³ b 61·23 m³
   c 1004·8 cm³ d 153·07 mm³
. a 153·86 cm³ b 7·8 cm
0. 27468·72 kg   11. 4·82 litres
2. 3709·125 cm³
3. a 602·88 cm³ b 348·54 cm³

Exercise 16·6 - page 129

. 502·4 cm²
. 621·72 cm²
. a 20 cm b 7536 cm²
. a 314 cm² b 1004·8 cm² c 1632·8 cm²
. 238·64 cm² 188·4 cm² one on left
. 6104·16 cm²   7. 17·62 m²
. 1075 ml

Exercise 16·7 - page 130

. 7234·56 cm³   2. 33493 mm³
. 523·33 cm³
. a 32708·33 cm³ b 32·7 litres
. 197820 cm³   6. 26451·4 cm³
. a 1216 cm³ b 9764·48 g

Remember Remember Ch 16 - page 131

. a 648 cm³ b 468 cm²
2. 288 litres
3. a 495 cm³ b 4500 cm³
4. V = 28260cm³ = 28·26 litres
5. a 5000 ml b 63·7 cm
6. a 256 cm³ b 297 cm³
7. 565·2 cm³
8. 6908 cm²
9. a 113·04 cm² b 527·52 cm²
   c 753·6 cm²
0. 17·15 m³
1. 28·94 litres
2. 10098·24 cm³

Answers to Chapter 17 Page 146

Exercise 17·1 - page 132

. a

T	1	2	3	4	5	6
L	3	6	9	12	15	18

b 3 c L = 3T d 150 e 24

2. a

H	1	2	3	4	5	6
L	6	12	18	24	30	36

b 6 c L = 6H

3. a $y = 5x$ b 40 c 15
4. a $T = 17p$ b 170 c 20
5. a $w = 0·5z$ b 20 c 60

Exercise 17·2 - page 133

1. a

T	1	2	3	4
L	3	5	7	9

b 2 c L = 2T + 1
d 21 e 30

2. (i) a

P	1	2	3	4
L	5	9	13	17

b 4 c L = 4P+1

(ii) a

H	1	2	3	4
L	6	11	16	21

b 5 c L = 5H+1

3. a

R	1	2	3	4
B	4	6	8	10

b B = 2R + 2 c 22 d 19
4. a B = 2R + 6 b 46 c 15
5. a S = 3P - 3 b 27 c 20
6. a B = 4P - 4 b 76 c 20
   d £46
7. a L = 2S + 1 b 23 c 85
8. a T = 5·7t - 3·1 b 93·8
   c 15 d 27 mins 23 secs
9. a G = 8p + 26 b 170 c 34
10. a H = 9a - 3 b 897 c 6
11. a V = -1·1q + 6·2 b 32·05 c 11
12. a t = 2g + 2 b 32 c 40

Exercise 17·3 - page 135

1. a (i) 30 (ii) 42
   (iii) 56 (iv) 90
   b $n^2 + n$
2. a (i) 16 (ii) 20 (iii) 24 (iv) 28
   b $(n + 2)^2 - n^2$
3. a (i) 15 (ii) 21 (iii) 28 (iv) 36
   b 1, 3, 6, 10, 15, 21, 28, ...
   c same number pattern
   d $\frac{1}{2}(n \times (n + 1)) = \frac{1}{2}(n^2 + n)$
4. a 1, 3, 6, 10, 15, 21.
   b check diagrams
   c (i) 28, 36 (ii) 45, 55 (iii) 66, 78

Exercise 17·4 - page 136

1. 66
2. 204
3. 153
4. 170
5. a 1 073 741 824 b 53·69 km

Exercise 17·5 - page 136

1. a (i) 31 (ii) 61
   b $(n + 1)^2 - n^2 = 2n + 1$
2. a (i) 5050 (ii) 500 500
   b $S_n = \frac{n}{2}(n + 1)$
3. a (i) $5^3 + 1 = (5 + 1)(5^2 - 5 + 1)$
   (ii) $8^3 + 1 = (8 + 1)(8^2 - 8 + 1)$
   b $(n + 1)(n^2 - n + 1)$
4. a 12 + 5 - 7   15 + 6 - 9
   b $2n + 2$
5. a 12 × 14 b $n(n + 2)$
6. a (10 × 11 × 21) ÷ 6 b $(n(n + 1)(2n + 1)) ÷ 6$
7. a 2·5 × 10 × 11 b 2·5 × n × (n + 1)
8. a $7 = 4^2 - 3^2$ b $19 = 10^2 - 9^2$
   c $2n - 1 = n^2 - (n - 1)^2$
   d $(2n - 1)(2n + 1) = 4n^2 - 1 = (2n)^2 - 1$
      even - 1 = odd
9. a (21 × 22) - 1 = 461
   b $(n + 1)(n + 2) - 1 = n^2 + 3n + 1$

Remember Remember Ch 17 - page 138

1. a

P	1	2	3	4
L	5	10	15	20

b 5 c L = 5P d 200 e 15
2. a B = 1·5h b 21 c 42
3. a

R	1	2	3	4
L	4	7	10	13

b L = 3R + 1 c 61 d 40
4. a T = 3P + 5 b 128 c 12
5. a K = S + 11 b 30 c 79
6. M = 3G - 5 b 55 c 111
7. a V = 0·5d - 1 b 19·5 c 396
8. 2, 10, 26, 50, 82
9. a 216 b 1000 cm³
   c $n \times n \times n = n^3$ d 200 cm

Answers to Chapter 18 Page 139

Exercise 18·1 - page 139

1.

2. a  b

c d
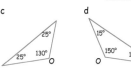

3. a b
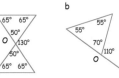

c d
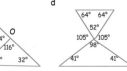

e f

g h

i j
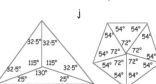

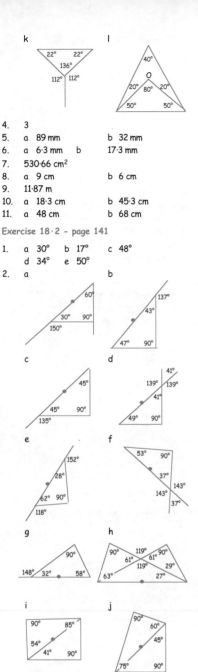

4.   3
5.   a 89 mm   b 32 mm
6.   a 6·3 mm   b   17·3 mm
7.   530·66 cm²
8.   a 9 cm   b 6 cm
9.   11·87 m
10. a 18·3 cm   b 45·3 cm
11. a 48 cm   b 68 cm

Exercise 18·2 - page 141

1.   a 30°   b 17°   c 48°
     d 34°   e 50°
2.   a   b

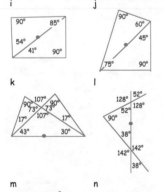

3.   13 cm
4.   a 21·54 cm   b 13·42 mm
     c 12·49 cm   d 21·56 cm

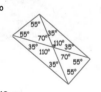

---

5.   17·6 cm   6. 907·46 mm²
7.   6·3 m   8. 8·28 m
9.   Check if 5·1² + 6·8² = 8·5².
     It does .
     It is a right angled triangle.
10. a 40 cm b 24 cm c 872 cm²

Exercise 18·3 - page 143

1.   a 90°   b 55°
2.   a 38°   b 75°   c 15°   d 60°
     e 45°   f 47°   g 32°
3.   a   b

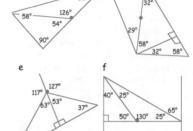

c   d

e   f

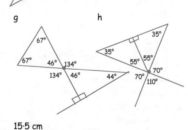

g   h

4.   15·5 cm
5.   a 9·2 cm   b 3·4 cm
6.   346·185 cm²   7. 21·2 cm
8.   2·4 cm
9.   a 18 cm   b 22·6 cm
10. 8·95 cm   11. 62·1 cm

Exercise 18·4 - page 145

1.   a 125°
2.   ∠AOB = 138° ∠CAO = 90° ∠CBO = 90°
3.   a 24°   b 132°   c 66°   d 24°
4.   22·4 cm
5.   706·5 cm²
6.   a (i) 10 cm (ii) 28 cm   b 26·2 cm
7.   60·9 cm

Remember Remember Ch 18 - page 146

1.   a 10   b 40   c 42·5
     d 70   e 40   f 37·5
     g 17·5   h 53   i 27
2.   65°
3.   a 6   b 7·81   c 20·6
4.   a AB = 50 – 10 – 10 = 30
     b 53 cm

Non-Calculator Exercise 6 - page 149

1.   a 64000 b 893   c –3   d 109
     e 10400 f 172   g 243   h 1
2.   a 70·024 b 4716   c 31·5   d 0·1133
3.   400
4.   a 6300 km   b 21·68 cm

---

     c 375 ml   d 11 mins 40 secs
5.   a ¹/₃   b ²/₅   c ¹/₃₈
6.   a 2¹/₄   b ³/₁₀   c 128
     d 28   e 4⁵/₈   f 7¹/₂
7.   a £4·50 b 96p   c 1600
     d 40p   e 120   f 800
8.   a –31   b –48   c –18
     d –19   e –78   f 75
     g 900   h –9   i 45
     j –9   k 19
9.   (7, 0)
10. a 2355 b 1815   c 0945
11. a 6 hrs 36 mins   b 9 hrs 39 mins
12. 1500 km
13. 314 m²
14. 12 cm

Answers to Chapter 19 Page 150

Exercise 19·1 - page 151

1.   a 0·424 b 1·072 c 1·376 d 11·430
     e 1·428 f 0·287 g 0·070 h 2·050
     i 8·144 j 1·000 k 2·174 l 0·061
2.   Yes, it is !
3.   a 16 cm b 10 cm c 1·6   d 1·6

Exercise 19·2 - page 151

1.   32·2 cm
2.   a 10·0 b 7·4   c 5·7
     d 78·6 e 7·7   f 20·8 (all cm)
3.   56 m   4. 8·1 m 5. 15·5 m
6.   125 m   7. 41·3 m 8. 51·2 ft

Exercise 19·3 - page 153

1.   a 25°   b 56°   c 14°   d 6°
     e 45°   f 38°   g 22°   h 12°
     i 66°   j 85°
2.   21·8°   3. a 24·0° b 32·1°
4.   a 38·7° b 45·0° c 71·6°
     d 20·7° e 28·1° f 52·4°
5.   31·7°   6. 70·7° 7. 13·6°
8.   a 10·3° b 100·3°

Exercise 19·4 - page 155

1.   a 0·766 b 0·500 c 0·866 d 0·995
     e 0·122 f 0·477 g 0·339 h 0·951
     i 0·99.. j 1·000
2.   a 23·6° b 12·4° c 26·4° d 73·7°
     e 7·2° f 10·5° g 30·0° h 14·5°
     i 19·5° j 36·0°
3.   a 17·8 b 8·8   c 105·0
     d 207·4 e 2·4   f 17·8 (all cm)
4.   1·75 m   5. 0·92 m 6. 1·5 km   7. 6·3 m
8.   a 60°   b 8·7 m c 8·7 m same !
9.   a 23·6° b 41·8° c 10·8°
     d 56·4° e 58·8° f 38·7°
10. 53·1°   11. 13·7° 12. 15·5° 13. 14·9°

Exercise 19·5 - page 158

1.   a 0·766   b 0·174   c 0·500
     d 0·866   e 0·996   f 0·609
2.   a 36·9°   b 69·1°   c 83·6°
     d 32·9°   e 79·5°   f 29·0°
3.   a 4·2 cm   b 5·7 cm   c 6·2 cm
4.   22·3 cm 5. 2·71 m 6. 27·5 cm 7. 10·6 cm
8.   39·7°   9. a 33·6° b 56·4°   10. 81·1°

Exercise 19·6 - page 160

1.   a 6·7   b 50·5   c 172·9 (all cm)
2.   8·12 m
3.   a 37·1 cm b 8·1 cm   c 247·2 mm
4.   3·1 m

5. a 20·9cm b 19·9cm c 306·7 mm
6. 15·8 cm 7. 51·6 cm 8. 10·3 cm

Exercise 19·7 - page 162
1. a 5·1 b 15·1 c 10·0
   d 14·0 e 10·1 f 24·2 (all cm)
2. a 57·3° b 39·9° c 11·7°
   d 35·7° e 64·6° f 30·0°
3. 39·4 m
4. 38·5°
5. 45·4 ft
6. a 7·8 m b 7·1 m 7. 13·5 m
8. 18·0 km 9. 12·8° Yes, ok
10. 118° 11. 108 cm² 12. 3·99 m
13. 36° - Yes, ok

Remember Remember Ch 19 - page 165
1. a 10·6 cm b 39·2° c 27·7 cm
2. 64·3° 3. 33 m
4. 302 m
5. a 149·8 m & 83·9 m b 66 m
6. 036° 7. 33·1 cm

Answers to Chapter 20 Page 166

Exercise 20·1 - page 167
1. A - H, B - C, D - J, E - I, F - G.
2. a both ratios 1:2 b both ratios 2:5
   c both ratios 3:1 d both ratios 4:3
3. B and D might be similar
4. a (i) 2 (ii) 18 cm b 3·5, 77 cm
   c 1·5 0·45 cm d 20, 15 m
5. a $\frac{1}{3}$, 4 cm b $\frac{2}{5}$, 24 cm
   c 0·7, 2·94 d 0·02, 30 cm
6. 9 cm
7. 7·2 m
8. a 5 cm b 1·5 cm
9. 9 cm
10. 17·5 cm
11. a 7·5 cm b 8 cm c 37·5 mm, 60 mm
12. a $\frac{5}{8}$ b 8

Exercise 20·2 - page 169
1. (a) and (c) are similar
2. (a) and (c) are similar
3. 77 cm
4. 7 cm
5. 20 cm
6. a All angles the same b 1·6 cm
7. a All angles the same b $23\frac{1}{3}$ cm
8. a Yes all angles the same b 13 cm
9. 6·75 m

Exercise 20·3 - page 171
1. a (i) 0·5 (ii) 5 b (i) 1·5 (ii) 9
   c (i) $\frac{2}{5}$ (ii) 2 d (i) 1·25 (ii) 25
2. a use corresponding angles to help show
   all angles are the same
   b 32 km c (i) 60 km (ii) 68 km
3. a 240 mm b 144 mm
4. a All angles the same - corresponding
   b (i) 15 cm (ii) 12 cm
5. 3·6 m
6. a 6 b 3 c 5 d $6\frac{2}{3}$
7. b $\frac{1}{2}$ c 6
8. Check diagrams a = 4·5 b = 12
   c = 12 d = 7·5 x = 23 y = 13

Exercise 20·4 - page 173
1. a 2 cm b 4
2. 9

3. 1750 cm²
4. 7·2 cm² 5. 562·5 cm² 6. 1760 m²
7. 60 cm² 8. 520 sq.inches 9. 306 cm²
10. 20 mm²
11. 30 cm²
12. a All angles same b 4 c 3·2 cm
    d $\frac{1}{16}$ e 0·4 cm²
13. 27 cm

Exercise 20·5 - page 175
1. 512 cm³ 2. 810 ml
3. 320 ml 4. 166·25 cm³
5. £6·75 6. £6·86
7. a 12 cm b 1·92 litres
8. 16 tonnes 9. £1·28
10. a (i) $\frac{3}{4}$ (ii) $\frac{5}{6}$
    b 900cm² c 625 cm³
11. 20 cm

Remember Remember Ch 20 - page 177
1. Same ratio, 0·74
2. a 1·25 b 112·5 cm
3. 8 cm
4. a All angles the same b 24 cm
5. a = 7·5 b = 3
6. 27 cm²
7. a 12 cm b 421·875 ml
8. £1·28

Answers to Chapter 21 Page 178

Exercise 21.1 - page 178
1. a $8\frac{1}{2}$ b $4\frac{5}{6}$ c $1\frac{8}{9}$
2. a $3\frac{1}{3}$ b $4\frac{3}{4}$ c $5\frac{1}{6}$
   d $5\frac{1}{2}$ e $7\frac{2}{5}$ f $6\frac{3}{8}$
3. a $2\frac{3}{5}$ b $3\frac{5}{6}$ kg c $5\frac{2}{5}$ l
4. $4\frac{1}{3}$
5. a $3\frac{1}{2}$ b $3\frac{1}{2}$ c $3\frac{1}{4}$
   d $4\frac{1}{5}$ e $2\frac{1}{3}$ f $3\frac{3}{4}$
6. a 4 b 8 c 11
7. a 9 b 2 c 11 d $\frac{11}{3}$
8. $\frac{23}{5}$
9. a $\frac{11}{3}$ b $\frac{38}{7}$ c $\frac{34}{5}$
10. a $\frac{5}{2}$ b $\frac{15}{4}$ c $\frac{53}{5}$
    d $\frac{49}{8}$ e $\frac{29}{3}$ f $\frac{27}{10}$
11. a 6 b 14 c 9 d 19
12. a 6 b 8 c 13
13. a 20 b 9 c 15 14. $6\frac{2}{5}$

Exercise 21.2 - page 179
1. a $\frac{4}{5}$ b $\frac{2}{9}$ c $\frac{3}{5}$ d $\frac{3}{8}$
2. a $1\frac{2}{7}$ b $\frac{8}{9}$ c $\frac{1}{4}$
   d $1\frac{1}{5}$ e $\frac{5}{11}$ f $\frac{2}{5}$
3. a 7 b $4\frac{1}{2}$ c $6\frac{2}{3}$
   d $6\frac{2}{9}$ e $4\frac{1}{2}$ f $11\frac{5}{7}$
4. $\frac{2}{5}$ km
5. $7\frac{1}{4}$
6. $9\frac{2}{5}$ kg
7. a $3\frac{1}{4}$ m b $4\frac{1}{2}$ l
   c $7\frac{3}{7}$ km d $\frac{7}{8}$ e $38\frac{1}{5}$ kg
8. a $3\frac{2}{5}$ ft b 16 ft
9. a 5 tonnes b $5\frac{3}{8}$ tonnes c $5\frac{3}{4}$ tonnes
10. $8\frac{1}{8}$ inches.

Exercise 21.3 - page 181
1. a $1\frac{1}{12}$ b $\frac{2}{15}$ c $\frac{1}{8}$ d $1\frac{11}{21}$
2. a $\frac{11}{15}$ b $\frac{1}{4}$ c $1\frac{5}{12}$ d $\frac{17}{20}$
   e $\frac{1}{3}$ f $\frac{5}{24}$ g $1\frac{1}{10}$ h $\frac{1}{18}$
3. a $1\frac{1}{12}$ b $\frac{1}{8}$ c $\frac{19}{30}$ d $\frac{37}{60}$
4. a $9\frac{1}{6}$ b $3\frac{1}{12}$ c $4\frac{3}{8}$ d $9\frac{3}{10}$
   e $2\frac{7}{30}$ f $3\frac{17}{24}$ g $7\frac{1}{18}$ h $4\frac{3}{20}$
5. a $3\frac{3}{4}$ b $4\frac{2}{5}$
6. a $1\frac{2}{3}$ b $4\frac{2}{9}$
7. $2\frac{5}{8}$ m 8. $4\frac{2}{5}$ km
9. a $3\frac{9}{10}$ b $1\frac{31}{40}$
10. a $2\frac{7}{10}$ b $4\frac{23}{30}$ c $1\frac{3}{4}$ d $1\frac{5}{8}$
    e $2\frac{5}{6}$ f $4\frac{9}{14}$ g $4\frac{19}{30}$ h $2\frac{23}{30}$

Exercise 21.4 - page 183
1. a $\frac{8}{15}$ b $\frac{5}{18}$
2. a $\frac{4}{15}$ b $\frac{1}{2}$ c $\frac{4}{21}$ d $\frac{1}{4}$
   e $\frac{3}{10}$ f $\frac{1}{3}$ g $\frac{11}{40}$ h $\frac{1}{5}$
3. $\frac{5}{16}$ sq m
4. $\frac{3}{10}$
5. a $3\frac{1}{2}$ b $7\frac{1}{12}$
6. a $5\frac{5}{6}$ b $10\frac{1}{2}$ c 20 d 6
   e 10 f $15\frac{7}{12}$ g $5\frac{19}{30}$ h $11\frac{1}{10}$
   i $6\frac{5}{12}$ j $26\frac{2}{5}$ k 9 l $5\frac{1}{5}$

Remember Remember Ch 21 - page 184
1. a $5\frac{4}{5}$ b $5\frac{3}{4}$ c $7\frac{3}{5}$
2. a $\frac{17}{3}$ b $\frac{33}{5}$ c $\frac{97}{9}$ 3. 14
4. a $\frac{6}{7}$ b $\frac{1}{4}$ c $\frac{1}{2}$ d $6\frac{1}{5}$
   e $\frac{7}{12}$ f $6\frac{7}{15}$ g $3\frac{11}{40}$ h $1\frac{5}{6}$
5. a $\frac{3}{10}$ b $\frac{14}{27}$ c 1 d $\frac{3}{7}$
   e $2\frac{1}{4}$ f $2\frac{2}{9}$ g $4\frac{1}{5}$ h 12
6. $10\frac{3}{4}$ 7. $9\frac{9}{10}$ 8. $19\frac{7}{8}$ kg
9. 3 10. $\frac{1}{5}$

Non-Calculator Exercise 7 - page 187
1. a 4752 b 587 c 9372 d 11106
   e 21000 f 3200000 g 100·4 h 4232
2. 11°C
3. a 14 b -1·112 c 45·433 d 1·7
   e 0·36 f 95·076 g 6·9 h 5·05
4. a 240 b £57·60 c 1200 d 99
5. a $\frac{5}{6}$ b $4\frac{5}{7}$ c 22 d $\frac{1}{16}$
6. £20
7. a 9 b $-4\frac{3}{4}$
8. a 89p b £4·80 c £22·47
   d £12·75 e £43 f £40
9. £3375
10. a -1 b -54 c 26 d 60
    e -48 f -96 g 121 h -9
    i -72 j -4 k -1 l 15
11. a £490 b £210
12. 30th March
13. 94·2 cm

Answers to Chapter 22 Page 188

Exercise 22.1 - page 188
1. a 6 b 15 c 25 d 0·7
   e 135 f 26·4 g 0
2. a 6 b 44 c 2·8 d 133
3. a 17·5 b 18 c 107
   d 0·65 e 0 f 5

4. a 8 b 23 c 1·8
   d 2 e 1124 f 0·75
5. (i) a 8 b 28 c 8
   d 1·5 e 16 f 5
   (ii) a 7 b 44 c 4·6
   d 2 e 189 f 0·55
6 a 55 b Mean = 11, Med = 5, Mode = 2
   c Median
   d Only one value > mean. Mode - lowest.
7. a Mean 6 Median 3 Mode 3
   b Mean 5·3 Median 5·4 Mode 5·4
   c Mean 271 Median 303 Mode 307
   d Mean 44·25 Median 41 Mode 40
   e Mean 65·5 Median 65·5 Mode 67
   f Mean 13 400 Med 13 000 Mode 10 000
   g Mean 1 Med -1 Mode -5
8. a 23 b Mode 45 Median 53
   c Median, since mode is the lowest value.
9. a Mean = 7·8, Med = 8, Mode = 8 b 4
10. a 12·9, 27 b 38·5, 99 c 2550·5
11. a Each uses mean, median and mode.
    b Mean indicates more "central" value.
12. 10·5 kg 13. 17 14. 78
15. a No. Mean, median & mode all 59. b 70
16. 93 17. 57
18. Not possible. Score needed is 101%!

Exercise 22.2 - page 191
1. a 0, 6, 22, 21, 16 => Total = 65
   b 30 c 65 d 2·2 e 2 f 2
2. a 6, 21, 36, 20, 12 => Total = 95
   b 25 c 95 d 3·8 e 4 f 4
3. a (i) 10, 36, 28, 10, 24 => Total = 108
        Mean = 3·6, Mode = 3, Median = 3
     (ii) 2, 36, 12, 48, 11, 12 => Total = 121
        Mean = 6·05, Mode = 4, Med = 5
     (iii) 9, 24, 10, 42, 0, 8, 0, 10, Tot = 103
        Mean = 5·2, Mode = 6, Med = 5
4. (ii) 10 (iii) 7
5. a 25 b 8 c 12·7 d 12 e 12
6. a 104, 196, 45, 144, 187 => Tot = 676
   b Mode 14, Range 4, Mean 15, Median 15

Exercise 22.3 - page 193
1 a CF = 5, 15, 27, 52, 69, 77, 80
   b 80 c 69 d 4
2. a CF = 1, 11, 27, 34, 37, 39, 40, med = 4
   b CF = 2, 8, 16, 36, 78, 92, 100, med = 7
   c CF = 4, 6, 13, 24, 43, 50, 51, med = 25
3. a 15(6), 16(5), 17(5), 18(3), 19(5), 20(1)
   b (90 + 80 + 85 + 54 + 95 + 20) ÷ 25 = 17·0
   c CF = 6, 11, 16, 19, 24, 25, med = 17

Remember Remember Ch 22 - page 194
1. a mean 13 med 10 mode 10 range 15
   b mean 7·5 med 7·4 mode 7·4 range 3·6
   c mean 222 med 208 mode 208 range 285
   d mean 45·1 med 42 mode 42 range 32
   e mean -1 med 1 mode -9 or 3 range 20
   f mean 5 med 5 mode 5½ range 7½
2. £110·35
3. 34
4. a No, mean = 119, med = 117·5, mode = 117
   b 130
5. a 33p b 33p c 4p d 32·9p
6. a 34 b 35

Answers to Chapter 23 Page 195

Exercise 23.1 - page 195
1. a 10 b 11 c 23 d 5
2. See Graph 3. See Graph
4. a (i) 30 (ii) 40 (iii) 50 b 27 c 200

5. See Graph 6. See Graph

Exercise 23.2 - page 196
1. a i 4/10 ii 1/10 iii 2/10 iv 3/10
   b burger, soup, pizza, salad.
2. a i 40% ii 30% iii 20%
   b i 60 ii 270
3. a i 25% ii 40% iii 15% iv 20%
   b i 75 ii 200
4 Pie Chart with Football taking up 10 sects, Rugby 4, Tennis 1, Hockey 3 & Netball 2.
5. Pie Chart - Pasta 7 sections, Carrots 8, Tomato 3, Rest 2.
6. Pie Chart - Dogs 8 sections, Cats 6, 3 fish 3 mice.
7. Pie Chart - Season 10 sections, Tickets 5, Juvenile 3, Rest 2.

Exercise 23.3 - page 197
1. a 40° 180° 20° 120°
   b Pie chart with these angles. Check.
2. a 40° 160° 144° 16°
   b Pie chart with these angles. Check.
3. a 120° 144° 84° 12°
   b Pie chart with these angles. Check.
4. a 180° 100° 20° 60°
   Pie chart with angles listed above. Check
   b 200° 80° 50° 30°
   Pie chart with angles listed above. Check
   c 200° 120° 35° 5°
   Pie chart with angles listed below. Check
5. a A - 9 B - 8 AB - 8 O - 15
   b Pie chart with angles listed below :-
   A - 81° B - 72° AB - 72° O - 135°

Remember Remember Ch 23 - page 199
1. See Bar Graph
2. See Line Graph
3. a 230° b i 135 ii 60 c 345
4. a 120° 84° 144° 12°
   b Pie chart with angles listed above. Check
5.
```
12 | 3 3              b £144  c £150·50
13 | 3 8
14 | 4 4 4 4
15 | 0 0 1 5 7 8
16 | 0 0 6
17 | 0 0 2     16/6 = 166
```

Answers to Chapter 24 Page 200

Exercise 24.1 - page 200
1. impossible
2. evens
3. unlikely
4. likely
5. unlikely
6. certain
7. impossible
8. certain

Exercise 24.2 - page 200
1. 1/3
2. a 1/6 b 1/3 c 1/2 d 0
3. a 1/6
   b (i) 1/6 (ii) 1/2 (iii) 0 (iv) 1/6
4. a 1/4 b 1/3 c 5/12 d 1/2
5. a 1/5 b 7/10 c 1/10 d 9/10
6. a 1/3 b 2/9 c 1/6
   d 1/9 e 1/12 f 1/18
   g 1/36 h 7/18 i 11/18
7. a 5/11 b 2/11 c 5/11 d 6/11

8. 4/7
9. a HHH, HHT, HTH, THH,
      HTT, THT, TTH, TTT,
   b (i) 1/8 (ii) 3/8
10. a 1/20 b 2/5 c 1/2 d 2/5
11. 3 more green
12. 0·75
13. 36 boys, 24 girls
14. a 1/2 b 1/4 c 1/13
    d 1/52 e 3/13
15. a 1/18 b 1/6 c 1/36 d 1/2
16. a 9/55 b 11/61 c 0·16, 0·18
    d 0·18 better chance
17. Daria 0·18 chance (Celia only 0·12)
18. Rain 0·158 (snow only 0·156)
19. Rivaldo 0·429 (Jonson 0·4, Erikton 0·417)

Remember Remember Ch 24 - page 202
1. a impossible b evens c unlikely
2. 10/13
3. a 1/8 b 1/2 c 1/2 d 0
4. 0·55
5. a 18 b 6
6. a 1/44 b 1/44 c 1/22 d 1/11
7. Box 1 - 0·46, Box 2 - 0·45 - Box 1 better

Answers to Chapter 25 Page 204

Revision Exercise - page 204
1. a 14 b 0·067 c 23000
2. a 22·41 b 6·29 c 1·68
3. a 7 b $-10p^2$ c 4 d 0
   e 30p f -4 g $49a^2b^2$ h -6t
4. a 41 b 123 c 49
5. a $7·80 b 9 c 108 ml d £2000
6. £16·20 25%
7. Both wrong - same price both ways
8. a $-x$ b $-2 + 6x$
9. a $2a(2a - 3)$ b $8y(3x^2 - 5y)$
10.

11. a 2 b 6
12. a 74·5 65·5 b 9·01 8·97
13. a 0·25 ± 0·2 b 0·061 ± 0·008
14. a 299 euros b £300
15. £930
16. a £23550 b £1962·50
17. a V = 850 - 20t b Wed 6.30 am
18. a $10^3 + 3 \times 10^2 \times 11 + 3 \times 10 \times 11^2 + 11^3$
    b $x^3 + 3x^2 + 3x + 1$
    c $(a + b)^3$
19. a 5·5 b 5 c 5 d 2
    e 4 f 30/13 g 10/9 h 85/6
    i $-19/5$ j 9 k 7
20. a $x < 6$ b $x < -6$ c $x \geq 5$
    d $x \leq 3$ e $x < 18$
21. < 10 in a packet
22. a $1·85 \times 10^5$ b $3·7 \times 10^{-3}$
23. a 178000000 b 0·0006
24. a $8·37 \times 10^3$ b $2·72 \times 10^{16}$
25. $1·8414 \times 10^{-2}$
26. 8 mins 12 secs

7. 95·1cm

8. 209·76cm²

9. a 15·9cm   b 7·98cm

10. a (-1,2) (-5,2) (-5,4)
    b (-1,-2) (-5,-2) (-5,-4)
    c (-5, 0), (-1, 0), (-1, 2)

11. 77·8m

12. a 6 cm   b 31cm

13. 1728 km

14. 93 km/hr

15. 3hr 36 min

16. G £80000   F £120000   C £140000

17. a 36   b 25

18. 36 mins

19. a 540 cm³   b 226080 cm³
   c 201 cm³   d 32708 cm³

20. a 527·52 cm²   b 835·24 cm³

21. 9·5 cm

22. a 4·19 cm³   b 2·1 cm

23. a 4500 cm²   b 540000 cm³

24. a $y = -4x - 3$ b $y = \frac{1}{2}x + 3$
   c $y = 4x - 4$ d $y = -\frac{1}{2}x + 3$

25. a $y = \frac{1}{4}x + 2$ b $p = 4$

26. a $P = -10t + 200$ b 130   c 20

27. a 125°   b 24°   c 52°

28. 18cm

29. a 10cm   b 218cm²

30. 28°

31. 4·33m

32. 48 mm²

33. 67·5 ml

34. a $1\frac{1}{4}$ b $\frac{1}{2}$ c $\frac{19}{40}$ d $9\frac{3}{4}$
   e $6\frac{1}{15}$ f $5\frac{1}{2}$ g $2\frac{7}{12}$ h $2\frac{7}{10}$

35. a $\frac{5}{14}$ b $\frac{18}{55}$ c $3\frac{1}{4}$
   d 8   e $2\frac{1}{5}$ f $\frac{5}{8}$

36. a Table b 6   c 7
   d 7   e 7·2

37. mean 4   median 3   mode 2   range 8

38. 6 yrs old

39. a 144°   b 300

40. a 40%   b 180   c 54°

41. $\frac{1}{12}$

42. Church better ... $\frac{1}{80}$ better than $\frac{1}{90}$

43. 30 gums

44. a 10·1 cm   b 14·9 cm   c 42·1°

45. 6·8 m

46. 079° (approx)

47. 18·4°

48. Safe - only 13·7°

49
```
1 | 2 7 9
2 | 1 2 5 5 8
3 | 0 2 3 6 7 8 9
4 | 2 5 5 7 9
5 | 1 3 8
6 | 0
```